HAVANA

CHRISTOPHER P. BAKER

Contents

Clockwise from top left: dancers in Escuela Nacional de Ballet, Universidad de la Habana; view towards Habana Vieja from Casablanca; neoclassical columns of colonial buildings in Plaza Vieja.

DISCOVER
Havana

Set foot in Havana and you will succumb to its enigmatic allure. Countless writers have commented on the exhilarating sensations that engulfed them in this most beautiful and beguiling of Caribbean cities. It is impossible to resist the city's mysteries and contradictions.

Havana has a flavor all its own, a merging of colonialism, capitalism, and Communism into one. One of the great historical cities of the New World, Havana is a far cry from most Caribbean capitals. The buildings come in a spectacular amalgam of styles—from the academic classicism of aristocratic homes, rococo residential exteriors, Moorish interiors, and art deco and art nouveau to stunning exemplars of 1950s moderne.

At the heart of the city is enchanting Habana Vieja (Old Havana), a living museum containing of Spanish-colonial buildings, Baroque churches, *casas particulares*, and world-class cuisine.

Havana awaits!

Clockwise from top left: swimming pool of Hotel Nacional; dining out in Vedado; art deco lobby; classic car on Calle Agramonte; Sacra Catedral Ortodoxa Rusa.

Planning Your Trip

Neighborhoods

Habana Vieja

The finest collection of **Spanish colonial buildings** in the Americas lines Habana Vieja's **cobbled streets.** Stroll the tree-lined Prado, hang out in **Hemingway's old haunts,** and people-watch in quintessentially Cuban plazas.

Centro Habana

Although its once-regal mansions are now dilapidated, this area features **shopping** along **Calle San Rafael** and in **Cuatro Caminos,** the country's largest **farmers market,** and the **Malecón**—Havana's seafront drive and undisputed social gathering spot.

Cerro and Diez de Octubre

South of Habana Vieja and Centro the land rises gently to Cerro, which developed during the **19th century** as the place where many wealthy families maintained **summer homes** on the cooler *cerro* (hill). The area is replete with once-stately *quintas* in **neoclassical, beaux-arts,** and **art nouveau** styles.

Vedado and Plaza de la Revolución

Hilly Vedado is Havana at its middle-class best, with the **University of Havana,** historic **Plaza de la Revolución,** and **prime hotels** and **restaurants** like the lavish **Hotel Nacional.** Walking **La Rampa** will lead you to cinemas, nightclubs, art deco buildings, and the best ice cream in the city at **Parque Coppelia.**

Playa: Miramar and Beyond

With their **luxurious residences** and new apartment buildings, Playa and Miramar are the face of Cuba's **quasi-capitalist makeover**—and possibly its future. The shoreline along 1ra Avenida rivals Miami's South Beach—not so many miles yet worlds away—and the famed **Tropicana nightclub** in Marianao is a must-see.

Suburban Havana

Venture outside the city to check out the **national zoo, Parque Lenin, ExpoCuba, Hemingway's former home,** charming **provincial towns, botanical gardens,** and the popular beaches of **Playas del Este.**

Before You Go

Seasons

Cuba has fairly distinct seasons: a relatively dry and mild **winter** (November-April) and a hot and wet **summer** (May-October). Early **spring** is the ideal time to travel, especially in the Oriente (the eastern provinces), which can be insufferably hot in summer. Christmas and New Year's are the busiest periods; many accommodations and car rental agencies sell out then, and finding a domestic flight is nearly impossible. Hotel prices are usually lower in summer—the low season (*temporada baja*)—when hurricanes are a slim possibility. Tropical storms can lash the island even in winter, however.

Transportation

Most international visitors fly into either Havana's **José Martí International Airport** or Varadero's **Juan Gualberto Gómez International Airport**. Cuba is a large island (more than 1,000 kilometers east-west). In Havana, getting around is simple thanks to an efficient **taxi** system. Traveling between cities by public transportation, however, can be a challenge. **Víazul tourist buses** connect major cities and resorts, as do domestic flights. Renting a car is recommended for serendipitous travelers, but cars are in short supply and roads are full of hazards.

Passports and Visas

Visitors to Cuba need a **passport** valid for at least six months beyond their intended length of stay; a **ticket** for onward travel; and a **tourist visa**, typically issued when you check in for your plane to Cuba. Stays of up to 30 days are permitted (90 days for Canadians), extendable one time.

U.S. Citizens

U.S. law bans travel by individuals who don't fit into one of the 12 license categories of allowable travel. However, every U.S. citizen qualifies for individual travel under the "people-to-people" license category. Travel is preapproved and self-policing. The U.S. government will take you at your word when your stated purpose is "meaningful interaction with Cubans." However, "tourism" is not allowed. For more details, see page 184.

The Best of Havana

The following fast-paced itinerary combines a sampling of the top sights and experiences for those intent on seeing the best Havana has to offer.

Days 1-2

Arrive at José Martí International Airport in **Havana;** transfer to a hotel or *casa particular* in Habana Vieja or the Vedado district. Take a self-guided walking tour of **Habana Vieja,** including the **Plaza de Armas, Plaza de la Catedral,** and **Plaza Vieja,** and taking in the key museums, galleries, and shops along the surrounding streets. Return at night to savor the plazas lit by traditional gas lanterns. Don't fail to sip a *mojito* at **La Bodeguita del Medio.**

Day 3

This morning, concentrate your time around **Parque Central** and **Paseo de Martí.** You'll want to visit the **Capitolio Nacional,** the **Museo Nacional de Bellas Artes,** and the **Museo de la Revolución.** A daiquiri at **El Floridita** is a must! At dusk, walk the **Malecón.**

Day 4

Spend the morning exploring the streets of **Vedado,** being sure to call in at the **Hotel Nacional,** the **Hotel Habana Libre Tryp,** and **Universidad de la Habana.** After cooling off with an ice cream at **Coppelia** (with pesos in hand, stand in line with the Cubans), hail a taxi to take you to **Cementerio Colón** and **Plaza de la Revolución.**

Day 5

Rent a car and set out on a tour of **suburban Havana,** calling in at **Museo**

Plaza Vieja, Habana Vieja

Ernest Hemingway. Then head west along the Autopista Habana-Pinar to **Las Terrazas,** an eco-resort and rural community in the heart of the Sierra del Rosario. Hike the trails and visit the artists' studios. Overnight at Hotel Moka and fly home the next morning.

¡Viva la Revolución!

Many a traveler departs Havana wearing a T-shirt emblazoned with the world-renowned image of Che Guevara. That doesn't necessarily indicate a fondness for Communism, or even Che. Still, thousands of visitors *do* arrive every year to pay homage to, or at least learn about, the *revolución.* Whatever your politics, following the footsteps of revolutionaries makes for a fascinating historical journey.

Day 1

Arrive at José Martí International Airport in **Havana;** transfer to a hotel or *casa particular* in Habana Vieja or the Vedado district.

Day 2

Start the day with a visit to the **Museo de la Revolución,** housed in the former presidential palace of corrupt dictator Fulgencio Batista, whom the Revolution overthrew. Of course, you'll want to spend some time viewing the other fascinating sites nearby. In the afternoon, your tour of **Habana Vieja** should include the **Museo Casa Natal de José Martí,** birthplace of the national hero whom Fidel Castro named the "intellectual author" of the Revolution; and **Casa-Museo del Che,** near the Fortaleza de San Carlos de la Cabaña.

Day 3

Today, concentrate your sightseeing around **Vedado.** Must-see sights include the **Casa Museo Abel Santamaría,** a former apartment that was the secret headquarters for Castro's 26th of July Movement; the **Universidad de la Habana,** where the **Escalinata** (staircase) was a venue for clashes with Batista's police; **Galería 23 y 12,** where Castro first announced that Cuba was socialist; **Plaza de la Revolución,** the seat of Communist government; and **Centro Estudios de Che.**

Music and dance are the pulsing undercurrent of Cuban life. Spanning the spectrum from traditional *son* to high culture, here are key venues and experiences not to miss in Havana.

Soulful Traditions

The **Tablao de Pancho** hosts a supper show with old-time crooners belting out songs from *Buena Vista Social Club.*

For *bolero,* head to **Café Concierto Gato Tuerto,** a 1950s lounge club where you expect the "Rat Pack" to stroll in any moment.

The **Conjunto Folklórico Nacional** will wow you with traditional Afro-Cuban dance to the beat of the drums.

Salsa is at its sizzling best at the **Casa de la Música,** where salsa dance lessons are also hosted.

No visit to Havana is complete without a visit to the **Tropicana** for a sexy cabaret show like no other.

High Culture

Cubans astound with their fond appreciation of ballet, theater, and classical and choral music, and Havana is replete with venues.

The **Basilica de San Francisco de Asís** hosts classical and chamber ensembles most Saturday evenings. Nearby, the intimate **Iglesia de San**

Gran Teatro de la Habana

Francisco de Paula is *the* venue to hear choral groups.

The acclaimed **Ballet Nacional de Cuba** typically performs at the **Gran Teatro de la Habana.** The Teatro Nacional hosts the Orquesta Sinfónica Nacional de Cuba. The Gran Teatro's chic **Adagio Barconcert** lounge bar hosts live classical and jazz ensembles.

Havana boasts several jazz venues, including the snazzy **Café Miramar** and intimate **Privé.**

Cars, Cigars, and Cabarets

Before 1959, Havana was the hottest spot in the Caribbean, notorious for its glittering cabarets, smooth rum, and chrome-laden Cadillacs. The good news is that the tail fins of '57 Eldorados still glint beneath the floodlit mango trees of nightclubs such as the famous Tropicana.

Days 1-2

Arrive in Havana; transfer to a hotel or *casa particular* in **Habana Vieja** or **Vedado**. Concentrate your time around **Parque Central**, where the highlight will be all the American classic cars parked nearby. Rent a 1950s auto and tour the city. Visit **Fábrica de Tabaco H. Upmann** to get the low-down on cigar production and buy some premium smokes. Enjoy dinner at **La Guarida** restaurant and then thrill to the spectacle of the Hotel Nacional's **Cabaret Parisien.**

Day 3

Today, follow Hemingway's ghost. Drive out to the village of San Miguel del Padrón and the **Museo Ernest Hemingway,** in the author's former home. Afterwards, head to **Cojímar** for a seafood lunch at **La Terraza** restaurant, once popular with Papa and his former skipper, late local resident Gregorio Fuentes. Return to Havana for a *mojito* at **La Bodeguita del Medio.** Explore **Plaza de la Catedral** and **Plaza de Armas,** stopping in at the **Hotel Ambos Mundos** (Room 511, where Hemingway was a longtime guest, is a museum) and the **Museo del Ron,** which gives insight into production of Cuba's fine rums. This evening, sample the daiquiris at **El Floridita.**

Days 4-5

Head to chic **Club Habana**, a private club open to nonmembers for a fee. Relax on the fine beach, partake of water sports, and sample cocktails and fine cigars. After dinner at **El Cocinero** *paladar*, head to the **Tropicana** for the sauciest cabaret in Cuba, now in its seventh decade of stiletto-heeled paganism. Fly home the next morning.

entrance to La Guarida restaurant

Havana

Havana is the political, cultural, and industrial heart of the nation.

It lies 150 kilometers (93 miles) due south of Florida on Cuba's northwest coast. It is built on the west side of the sweeping Bahía de la Habana and extends west 12 kilometers to the Río Jaimanitas and south for an equal distance.

Countless writers have commented on the exhilarating sensation that engulfs visitors to this most beautiful and beguiling of Caribbean cities. Set foot one time in Havana and you can only succumb to its enigmatic allure. It is impossible to resist the city's mysteries and contradictions.

Havana (pop. 2.2 million) has a flavor all its own, a merging of colonialism, capitalism, and Communism into one. One of the great historical cities of the New World, Havana is a far cry from the Caribbean backwaters that call themselves capitals elsewhere in the Antilles. Havana is a city, notes architect Jorge Rigau, "upholstered in columns, cushioned by colonnaded arcades." The buildings come in a spectacular amalgam of styles—from the academic classicism of aristocratic homes, rococo residential exteriors, Moorish interiors, and art deco and art nouveau to stunning exemplars of 1950s moderne.

At the heart of the city is enchanting Habana Vieja (Old Havana), a living museum inhabited by 60,000 people and containing perhaps the finest collection of Spanish-colonial buildings in all the Americas. Baroque churches, convents, and castles that could have been transposed from Madrid or Cádiz still reign majestically over squares embraced by the former palaces of Cuba's ruling gentry and cobbled streets still haunted by Ernest Hemingway's ghost. Hemingway's house, Finca Vigía, is one of dozens of museums dedicated to the memory of great men and women. And although older monuments of politically incorrect heroes were pulled

---

Previous: 1959 Cadillac outside Hotel Nacional; Plaza Vieja, Habana Vieja.

Look for ★ to find recommended sights, activities, dining, and lodging.

Highlights

© AVALON TRAVEL

★ **Museo Nacional de Bellas Artes:** Divided into national and international sections, this art gallery is among the world's finest (pages 28 and 33).

★ **Capitolio Nacional:** Cuba's former congressional building is an architectural glory reminiscent of Washington's own capitol (page 28).

★ **Plaza de la Catedral:** This small, atmospheric plaza is hemmed in by colonial mansions and a baroque cathedral (page 36).

★ **Plaza de Armas:** The restored cobbled plaza at the heart of Old Havana features tons of charm; don't miss the Castillo de la Real Fuerza and Palacio de los Capitanes Generales (page 44).

★ **Plaza Vieja:** Undergoing restoration, this antique plaza offers offbeat museums, Havana's only brewpub, flashy boutiques, and heaps of ambience (page 50).

★ **Hotel Nacional:** A splendid landmark with magnificent architecture and oodles of history, this hotel is a great place to relax with a *mojito* and cigar while soaking in the heady atmosphere of the past (page 69).

★ **Necrópolis Cristóbal Colón:** This is one of the New World's great cemeteries, with dramatic tombstones that comprise a who's who of Cuban history (page 78).

★ **Parque Histórico Militar Morro-Cabaña:** An imposing castle complex contains the Castillo de los Tres Reyes del Morro and massive Fortaleza de San Carlos de la Cabaña, with cannons in situ and soldiers in period costume (page 93).

★ **Tropicana:** Havana at its most sensual, the Tropicana hosts a spectacular cabaret with more than 200 performers and dancers (page 105).

★ **Museo Ernest Hemingway:** "Papa's" former home is preserved as it was on the day he died. His sportfishing boat, the *Pilar*, stands on the grounds (page 173).

down, they were replaced by dozens of monuments to those on the correct side of history.

The heart of Habana Vieja has been restored, and most of the important structures have been given facelifts, or better, by the City Historian's office. Some have even metamorphosed into boutique hotels. Nor is there a shortage of 1950s-era modernist hotels steeped in Mafia associations. And hundreds of *casas particulares* provide an opportunity to live life alongside the *habaneros* themselves. As for food, Havana is in the midst of a gastro-revolution. A dynamic new breed of *paladar* (private restaurant) owner is now offering world-class cuisine in spectacular settings. Streets from Habana Vieja to Vedado resound with the sound of jackhammers. Pockets of gentrification—an inconceivable word for Cuba until now—are emerging as the rapprochement with the United States and the tourism boom it has fostered are translating into money, money, money and a surge of private investment in boutique bars, boutiques, and chic *casas particulares* billed as boutique "hotels."

Nonetheless, it's increasingly hard to find a vacant hotel room: Havana is jam-packed with *yanqui* visitors making the most of the heretofore forbidden fruit. A series finale of *House of Lies*, plus segments of *Fast & Furious 8*, have been filmed in Havana as Hollywood, too, has cottoned on. In 2017, U.S. cruise ships arrived, flooding the plazas with tour groups. The arts scene remains unrivaled in Latin America, with first-rate museums and galleries—not only formal galleries, but informal ones where contemporary artists produce unique works of amazing profundity and appeal. There are tremendous crafts markets and boutique stores. Afro-Caribbean music is everywhere, quite literally on the streets. Lovers of sizzling salsa have dozens of venues from which to choose. Havana even has a hot jazz scene. Classical music and ballet are world class. And neither Las Vegas nor Rio de Janeiro can compare with Havana for sexy cabarets, with top billing now, as back in the day, belonging to the Tropicana.

PLANNING YOUR TIME

Havana is so large, and the sights to be seen so many, that one week is the bare minimum needed. Metropolitan Havana sprawls over 740 square kilometers (286 square miles) and incorporates 15 *municipios* (municipalities). Havana is a collection of neighborhoods, each with its own distinct character. Because the city is so spread out, it is best to explore Havana in sections, concentrating your time on the three main districts of touristic interest—Habana Vieja, Vedado, and Miramar—in that order.

If you have only one or two days in Havana, book a get-your-bearings trip by HabanaBusTour or hop on an organized city tour offered by Havanatur or a similar agency. This will provide an overview of the major sights. Concentrate the balance of your time around Parque Central, Plaza de la Catedral, and Plaza de Armas. Your checklist of must-sees should include the **Capitolio Nacional, Museo de la Revolución, Museo Nacional de Bellas Artes, Catedral de la Habana, Museo de la Ciudad de la Habana,**

Havana

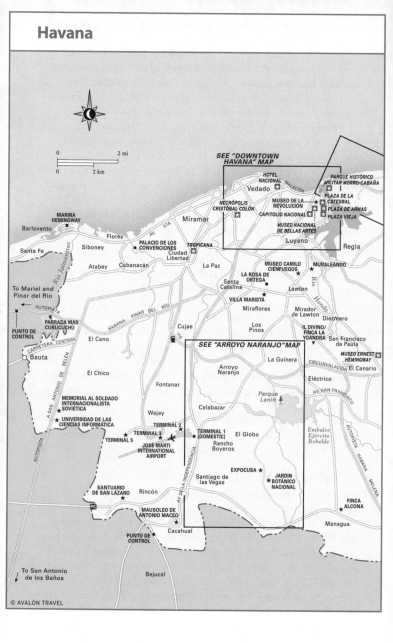

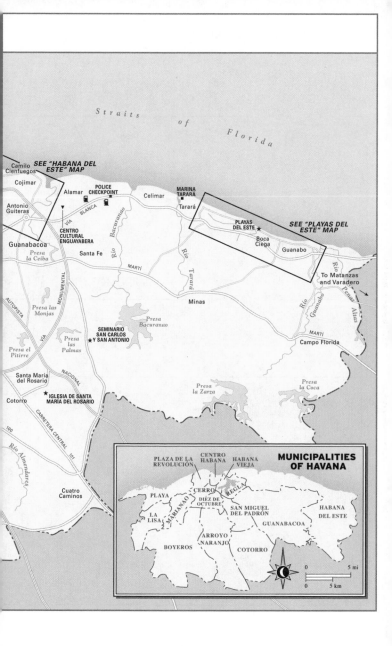

Straits of Florida

SEE "HABANA DEL ESTE" MAP

Camilo Cienfuegos
Cojímar
Antonio Guiteras
Guanabacoa

Alamar
POLICE CHECKPOINT
Celimar
MARINA TARARÁ
Tarará

VÍA BLANCA

CENTRO CULTURAL ENGUAYABERA

Santa Fe

Río Bacuranao

Río Tarará

PLAYAS DEL ESTE ★

Boca Ciega
Guanabo

SEE "PLAYAS DEL ESTE" MAP

To Matanzas and Varadero

Río Guanabo

Río Peñas Altas

MARTÍ

Presa la Ceiba

MONUMENTAL

Presa las Monjas

AUTOPISTA

Presa el Pitirre

VÍA NACIONAL

Presa las Palmas

Minas

SEMINARIO SAN CARLOS Y SAN ANTONIO ★

Presa Bacuranao

MARTÍ

Campo Florida

Santa María del Rosario

Presa la Zarza

Presa la Coca

Cotorro

★ IGLESIA DE SANTA MARÍA DEL ROSARIO

CARRETERA CENTRAL 101

Río Almendares

100

Cuatro Caminos

MUNICIPALITIES OF HAVANA

PLAZA DE LA REVOLUCIÓN
CENTRO HABANA
HABANA VIEJA

PLAYA

CERRO
MARIANAO
DIÉZ DE OCTUBRE

REGLA

SAN MIGUEL DEL PADRÓN

GUANABACOA

HABANA DEL ESTE

LA LISA

BOYEROS

ARROYO NARANJO

COTORRO

0   5 mi
0   5 km

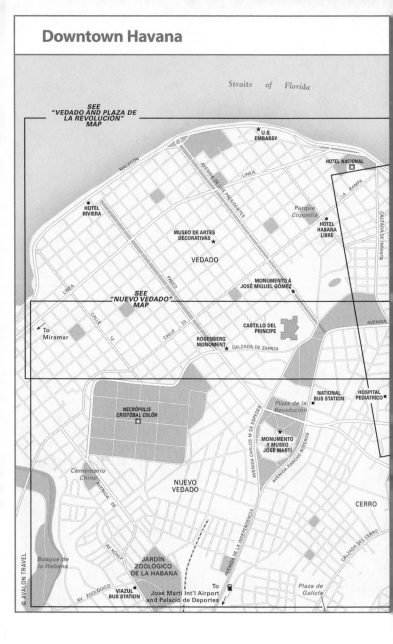

Downtown Havana

Straits of Florida

SEE "VEDADO AND PLAZA DE LA REVOLUCIÓN" MAP

U.S. EMBASSY

HOTEL NACIONAL

LA RAMPA

MALECÓN

LINEA

AVENIDA DE LOS PRESIDENTES

CALZADA DE INFANTA

HOTEL RIVIERA

Parque Coppelia

HOTEL HABANA LIBRE

MUSEO DE ARTES DECORATIVAS

VEDADO

PASEO

MONUMENTO A JOSÉ MIGUEL GÓMEZ

LINEA

SEE "NUEVO VEDADO" MAP

AVENIDA

To Miramar

CALLE 12

CALLE 23

CASTILLO DEL PRINCIPE

ROSENBERG MONUMENT

CALZADA DE ZAPATA

NATIONAL BUS STATION

HOSPITAL PEDIÁTRICO

NECRÓPOLIS CRISTÓBAL COLÓN

Plaza de la Revolución

AVENIDA CARLOS M DE ESPEDES

MONUMENTO Y MUSEO JOSÉ MARTÍ

AVENIDA RANCHO BOYEROS

Cementerio Chino

NUEVO VEDADO

CERRO

AVENIDA 26

AVENIDA DE LA INDEPENDENCIA

CALZADA DEL CERRO

AV KOHLY

Bosque de la Habana

JARDÍN ZOOLÓGICO DE LA HABANA

AV. ZOOLOGICO

VIAZUL BUS STATION

To José Martí Int'l Airport and Palacio de Deportes

Plaza de Galicia

© AVALON TRAVEL

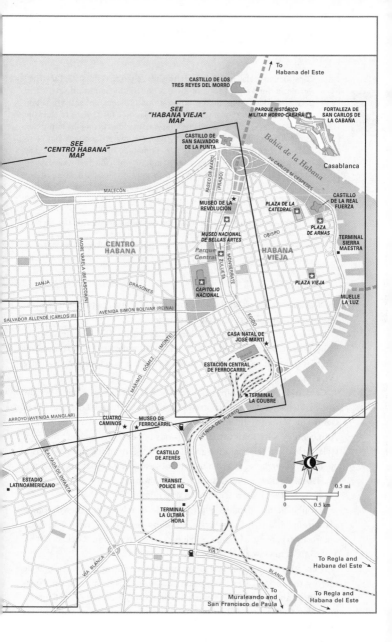

Havana's City Walls

Construction of Havana's fortified city walls began on February 3, 1674. They ran along the western edge of the bay and, on the landward side, stood between today's Calle Egido, Monserrate, and Zulueta. Under the direction of engineer Juan de Siscaras, African slaves labored for 23 years to build the 1.4-meter-thick, 10-meter-tall wall that was intended to ring the entire city, using rocks hauled from the coast. The 4,892-meter-long wall was completed in 1697, with a perimeter of five kilometers. The damage inflicted by the British artillery in 1762 was repaired in 1797, when the thick wall attained its final shape. It formed an irregular polygon with nine defensive bastions with moats and steep drops to delay assault by enemy troops. In its first stage it had just two entrances (nine more were added later), opened each morning and closed at night upon the sound of a single cannon.

As time went on, the *intramuros* (the city within the walls) burst its confines. In 1841, Havana authorities petitioned the Spanish crown for permission to demolish the walls. The demolition began in 1863, when African slave-convicts were put to work to destroy what their forefathers had built.

and **Parque Histórico Militar Morro-Cabaña**, featuring two restored castles attended by soldiers in period costume.

Habana Vieja, the original colonial city within the 17th-century city walls (now demolished), will require at least three days to fully explore. You can base yourself in one of the charming historic hotel conversions close to the main sights of interest.

Centro Habana has many *casas particulares* and fine restaurants but few sites of interest, and its rubble-strewn, dimly lit streets aren't the safest. Skip Centro for **Vedado,** the modern heart of the city that evolved in the early 20th century, with many ornate mansions in beaux-arts and art nouveau style. Its leafy streets make for great walking. Many of the city's best *casas particulares* are here, as are most businesses, *paladares,* and nightclubs. The **Hotel Nacional, Universidad de la Habana, Cementerio Colón,** and **Plaza de la Revolución** are sights not to miss.

If you're interested in beaux-arts or art deco architecture, then the once-glamorous **Miramar, Cubanacán,** and **Siboney** regions, west of Vedado, are worth exploring. Miramar also has excellent restaurants, deluxe hotels, and some of my favorite nightspots.

Most other sections of Havana are run-down residential districts of little interest to tourists. A few exceptions lie on the east side of Havana harbor. **Regla** and neighboring **Guanabacoa** are together a center of Santería and Afro-Cuban music. The 18th-century fishing village of **Cojímar** has Hemingway associations, and the nearby community of **San Miguel del Padrón** is where the great author lived for 20 years. A visit to his home, **Finca Vigía,** today the Museo Ernest Hemingway, is de rigueur. Combine it with a visit to the exquisite colonial **Iglesia de Santa María del Rosario.**

About 15 kilometers east of the city, long, white-sand beaches—the **Playas del Este**—prove tempting on hot summer days.

In the suburban district of **Boyeros,** to the south, the **Santuario de San Lázaro** is an important pilgrimage site. A visit here can be combined with the nearby **Mausoleo Antonio Maceo,** where the hero general of the independence wars is buried outside the village of Santiago de las Vegas. A short distance east, the **Arroyo Naranjo** district has **Parque Lenin,** a vast park with an amusement park, horseback rides, boating, and more. Enthusiasts of botany can visit the **Jardín Botánico Nacional.**

Despite Havana's great size, most sights of interest are highly concentrated, and most exploring is best done on foot.

HISTORY

The city was founded in July 1515 as San Cristóbal de la Habana, and was located on the south coast, where Batabanó stands today. The site was a disaster. On November 25, 1519, the settlers moved to the shore of the flask-shaped Bahía de la Habana. Its location was so advantageous that in July 1553 the city replaced Santiago de Cuba as the capital of the island.

Every spring and summer, Spanish treasure ships returning from the Americas crowded into Havana's sheltered harbor before setting off for Spain in an armed convoy—*la flota.* By the turn of the 18th century, Havana was the third-largest city in the New World after Mexico City and Lima. The 17th and 18th centuries saw a surge of ecclesiastical construction and a perimeter wall was built.

In 1762, the English captured Havana but ceded it back to Spain the following year in exchange for Florida. The Spanish lost no time in building the largest fortress in the Americas—San Carlos de la Cabaña. Under the supervision of the new Spanish governor, the Marqués de la Torre, the city attained a new focus and rigorous architectural harmony. The first public gas lighting arrived in 1768. Most of the streets were cobbled. Along them, wealthy merchants and plantation owners erected beautiful mansions fitted inside with every luxury in European style.

By the mid-19th century, Havana was bursting its seams. In 1863, the city walls came tumbling down. New districts went up westward, and graceful boulevards pushed into the surrounding countryside, lined with a parade of *quintas* (summer homes) fronted by classical columns. By the mid-1800s, Havana had achieved a level of modernity that surpassed that of Madrid.

Following the Spanish-Cuban-American War, Havana entered a new era of prosperity. The city spread out, its perimeter enlarged by parks, boulevards, and dwellings in eclectic, neoclassical, and revivalist styles, while older residential areas settled into an era of decay.

By the 1950s Havana was a wealthy and thoroughly modern city with a large and prospering middle class, and had acquired skyscrapers such as the Focsa building and the Hilton (now the Habana Libre). Ministries were being moved to a new center of construction (today the Plaza de la

Revolución), inland from Vedado. Gambling found new life, and casinos flourished.

Following the Revolution in 1959, a mass exodus of the wealthy and the middle class began, inexorably changing the face of Havana. Tourists also forsook the city, dooming Havana's hotels, restaurants, and other businesses to bankruptcy. Festering slums and shantytowns marred the suburbs. The government ordered them razed. Concrete apartment blocks were erected on the outskirts. That accomplished, the Revolution turned its back on the city. Havana's aged housing and infrastructure, much of it already decayed, have ever since suffered neglect.

Tens of thousands of poor peasant migrants poured into Havana from Oriente. The settlers changed the city's demographic profile: Most of the immigrants were black; today, as many as 400,000 *"palestinos,"* immigrants from Santiago and the eastern provinces, live in Havana.

Finally, in the 1980s, the revolutionary government established a preservation program for Habana Vieja, and the Centro Nacional de Conservación, Restauración, y Museología was created to inventory Havana's historic sites and implement a restoration program that would return the ancient city to pristine splendor. Much of the original city core now gleams afresh with confections in stone, while the rest is left to crumble.

Sights

HABANA VIEJA

Habana Vieja (4.5 square km) is defined by the limits of the early colonial settlement that lay within fortified walls. The legal boundary of Habana Vieja includes the Paseo de Martí (Prado) and everything east of it.

Habana Vieja is roughly shaped like a diamond, with the Castillo de la Punta its northerly point. The Prado runs south at a gradual gradient from the Castillo de la Punta to Parque Central and, beyond, Parque de la Fraternidad. Two blocks east, Avenida de Bélgica parallels the Prado, tracing the old city wall to the harborfront at the west end of Desamparados. East of Castillo de la Punta, Avenida Carlos Manuel de Céspedes (Avenida del Puerto) runs along the harbor channel and curls south to Desamparados.

The major sites of interest are centered on Plaza de Armas, Plaza de la Catedral, Plaza Vieja, and Parque Central. Each square has its own flavor. The plazas and surrounding streets shine after a complete restoration that now extends to the area east of Avenida de Bélgica and southwest of Plaza Vieja, between Calles Brasil and Merced. This was the great ecclesiastical center of colonial Havana and is replete with churches and convents.

Habana Vieja is a living museum—as many as 60,000 people live within the confines of the old city wall—and suffers from inevitable ruination brought on by the tropical climate, hastened since the Revolution by years of neglect. The grime of centuries has been soldered by tropical heat into the chipped cement and faded pastels. Beyond the restored areas, Habana Vieja is a quarter of sagging, mildewed walls and half-collapsed balconies. The much-deteriorated (mostly residential) southern half of Habana Vieja requires caution.

The past few years have witnessed a spectacular tourist boom. Gentrification is sweeping pockets of Habana Vieja. Suddenly every third building in this overcrowded, once sclerotic northern extreme of Habana Vieja is in the throes of a remake as a boutique B&B, hip restaurant, or—what's this?—a gourmet *heladería* selling homemade gelato. You'll want to avoid Habana Vieja when the cruise ships are in.

Paseo de Martí (Prado)

Paseo de Martí, colloquially known as the Prado, is a kilometer-long tree-lined boulevard that slopes southward, uphill, from the harbor mouth to Parque Central. The beautiful boulevard was initiated by the Marqués de la Torre in 1772 and completed in 1852, when it had the name Alameda de Isabella II. It lay *extramura* (outside the old walled city) and was Havana's most notable thoroughfare. Mansions of aristocratic families rose on each side and it was a sign of distinction to live here. The *paseo*—the daily carriage ride—along the boulevard was an important social ritual, with bands at regular intervals to play to the parade of *volantas* (carriages).

French landscape artist Jean-Claude Nicolas Forestier remodeled the Prado to its present form in 1929. It's guarded by eight bronze lions, with an elevated central walkway bordered by an ornate wall with alcoves containing marble benches carved with scroll motifs. At night, it is lit by brass gas lamps with globes atop wrought-iron lampposts in the shape of griffins. Schoolchildren sit beneath shade trees, listening to lessons presented alfresco. An art fair is held on Sundays.

Heading downhill from Neptuno, the first building of interest, on the east side at the corner of Virtudes, is the former **American Club**—U.S. expat headquarters before the Revolution. The **Palacio de Matrimonio** (Prado #306, esq. Ánimas, tel. 07/866-0661, Tues.-Fri. 8am-6pm), on the west side at the corner of Ánimas, is where many of Havana's wedding ceremonies are performed. The palace, built in 1914, boasts a magnificent neobaroque facade and spectacularly ornate interior.

The Moorish-inspired **Hotel Sevilla** (Trocadero #55) is like entering a Moroccan medina. It was inspired by the Patio of the Lions at the Alhambra in Granada, Spain. The hotel opened in 1908. The gallery walls are festooned with black-and-white photos of famous figures who have stayed here, from singer Josephine Baker and boxer Joe Louis to Al Capone, who took the entire sixth floor (Capone occupied room 615).

At Trocadero, budding dancers train for potential ballet careers in the **Escuela Nacional de Ballet** (National School of Ballet, Prado #207, e/ Colón y Trocadero, tel. 07/861-6629, cuballet@cubarte.cult.cu; entry by permission only). On the west side, the **Casa de los Científicos** (Prado #212, esq. Trocadero, tel. 07/862-1607), the former home of President José

Habana Vieja

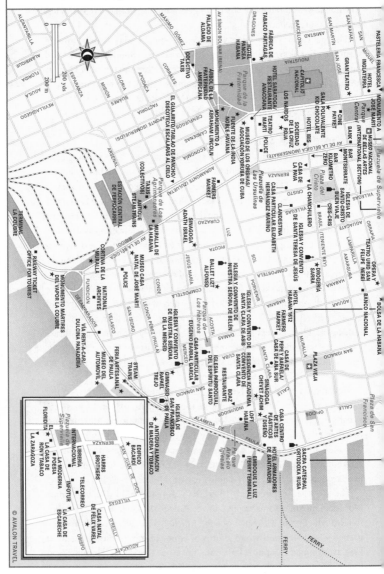

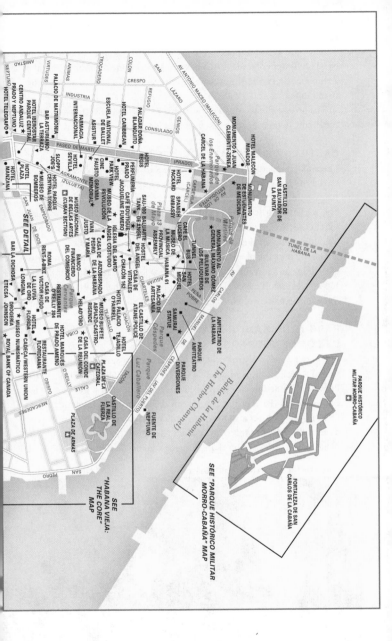

Miguel Gómez, first president of the republic, is now a hotel; pop in to admire the fabulous stained glass and the chapel.

At Prado and Colón, note the art deco **Cine Fausto,** an ornamental band on its upper facade; two blocks north, examine the mosaic mural of a Nubian beauty on the upper wall of the **Centro Cultural de Árabe** (between Refugio and Trocadero).

The bronze **statue of Juan Clemente-Zenea** (1832-1871), at the base of the Prado, honors a nationalist poet shot for treason in 1871.

CASTILLO DE SAN SALVADOR DE LA PUNTA

The small, recently restored **Castillo de San Salvador de la Punta** (Av. Carlos M. de Céspedes, esq. Prado y Malecón, tel. 07/860-3195, Wed.-Sun. 10am-6pm, CUC1) guards the entrance to Havana's harbor channel at the base of the Prado. It was built in 1589 directly across from the Morro castle so that the two fortresses could catch invaders in a crossfire. A great chain was slung between them each night to secure Havana harbor.

Gazing over the plaza on the west side of the castle is a life-size statue of Venezuelan general Francisco de Miranda Rodríguez (1750-1816), while 100 meters east of the castle is a statue of Pierre D'Iberville (1661-1706), a Canadian explorer who died in Havana.

PARQUE DE MÁRTIRES AND PARQUE DE LOS ENAMORADOS

The park immediately south of the Castillo de San Salvador, on the south side of Avenida Carlos Manuel de Céspedes, at the base (and east) of the Prado, is divided in two by Avenida de los Estudiantes. **Parque de los Enamorados** (Park of the Lovers), on the north side of Avenida de los Estudiantes, features a statue of an Indian couple, plus the **Monumento de Estudiantes de Medicina,** a small Grecian-style temple shading the remains of a wall used by Spanish firing squads. On November 27, 1871,

dancers at the Escuela Nacional de Ballet

eight medical students met their deaths after being falsely accused of desecrating the tomb of a prominent loyalist. A trial found them innocent, but enraged loyalist troops held their own trial and shot the students, who are commemorated each November 27.

Parque de Mártires (Martyrs' Park), on the south side of Avenida de los Estudiantes, occupies the ground of the former Tacón prison, built in 1838. Nationalist hero José Martí was imprisoned here 1869-1870. The **Carcel de la Habana** prison was demolished in 1939. Preserved are two of the punishment cells and the chapel used by condemned prisoners before being marched to the firing wall.

Parque Central

Spacious Parque Central is the social epicenter of Habana Vieja. The park—bounded by the Prado, Neptuno, Zulueta, and San Martín—is presided over by stately royal palms shading a marble **statue of José Martí**. It was sculpted by José Vilalta de Saavedra and inaugurated in 1905. Adjacent, baseball fanatics gather at a point called *"esquina caliente"* ("hot corner") to argue the intricacies of *pelota* (baseball).

The park is surrounded by historic hotels, including the triangular **Hotel Plaza** (Zulueta #267), built in 1909, on the northeast face of the square. In 1920, baseball legend Babe Ruth stayed in room 216, preserved as a museum with his signed bat and ball in a case. Much of the social action happens in front of the **Hotel Inglaterra** (Paseo de Martí #416), opened in 1856 and today the oldest Cuban hotel still extant. The sidewalk, known in colonial days as the Acera del Louvre, was a focal point for rebellion against Spanish rule. A plaque outside the hotel entrance honors the "lads of the Louvre sidewalk" who died for Cuban independence. Inside, the hotel boasts elaborate wrought-ironwork and exquisite Mudejar-style detailing, including arabesque archways and *azulejos* (patterned tile). A highlight is the sensuous life-size bronze statue of a Spanish dancer—*La Sevillana*—in the main

Parque Central, Habana Vieja

SIGHTS

bar. Hopefully the fin de siècle charm will survive the 2016 remake initiated by U.S. hotel company Starwood.

GRAN TEATRO DE LA HABANA ALICIA ALONSO

Immediately south of the Inglaterra, the **Gran Teatro** (Paseo de Martí #452, e/ San Rafael y Neptuno, tel. 07/862-9473, guided tours Tue.-Sat. 9am-5pm, CUC2) originated in 1837 as the Teatro Tacón, drawing operatic luminaries such as Enrico Caruso and Sarah Bernhardt. The current neobaroque structure dates from 1915, when a social club—the Centro Gallego—was built around the old Teatro Tacón for the Galician community.

The building's exorbitantly baroque facade drips with caryatids and has four towers, each tipped by a white marble angel reaching gracefully for heaven. It functions as a theater for the Ballet Nacional and Ópera Nacional de Cuba. The main auditorium, the exquisitely decorated 2,000-seat Teatro García Lorca, features a painted dome and huge chandelier. Smaller performances are hosted in the 500-seat Sala Alejo Carpentier and the 120-seat Sala Artaud. After a two-year restoration, it reopened in 2016 (in time for President Obama's speech here) and is spectacularly illuminated at night.

★ MUSEO NACIONAL DE BELLAS ARTES (INTERNATIONAL SECTION)

The international section of the **Museo Nacional de Bellas Artes** (National Fine Arts Museum, San Rafael, e/ Zulueta y Monserrate, tel. 07/863-9484 or 07/862-0140, www.bellasartes.cult.cu, Tues.-Sat. 9am-5pm, Sun. 10am-2pm, entrance CUC5, or CUC8 for both sections, guided tour CUC2) occupies the former Centro Asturiano, on the southeast side of the square. The building, lavishly decorated with neoclassical motifs, was erected in 1885 but rebuilt in Renaissance style in 1927 following a fire and housed the postrevolutionary People's Supreme Court. A stained glass window above the main staircase shows Columbus's three caravels.

The art collection is displayed on five floors covering 4,800 square meters. The works span the United States, Latin America, Asia, and Europe—including masters such as Gainsborough, Goya, Murillo, Rubens, Velásquez, and various Impressionists. The museum also boasts Latin America's richest trove of Roman, Greek, and Egyptian antiquities. It has a top-floor restaurant.

★ CAPITOLIO NACIONAL

The statuesque **Capitolio Nacional** (Capitol, Paseo de Martí, e/ San Martín y Dragones), one block south of Parque Central, dominates Havana's skyline. It was built between 1926 and 1929 as Cuba's Chamber of Representatives and Senate and designed after the U.S. Capitol. The 692-foot-long edifice is supported by colonnades of Doric columns, with semicircular pavilions at each end of the building. The lofty stone cupola rises 62 meters, topped by a replica of 16th-century Florentine sculptor Giambologna's famous bronze *Mercury*.

A massive stairway—flanked by neoclassical figures in bronze by Italian sculptor Angelo Zanelli that represent Labor and Virtue—leads to an entrance portico with three tall bronze doors sculpted with 30 bas-reliefs that depict important events of Cuban history. Inside, facing the door is the *Estatua de la República* (Statue of the Republic), a massive bronze sculpture (also by Zanelli) of Cuba's Indian maiden of liberty. At 17.5 meters (57 feet) tall, she is the world's third-largest indoor statue (the other two are the gold Buddha in Nava, Japan, and the Lincoln Memorial in Washington, DC). In the center of the floor a replica of a 24-carat diamond marks Kilometer 0, the point from which all distances on the island are calculated.

The 394-foot-long **Salón de los Pasos Perdidos** (Great Hall of the Lost Steps), so named because of its acoustics, is inlaid with patterned marble motifs and features bronze bas-reliefs, green marble pilasters, and massive lamps on carved pedestals of glittering copper. Renaissance-style candelabras dangle from the frescoed ceiling. The semicircular Senate chamber and Chamber of Representatives are at each end.

At press time the building remained closed for a three-year restoration and will supposedly reopen as the home of the Asemblea Nacional.

Parque de la Fraternidad and Vicinity

Paseo de Martí (Prado) runs south from Parque Central three blocks, where it ends at the junction with Avenida Máximo Gómez (Monte). Here rises the **Fuente de la India Noble Habana** in the middle of the Prado. Erected in 1837, the fountain is surmounted by a Carrara marble statue of the legendary Indian queen. In one hand she bears a cornucopia, in the other a shield with the arms of Havana. Four fish at her feet occasionally spout water.

The **Asociación Cultural Yoruba de Cuba** (Prado #615, e/ Dragones y Monte, tel. 07/863-5953, www.yorubacuba.org, daily 9am-5pm) has a rather prosaic upstairs **Museo de los Orishas** (CUC10, students CUC3) dedicated to the *orishas* of Santería; no photos are permitted. The constitution for the republic was signed in 1901 in the restored **Teatro Martí** (Dragones, esq. Zulueta), one block west of the Prado.

PARQUE DE LA FRATERNIDAD

The **Parque de la Fraternidad** (Friendship Park) was laid out in 1892 on an old military drill square, the Campo de Marte, to commemorate the fourth centennial of Columbus's discovery of America. The current layout by Jean-Claude Nicolas Forestier dates from 1928. The **Árbol de la Fraternidad Americana** (Friendship Tree) was planted at its center on February 24, 1928, to cement goodwill between the nations of the Americas. Busts and statues of outstanding American leaders such as Simón Bolívar and Abraham Lincoln watch over.

The **Palacio de Aldama** (Amistad #510, e/ Reina y Estrella), on the park's far southwest corner, is a grandiose mansion built in neoclassical style in 1844 for a wealthy Basque, Don Domingo Aldama y Arrechaga. Its facade

Restoring Old Havana

Old Havana has been called the "finest urban ensemble in the Americas." The fortress colonial town that burst its walls when Washington, DC, was still a swamp is a 140-hectare repository of antique buildings. More than 900 of Habana Vieja's 3,157 structures are of historical importance. Of these, only 101 were built in the 20th century. Almost 500 are from the 19th; 200 are from the 18th; and 144 are from the 16th and 17th. Alas, many buildings are crumbling into ruins.

In 1977, the Cuban government named Habana Vieja a National Monument. In 1982, UNESCO named Habana Vieja a World Heritage Site worthy of international protection. Cuba formalized a plan to rescue much of the old city from decades of neglect under the guidance of Eusebio Leal Spengler, the official city historian, who runs the **Oficina del Historiador de la Ciudad de La Habana** (Av. del Puerto, esq. Obrapí, Habana Vieja, tel. 07/861-5001, www.ohch.cu). Leal, who grew up in Habana Vieja, is a member of Cuba's National Assembly, the Central Committee of the Communist Party, and the all-important Council of State.

The ambitious plan stretches into the future and has concentrated on four squares: Plaza de Armas, Plaza de la Catedral, Plaza Vieja, and Plaza de San Francisco. The most important buildings have received major renovations; others have been given facelifts. Priority is given to edifices with income-generating tourist value. Structures are ranked into one of four levels according to historical and physical value. The top level is reserved for museums; the second level is for hotels, restaurants, offices, and schools; and the bottom levels are for housing.

Until 2016, **Habaguanex** (Calle Oficios 52, e/ Obrapía y Lamparilla, Plaza de San Francisco, Havana, tel. 07/204-9201, www.habaguanex.ohc.cu) was responsible for opening and operating commercial entities such as hotels, restaurants, cafés, and shops. The profits helped finance further infrastructural improvements; 33 percent of revenues are supposedly devoted to social projects such as theaters, schools, and medical facilities. In 2016, the military's Business Administration Group, GAESA, took control of Habaguanex. Word is that the businesses will be dispersed to subsidiaries of GAESA: the hotels to Gaviota, the restaurants to CIMEX, and the shops to TRD Caribe.

Still, there is little evidence of actual homes being restored. In southern Habana Vieja, where there are relatively few structures of touristic interest, talk of restoration raises hollow laughs from the inhabitants occupying overcrowded *solares* (slums).

is lined by Ionic columns and the interior features murals of scenes from Pompeii. It is not open to the public.

To the park's northeast side, a former graveyard for rusting antique steam trains has been cleared to make way for a new hotel, **Pancea Havana Cuba.**

FÁBRICA DE TABACO PARTAGÁS

The original **Partagás Cigar Factory** (Industria #520, e/ Dragones y Barcelona), on the west side of the Capitolio, features a four-story classical

Visiting Havana's Cigar Factories

cigar factories produce for export

You'll forever remember the pungent aroma of a cigar factory. The factories, housed in colonial buildings, remain much as they were in the mid-19th century. Though now officially known by ideologically sound names, they're still commonly referred to by their prerevolutionary names. (Note that the factory names switch between factories with annoying regularity when one or more close for repair.) Each specializes in cigar brands of a particular flavor—the government assigns to certain factories the job of producing particular brands.

You must book in advance through a state tour desk or agency (CUC10). No cameras or bags are permitted.

Fábrica Corona (20 de Mayo #520, e/ Marta Abreu y Línea, Cerro, tel. 07/873-0131, Mon.-Fri. 9am-11am and 1pm-3pm) is a modern cigar factory producing Hoyo de Monterey, Punch, and other labels.

Fábrica de Tabaco H. Upmann (Padre Varela, e/ Desagüe y Peñal Verno, Centro Habana, tel. 07/878-1059 or 07/879-3927, 9am-1pm), formerly the Fábrica de Tabaco Romeo y Julieta, makes about a dozen brand names and is the best factory to visit.

Fábrica de Tabaco Partagás (Luceña, esq. Penalver, Centro Habana), formerly the El Rey del Mundo factory, opened in 2011 to house the Partagás workers. Cramped and noisy, it is not as rewarding to visit.

Spanish-style facade capped by a roofline of baroque curves topped by lions. It closed in 2010 for repair and remained so at press time, with little sign of progress. The cigar-making facility moved to the former **El Rey del Mundo factory** (Luceña #816, esq. Penalver, Centro Habana) and is open for tours. The factory specialized in full-bodied Partagás cigars, started in 1843 by Catalan immigrant Don Jaime Partagás Ravelo. Partagás was murdered in 1868—some say by a rival who discovered that Partagás was having an affair with his wife—and his ghost is said to haunt the building. A tobacco shop and cigar lounge remain open on the ground floor (tel. 07/863-5766).

Calle Agramonte, more commonly referred to by its colonial name of Zulueta, parallels the Prado and slopes gently upward from Avenida de los Estudiantes to the northeast side of Parque Central. Traffic runs one-way uphill.

At its north end is the **Monumento al General Máximo Gómez.** This massive monument of white marble by sculptor Aldo Gamba was erected in 1935 to honor the Dominican-born hero of the Cuban wars of independence who led the Liberation Army as commander-in-chief. Gómez (1836-1905) is cast in bronze, reining in his horse.

One block north of Parque Central, at the corner of Zulueta and Ánimas, is **Sloppy Joe's,** commemorated as Freddy's Bar in Hemingway's *To Have and Have Not.* Restored in 2013, it reopened its doors after decades lying shuttered and near-derelict.

The old Cuartel de Bomberos fire station houses the tiny **Museo de Bomberos** (Museum of Firemen, Zulueta #257, e/ Neptuno y Ánimas, tel. 07/863-4826, Tues.-Fri. 9:30am-5pm, free), displaying a Merryweather engine from 1894 and antique firefighting memorabilia.

Immediately beyond the Museo Nacional de Bellas Artes and Museo de la Revolución is **Plaza 13 de Marzo,** a grassy park named to commemorate the ill-fated attack of the presidential palace by student martyrs on March 13, 1957. At the base of Zulueta, at the junction with Cárcel, note the flamboyant art nouveau building housing the **Spanish Embassy.**

MUSEO DE LA REVOLUCIÓN

The ornate building facing north over Plaza 13 de Marzo was initiated in 1913 to house the provincial government. Before it could be finished (in 1920), it was earmarked as the Palacio Presidencial (Presidential Palace), and Tiffany's of New York was entrusted with its interior decoration. It was designed by Belgian Paul Belau and Cuban Carlos Maruri in an eclectic style, with a lofty dome. Following the Revolution, the three-story palace was converted into the dour **Museo de la Revolución** (Museum of the Revolution, Refugio #1, e/ Zulueta y Monserrate, tel. 07/862-4091, daily 9am-5pm, CUC8, cameras CUC2, guide CUC2). It is fronted by a SAU-100 Stalin tank used during the Bay of Pigs invasion in 1961 and a semi-derelict watchtower, **Baluarte de Ángel,** erected in 1680.

The marble staircase leads to the Salón de los Espejos (the Mirror Room), a replica of that in Versailles (replete with paintings by Armando Menocal); and Salón Dorado (the Gold Room), decorated with gold leaf and highlighted by its magnificent dome.

Rooms are divided chronologically. Maps describe the progress of the revolutionary war. Guns and rifles are displayed alongside grisly photos of dead and tortured heroes. The Rincón de los Cretinos (Corner of Cretins) pokes fun at Batista, Ronald Reagan, and George Bush. There's a café to the rear.

At the rear, in the former palace gardens, is the **Granma Memorial,** preserving the vessel that brought Castro and his revolutionaries from Mexico to Cuba in 1956. The *Granma* is encased in a massive glass structure. It's surrounded by vehicles used in the revolutionary war: armored vehicles, the bullet-riddled "Fast Delivery" truck used in the student commandos' assault on the palace on March 13, 1957 (Batista escaped through a secret door), and Castro's Toyota jeep from the Sierra Maestra. There's also a turbine from the U-2 spy plane downed during the missile crisis in 1962, plus a Sea Fury aircraft and a T-34 tank.

★ MUSEO NACIONAL DE BELLAS ARTES (CUBAN SECTION)

The Cuban section of the **Museo Nacional de Bellas Artes** (National Fine Arts Museum, Trocadero, e/ Zulueta y Monserrate, tel. 07/863-9484 or 07/862-0140, www.bellasartes.cult.cu, Tues.-Sat. 9am-5pm, Sun. 10am-2pm, entrance CUC5, or CUC8 for both sections, guided tour CUC2) is housed in the soberly classical Palacio de Bellas Artes. The museum features an atrium garden from which ramps lead to two floors exhibiting a complete spectrum of Cuban paintings, engravings, sketches, and sculptures. Works representing the vision of early 16th- and 17th-century travelers merge into colonial-era pieces, early 20th-century Cuban interpretations of Impressionism, Surrealism, and works spawned by the Revolution.

Monserrate (Avenida de los Misiones)

Avenida de los Misiones, or Monserrate as everyone knows it, parallels Zulueta one block to the east (traffic is one-way, downhill) and follows the space left by the ancient city walls. At the base of Monserrate, at its junction with Calle Tacón, is the once lovely **Casa de Pérez de la Riva** (Capdevila #1), built in Italian Renaissance style in 1905. It was closed for restoration at press time and is due to reopen as the Museo de la Música.

Immediately north is a narrow pedestrian alley (Calle Aguiar e/ Peña

Museo de la Revolución

Pobre y Capdevila) known as **Callejón de los Peluqueros** (Hairdressers' Alley). Adorned with colorful murals, it's the venue for the community **ArteCorte** project—the inspiration of local stylist Gilberto "Papito" Valladares—and features barber shops, art galleries, and cafés. **Papito** (Calle Aguiar #10, tel. 07/861-0202) runs a hairdressers' school and salon that doubles as a barbers' museum.

IGLESIA DEL SANTO ÁNGEL CUSTODIO

The Gothic **Iglesia del Santo Ángel Custodio** (Monserrate y Cuarteles, tel. 07/861-8873), immediately east of the Palacio Presidencial, sits atop a rock known as Angel Hill. The church was founded in 1687 by builder-bishop Diego de Compostela. The tower dates from 1846, when a hurricane toppled the original, while the facade was reworked in neo-Gothic style in the mid-19th century. Cuba's national hero, José Martí, was baptized here on February 12, 1853.

The church was the setting for the tragic marriage scene that ends in the violent denouement on the steps of the church in the 19th-century novel *Cecilia Valdés* by Cirilo Villaverde. A bust of the author and a statue of Cecilia grace the **Plazuela de Santo Ángel** outside the main entrance (the corner of Calles Compostela and Cuarteles). This colorful little plaza is a popular venue for music-video and film shoots.

EDIFICIO BACARDÍ

The **Edificio Bacardí** (Bacardí Building, Monserrate #261, esq. San Juan de Dios), former headquarters of the Bacardí rum empire, is a stunning exemplar of art deco design. Designed by Cuban architect Esteban Rodríguez and finished in December 1929, it is clad in Swedish granite and local limestone. Terra-cotta of varying hues accents the building, with motifs showing Grecian nymphs and floral patterns. It's crowned by a Lego-like pyramidal bell tower topped with a brass bat—the famous Bacardí motif. The building now houses various offices. The **Café Barrita** bar (daily 9am-6pm), a true gem of art deco design, is to the right of the lobby, up the stairs.

EL FLORIDITA

The famous restaurant and bar **El Floridita** (corner of Monserrate and Calle Obispo, tel. 07/867-1299, www.floridita-cuba.com, daily 11:30am-midnight) has been serving food since 1819, when it was called Pina de Plata. You expect a spotlight to come on and Desi Arnaz to appear conducting a dance band, and Hemingway to stroll in as he would every morning when he lived in Havana and drank with Honest Lil, the Worst Politician, and other real-life characters from his novels. A life-size bronze statue of Hemingway, by sculptor José Villa, leans on the dark mahogany bar where Constante Ribailagua once served frozen daiquiris to the great writer (Hemingway immortalized both the drink and the venue in his novel *Islands in the Stream*) and such illustrious guests as Gary Cooper, Tennessee Williams, Marlene Dietrich, and Jean-Paul Sartre.

El Floridita has been spruced up for tourist consumption with a 1930s art deco polish. They've overpriced the place, but sipping a daiquiri here is a must. Depsite the restaurant's fantastic fin de siècle ambience, dining is subpar.

PLAZA DEL CRISTO

Plaza del Cristo lies at the west end of Amargura, between Lamparilla and Brasil, one block east of Monserrate. It was here that Wormold, the vacuum-cleaner salesman turned secret agent, was "swallowed up among the pimps and lottery sellers of the Havana noon" in Graham Greene's *Our Man in Havana.* Wormold and his daughter, Millie, lived at the fictional 37 Lamparilla.

The plaza is dominated by the tiny **Iglesia de Santo Cristo Buen Vieja** (Villegas, e/ Amargura y Lamparilla, tel. 07/863-1767, daily 9am-noon), dating from 1732, but with a Franciscan hermitage dating from 1640. Buen Viaje was the final point of the Vía Crucis (the Procession of the Cross) held each Lenten Friday and beginning at the Iglesia de San Francisco de Asís. The church, named for its popularity among sailors, who pray here for safe voyages, has an impressive cross-beamed wooden ceiling and exquisite altars, including one to the Virgen de la Caridad showing three boatmen being saved from a tempest.

The handsome **Iglesia y Convento de Santa Teresa de Jesús** (Brasil, esq. Compostela, tel. 07/861-1445), two blocks east of Plaza del Cristo, was built by the Carmelites in 1705. The church is still in use, although the convent ceased to operate as such in 1929, when the nuns were moved out and the building was converted into a series of homes.

Across the road is the **Drogería Sarrá** (Brasil, e/ Compostela y Habana, tel. 07/866-7554, daily 9am-5pm, free), a fascinating apothecary that is now the **Museo de la Farmacia Habanera.** Its paneled cabinets are still stocked with herbs and pharmaceuticals in colorful old bottles and ceramic jars.

The Harbor Channel

Throughout most of the colonial era, sea waves washed up on a beach that lined the southern shore of the harbor channel and bordered what is today Calle Cuba and, eastward, Calle Tacón, which runs along the site of the old city walls forming the original waterfront. In the early 19th century, the area was extended with landfill, and a broad boulevard—**Avenida Carlos Manuel de Céspedes** (Avenida del Puerto)—was laid out along the new harborfront. **Parque Luz Caballero,** between the *avenida* and Calle Tacón, is pinned by a statue of José de la Luz Caballero (1800-1862), a philosopher and nationalist. In 2014, a statue of feudal samurai Hasekura Tsunenaga (the first Japanese to visit Cuba, in 1614) was erected.

Overlooking the harborfront at the foot of Empedrado is the **Fuente de Neptuno** (Neptune Fountain), erected in 1838.

The giant and beautiful modernist glass cube at the Avenida del Puerto and Calle Narciso López, by Plaza de Armas, is the **Cámara de Rejas,** the new sewer gate. Educational panels tell the history of Havana's sewer system.

CALLES CUBA AND TACÓN

Calle Cuba extends east from the foot of Monserrate. At the foot of Calle Cuarteles is the Palacio de Mateo Pedroso y Florencia, known today as the **Palacio de Artesanía** (Artisans Palace, Cuba #64, e/ Tacón y Peña Pobre, Mon.-Sat. 9am-8pm, Sat. 9am-2pm, free), built in Moorish style for nobleman Don Mateo Pedroso around 1780. Pedroso's home displays the typical architectural layout of period houses, with stores on the ground floor, slave quarters on the mezzanine, and the owner's dwellings above. Today it houses craft shops, boutiques, and folkloric music.

Immediately east is **Plazuela de la Maestranza,** where a remnant of the old city wall is preserved. On its east side, in the triangle formed by the junction of Calles Cuba, Tacón, and Chacón, is a medieval-style fortress, **El Castillo de Atane,** a police headquarters built in 1941 as a pseudo-colonial confection.

The Seminario de San Carlos y San Ambrosio, a massive seminary running the length of Tacón east of El Castillo de Atane, was established by the Jesuits in 1721 and is now the **Centro Cultural Félix Varela** (e/ Chacón y Empedrado, tel. 07/862-8790, www.cfv.org.cu, Mon.-Sat. 9am-4pm, free). The downstairs cloister is open to the public.

The entrance to the seminary overlooks an excavated site showing the foundations of the original seafront section of the city walls, here called the **Cortina de Valdés.**

Tacón opens to a tiny *plazuela* at the junction with Empedrado, where horse-drawn cabs called *calezas* offer guided tours. The **Museo de Arqueología** (Tacón #12, e/ O'Reilly y Empedrado, tel. 07/861-4469, Tues.-Sat. 9am-2pm, CUC1) displays pre-Columbian artifacts, plus ceramics and items from the early colonial years. The museum occupies Casa de Juana Carvajal, a mansion first mentioned in documents in 1644, and features floor-to-ceiling murals depicting 18th-century life.

★ Plaza de la Catedral

The exquisite cobbled **Plaza de la Catedral** (Cathedral Square) was the last square to be laid out in Habana Vieja. It occupied a lowly quarter where rainwater and refuse collected (it was originally known as the Plazuela de la Ciénaga—Little Square of the Swamp). A cistern was built in 1587, and only in the following century was the area drained. Its present texture dates from the 18th century. The square is Habana Vieja at its most quintessential, the atmosphere enhanced by women in traditional costume who will pose for your camera for a small fee.

CATEDRAL SAN CRISTÓBAL DE LA HABANA

On the north side of the plaza and known colloquially as Catedral Colón (Columbus Cathedral) is the **Catedral San Cristóbal de la Habana** (St.

Christopher's Cathedral, tel. 07/861-7771, Mon.-Fri. 9am-5pm, Sat.-Sun. 9am-noon, tower tour CUC1), initiated by the Jesuits in 1748. The order was kicked out of Cuba by Carlos III in 1767, but the building was eventually completed in 1777 and altered again in the early 19th century. The original baroque interior (including the altar) is gone, replaced in 1814 by a classical interior.

The baroque facade is adorned with clinging columns and ripples like a great swelling sea; Cuban novelist Alejo Carpentier thought it "music turned to stone." A royal decree of December 1793 elevated the church to a cathedral. A second bell tower, narrower than the first, was added. Columns divide the rectangular church into three naves. The neoclassical main altar is made of wood; the murals above are by Italian painter Guiseppe Perovani. The chapel immediately to the left has several altars. Note the wooden image of Saint Christopher, patron saint of Havana, dating to 1633.

The Spanish believed that a casket brought to Havana from Santo Domingo in 1796 and that resided in the cathedral for more than a century held the ashes of Christopher Columbus. It was returned to Spain in 1899. All but the partisan *habaneros* now believe that the ashes were those of Columbus's son Diego.

CASA DE LOS MARQUESES DE AGUAS CLARAS

This splendid mansion, on the northwest side of the plaza, was built during the 16th century by Governor General Gonzalo Pérez de Angulo and has since been added to by subsequent owners. Today a café occupies the portico; the inner courtyard, with its fountain, houses the Restaurante El Patio. The upstairs restaurant offers splendid views over the plaza. Sunlight pouring in through stained glass *mediopuntos* saturates the floors with shifting colors.

Plaza de la Catedral

Habana Vieja: The Historic Core

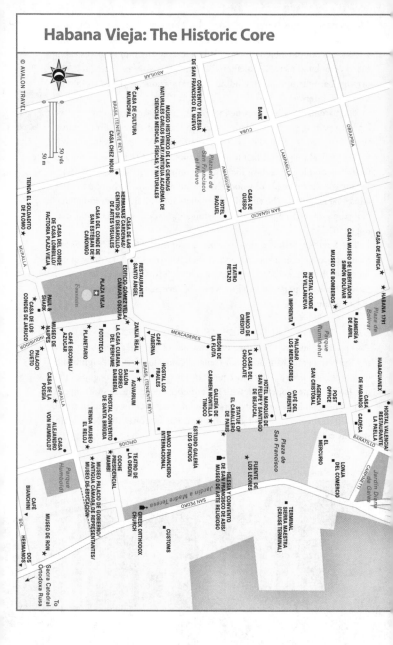

© AVALON TRAVEL

0   50 yds
0   50 m

AGUILAR

BRASIL (TENIENTE REY)

CONVENTO Y IGLESIA DE SAN FRANCISCO EL NUEVO

CASA DE CULTURA MUNICIPAL

MUSEO HISTÓRICO DE LAS CIENCIAS NATURALES CARLOS FINLAY/ANTIGUA ACADEMIA DE CIENCIAS MÉDICAS, FÍSICAS, Y NATURALES

CASA CHEZ NOUS

TIENDA EL SOLDADITO DE PLOMO

CASA DEL CONDE DE CASA LOMBILLO/ FACTORÍA PLAZA VIEJA

MURALLA

HERMANAS CÁRDENAS/ CENTRO DE DESARROLLO DE ARTES VISUALES

CASA DE LAS

CASA DEL CONDE DE SAN ESTEBAN DE CAÑONGO

PAUL & SHARK

CASA DE LOS CONDES DE JARUCO

INQUISIDOR

MUSEO DE NAIPES

PLAZA VIEJA

Fountain

EDIFICIO GÓMEZ VILA/ CÁMARA OSCURA

RESTAURANTE SANTO ANGEL

CAFÉ ESCORIAL/ AZÚCAR

PALACIO CUETO

CASA DE LA POESÍA

CASA ALEJANDRO VON HUMBOLDT

PLANETARIO

FOTOTECA

LA CASA CUBANA DEL PERFUME

ZANJA REAL

CAFÉ TABERNA

MERCADERES

SALÓN CORREO BARBERÍA

AQUARIUM

BRASIL (TENIENTE REY)

HOSTAL LOS FRAILES

TIENDA MUSEO EL RELOJ

HOSTAL CONVENTO DE SANTA BRÍGIDA

MURALLA

OFICIOS

MESÓN DE LA FLOTA

GALERÍA DE CARMEN MONTILLA TINOCO

LA CASA DEL CHOCOLATE

BANCO DE CRÉDITO

TEATRO RETAZO

HOTEL RAQUEL

AMARGURA

SAN IGNACIO

CASA DE QUESO

Plazuela de San Francisco el Nuevo

BANK

CUBA

LAMPARILLA

OBRAPÍA

CASA MUSEO DE LIBERTADOR SIMÓN BOLÍVAR

HOSTAL CONDE DE VILLANUEVA

LA IMPRENTA

MUSEO DE BOMBEROS

CASA DE ÁFRICA

HABANA 1791

Parque Rumiñahui

ARMERÍA 9 DE ABRIL

Plaza de Bolívar

PALADAR LOS MERCADERES

AGENCIA SAN CRISTÓBAL

CAFÉ DEL ORIENTE

HOTEL MARQUÉS DE SAN FELIPE Y SANTIAGO DE BEJUCAL

STATUE OF EL CABALLERO DE PARÍS

HABAGUANEX

CASA DE HABANOS

POST OFFICE

CADECA

HOSTAL VALENCIA/ RESTAURANTE LA PAELLA

LA PAELLA

BARATILLO

EL MERCURIO

LONJA DEL COMERCIO

Jardín Diana de Gales

Camilo Cienfuegos

ESTUDIO GALERÍA LOS OFICIOS

BANCO FINANCIERO INTERNACIONAL

TEATRO DE LA ORDEN

COCHE PRESIDENCIAL MAMBÍ

MUSEO PALACIO DE GOBIERNO/ ANTIGUA CÁMARA DE REPRESENTANTES/ MUSEO DE EDUCACIÓN

IGLESIA Y CONVENTO DE SAN FRANCISCO DE ASÍS/ MUSEO DE ARTE RELIGIOSO

FUENTE DE LOS LEONES

Plaza de San Francisco

TERMINAL SIERRA MAESTRA (CRUISE TERMINAL)

Jardín a Madre Teresa

SAN PEDRO

GREEK ORTHODOX CHURCH

Parque Humboldt

CAFÉ BIANCHINI

MUSEO DE RON

SOL

DOS HERMANOS

CUSTOMS

To Sacra Catedral Ortodoxa Rusa

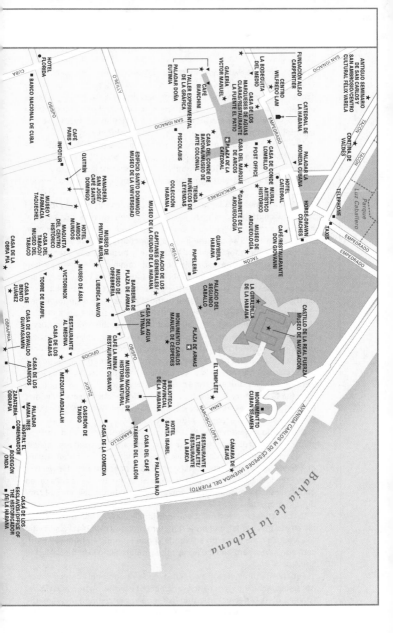

ANTIGUO SEMINARIO DE SAN CARLOS Y SAN AMBROSIO/CENTRO CULTURAL FÉLIX VARELA

HOTEL FLORIDA

BANCO NACIONAL DE CUBA

FUNDACIÓN ALEJO CARPENTIER

LA BODEGUITA DEL MEDIO

CENTRO WILFREDO LAM

CATEDRAL DE LA HABANA

CORTINA DE VALDÉS

CAFÉ PARIS

INFOTUR

GALERÍA VICTOR MANUEL

PALADAR DOÑA EUTIMIA

TALLER EXPERIMENTAL DE LA GRÁFICA

CASA DE LOS MARQUESES DE AGUAS CLARAS/RESTAURANTE LA FUENTE EL PATIO

CAFÉ BIANCHINI

PALADAR LA MONEDA CUBANA

TELEPHONE

TAXIS

EMPEDRADO

PISCOLABIS

CASA DEL CONDE DE BAYONA/MUSEO DE ARTE COLONIAL

PLAZA DE LA CATEDRAL

CASA DEL MARQUÉS DE ARCOS

POST OFFICE

MURAL ARTÍSTICO HISTÓRICO

PALADAR DOÑA EUTIMIA

HOTEL CATEDRAL

CAFÉ/RESTAURANTE DON GIOVANNI

HORSE-DRAWN COACHES

EMPEDRADO

QUITRIN

PANADERÍA SAN JOSÉ/ CAFÉ SANTO DOMINGO

EDIFICIO SANTO DOMINGO/ MUSEO DE LA UNIVERSIDAD

TIENDA MUÑECOS DE LEYENDAS

COLECCIÓN HABANA

GABINETE DE LA ARQUEOLOGÍA

MUSEO DE ARQUEOLOGÍA

GUAYABERA HABANA

MUSEO DE LA CIUDAD DE LA HABANA

CAPITANES GENERALES

PAPELERÍA

HOTEL AMBOS MUNDOS

MUSEO DEL TABACO/ MUSEO DEL CENTRO HISTÓRICO

MAQUETA DEL CENTRO HISTÓRICO

MUSEO DE PINTURA MURAL

MUSEO DE ASIA

PALACIO DE LOS CAPITANES GENERALES/ PLAZA DE ARMAS

PALACIO DEL SEGUNDO CABO

CASTILLO DE LA REAL FUERZA MUSEO DE NAVEGACIÓN

LA GIRALDILLA DE LA HABANA

CASA DE LA OBRA PÍA

CASA DEL TABACO

LIBRERÍA NAVIO

BARBERÍA DE PLAZA DE ARMAS

CASA DE LA TINAJA

MONUMENTO MANUEL DE CÉSPEDES

PLAZA DE ARMAS

EL TEMPLETE

MONUMENTO A CUBAN SEAMEN

HOTEL SANTA ISABEL

CASA DE BENITO JUÁREZ

TORRE DE MARFIL

MUSEO DE ORFEBRERÍA

RESTAURANTE AL MEDINA

CASA DE LOS ÁRABES

CAFÉ LA MINA/ RESTAURANTE CUBANO

MUSEO NACIONAL DE HISTORIA NATURAL

CÁMARA DE RELAS

CASA DE OSWALDO GUAYASAMÍN

CASA DE LOS ÁBANICOS

MEZQUITA ABDALLAH

BIBLIOTECA PROVINCIAL DE LA HABANA

RESTAURANTE EL TEMPLETE/ RESTAURANTE LA BARCA

ZAPATERÍA OBRAPÍA

PALADAR MAMA INÉS

CASERÓN DE TANGO

PALADAR NAO

TABERNA DEL GALEÓN

HOSTAL EL COMENDADOR

CASA DEL CAFÉ

CASA DE LA COMEDIA

BODEGÓN ONDA

CASA DE LOS ESCLAVOS/OFFICE OF THE HISTORICADOR DE LA HABANA

Bahía de La Habana

Cuban Colonial Architecture

Cuba boasts the New World's finest assemblage of colonial buildings. Spanning four centuries, these palaces, mansions, churches, castles, and more simple structures catalog a progression of styles. The academic classicism of aristocratic 18th-century Spanish homes blends with 19th-century French rococo, while art deco and art nouveau exteriors from the 1920s fuse into the cool, columned arcades of ancient palaces in Mudejar style.

The 17th-century home was made of limestone and modeled on the typical Spanish house, with a simple portal, balconies, and tall, generously proportioned rooms. By the 18th century, those houses that faced onto squares had adopted a *portico* and *loggia* (supported by arched columns) to provide shelter from sun and rain.

Colonial homes grew larger with ensuing decades and typically featured two small courtyards, with a dining area between the two, and a central hallway, or *zaguán,* big enough for carriages and opening directly from the street. Arrayed around the ground floor courtyard were warehouses, offices, and other rooms devoted to the family business, with stables and servants' quarters to the rear, while the private family quarters were sequestered above, around the galleried second story reached by a stately inner stairway. The design was unique to Havana houses. Commercial activity on the ground floor was relegated to those rooms (*dependencias*) facing the street (these were usually rented out to merchants). Laundry and other household functions were relegated to the inner, second patio, or *traspatio,* hidden behind massive wooden doors often flanked by pillars that in time developed ornate arches. The formal layout of rooms on the ground floor was usually repeated on the main, upper story. Another design borrowed from Spain was the *entresuelo,* a mezzanine of half-story proportions tucked between the two stories and used to house servants.

By the 19th century, the wealthy were building neoclassical-style summer homes *(quintas)* in Havana's hilly suburbs. Many, however, were influenced by the Palladian style, fashionable in Europe.

Ground-floor windows were full height from ground level and featured shutter-doors to permit a free flow of air. Later windows acquired ornate grilled *rejas* (bars). In the 19th century, glass was introduced, though usually only for decoration in multicolored stained glass panes inserted between or above the louvered wooden panels. Meanwhile, ornate metal grills called *guardavecinos* were adopted for upper stories to divide balconies of contiguous properties.

Certain styles evolved unique to individual cities, as with the *arco mixtilíneo* (doorway lintel) and projecting turned-wood roof brackets unique to Camagüey; the gingerbread wooden homes (imported from Key West) common in Varadero; and the trompe l'oeil murals found in homes of Sancti Spíritus.

Cuban structures were heavily influenced by traditional Mudejar (Moorish) styles, including inner patios, ornamented window guards, and *vitrales* (stained glass windows, including half-moon *mediopuntos*) in geometric designs to diffuse sunlight, saturating a room with shifting color.

CASA DEL CONDE DE BAYONA

This simple two-story structure, on the south side of the square, is a perfect example of the traditional Havana merchant's house of the period, with side stairs and an *entresuelo* (mezzanine of half-story proportions). It was built in the 1720s for Governor General Don Luis Chacón. Today it houses the **Museo de Arte Colonial** (Colonial Art Museum, San Ignacio #61, tel. 07/862-6440, daily 9:30am-5pm, entrance CUC2, cameras CUC5, guides CUC1), which re-creates the lavish interior of an aristocratic colonial home. One room is devoted to colorful stained glass *vitrales*.

CALLEJÓN DEL CHORRO

At the southwest corner of the plaza, this short cul-de-sac is where a cistern was built to supply water to ships in the harbor. The *aljibe* (cistern) marked the terminus of the Zanja Real (the "royal ditch," or *chorro*), a covered aqueduct that brought water from the Río Almendares some 10 kilometers away.

The **Casa de Baños,** which faces onto the square, looks quite ancient but was built in the 20th century in colonial style on the site of a bathhouse erected over the *aljibe.* Today the building contains the **Galería Victor Manuel** (San Ignacio #56, tel. 07/861-2955, daily 9am-8pm), selling quality arts.

At the far end of Callejón del Chorro is the not-to-be-missed **Taller Experimental de la Gráfica** (tel. 07/864-7622, tgrafica@cubarte.cult.cu, Mon.-Fri. 9am-4pm), a graphics cooperative where you can watch artists make prints for sale using antique presses and lithographic stones.

CASA DE CONDE DE LOMBILLO

On the plaza's east side is the **Casa de Conde de Lombillo** (tel. 07/860-4311, Mon.-Fri. 9am-5pm, Sat. 9am-1pm, free). Built in 1741, this former home of a slave trader houses a small post office (Cuba's first), as it has since 1821. The building now holds historical lithographs. The mansion adjoins the **Casa del Marqués de Arcos,** built in the 1740s for the royal treasurer. What you see is the rear of the mansion; the entrance is on Calle Mercaderes, where the building facing the entrance is graced by the *Mural Artístico-Histórico,* by Cuban artist Andrés Carrillo. A restoration of the mansion was completed in 2017; the venue now hosts the **Café Literario Marque de Arcos** café, library, and exhibition space.

The two houses are fronted by a wide portico supported by thick columns. Note the mailbox set into the wall, a grotesque face of a tragic Greek mask carved in stone, with a scowling mouth as its slit. A life-size bronze statue of Spanish flamenco dancer Antonio Gades (1936-2004) leans against one of the columns.

CENTRO WILFREDO LAM

The **Centro Wilfredo Lam** (San Ignacio #22, esq. Empedrado, tel. 07/864-6282, www.wlam.cult.cu, Tues.-Sat. 10am-5pm), on cobbled Empedrado, on the northwest corner of the plaza, occupies the former mansion of the

A Walk Down Calle Mercaderes

Cobbled Calle Mercaderes between Obispo and Plaza Vieja, four blocks south, is full of attractions. Setting out toward Plaza Vieja from the Hotel Ambos Mundos, after 20 meters you'll pass the charming **Casa de Ásia** (Mercaderes #111, tel. 07/863-9740, Tues.-Sat. 9:15am-4:45pm, Sun. 9:15am-12:45pm, entrance CUC1, cameras CUC2, videos CUC10) on your left, containing an array of carved ivory, silverware, mother-of-pearl furniture, kimonos, and Asian armaments. Opposite, call in to the **Maqueta de Centro Histórico** (Model of the Historic Center, Calle 28 #113, e/ 1ra y 3ra, tel. 07/206-1268, maqueta@gdic.cu, Tues.-Sat. 9:30am-6:30pm, adults CUC3, students, seniors, and children CUC1, guided tour CUC1, cameras CUC2); this 1:500 scale model of Habana Vieja measures eight by four meters, with every building delineated and color coded by use. Guides give a spiel.

On the west side, 20 meters farther south, the **Casa del Tabaco** houses the **Museo del Tabaco** (Mercaderes #120, tel. 07/861-5795, Tues.-Sat. 10am-5pm, Sun. 9am-1pm, free), a cigar museum upstairs.

At the end of the block, at the corner of Obrapía, the **Casa de Benito Juárez** (also called Casa de México, Mercaderes #116, tel. 07/861-8166, Tues.-Sat. 9:30am-4:45pm, Sun. 9:30am-1pm, entrance by donation) displays artwork and costumes from Mexico, including priceless Aztec jewelry.

Turn west onto Obrapía to visit the **Casa de la Obra Pía** (House of Charitable Works, Obrapía #158, tel. 07/861-3097, Tues.-Sat. 9:30am-5pm, Sun. 9:30am-noon, free), 20 meters west of Mercaderes. This splendid mansion was built in 1665 by Capitán Martín Calvo de la Puerta y Arrieta, the Cuban solicitor general. (The house and street are named for his *obra pía*, or pious act, of devoting a portion of his wealth to sponsoring five orphan girls every year.) The family coat of arms, surrounded by exuberant baroque stonework,

counts of Peñalver. This art center displays works by the eponymous Cuban artist as well as artists from Latin America. The institution studies and promotes contemporary art from around the world.

LA BODEGUITA DEL MEDIO

No visit to Havana is complete without popping into **La Bodeguita del Medio** (Empedrado #207, tel. 07/866-8857, daily 10am-midnight), half a block west of the cathedral. This neighborhood hangout was originally the coach house of the mansion next door. Later it was a bodega, a mom-and-pop grocery store where Spanish immigrant Ángel Martínez served food and drinks.

Today troubadours move among thirsty *turistas* and the house drink is the somewhat weak *mojito*. Adorning the walls are posters, paintings, and faded photos of Ernest Hemingway, Carmen Miranda, and other famous visitors. The walls were once decorated with the signatures and scrawls of visitors dating back decades. Alas, a renovation wiped away much of the original charm; the artwork was erased and replaced in ersatz style, with visitors being handed blue pens (famous visitors now sign a chalkboard). The most famous graffiti is credited to Hemingway: *"Mi mojito* is emblazoned above the massive portal, brought from Cádiz in 1686. The mansion features art galleries. Across the street, the **Casa de África** (Obrapía #157, e/ Mercaderes y San Ignacio, tel. 07/861-5798, africa@patrimonio. ohc.cu, Tues.-Sat. 9:30am-5pm, Sun. 9:30am-noon, CUC2) celebrates African culture and is full of African art and artifacts. On the third floor is a collection of paraphernalia used in Santería.

One block east, between Mercaderes and Oficios, is the **Casa de Oswaldo Guayasamín** (Obrapía #112, tel. 07/861-3843, Tues.-Sat. 9am-5:30pm, Sun. 9am-1:30pm, free), housing a museum of art by the Ecuadorian painter, who lived and worked here for many years. Next door is the **Casa de los Abanicos** (Obrapía #107, tel. 07/863-4452, Mon.-Sat. 10am-7pm, Sun. 10am-1pm, free), where traditional Spanish fans (*abanicos*) are made by hand.

Return to Mercaderes and pop into **Habana 1791** (Mercaderes #176, tel. 07/861-3525, Mon.-Sat. 10am-7pm, Sun. 10am-1pm), on the southwest corner of Obrapía, where traditional fragrances are made and sold. Continue south half a block past the small **Plaza de Bolívar** to the **Armería 9 de Abril** (Mercaderes #157, tel. 07/861-8080, Mon.-Sat. 9am-5pm, CUC1), a museum that commemorates four members of Castro's 26th July Movement killed in an assault on the armory on April 9, 1958.

One block south, the corner of Mercaderes and Armagura is known as the Cruz Verde (Green Cross) because it was the first stop on the annual Vía Crucis pilgrimage. Here is the **Museo de Chocolate** (tel. 07/866-4431, daily 9am-11pm), selling sweets and featuring a museum relating the history of chocolate.

en La Bodeguita, mi daiquirí en El Floridita," he supposedly scrawled on the sky-blue walls. According to Tom Miller in *Trading with the Enemy,* Martínez concocted the phrase as a marketing gimmick after the writer's death. Errol Flynn thought it "A Great Place to Get Drunk."

CASA DEL CONDE DE LA REUNIÓN

Built in the 1820s, at the peak of the baroque era, this home has a trefoil-arched doorway opening onto a *zaguán* (courtyard). Exquisite *azulejos* (painted tiles) decorate the walls. Famed novelist Alejo Carpentier used the house as the main setting for his novel *El Siglo de las Luces* (The Enlightenment). A portion of the home, which houses the Centro de Promoción Cultural, is dedicated to his memory as the **Fundación Alejo Carpentier** (Empedrado #215, tel. 07/861-5506, www.fundacioncarpentier. cult.cu, Mon.-Fri. 8:30am-4:30pm, free).

One block west, tiny **Plazuela de San Juan de Dios** (Empedrado, e/ Habana y Aguiar) is pinned by a white marble facsimile of *Don Quixote* author Miguel de Cervantes sitting in a chair, pen in hand, lending the plaza its colloquial name: Parque Cervantes. Visitors on the revolutionary trail should continue one block north up Aguiar to Calle Tejadillo. To the right is the **Museo Bufete Aspiazo-Castro-Risende** (Tejadillo #57; tel. 07/861-5001, by appointment), the office where Fidel Castro worked as a lawyer 1950-1952. The **Arzobispado de la Habana,** the 18th-century home of the archbishop, is one block west at the corner of Tejadillo and Habana. The lovely interior is closed to public view.

★ Plaza de Armas

The oldest and most important plaza in Habana Vieja, handsome Arms Square was laid out in 1519 and named Plaza de Iglesia for a church that was demolished in 1741 after an English warship, the ill-named HMS *Invincible,* was struck by lightning and exploded, sending its main mast sailing down on the church. Later, Plaza de Armas evolved to become the settlement's administrative center, when military parades and musical concerts were held and the gentry would take their evening promenade.

Off the southeast corner of the square, tucked off Calle Baratillo, is an enclosed plazuela—the setting for **Feria de Publicaciones y Curiosidades,** with stalls selling tatterdemalion antiquarian books and small antiquities.

PALACIO DE LOS CAPITANES GENERALES

The somber yet stately **Palacio de los Capitanes Generales** (Palace of the Captains-Generals) was completed in 1791 and became home to 65 governors of Cuba between 1791 and 1898. After that, it was the U.S. governor's residence, the early seat of the Cuban government (1902-1920), and Havana's city hall (1920-1967).

The palace is fronted by a loggia supported by Ionic columns and by "cobblewood," laid instead of stone to soften the noise of carriages and thereby lessen the disturbance of the governor's sleep. The three-story structure surrounds a courtyard that contains a statue of Christopher Columbus by Italian sculptor Cucchiari. Arched colonnades rise on all sides. In the southeast corner, a hole containing the coffin of a nobleman

Cuban man painting in Plaza de Armas

is one of several graves from the old Cementerio de Espada. To the north end of the loggia is a marble **statue of Fernando VII.**

Today, the palace houses the **Museo de la Ciudad de la Habana** (City of Havana Museum, Tacón #1, e/ Obispo y O'Reilly, tel. 07/861-5001, Tues.-Sun. 9:30am-5pm, last entry at 4pm, entrance CUC3, cameras CUC5, guide CUC5). The stairs lead up to palatially furnished rooms. The Salón del Trono (Throne Room), made for the king of Spain but never used, is of breathtaking splendor. The museum also features the Salón de las Banderas (Hall of Flags), with magnificent artwork that includes *The Death of Antonio Maceo* by Menocal, plus exquisite collections illustrating the story of the city's (and Cuba's) development and the 19th-century struggles for independence.

PALACIO DEL SEGUNDO CABO

On the park's northwest corner, the austere **Palacio del Segundo Cabo** (Palace of the Second Lieutenant, O'Reilly #14, tel. 07/862-8091, Mon.-Fri. 6am-midnight) dates from 1770, when it was designed as the city post office. Later it became the home of the vice governor-general and, after independence, the seat of the Senate. Today it is a cultural center.

CASTILLO DE LA REAL FUERZA

The pocket-size **Castillo de la Real Fuerza** (Royal Power Castle, O'Reilly #2, tel. 07/864-4490, Tues.-Sun. 9:30am-5pm, entrance CUC3, cameras CUC5), on the northeast corner of the plaza, was begun in 1558 and completed in 1577. It's the oldest of the four forts that guarded the New World's most precious harbor. Built in medieval fashion, with walls 6 meters wide and 10 meters tall, the castle forms a square with enormous triangular bulwarks at the corners, their sharp angles slicing the dark waters of the moat. It was almost useless from a strategic point of view, being landlocked far from the mouth of the harbor channel and hemmed in by surrounding buildings that would have formed a great impediment to its cannons in any attack. The governors of Cuba lived here until 1762.

Visitors enter via a courtyard full of cannons and mortars. Note the royal coat of arms carved in stone above the massive gateway as you cross the moat by a drawbridge.

The castle houses the not-to-be-missed **Museo de Navegación** (Naval Museum), displaying treasures from the golden age when the riches of the Americas flowed to Spain. The air-conditioned Sala de Tesoro gleams with gold bars and coins, plus precious jewels, bronze astrolabes, and silver *reales* ("pieces of eight"). The jewel in the crown is a four-meter interactive scale model of the *Santisima Trinidad* galleon, built in Havana 1767-1770 and destroyed at the Battle of Trafalgar.

A cylindrical bell tower rising from the northwest corner is topped by a bronze weathervane called **La Giraldilla de la Habana** showing a voluptuous figure with hair braided in thick ropes; in her right hand is a palm tree and in her left a cross. This figure is the official symbol of Havana. The

El Caballero de París

Many myths surround the enigmatic real-life character known as the "Gentleman of Paris." Born in 1899 to a humble family in Vilaseca, Galicia, Spain, José María López Lledín migrated to Cuba at the age of 13. He worked in various menial jobs until some time in the late 1920s, when he was imprisoned, supposedly for a crime he did not commit. The event unhinged him. By the time of his release he'd gone mad.

His hair long and curly, with pointed beard, and wearing a dark suit and cape, José took to the streets as a likable tramp. For five decades he roamed Havana's streets as El Caballero de París. He never begged for alms but offered gallant words to the ladies, pens and pencils to kids, or perhaps a leaf or a verse in reward for favors. *Habaneros* regarded him with affection.

Eventually his health declined and with it his ragged appearance. He was admitted to the psychiatric hospital, where he died in 1985. He was buried in the Santiago de las Vegas cemetery. In 1999, his body was exhumed and relocated to the crypt of the **Iglesia y Convento de San Francisco de Asís.**

vane is a copy; the original, which now resides in the foyer, was cast in 1631 in honor of Isabel de Bobadilla, the wife of Governor Hernando de Soto, the tireless explorer who fruitlessly searched for the fountain of youth in Florida. De Soto named his wife governor in his absence—the only female governor ever to serve in Cuba. For four years she scanned the horizon in vain for his return.

Immediately east of the castle, at the junction of Avenida del Puerto and O'Reilly, is an obelisk to the 77 Cuban seamen killed during World War II by German submarines.

EL TEMPLETE

A charming copy of a Doric temple, **El Templete** (The Pavilion, daily 9:30am-5pm, CUC1.50 including guide) stands on the northeast corner of the Plaza de Armas. It was inaugurated on March 19, 1828, on the site where the first mass and town council meeting were held in 1519, beside a massive ceiba tree. The original ceiba was felled by a hurricane in 1828 and replaced by a column fronted by a small bust of Christopher Columbus. A ceiba has since been replanted and today shades the tiny temple; its interior features a wall-to-ceiling triptych depicting the first mass, the council meeting, and El Templete's inauguration. In the center of the room sits a bust of the artist, Jean-Baptiste Vermay (1786-1833).

PALACIO DEL CONDE DE SANTOVENIA

Immediately south of El Templete is the former **Palacio del Conde de Santovenia** (Baratillo, e/ Narciso López y Baratillo y Obispo). Its quintessentially Cuban-colonial facade is graced by a becolumned portico and, above, wrought-iron railings on balconies whose windows boast stained glass *mediopuntos*. The *conde* (count) in question was famous for hosting elaborate parties, most notoriously a three-day bash in 1833 to celebrate the accession to the throne of Isabel II that climaxed with the ascent of a gaily decorated gas-filled balloon. Later that century the building served as a hotel. Today it's the Hotel Santa Isabel. President Carter stayed here during his visit to Havana in 2002.

MUSEO NACIONAL DE HISTORIA NATURAL

On the south side of the plaza, the **Museo Nacional de Historia Natural** (Natural History Museum, Obispo #61, e/ Oficios y Baratillo, tel. 07/863-9361, museo@mnhnc.inf.cu, Tues.-Sun. 9:30pm-5pm, CUC3) covers evolution in a well-conceived display. The museum houses collections of Cuban flora and fauna—many in clever reproductions of their natural environments—plus stuffed tigers, apes, and other beasts from around the world. Children will appreciate the interactive displays.

Immediately east, the **Biblioteca Provincial de la Habana** (Havana Provincial Library, tel. 07/862-9035, Mon.-Fri. 8:15am-7pm, Sat. 8:15am-4:30pm, Sun. 8:15am-1pm) once served as the U.S. Embassy.

One block south along Calle Oficios, at the corner of Justiz, the former Depósito del Automóvil has been beautifully restored as **Mezquita Abdallah** (Oficios #18, no tel.)—a mosque and the only place in Havana where Muslims can practice the Islamic faith. The prayer hall is decorated with hardwoods inlaid with mother-of-pearl. Only Muslims may enter, but you can peer in at the beautiful Mughal architecture through glass-panel doors.

Across the street, the **Casa de los Árabes** (Arabs' House, Oficios #12, tel. 07/861-5868, Tues.-Sat. 9am-4:30pm, Sun. 9am-1pm, free) comprises two Moorish-inspired 17th-century mansions that house a small yet impressive museum dedicated to a Levantine and Islamic theme.

Plaza de San Francisco

Cobbled Plaza de San Francisco, two blocks south of Plaza de Armas, at Oficios and the foot of Amargura, faces onto Avenida del Puerto. During the 16th century this area was the waterfront. Iberian emigrants disembarked, slaves were unloaded, and galleons were replenished and treasure fleets loaded for the passage to Spain. A market developed on the plaza, which became the focus of the annual Fiesta de San Francisco each October 3, when a gambling fair was established. At its heart is the **Fuente de los Leones** (Fountain of the Lions) by Giuseppe Gaggini, erected in 1836.

The five-story neoclassical building on the north side is the **Lonja del Comercio** (Goods Exchange, Amargura #2, esq. Oficios, tel. 07/866-9588, Mon.-Sat. 9am-6pm), dating from 1907, when it was built as a center for commodities trading. Restored, it houses offices of international corporations, news bureaus, and tour companies. The dome is crowned by a bronze figure of the god Mercury.

Behind the Lonja del Comercio, entered by a wrought-iron archway

A Walk Along Calle Obispo

Pedestrians-only Calle Obispo links Plaza de Armas with Parque Central and is Habana Vieja's busiest shopping street.

Begin at Plaza Albear and walk east. Fifty meters on your left you'll pass the Infotur office. Crossing Calle Havana, five blocks east of Plaza Albear, you arrive at Havana's erstwhile "Wall Street," centered on Calles Obispo, Cuba, and Aguiar, where the main banks were concentrated prior to the Revolution. The **Museo Numismático** (Coin Museum, Obispo, e/ Habana y Aguiar, tel. 07/861-5811, Tues.-Sat. 9am-5pm, Sun. 9:30am-12:45pm, CUC1) displays a broad-ranging collection of coins and banknotes spanning the Greco, Roman, and Phoenician epochs, as well as Spanish coins plus Cuban money from the republican era. Across the street is the **Museo 28 de Septiembre** (Obispo #310, tel. 07/864-3253, daily 9am-5:30pm, CUC2), a dour museum telling the history of the Committees for the Defense of the Revolution.

Continue one block to **Drogería Johnson** (Obispo #361, tel. 07/862-3057, daily 9am-5pm), an ancient apothecary that still operates as a pharmacy.

At the corner of Calle Cuba you reach the former **Banco Nacional de Cuba** (Obispo #211, esq. Cuba), in a splendid neoclassical building fronted by fluted Corinthian columns; it is occupied by the Ministerio de Finanzas y Precios (Ministry of Finance and Prices). Beyond, don't miss the **Museo y Farmacia Taquechel** (Obispo #155, esq. Aguiar, tel. 07/862-9286, daily 9am-6pm, free), another fascinating and dusty old apothecary with mixing vases, mortars and pestles, and colorful ceramic jars.

Across the street, on the north side of Obispo, is the **Edificio Santo Domingo,** a looming contemporary building occupying the site of the Convento de Santo Domingo, which between 1727 and 1902 housed the original University of Havana. The building has been remodeled with a replica of the original baroque doorway and campanile containing the original bell. Today it houses the university's school of restoration. On the north side is the **Museo de la Universidad** (Calle O'Reilly, no tel., Tues.-Sat. 9:30am-5pm, Sun. 9:30am-1pm), displaying miscellany related to the early university.

Fifty meters beyond Museo y Farmacia Taquechel you'll arrive at the rose-pink **Hotel Ambos Mundos** (Obispo #153, esq. Mercaderes, tel. 07/860-9530), dating from 1925. Off and on throughout the 1930s, Hemingway laid his head in room 511, where he wrote *The Green Hills of Africa* and *Death in the Afternoon*. The room is today a museum (daily 10am-5pm, CUC2). Hemingway's quarters have been preserved, with furnishings from his home, Finca Vigía, including his typewriter.

One block farther brings you to a 50-meter-long cobbled pedestrian section and the oldest mansion in Havana: The **Casa del Agua la Tinaja** (Obispo #111) sells mineral water (CUC0.25 a glass). The **Museo de la Orfebrería** (Museum of Silverwork, Obispo #113, tel. 07/863-9861, Tues.-Sat. 9:30am-5pm, Sun. 9:30am-1pm, free) is crammed with silver and gold ornaments from the colonial era, including a splendid collection of swords and firearms. Next door, the **Museo de Pintura Mural** (Painted Mural Museum, Obispo #119, tel. 07/864-2354, Tues.-Sat. 9:30am-5pm, Sun. 9:30am-1pm) displays colonial murals, plus a *quitrín*, the traditional low-slung, horse-drawn cart of the colonial nobility.

Another 50 meters brings you to Plaza de Armas.

topped by a most-uncommunist fairytale crown, is the **Jardín Diana de Gales** (Baratillo, esq. Carpinetti, daily 9am-6pm), a park unveiled in 2000 in memory of Diana, Princess of Wales. The three-meter-tall column is by acclaimed Cuban artist Alfredo Sosabravo. There's also an engraved Welsh slate and stone plaque from Althorp, Diana's childhood home, donated by the British Embassy.

The garden backs onto the **Casa de los Esclavos** (Obrapía, esq. Av. del Puerto), a slave-merchant's home that now serves as the principal office of the city historian.

IGLESIA Y CONVENTO DE SAN FRANCISCO DE ASÍS

Dominating the plaza on the south side, the **Iglesia y Convento de San Francisco de Asís** (Oficios, e/ Amargura y Brasil, tel. 07/862-9683, daily 9am-5:30pm, entrance CUC2, guide CUC1, cameras CUC2, videos CUC10) was completed in 1730 in baroque style with a 40-meter bell tower. The church was eventually proclaimed a basilica, serving as Havana's main church. It was from here that the processions of the Vía Crucis (Procession of the Cross) departed every Lenten Friday, ending at the Iglesia del Santo Cristo del Buen Vieja. The devout passed down Calle Amargura (Street of Bitterness), where stations of the cross were set up at street corners. After the Protestant English worshiped here in 1762, the Catholic Spanish considered it desecrated and it was never again used for religious purposes.

The main nave, with its towering roof supported by 12 columns, each topped by an apostle, features a trompe l'oeil that extends the perspective of the nave. The sumptuously adorned altars are gone, replaced by a huge crucifix suspended above a grand piano. (The cathedral serves as a concert hall, with classical music performances hosted 6pm Sat. and 11am Sun. Sept.-June.) Aristocrats were buried in the crypt; some skeletons can be seen through clear plastic set into the floor. Climb the campanile (CUC1) for a panoramic view. A side nave contains the **Museo de Arte Sacro,** featuring religious icons.

A life-size bronze statue (by José Villa Soberón) of an erstwhile and once-renowned tramp known as **El Caballero de París** (Gentleman of Paris) graces the sidewalk in front of the cathedral entrance. Many Cubans believe that touching his beard will bring good luck.

On the basilica's north side is **Jardín Madre Teresa de Calcuta,** a garden dedicated to Mother Teresa. It contains the small **Iglesia Ortodoxa Griega,** a Greek Orthodox church opened in 2004.

CALLE OFICIOS

Facing the cathedral, cobbled Calle Oficios is lined with 17th-century colonial buildings that possess a marked Mudejar style, exemplified by their wooden balconies. Many of the buildings have been converted into art galleries, including **Galería de Carmen Montilla Tinoco** (Oficios #162, tel. 07/866-8768, Mon.-Sat. 9am-5pm, free); only the front of the house remains, but the architects have made creative use of the empty shell. Next door, **Estudio Galería Los Oficios** (Oficios #166, tel. 07/863-0497, Mon.-Sat. 9:30am-5pm, Sun. 9am-1pm, free) displays works by renowned artist Nelson Domínguez.

Midway down the block, cobbled Calle Brasil extends west about 80 meters to Plaza Vieja. Portions of the original colonial-era aqueduct (the Zanja Real) are exposed. Detour to visit the **Aqvarium** (Brasil #9, tel. 07/863-9493, Tues.-Sat. 9am-5pm, Sun. 9am-1pm, CUC1, children free), displaying tropical fish. Next door, **La Casa Cubana del Perfume** (Brasil #13, tel. 07/866-3759, Mon.-Sat. 10am-7pm, Sun. 10am-1pm) displays colonial-era distilleries, has aromatherapy demos, and sells handmade perfumes made on-site.

Back on Oficios, the former Casa de Don Lorenzo Montalvo houses a convent and the **Hostal Convento de Santa Brígida.** To its side, the **Coche Presidencial Mambí** railway carriage (Mon.-Fri. 8:30am-4:45pm, CUC1) stands on rails at Oficios and Churruca. It served as the official presidential carriage of five presidents, beginning in 1902 with Tomás Estrada Palma. Its polished hardwood interior gleams with brass fittings.

The door inset in the wall behind the carriage opens to the Salón Blanco, housing **El Genio de Leonardi da Vinci Exhibición Permanente** (no tel., Tues.-Sat. 9:30am-4pm, CUC2), dedicated to the Renaissance genius. It displays copies (and contemporary reinterpretations) of his artwork, plus magnificent 3-D models of his inventions—from bicycles, gliders, and helicopters to a diving suit—all labeled in various languages. Da Vinci (1452-1519) died the year of Havana's founding.

Immediately east of the Coche is the **Museo Palacio de Gobierno** (Government Palace Museum, Oficios #211, esq. Muralla, tel. 07/863-4358, Tues.-Sat. 9:30am-5pm, Sun. 9:30am-1pm). This 19th-century neoclassical building housed the Cámara de Representantes (Chamber of Representatives) during the early republic. Later it served as the Ministerio de Educación (1929-1960) and, following the Revolution, housed the Poder Popular Municipal (Havana's local government office). Today it has uniforms, documents, and other items relating to its past use, and the office of the President of the Senate is maintained with period furniture. The interior lobby is striking for its magnificent stained glass skylight.

The **Tienda Museo el Reloj** (Watch Museum, Oficios, esq. Muralla, tel. 07/864-9515, Mon.-Sat. 10am-7pm, Sun. 10am-1pm) doubles as a watch and clock museum, and a deluxe store selling watches and pens made by Cuervo y Sobrinos, a Swiss-Italian company that began life in Cuba in 1882.

On the southeast side of Oficios and Muralla is **Casa Alejandro Von Humboldt** (Oficios #254, tel. 07/863-9850, Tues.-Sat. 9am-5pm, Sun. 9am-noon, CUC1), a museum dedicated to the German explorer (1769-1854) who lived here while investigating Cuba in 1800-1801.

★ Plaza Vieja

The last of the four main squares to be laid out in Habana Vieja, **Plaza Vieja** (Old Square, bounded by Calles Mercaderes, San Ignacio, Brasil, and

Muralla) originally hosted a covered market. It is surrounded by mansions and apartment blocks where, in colonial times, residents looked down on executions and bullfights.

In the 20th century the square sank into disrepair. Today it is in the final stages of restoration. Even the white Carrara marble fountain—an exact replica of the original by Italian sculptor Giorgio Massari—has reappeared. Two decades ago, most buildings were squalid tenements; the tenants have since moved out as the buildings metamorphosed into boutiques, restaurants, museums, and luxury apartments for foreign residents.

Various modern sculptures grace the park. At the southeast corner is *Viaje Fantástico,* by Roberto Fabelo—a bronze figure of a bald, naked woman riding a rooster.

EAST SIDE

The tallest building is the **Edificio Gómez Villa,** on the square's northeast corner. Take the elevator to the top for views over the plaza and to visit the **Cámara Oscura** (tel. 07/866-4461, daily 9am-5:30pm, CUC2). The optical reflection camera revolves 360 degrees, projecting a real-time picture of Havana at 30 times the magnification onto a two-meter-wide parabola housed in a completely darkened room.

The shaded arcade along the plaza's east side leads past the Casa de Juan Rico de Mata, today the headquarters of **Fototeca** (Mercaderes #307, tel. 07/862-2530, fototeca@cubarte.cult.cu, Tues.-Sat. 10am-5pm), the state-run agency that promotes the work of Cuban photographers. It hosts photo exhibitions.

Next door, the **Planetario Habana** (Mercaderes #309, tel. 07/864-9544, shows Wed.-Sat. 9:30am-5pm, Sun. 9:30am-12:30pm, CUC10 adults, children under 12 free) delights visitors with its high-tech interactive exhibitions on space science and technology. A scale model of the solar system spirals around the sun in the 66-seat theater.

Plaza Vieja at night

The old **Palacio Cueto,** on the southeast corner of Plaza Vieja, is a phenomenal piece of Gaudí-esque art nouveau architecture dating from 1906. It awaits restoration as a hotel.

SOUTH SIDE

On the southeast corner, the Casa de Marqués de Prado Amero today houses the **Museo de Naipes** (Museum of Playing Cards, Muralla #101, tel. 07/860-1534, Tues.-Sat. 9:30am-5pm, Sun. 9am-2:30pm, entrance by donation), displaying playing cards through the ages.

The 18th-century **Casa de los Condes de Jaruco** (House of the Counts of Jaruco, Muralla #107), or "La Casona," on the southeast corner, was built between 1733 and 1737. It is highlighted by mammoth doors that open into a cavernous courtyard surrounded by lofty archways festooned with hanging vines. Art galleries (Tues.-Sat. 9am-5pm) occupy the downstairs.

WEST SIDE

On the plaza's southwest corner, cool off with a chilled beer brewed onsite in the **Factoría de Plaza Vieja** (San Ignacio #364, tel. 07/866-4453, daily 11am-1am), in the former Casa del Conde de Casa Lombillo. The copper stills are displayed in the main bar, where a 1913 Ford delivery truck now sits amid artworks by such famous Cuban artists as Kcho and Nelson Domínguez. Accessed via a door next to the brewpub is the **Taller de Luthiería** (tel. 07/801-8339), a workshop run by Habaguanex that repairs string instruments.

The **Casa del Conde de San Estéban de Cañongo** (San Ignacio #356, tel. 07/868-3561, Mon.-Fri. 9:30am-5:30pm, Sat. 9:30am-1pm) is today a cultural center. Adjoining, on the northwest corner of the plaza, is the Casa de las Hermanas Cárdenas, housing the **Centro de Desarollo de Artes Visuales** (San Ignacio #352, tel. 07/862-2611, Tues.-Sat. 10am-6pm). The inner courtyard is dominated by an intriguing sculpture by Alfredo Sosabravo. Art education classes are given on the second floor. The top story has an art gallery.

Well worth the side trip is **Hotel Raquel** (San Ignacio, esq. Amargura, tel. 07/860-8280), one block north of the plaza. This former 1908 bank and warehouse is an architectural jewel with a stunning stained glass atrium ceiling and art nouveau facade. The hotel is themed to honor the city's former Jewish community.

MUSEO HISTÓRICO DE LAS CIENCIAS NATURALES CARLOS FINLAY

One block west and one north of the plaza is the **Museo Histórico de las Ciencias Naturales Carlos Finlay** (Museum of Natural History, Cuba #460, e/ Amargura y Brasil, tel. 07/863-4824, Mon.-Fri. 9am-5pm, Sat. 9am-1pm, CUC2). Dating from 1868 and once the headquarters of the Academy of Medical, Physical, and Natural Sciences, today it contains a pharmaceutical collection and tells the tales of Cuban scientists' discoveries and innovations. The Cuban scientist Dr. Finlay is honored, of course; it was he who on August 14, 1881, discovered that yellow fever is transmitted by the *Aedes aegipti* mosquito. The museum also contains, on the third floor, a reconstructed period pharmacy.

Adjoining the museum to the north, the **Convento y Iglesia de San Francisco el Nuevo** (Cuba, esq. Amargura, tel. 07/861-8490, free) was completed in 1633 for the Augustine friars. It was consecrated anew in 1842, when it was given to the Franciscans, who then rebuilt it in renaissance style in 1847. The church has a marvelous domed altar and nave.

Southern Habana Vieja

The mostly residential and dilapidated southern half of Habana Vieja, south of Calle Brasil, was the ecclesiastical center of Havana during the colonial era and is studded with churches and convents. This was also Havana's Jewish quarter.

Southern Habana Vieja is enclosed by Avenida del Puerto, which swings along the harborfront and becomes Avenida San Pedro, then Avenida Leonor Pérez, then Avenida Desamparados as it curves around to Avenida de Bélgica (colloquially called Egido). The waterfront boulevard is overshadowed by warehouses. Here were the old P&O docks where the ships from Miami and Key West used to land and where Pan American World Airways had its terminal when it was still operating the old clipper flying boats.

CALLE EGIDO

Egido follows the hollow once occupied by Habana Vieja's ancient walls. It is a continuation of Monserrate and flows downhill to the harbor. The **Puerta de la Tenaza** (Egido, esq. Fundición) is the only ancient city gate still standing; a plaque inset in the wall shows a map of the city walls as they once were. About 100 meters south, on Avenida de Puerto, the **Monumento Mártires del Vapor La Coubre** is made of twisted metal fragments of *La Coubre,* the French cargo ship that exploded in Havana harbor on March 4, 1960 (the vessel was carrying armaments for the Castro government). The monument honors the seamen who died in the explosion.

Egido's masterpiece is the **Estación Central de Ferrocarril** (esq. Arsenal), or Terminal de Trenes, Havana's railway station. Designed in 1910, it blends Spanish Revival and Italian Renaissance styles and features twin towers displaying the shields of Havana and Cuba (and a clock permanently frozen at 5:20). It is built atop the former Spanish naval shipyard. It closed in 2015 for a long restoration that will incorporate contemporary architecture.

On the station's north side, the small, shady **Parque de los Agrimensores** (Park of the Surveyors) features a remnant of the **Cortina de la Habana,** the old city wall. The park is now populated by steam trains retired from hauling sugarcane; the oldest dates from 1878.

Two blocks north of the park, do not miss the **Mercado Agropecuario**

Jews in Cuba

Today, Havana's Jewish community (La Comunidad Hebrea) numbers only about 1,500, about 5 percent of its prerevolutionary size, when it supported five synagogues and a college.

The first Jew in Cuba, Luis de Torres, arrived with Columbus in 1492 as the explorer's translator. He was followed in the 16th century by Jews escaping persecution at the hands of the Spanish Inquisition. Later, Jews emigrating from Eastern Europe passed through Cuba en route to the United States in significant numbers until the United States slammed its doors in 1924, after which they settled in Cuba.

By the 1950s, about 20,000 Jews lived in Havana, concentrated around Calle Belén and Calle Acosta, which bustled with kosher bakeries, cafés, and clothes stores. Following the Revolution they became part of the Cuban diaspora. About 95 percent of them fled.

Although the Castro government discouraged Jews from practicing their faith, Jewish religious schools were the only parochial schools allowed to remain open after the Revolution. The government has always made matzo available and even authorized a kosher butcher shop to supply meat for observant Jews.

Jewish Heritage Sites

Habana Vieja's Jewish quarter features the **Sinagoga Adath Israel** (Picota #52, esq. Acosta, tel. 07/861-3495, adath@ip.etecsa.cu, by appointment), with a wooden altar carved with scenes from Jerusalem and historic Havana. Nearby is the **Parque de Los Hebreos** (Calle Acosta esq. Damas), with a giant menorah. **Chevet Achim** (Inquisidor, e/ Luz y Santa Clara, tel. 07/832-6623, by appointment) was built in 1914 and is the oldest synagogue

Egido (e/ Apodaca y Corrales), Havana's most colorful farmers market. Take (and hold on to) your camera! Head two blocks west, then turn left onto **Cárdenas.** The two blocks between Misión y Apodaca feature some astounding examples of Gaudi-style art nouveau architecture (especially noteworthy are #103, #107, and #161).

MUSEO CASA NATAL DE JOSÉ MARTÍ

The birthplace of Cuba's preeminent national hero, **Museo Casa Natal de José Martí** (Leonor Pérez #314, esq. Av. de Bélgica, tel. 07/861-3778, Tues.-Sat. 9am-5pm, entrance CUC1, guide CUC1, cameras CUC2, videos CUC10) sits one block south of the railway station at the end of a street named after Martí's mother. The leader of the independence movement was born on January 28, 1853, in this simple house with terra-cotta tile floors. The house displays many of his personal effects, including an *escritorio* (writing desk) and even a lock of Martí's hair.

IGLESIA Y CONVENTO DE NUESTRA SEÑORA DE BELÉN

The **Iglesia y Convento de Nuestra Señora de Belén** (Church and Convent of Our Lady of Bethlehem, Compostela y Luz, tel. 07/860-3150, in Cuba. The building is owned and maintained by the Centro Sefardi but is not used.

In Vedado, the Casa de la Comunidad Hebrea de Cuba (Calle I #253, e/ 13 y 15, tel. 07/832-8953, patronato.ort@enet.uc, Mon.-Fri. 9:30am-5pm), or Patronato, is the Jewish community headquarters. Services at the adjacent Bet Shalon Sinagogo are Friday at 7:30pm (May-Sept.) or 6pm (Oct.-Apr.) and Saturday at 10am (year-round). Nearby, the Centro Sefardí (Calle 17 #462, esq. E, tel. 07/832-6623, judiosefarad@yahoo.com) hosts a Holocaust museum.

Guanabacoa, on the east side of Havana harbor, has two Jewish cemeteries. The Cementerio de la Comunidad Religiosa Ashkenazi (Av. de la Independencia Este, e/ Obelisco y Puente, Mon.-Fri. 8am-11am and 2pm-5pm), also known as the United Hebrew Congregation Cemetery, is for Ashkenazim. It is entered by an ocher-colored Spanish-colonial frontispiece with a Star of David. A Holocaust memorial immediately to the left of the gate stands in memory of the millions who lost their lives to the Nazis. Behind the Ashkenazi cemetery is the Cementerio de la Unión Sefardi (Calle G, e/ 5ta y Final, daily 7am-5pm), for Sephardic Jews. It too has a memorial to Holocaust victims.

Jewish Aid Organizations

The following organizations send humanitarian aid to Cuba and/or offer organized trips: the B'nai B'rith International (tel. 877/222-9590, www.bnaibrith.org/cuba-missions.html), the Cuba-America Jewish Mission (www.cajm.org), and Jewish Solidarity (tel. 305/642-1600, http://jewish-cuba.org/solidarity).

Mon.-Sat. 10am-4pm, Sun. 9am-1pm, free; visits only with a prearranged guide with Agencia San Cristóbal), the city's largest religious complex, occupies an entire block. The convent, completed in 1718, was built to house the first nuns to arrive in Havana and later served as a refuge for convalescents. In 1842, Spanish authorities ejected the religious order and turned the complex over to the Jesuits, who established a college for the sons of the aristocracy. As the nation's official weather forecasters, they erected the Observatorio Real (Royal Observatory) atop the tower in 1858; it was in use until 1925. The church and convent are linked to contiguous buildings across the street by an arched walkway—the Arco de Belén (Arch of Bethlehem)—spanning Acosta.

IGLESIA Y CONVENTO DE SANTA CLARA DE ASÍS

Partially restored, the Iglesia y Convento de Santa Clara de Asís (Convent of Saint Clair of Assisi, Cuba #610, e/ Luz y Sol, tel. 07/761-3335), two blocks east of Belén, is a massive former nunnery completed in 1644. The nuns moved out in 1922. It is a remarkable building, with a lobby full of beautiful period pieces. The cloistered courtyard is surrounded by columns. Note the 17th-century fountain of a Samaritan woman, and the beautiful

José Martí

José Martí, the "Apostle of the Nation," is the most revered figure in Cuban history: the canonical avatar of Cuba's independece movement and the "ideological architect" of the Cuban Revolution, according to Fidel Castro. There is hardly a quadrant in Havana that does not have a street, square, or major building named in his honor.

José Julian Martí de Pérez was born in 1853 in Habana Vieja. His father was from Valencia, Spain, and became a policeman in Cuba; his mother came from the Canary Islands. When the Ten Years War erupted in 1868, Martí was 15 years old. Already he sympathized with the nationalist cause. At the age of 16, he published his first newspaper, *La Patria Libre* (Free Fatherland). Martí was sentenced to six years' imprisonment, including hard labor. Martí suffered a hernia and gained permanent scars from his shackles. In 1871, his sentence was commuted to exile on the Isla de Pinos, and briefly thereafter he was exiled to Spain, where he earned a degree in law and philosophy. Later, he settled in Mexico, where he became a journalist, and in Guatemala, where he taught. In 1878, as part of a general amnesty, he was allowed to return to Cuba but was then deported again. He traveled through France and Venezuela and, in 1881, to the United States, where he settled in New York for the next 14 years. He worked as a reporter and acted as a consul for Argentina, Paraguay, and Uruguay.

The Pen and the Sword

Dressed in his trademark black frock coat and bow tie, with his thick moustache waxed into pointy tips, Martí devoted his time to winning independence for Cuba. He wrote poetry wedding the rhetoric of nationalism to calls for social justice. He was one of the most prolific and accomplished Latin American writers of his day.

cloister roof carved with geometric designs—a classic *alfarje*—in the Salón Plenario, a marble-floored hall of imposing stature. Wooden carvings abound. The second cloister contains the so-called Sailor's House, built by a wealthy ship owner for his daughter, whom he failed to dissuade from a life of asceticism.

IGLESIA PARROQUIAL DEL ESPÍRITU SANTO

The **Iglesia Parroquial del Espíritu Santo** (Parish Church of the Holy Ghost, Acosta #161, esq. Cuba, tel. 07/862-3410, Mon.-Fri. 8am-noon and 3pm-6pm), two blocks south of Santa Clara de Asís, is Havana's oldest church, dating from 1638 (the circa-1674 central nave and facade, as well as the circa-1720 Gothic vault, are later additions), when it was a hermitage for the devotions of free blacks. Later, King Charles III granted the right of asylum here to anyone hunted by the authorities.

The church's many surprises include a gilded, carved wooden pelican in a niche in the baptistry. The sacristy, where parish archives dating back through the 17th century are preserved, boasts an enormous cupboard full of baroque silver staffs and incense holders. Catacombs to the left of the

He admired the liberty of America but became a staunch anticolonialist, and his voluminous writings are littered with astute critiques of U.S. culture and politics. He despised the expansionist nature of the United States. "It is my duty...to prevent, through the independence of Cuba, the U.S.A. from spreading over the West Indies and falling with added weight upon other lands of Our America. All I have done up to now and shall do hereafter is to that end."

Prophetically, Martí's writings are full of invocations to death. It was he who coined the phrase *"La Victoria o el Sepulcro"* (Victory or the Tomb), which Fidel Castro has turned into a call for *"Patria o Muerte"* (Patriotism or Death).

Theory into Action

Having established himself as the acknowledged political leader of the independence cause, he melded the various exile factions together and integrated the cause of Cuban exiled workers into the crusade—they contributed 10 percent of their earnings to his cause. He also founded La Liga de Instrucción, which trained revolutionary fighters.

In 1895, Martí was named major general of the Armies of Liberation; General Máximo Gómez was named supreme commander. On April 11, 1895, Martí, Gómez, and four followers landed at Cajobabo, in a remote part of eastern Cuba. Moving through the mountains, they finally linked up with Antonio Maceo and his army of 6,000. The first skirmish with the Spanish occurred at Dos Ríos on May 19, 1895. Martí was the first casualty. He had determined on martyrdom and committed sacrificial suicide by riding head-long into the enemy line.

The **Centro de Estudios Martiana** (Calzada #807 e/ Calles 2 y 4, Vedado, Havana, tel. 07/836-4966, www.josemarti.cu) studies his life and works.

nave are held up by subterranean tree trunks. You can explore the eerie vault that runs under the chapel, with the niches still containing the odd bone. Steps lead up to the bell tower.

IGLESIA Y CONVENTO DE NUESTRA SEÑORA DE LA MERCED

Iglesia y Convento de Nuestra Señora de la Merced (Our Lady of Mercy, Cuba #806, esq. Merced, tel. 07/863-8873, daily 8am-noon and 3pm-6pm) is Havana's most impressive church, thanks to its ornate interior multiple dome paintings and walls entirely painted in early-20th-century religious frescoes. The church, begun in 1755, has strong Afro-Cuban connections (the Virgin of Mercy is also Obatalá, goddess of earth and purity), drawing devotees of Santería. Each September 24, scores of worshippers cram in for the Virgen de la Merced's feast day. More modest celebrations are held on the 24th of every other month.

Boxing fans might nip across the street to **Gimnasio Rafael Trejo** (Cuba #815, tel. 07/862-0266, Fri. 7pm), where young boxers train in a tumble-down open-air facility.

The 100-meter-long Alameda de Paula promenade runs alongside the waterfront boulevard between Luz and Leonor Pérez. Lined with marble and iron street lamps, the promenade is the midst of a two-decades-long remodeling project. In 2016, it gained a new ferry terminal and statues.

The raised central median that is the Alameda proper begins on the south side of **Parque Aracelio Iglesias** (Av. del Puerto y Luz), where passengers alight ferries at Emboque de Luz terminal. Two blocks south at Calle Jesús María stands a carved column with a fountain at its base, erected in 1847 in homage to the Spanish navy. It bears an unlikely Irish name: **Columna O'Donnell**, for the Capitán-General of Cuba, Leopoldo O'Donnell, who dedicated the monument. It is covered in relief work on a military theme and crowned by a lion with the arms of Spain in its claws.

At the southern end of the Alameda, **Iglesia de San Francisco de Paula** (San Ignacio y Leonor Pérez, tel. 07/860-4210, daily 9am-5pm) highlights the circular Plazuela de Paula. The quaint, restored church features marvelous artworks including stained glass pieces. It is used for baroque and chamber concerts. To its east, occupying a waterfront wharf, is the **Antiguo Almacén de Madera y el Tabaco** (daily noon-midnight), a beer hall with an on-site brewery.

A stone's throw south, the **Centro Cultural Almacenes de San José** (Av. Desamparados at San Ignacio, tel. 07/864-7793, daily 10am-6pm), or Feria de la Artesanía—the city's main arts and crafts market—also occupies a former waterfront warehouse. Several antique steam trains sit on rails outside. Immediately to the south is the **Museo de Automóviles** (Automobile Museum, Desemparados esq. Damas, tel. 07/863-9942, automovil@bp.patrimonio.ohc.cu, Tues.-Sat. 9:30am-5pm, Sun. 9am-1pm, entrance CUC1.50, cameras CUC2, videos CUC10), displaying an eclectic range of 30 antique automobiles—from a 1905 Cadillac to singer Benny More's 1953 MGA and revolutionary leader Camilo Cienfuegos's 1959 mint Oldsmobile. Classic Harley-Davidson motorcycles are also exhibited.

MUSEO DEL RON

Two blocks north of Luz is the Fundación Destilería Havana Club, or **Museo del Ron** (Museum of Rum, Av. San Pedro #262, e/ Muralla y Sol, tel. 07/861-8051, daily 9:30am-5:30pm, CUC7 including guide and drink). Occupying the former colonial mansion of the Conde de la Mortera, it's a must-see introduction to the manufacture of Cuban rum. Tours begin with an audiovisual presentation and include exhibits such as a mini-cooperage, *pailes* (sugar boiling pots), wooden *trapiches* (sugarcane presses), *salas* dedicated to an exposition on sugarcane, and the colonial sugar mills where the cane was pressed and the liquid processed. An operating production unit replete with bubbling vats and copper demonstrates the process. The highlight is a model of an early-20th-century sugar plantation at 1:22.5 scale, complete with working steam locomotives.

Hemingway once favored **Dos Hermanos** (Av. San Pedro #304, esq. Sol, tel. 07/861-3514), a simple bar immediately south of the museum.

SACRA CATEDRAL ORTODOXA RUSA

Immediately south of Dos Hermanos bar is the beautiful, gleaming white **Sacra Catedral Ortodoxa Rusa** (Russian Orthodox Cathedral, Av. del Puerto and Calle San Pedro, daily 9am-5:45pm), a 21st-century construction. Officially called the **Iglesia Virgen de María de Kazan,** it whisks you allegorically to Moscow with its bulbous, golden minarets. No photos are allowed inside, where a gold altar and chandeliers hang above gray marble floors.

CENTRO HABANA

Laid out in a near-perfect grid, mostly residential Centro Habana (Central Havana, pop. 175,000) lies west of the Paseo de Martí and south of the Malecón. The region evolved following demolition of the city walls in 1863. Prior, it had served as a glacis. The buildings are deep and tall, of four or five stories, built mostly as apartment units. Many houses are in a tumbledown state, and barely a month goes by without at least one building collapse.

The major west-east thoroughfares are the Malecón to the north and Zanja and Avenida Salvador Allende through the center, plus Calles Neptuno and San Rafael between the Malecón and Zanja. Three major thoroughfares run perpendicular, north-south: Calzada de Infanta, forming the western boundary; Padre Varela, down the center; and Avenida de Italia (Galiano), farther east.

In prerevolutionary days, Centro Habana hosted Havana's red-light district, and prostitutes roamed such streets as the ill-named Calle Virtudes (Virtues). Neptuno and San Rafael formed the retail heart of the city. The famous department stores of prerevolutionary days still bear neon signs promoting U.S. brand names from yesteryear.

Sacra Catedral Ortodoxa Rusa

Centro Habana

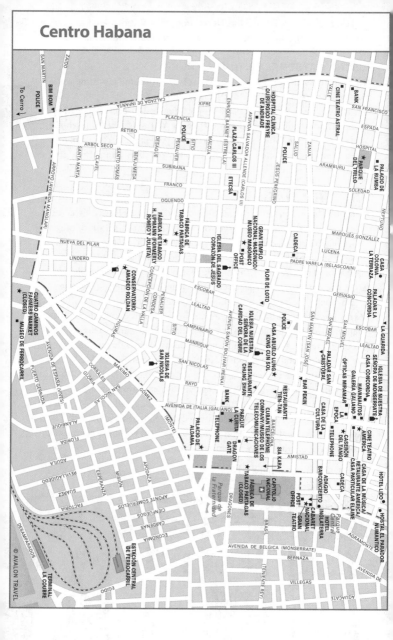

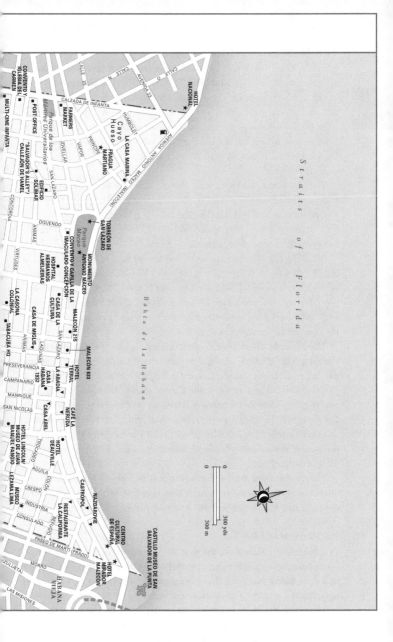

The Malecón (Centro)

Officially known as Avenida Antonio Maceo, and more properly the Muro de Malecón (literally "embankment," or "seawall"), Havana's seafront boulevard winds dramatically along the Atlantic shoreline between the Castillo de San Salvador de la Punta and the Río Almendares. The six-lane seafront boulevard was designed as a jetty wall in 1857 by Cuban engineer Francisco de Albear but not laid out until 1902, by U.S. governor General Leonard Wood. It took 50 years to reach the Río Almendares, almost five miles to the west.

The Malecón is lined with once-glorious high-rise houses, each exuberantly distinct from the next. Unprotected by seaworthy paint, they have proven incapable of withstanding the salt spray that crashes over the seawall. Many buildings have already collapsed, and an ongoing restoration has made little headway against the elements.

All along the shore are the worn remains of square baths—known as the "Elysian Fields"—hewn from the rocks below the seawall, originally with separate areas for men, women, and blacks. These **Baños del Mar** preceded construction of the Malecón. Each is about four meters square and two meters deep, with rock steps for access and a couple of portholes through which the waves wash in and out.

The Malecón offers a microcosm of Havana life: the elderly walking their dogs; the shiftless selling cigars and cheap sex to tourists; the young passing rum among friends; fishers tending their lines and casting off on giant inner tubes (*neumáticos*); and always, scores of couples courting and necking. The Malecón is known as "Havana's sofa" and acts, wrote Claudia Lightfoot, as "the city's drawing room, office, study, and often bedroom."

Every October 26, schoolchildren throw flowers over the seawall in memory of revolutionary leader Camilo Cienfuegos, killed in an air crash on that day in 1959.

The most intriguing site is *Primavera* (esq. Galiano), a fantastical bronze bust by sculptor Rafael San Juan. A tribute to Cuban women, with mariopas (the national flower) for hair, it went up for the 2015 Havana Biennial.

PARQUE MACEO

Dominating the Malecón to the west, at the foot of Avenida Padre Varela, is the massive bronze **Monumento Antonio Maceo,** atop a marble base in a plaza with a fountain. The classical monument was erected in 1916 in honor of the mulatto general and hero of the wars of independence who was known as the "Bronze Titan." The motley tower that stands at the west end of the plaza is the 17th-century **Torreón de San Lázaro.** Although it looks modern, it was built in 1665 to guard the former cove of San Lázaro.

To the south, the **Hospital Hermanos Almeijeiras** looms over the park; its basement forms Cuba's "Fort Knox." The **Convento y Capilla de la Inmaculada Concepción** (San Lázaro #805, e/ Oquendo y Lucena, tel.

mediately west of the hospital. This beautiful church and convent was built
in Gothic style in 1874 and features notable stained glass windows and a
painted altar.

Barrio Cayo Hueso

Immediately west of the Plaza Antonio Maceo, a triangular area bordered
roughly by the Malecón, San Lázaro, and Calzada de Infanta forms the
northwest corner of Centro Habana. Known as Barrio Cayo Hueso, the region dates from the early 20th century, when tenement homes were erected
atop what had been the Espada cemetery (hence the name, Cay of Bones).
Its several art deco inspirations include the **Edificio Solimar** (Soledad #205,
e/ San Lázaro y Ánimas) apartment complex, built in 1944.

The pseudo-castle at the corner of Calle 25 and the Malecón was before
the Revolution the **Casa Marina,** Havana's most palatial brothel.

Hallowed ground to Cubans, the tiny **Museo Fragua Martiana**
(Museum of Martí's Forging, Principe #108, esq. Hospital, tel. 07/870-7338,
fragua@comuh.uh.cu, Mon.-Fri. 9am-4pm, Sat. 9am-noon, free) occupies
the site of the former San Lázaro quarry, where national hero José Martí
and fellow prisoners were forced to break rocks. The museum displays
manuscripts and shackles. To its rear, the quarry has been turned into a
garden, with a life-size bronze statue of Martí.

Every January 27 the nighttime **La Marcha de las Antorchas** (March of
the Torches) takes place to celebrate Martí's birthday. Thousands of students walk with lit torches from the university (which oversees the site) to
the Fragua Martiana.

"SALVADOR'S ALLEY"

Almost every dance enthusiast in the know gravitates to **Callejón de
Hamel** (e/ Aramburu y Hospital) on Sunday for Afro-Cuban rumbas in an
alley adorned by local artist Salvador González Escalona with evocative
murals in sun-drenched yellow, burnt orange, and blazing reds, inspired
by Santería. The alley features a Santería shrine and fantastical totemic
sculptures. González, a bearded artist with an eye for self-promotion, has
an eclectic gallery, **Estudio-Galería Fambá** (Callejón de Hamel #1054,
tel. 07/878-1661, eliasasef@yahoo.es, daily 9:30am-6pm). Alas, *jineteros*
abound.

The area has several other sites associated with *santería*, including
Parque del Trillo (Calle San Miguel y Hospital), four blocks south. Note
the sacred ceiba trees on each corner; the plastic bags at their base contain
offerings. *Santero* **Abel Hierrezuelo Nolasco** (Calle Espada #268 Apt. 9
bajos, e/ San Lázaro y Concordia, no tel., by donation) displays an amazing collection of effigies.

Parque de los Mártires Universitarios (Infanta, e/ Calles Jovellar y
San Lázaro), one block west of Callejón de Hamel, honors students who
lost their lives during the fights against the Machado and Batista regimes.

Soaring over Calzada de Infanta, about 100 meters south of San Lázaro, **Convento y Iglesia del Carmen** (Infanta, e/ Neptuno y Concordia, tel. 07/878-5168, Tues.-Sun. 7:30am-noon and 3pm-7pm) is one of Havana's largest and most impressive churches. Built in baroque fashion, the church is capped by a 60.5-meter-tall tower topped by a sculpture of Our Lady of Carmen.

Galiano

This boulevard, lined with arcaded porticos, runs south from the Malecón to Avenida Salvador Allende and is Centro's main north-south artery. The **Hotel Lincoln** (Galiano, e/ Ánimas y Virtudes) was where Argentina's world-champion race-car driver Juan Manuel Fangio was kidnapped by Castro's revolutionaries in 1958 during the Cuban Grand Prix. Room 810 is today the **Museo de Juan Manuel Fangio** (open when not occupied), presenting a predictably one-sided version of the affair.

Cine América (Galiano #253, esq. Concordia, tel. 07/862-5416) dates from 1941 and is one of the world's great art deco theaters, albeit severely deteriorated. The foyer features a terrazzo floor inlaid with zodiac motifs and a map of the world, with Cuba at the center in polished brass. Kitty-corner, the rarely open **Iglesia de Nuestra Señora de Monserrate** dates from 1843.

Literature buffs might detour to **Casa Museo Lezama Lima** (Trocadero #162, e/ Crespo y Industria, tel. 07/863-4161, Tues.-Sat. 9am-5pm, Sun. 9am-1pm, entrance CUC2, guide CUC1), four blocks east of Galiano, in the former home of writer José Lezama Lima. The novelist is most famous for *Paradiso,* an autobiographical, sexually explicit, homoerotic baroque novel that viewed Cuba as a "paradise lost." Lima fell afoul of Fidel Castro and became a recluse until his death in 1975.

Barrio Chino

The first Chinese immigrants to Cuba arrived in 1847 as indentured laborers. Over ensuing decades, as many as 150,000 arrived to work the fields. They were contracted to labor for miserable wages insufficient to buy their return. Most stayed, and many intermarried with blacks. The Sino-Cuban descendants of those who worked off their indenture gravitated to Centro Habana, where they settled in the zones bordering the Zanza Real, the aqueduct that channeled water to the city. They were later joined by other Chinese. In time Havana's Chinese quarter, Barrio Chino, became the largest in Latin America. The vast majority of Chinese left Cuba immediately following the Revolution; those who stayed were encouraged to become "less Chinese and more Cuban."

Today, Barrio Chino is a mere shadow of its former self, with about 2,000 descendants still resident. Approximately a dozen social associations (*casinos*) attempt to keep Chinese culture alive. In 1995, the city fathers initiated Proyecto Integral Barrio Chino to revitalize the area and its culture. The **Casa de Artes y Tradiciones Chinas** (Salud #313, e/ Gervasio y Escobar, tel.

07/860-9976, barriochino@patrimonio.ohc.cu) features a small gallery and tai chi and dance classes. The **Casa Abuelo Lung Kong Cun Sol** (Dragones #364, e/ Manrique y San Nicolás, tel. 07/862-5388) exists to support elders in the Chinese community; on the third floor, the **Templo San Fan Kong** has an exquisitely carved gold-plated altar.

In 1995, the government of China funded a **Pórtico Chino** (Dragon Gate, or *paifang*) across Calle Dragones, between Amistad and Aguila, announcing visitors' entry from the east. The highlight is pedestrian-only **Callejón Cuchillo** (Knife Alley), lined with Chinese restaurants and aglow at night with Chinese lanterns.

Two blocks to the southwest, the **Iglesia Nuestra Señora de la Caridad del Cobre** (Manrique #570, esq. Salud, tel. 07/861-0945), erected in 1802, features exquisite statuary, stained glass, and a gilded altar. A shrine to the Virgen del Cobre draws worshippers (both Catholics and believers in santería come to worship her avatar, Ochún), who bring sunflowers to adorn the shrine.

Soaring over Barrio Chino is the eclectic-style former headquarters of the Cuban Telephone Company, inaugurated in 1927 and at the time the tallest building in Havana. Today utilized by Etecsa, the Cuban state-owned telephone company, it hosts the impressive **Museo de las Telecomunicaciones** (tel. 07/860-7574, Mon.-Fri. 10am-4pm), telling the history of the telephone in Cuba and with a functional and interactive antique telephone exchange.

Avenidas Simón Bolívar and Salvador Allende

Avenida Simón Bolívar (formerly Avenida Reina) runs west from Parque de la Fraternidad. It is lined with once-impressive colonial-era structures gone to ruin. Beyond Avenida Padre Varela (Belascoain), the street broadens into a wide boulevard called Avenida Salvador Allende, laid out in the early 19th century (when it was known as Carlos III) by Governor Tacón.

Barrio Chino, Centro Habana

The **Gran Templo Nacional Masónico** (Grand Masonic Temple, Av. Salvador Allende, e/ Padre Varela y Lucena) was established in 1951. Though no longer a Freemasons' lodge, it retains a mural in the lobby depicting the history of Masonry in Cuba. Upstairs, reached by a marble staircase, the **Museo Nacional Masónico** (tel. 07/878-4795, www.granlogiacuba.org/museo, Mon.-Fri. 2pm-6pm) has eclectic exhibits—from ceremonial swords to an antique steam-powered fire engine, plus busts honoring great American Masons (including George Washington, Abraham Lincoln, and Simón Bolívar).

One of the few structures not seemingly on its last legs, the **Iglesia del Sagrado Corazón de Jesús** (Church of the Sacred Heart of Jesus, Simón Bolívar, e/ Padre Varela y Gervasio, tel. 07/862-4979, daily 8am-noon and 3pm-6pm) is a Gothic inspiration that could have been transported from medieval England. It was built in 1922 with a beamed ceiling held aloft by great marbled columns. Gargoyles and Christian allegories adorn the exterior.

Cuatros Caminos

South of Avenidas Simón Bolívar and Salvador Allende, the down-at-the-heels neighborhoods of southern Centro Habana extend to Cuatros Caminos, an all-important junction where the **Mercado Agropecuario Cuatro Caminos** (Four Roads Farmers Market) takes up an entire block between Máximo Gómez and Cristina (also called Avenida de la México), and Manglar Arroyo and Matadero. The dilapidated 19th-century market hall closed in 2015 for restoration.

On the east side of Cristina, facing the market, is the **Museo de Ferrocarril** (Railway Museum, tel. 07/879-4414, Tues.-Sat. 9:30am-5pm, Sun. 9:30am-1pm, entrance CUC2, camera CUC5), housed in the former Estación Cristina. The exhibits include model trains, bells, signals, and even telegraph equipment that tell the history of rail in Cuba. Sitting on rails in its lobby is an 1843 steam locomotive (Cuba's first) called *La Junta*. Three other antique steam trains are displayed, along with various diesel locomotives.

FÁBRICA DE TABACO H. UPMANN

The most rewarding cigar factory tour in Havana is offered at **Fábrica de Tabaco H. Upmann** (H. Upmann Tobacco Factory, Padre Varela #852, e/ Desagüe y Peñal Verno, tel. 07/878-1059 or 07/879-3927, 9am-1pm, CUC10), five blocks northwest of Cuatro Caminos. The factory was founded in 1875 by Inocencia Álvarez and later became the Romeo y Julieta factory, making the famous brand of that name. At press time, it had become the temporary home of the H. Upmann brand, whose name it now bears. The facade, however, is topped by a scroll with the original name: "Cuesta Rey & Co."

To the rear is the old Fábrica El Rey del Mundo, decorated with Ionic columns. Today it operates as the temporary **Fábrica de Tabaco Partagás** (Luceña esq. Penalver, Centro Habana). A visit here is not as rewarding due to the cramped conditions. One block south is the **Conservatorio Amaeo Roldán** (Padre Varela, esq. Carmen), a music conservatory boasting a well-preserved classical facade.

CERRO AND DIEZ DE OCTUBRE

South of Habana Vieja and Centro the land rises gently to Cerro, which developed during the 19th century as the place to retire for the torrid midsummer months. Many wealthy families maintained two homes in Havana—one in town, another on the cooler *cerro* (hill). The area is replete with once-stately *quintas* (summer homes) in neoclassical, beaux-arts, and art nouveau styles. Alas, the region is terribly deteriorated and the majority of buildings transcend sordid.

Cerro merges east into the less-crowded municipality of Diez de Octubre, a relatively leafy and attractive residential area laid out during the 20th century comprising the district of Santo Suárez and, to its east, Luyanó.

Avenida Máximo Gómez and Calzada de Cerro

Avenida Máximo Gómez (popularly called Monte; the name changes to Calzada de Cerro west of Infanta) snakes southwest from Parque de la Fraternidad and south of Arroyo (Avenida Manglar), connecting Habana Vieja with Cerro. During the 19th century, scores of summer homes in classical style were erected. It has been described by writer Paul Goldberger as "one of the most remarkable streets in the world: three unbroken kilometers of 19th-century neoclassical villas, with colonnaded arcades making an urban vista of heartbreaking beauty." The avenue ascends southward, marching backward into the past like a classical ruin, with once-stunning arcades and houses collapsing behind decaying facades.

One of the most splendid mansions is the palatial **Quinta del Conde de Santovenia,** erected in 1845 in subdued neoclassical style with a 1929 neo-Gothic chapel addition. Today housing the **Hogar de Ancianos Santovenia** (Calzada de Cerro #1424, e/ Patria y Auditor, tel. 07/879-6072, visits by appointment Tues., Thurs., and Sat. 4pm-5pm and Sun. 10am-noon), it has served as a home for the elderly (*hogar de ancianos*) for more than a century. It's run by Spanish nuns.

Rising over the south of Cerro is **Estadio Latinoamericano** (Consejero Aranjo y Pedro Pérez, Cerro, tel. 07/870-6526), Havana's main baseball stadium. To its northwest is **Fábrica de Tabaco Corona** (20 de Mayo #520, e/ Marta Abreu y Línea, Cerro, tel. 07/873-0131, Mon.-Fri. 9am-11am and 1pm-3pm, CUC10 guided tours), a modern cigar factory producing Hoyo de Monterey, Punch, and other labels.

Proyecto Comunitario Muraleando

Founded in 2001, this art-focused community project spans roughly four blocks along Calle Aguilera southeast of Porvenir. Fourteen core residents have cleaned up their once trash-strewn neighborhood and turned the metal garbage pieces into fanciful art, such as the **Arco de Triunfo**—an arch made of old wheel rims. Walls have been brightened with colorful murals, including an international wall with murals by non-Cuban painters.

The headquarters is **El Tanque** (Aguilera, esq. 9 de Abril, Luyanó), a converted water tank that now holds a performance art space and art gallery. On weekends, it hosts free art workshops for adults and kids, plus a children's street party every month. A highlight is **Obelisko Amistad** (Friendship Obelisk), with plaques representing differing countries; visitors are invited to circle the column and ask for peace for the world.

About 1.5 km southwest, off Avenida Porvenir, is **Museo Casa Natal Camilo Cienfuegos** (Calle Pocito #228, esq. Lawton, tel. 07/698-3509, Tues.-Sat. 9:30am-3:30pm, Sun. 9:30am-noon, free), occupying a small house built in eclectic style in 1920 and where on February 6, 1932, was born Camilo Cienfuegos Gorriarán, who rose to be Fidel's chief of staff before dying in a mysterious plane crash in 1959. Furnished with original pieces, it has five rooms dedicated to his life as a child and, later, revolutionary commander.

VEDADO AND PLAZA DE LA REVOLUCIÓN

The *municipio* of Plaza de la Revolución (pop. 165,000), west of Centro Habana, comprises the leafy residential streets of Vedado and, to the southwest, the modern enclave of Nuevo Vedado and Plaza de la Revolución.

Vedado—the commercial heart of "modern" Havana—has been described as "Havana at its middle-class best." The University of Havana is here. So are many of the city's prime hotels and restaurants, virtually all its main commercial buildings, and block after block of handsome mansions and apartment houses in art deco, eclectic, beaux-arts, and neoclassical styles—luxurious and humble alike lining streets shaded by stately jagüeys dropping their aerial roots to the ground.

Formerly a vast open space between Centro Habana and the Río Almendares, Vedado (which means "forbidden") served as a buffer zone in case of attack from the west; construction was prohibited. In 1859, however, plans were drawn up for urban expansion. Strict building regulations called for 15 feet of gardens between building and street, and more in wider *avenidas*. Regularly spaced parks were mandated. The conclusion of the Spanish-Cuban-American War in 1898 brought U.S. money rushing in. Civic structures, hotels, casinos, department stores, and restaurants sprouted alongside nightclubs.

The sprawling region is hemmed to the north by the Malecón, to the east by Calzada de Infanta, to the west by the Río Almendares, and to the southeast by the Calzada de Ayestaran and Avenida de la Independencia. Vedado follows a grid pattern laid out in quadrants. Odd-numbered streets (*calles*) run east-west, parallel to the shore. Even-numbered *calles* run perpendicular. (To confuse things, west of Paseo, *calles* are even-numbered; east of Paseo, *calles* run from A to P.) The basic grid is overlaid by a larger grid of broad boulevards (*avenidas*) an average of six blocks apart: Calle L to the east, and Avenida de los Presidentes, Paseo, and Avenida 12 farther west.

Dividing the quadrants east-west is Calle 23, which rises (colloquially) as La Rampa from the Malecón at its junction with Calzada de Infanta. La Rampa runs uphill to Calle L and continues on the flat as Calle 23. Paralleling it to the north is a second major east-west thoroughfare, Línea (Calle 9), five blocks inland of the Malecón, which it meets to the northeast.

Vedado slopes gently upward from the shore to Calle 23 and then gently downward toward Plaza de la Revolución.

The Malecón (Vedado)

Extending west from Centro Havana, the Malecón runs along the bulging, wave-battered shorefront of northern Vedado, curling from La Rampa in the east to the Río Almendares in the west, a distance of three miles. The sidewalk is pitted underfoot, but a stroll makes for good exercise while taking in such sights as the **Monumento Calixto García** (Malecón y Av. de los Presidentes), featuring a bronze figure of the 19th-century rebel general on horseback; the **Hotel Habana Riviera** (Malecón y Paseo), opened by the Mafia in 1958 and recently remodeled to show off its spectacular modernist lobby; and the **Torreón de Santa Dorotea de la Luna de la Chorrera** (Malecón y Calle 20), a small fortress built in 1762 to guard the mouth of the Río Almendares. Immediately beyond "La Chorrera," the Restaurante 1830 features a Gaudí-esque garden that includes a dramatic cupola and a tiny island in Japanese style.

★ HOTEL NACIONAL

The landmark **Hotel Nacional** (Calles O y 21, tel. 07/836-3564) is dramatically perched atop a cliff at the junction of La Rampa and the Malecón. Now a national monument, this grande dame hotel was designed by the same architects who designed The Breakers in Palm Beach, which it closely resembles. It opened on December 30, 1930, in the midst of the Great Depression. In 1933, army officers loyal to Machado holed up here following Batista's coup; a gun battle ensued. More famously, in December 1946 Lucky Luciano called a mobster summit to discuss carving up Havana.

The Spanish Renaissance-style hotel was greatly in need of refurbishment when, in 1955, mobster Meyer Lansky persuaded General Batista to let him build a grand casino. Luminaries from Winston Churchill and the Prince of Wales to Marlon Brando have laid their heads here, as attested by the photos in the bar. It is still the preferred hotel for visiting bigwigs.

Beyond the Palladian porch, the vestibule is lavishly adorned with Mudejar patterned tiles. The sweeping palm-shaded lawns to the rear slope toward the Malecón, above which sits a battery of cannons from the independence wars. The cliff is riddled with defensive tunnels built since the 1970s.

The modernist **Hotel Capri** (Calles 21 y N), one block west of the Hotel

Vedado and Plaza de la Revolución

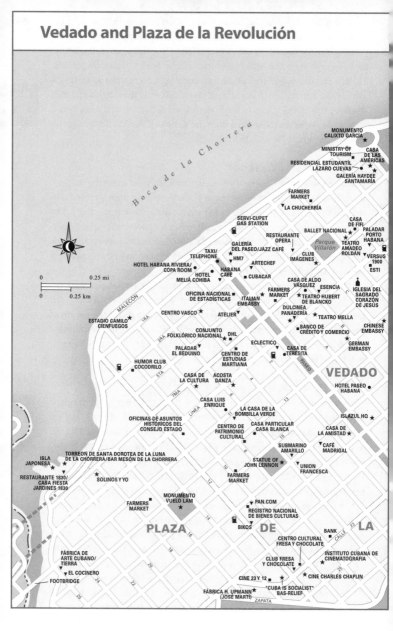

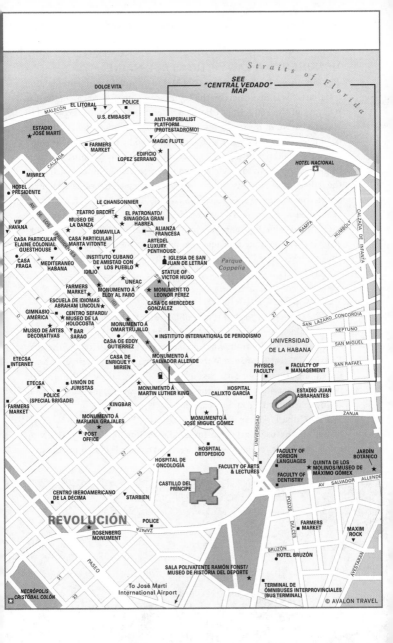

Nacional, was built in 1958 by the American gangster Santo Trafficante. It was a setting in the movies *The Godfather* and *Soy Cuba*.

MONUMENTO A LAS VÍCTIMAS DEL MAINE

The **Monumento a las Víctimas del Maine** (Maine Monument, Malecón y Calle 17) was dedicated by the republican Cuban government to the memory of the 260 sailors who died when the USS *Maine* exploded in Havana harbor in 1898, creating a prelude for U.S. intervention in the War of Independence. Two rusting cannons tethered by chains from the ship's anchor are laid out beneath 12-meter-tall Corinthian columns that were originally topped by an eagle with wings spread wide. Immediately after the failed Bay of Pigs invasion in 1961, a mob toppled the eagle; its body is now in the Museo de la Ciudad de la Habana, while the head hangs in the U.S. Embassy (the ambassador's residence in Siboney displays an original eagle, felled from the monument by a hurricane in 1925). The Castro government later dedicated a plaque that reads, "To the victims of the *Maine*, who were sacrificed by imperialist voracity in its eagerness to seize the island of Cuba."

PLAZA DE LA DIGNIDAD

The **Plaza de la Dignidad** (Plaza of Dignity, Malecón y Calzada), west of the Maine Monument, was created at the height of the Elián González fiasco in 1999-2000 from what was a grassy knoll in front of the U.S. Embassy. A **statue of José Martí** stands at the plaza's eastern end, bearing in one arm a bronze likeness of young Elián while with the other he points an accusatory finger at the embassy—*habaneros* joke that Martí is trying to tell them, "Your visas are that way!"

The Cuban government also built the **Tribuna Abierta Anti-Imperialista** (José Martí Anti-Imperialist Platform)—called jokingly by locals the *"protestadromo"*—at the west end of the plaza to accommodate

Hotel Nacional, Vedado

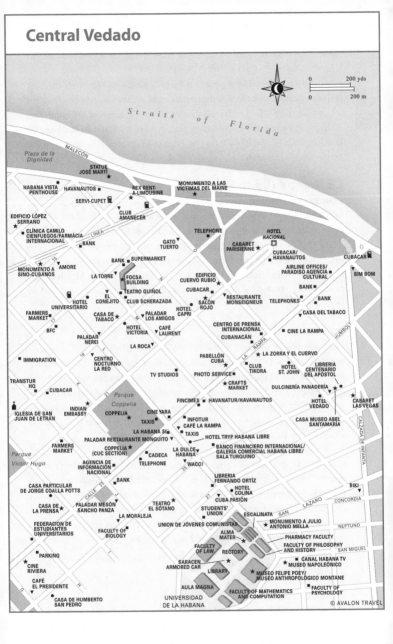

Central Vedado

Straits of Florida

MALECÓN

Plaza de la Dignidad

STATUE JOSÉ MARTÍ ★

MONUMENTO A LAS VICTIMAS DEL MAINE

HABANA VISTA PENTHOUSE ● HAVANAUTOS ■ REX RENT-A-LIMOUSINE ■

SERVI-CUPET ■

CLUB AMANECER ●

EDIFICIO LÓPEZ SERRANO ★

CLÍNICA CAMILO CIENFUEGOS/FARMÁCIA INTERNACIONAL ★

LÍNEA

BANK ■

GATO TUERTO ★

TELEPHONE ●

HOTEL NACIONAL ☆

CABARET PARISIENNE ★

CUBACAR/ HAVANAUTOS ■

CUBACAR ■

MONUMENTO A SINO-CUBANOS ★ AMORE ●

BANK ■ SUPERMARKET ■

AIRLINE OFFICES/ PARADISO AGENCIA CULTURAL ■

BIM BOM ●

LA TORRE ★ FOCSA BUILDING ★

EDIFICIO CUERVO RUBIO ★

BANK ■

HOTEL UNIVERSITARIO 🏨

EL CONEJITO ▼

TEATRO GUIÑOL ★

CLUB SCHERAZADA ●

CUBACAR ■

RESTAURANTE MONSEIGNEUR ▼

TELEPHONES ●

BANK ■

CASA DEL TABACO ■

FARMERS MARKET ■

CASA DE TABACO ★

PALADAR LOS AMIGOS ▼

SALÓN ROJO ★

HOTEL CAPRI 🏨

CENTRO DE PRENSA INTERNACIONAL CUBANACÁN ■

CINE LA RAMPA ★

BFC ■

HOTEL VICTORIA 🏨

CAFÉ LAURENT ▼

PALADAR NEREI ▼

LA ROCA ▼

LA RAMPA

LA ZORRA Y EL CUERVO ★

PABELLÓN CUBA ★

CLUB TIKORA ●

HOTEL ST. JOHN ■

LIBRERIA CENTENARIO DEL APÓSTOL ■

IMMIGRATION ●

CENTRO NOCTURNO LA RED ●

TV STUDIOS ■

PHOTO SERVICE ●

DULCERÍA PANADERÍA ■

TRANSTUR HQ ■

CUBACAR ■

Parque Coppelia

CRAFTS MARKET ★

FINCIMEX ■ HAVANATUR/HAVANAUTOS ■

HOTEL VEDADO ■

CABARET LAS VEGAS ★

IGLESIA DE SAN JUAN DE LETRÁN ★

INDIAN EMBASSY ■

COPPELIA ★

CINE YARA ★

TAXIS ■

INFOTUR ■ CAFÉ LA RAMPA ▼

CASA MUSEO ABEL SANTAMARÍA ■

Parque Víctor Hugo

FARMERS MARKET ■

LA HABANA Sí ■

PALADAR RESTAURANTE MONGÜITO ▼

COPPELIA (CUC SECTION) ★

TAXIS ■

HOTEL TRYP HABANA LIBRE ■

AGENCIA DE INFORMACIÓN NACIONAL ■

CADECA ■

TELEPHONE ●

LA DULCE HABANA ▼

WACO! ▼

BANCO FINANCIERO INTERNACIONAL/ GALERÍA COMERCIAL HABANA LIBRE/ SALA TURQUINO ■

BANK ■

LIBRERIA FERNANDO ORTÍZ ●

CALZADA DE INFANTA

CASA PARTICULAR DE JORGE COALLA POTTS ●

HOTEL COLINA ■

CUBA PASIÓN ●

BIKI

CASA DE LA PRENSA ★

PALADAR MESÓN SANCHO PANZA ▼

TEATRO EL SÓTANO ★

LA MORALEJA ▼

STUDENTS' UNION ■

ESCALINATA ★

SAN LÁZARO

CONCORDIA

FEDERACIÓN DE ESTUDIANTES UNIVERSITARIOS ■

UNION DE JÓVENES COMUNISTAS ■

MONUMENTO A JULIO ANTONIO MELLA ★

NEPTUNO

FACULTY OF BIOLOGY ■

ALMA MATER ★

PHARMACY FACULTY ■

PARKING ■

CINE RIVIERA ★

CAFÉ EL PRESIDENTE ▼

FACULTY OF LAW ■

SARACEN ARMORED CAR ■

RECTORY ■

LIBRARY ■

FACULTY OF PHILOSOPHY AND HISTORY ■

CANAL HABANA TV ■ MUSEO NAPOLEÓNICO ■

SAN MIGUEL

MUSEO FELIPE POEY/ MUSEO ANTHROPOLÓGICO MONTANE ★

FACULTY OF PSYCHOLOGY ■

CASA DE HUMBERTO SAN PEDRO ●

AULA MAGNA ★

FACULTY OF MATHEMATICS AND COMPUTATION ■

UNIVERSIDAD DE LA HABANA

0   200 yds
0   200 m

© AVALON TRAVEL

the masses bused in to taunt Uncle Sam. The concrete supports bear plaques inscribed with the names of Communist and revolutionary heroes, plus those of prominent North Americans, from Benjamin Spock to Malcolm X, at the fore of the fight for social justice.

At the western end of the plaza is the **U.S. Embassy** (formerly the U.S. Interests Section), where U.S. diplomats and CIA agents serve Uncle Sam's whims behind a veil of mirrored-glass windows. A forest of 138 huge flagstaffs, **El Monte de los Banderas,** was erected by Cuba in front of the building in 2007. Each black flag represents a year since the launch of the Ten Years War in 1868.

La Rampa (Calle 23)

Calle 23 rises from the Malecón to Calle L and climbs steadily past high-rise office buildings, nightclubs, cinemas, travel agencies, TV studios, and art deco apartment buildings. La Rampa (the Ramp) was the setting of *Three Trapped Tigers,* Guillermo Cabrera Infante's famous novel about swinging 1950s Havana; it was here that the ritziest hotels, casinos, and nightclubs were concentrated in the days before the Revolution. Multicolored granite tiles created by Wilfredo Lam and René Portocarrero are laid in the sidewalks.

PARQUE COPPELIA

At the top of La Rampa is **Parque Coppelia** (Calle 23 y L, Tues.-Sun. 10am-9:30pm), the name of a park in Havana, of the flying saucer-like structure at its heart, and of the brand of excellent ice cream served here. In 1966, the government built this lush park with a parlor in the middle as the biggest ice creamery in the world, serving up to an estimated 30,000 customers a day. Cuba's rich diversity can be observed standing in line at Coppelia on a sultry Havana afternoon.

The strange concrete structure, suspended on spidery legs and looming over the park, features circular rooms overhead like a four-leaf clover, offering views over open-air sections where *helado* (ice cream) is enjoyed beneath the dappled shade of lush jagüey trees. Each section has its own *cola* (line), proportional in length to the strength of the sun. Foreigners are usually sent to a section where you pay CUC1 per scoop, but the fun is standing in line with Cubans (you'll need *moneda nacional*).

HOTEL HABANA LIBRE

The 416-foot-tall **Hotel Habana Libre** (Free Havana Hotel, Calle L, e/ 23 y 25, tel. 07/834-6100) was *the* place to be after opening as the Havana Hilton in April 1958. Castro even had his headquarters here briefly in 1959. The modernist hotel is fronted by a massive mural—*Frutas Cubanas*—by ceramist Amelia Peláez, made of 6.7 million pieces in the style of Picasso. The mezzanine contains a mosaic mural, *Carro de la Revolución* (the Revolutionary Car) by Alfredo Sosabravo.

Of interest to students of Cuba's revolutionary history, this **museum** (Calle 25 #164, e/ Infanta y O, tel. 07/835-0891, Mon.-Sat. 9am-4pm, free) occupies a simple two-room, sixth-floor apartment (#603) where Fidel Castro's revolutionary movement, the M-26-7, had its secret headquarters in the former home of the eponymous martyr, brutally tortured and murdered following the attack on the Moncada barracks in 1953. Original furnishings include Fidel's work desk.

Universidad de la Habana and Vicinity

The **Universidad de la Habana** (University of Havana, Calle L y San Lázaro, tel. 07/878-3231, www.uh.cu, Mon.-Fri. 8am-6pm) was founded by Dominican friars in 1728 and was originally situated on Calle Obispo in Habana Vieja. The current edifices were built 1905-1911, when the school was inaugurated in its current location. During the 20th century the university was an autonomous "sacred hill" that neither the police nor the army could enter. The campus is off-limits on weekends and is closed July-August.

From Calle L, the university is entered via an immense, 50-meter-wide stone staircase: the 88-step **Escalinata** (staircase). A patinated bronze **statue of the Alma Mater** cast by Czech sculptor Mario Korbel in 1919 sits atop the staircase. The twice-life-size statue portrays a woman seated in a bronze chair with six classical bas-reliefs representing disciplines taught at the university. She is dressed in a tunic and extends her bare arms, beckoning all who desire knowledge.

The staircase is topped by a columned portico, beyond which lies the peaceful **Plaza Ignacio Agramonte,** surrounded by classical buildings. A **Saracen armored car** in the quadrant was captured in 1958 by students in the fight against Batista. The **Aula Magna** (Great Hall) features magnificent

Universidad de la Habana, Vedado

murals by Armando Menocal, plus the marble tomb of independence leader Félix Varela (1788-1853).

The **Monumento a Julio Antonio Mella,** across Calle L at the base of the Escalinata, contains the ashes of Mella, founder of the University Students' Federation and, later, of the Cuban Communist Party.

The Escuela de Ciencias (School of Sciences), on the south side of the quadrant, contains the **Museo de Ciencias Naturales Felipe Poey** (Felipe Poey Museum of Natural Sciences, tel. 07/877-4221, Mon.-Fri. 9am-noon and 1pm-4pm, free), displaying endemic species from alligators to sharks, stuffed or pickled for posterity. The museum dates from 1842 and is named for its French-Cuban founder. Poey (1799-1891) was versed in every field of the sciences and founded the Academy of Medical Sciences, the Anthropological Society of Cuba, and a half-dozen other societies. The **Museo Antropológico Montane** (Montane Anthropology Museum, tel. 07/879-3488, http://fbio.uh.cu/mmontane.php, Mon.-Fri. 9am-noon and 1pm-4pm, free), on the second floor, displays pre-Columbian artifacts.

MUSEO NAPOLEÓNICO

Who would imagine that so much of Napoleon Bonaparte's personal memorabilia would end up in Cuba? But it has, housed in the **Museo Napoleónico** (Napoleonic Museum, San Miguel #1159, e/ Ronda y Masón, tel. 07/879-1412, mnapoleonico@patrimonio.ohc.cu, Tues.-Sat. 9:30am-5pm, Sun. 9:30am-12:30pm, entrance CUC3, cameras CUC5, guide CUC2) in a three-story Florentine Renaissance mansion on the south side of the university. The collection (7,000 pieces) was the private work of Orestes Ferrara, one-time Cuban ambassador to France. Ferrara brought back from Europe such precious items as the French emperor's death mask, his watch, toothbrush, and the pistols Napoleon used at the Battle of Borodino. Other items were seized from Julio Lobo, the former National Bank president, when he left Cuba for exile. The museum, housed in Ferrara's former home (Ferrara was also forced out by the Revolution), is replete with busts and portraits of the military genius, plus armaments and uniforms.

CALLE 17

This street stretches west from the Monumento a las Víctimas del Maine and is lined with remarkable buildings, beginning with the landmark 35-story **Focsa** (Calle 17 e/ M y N), a V-shaped apartment block built 1954-1956 as one of the largest reinforced concrete structures in the world. The **Instituto Cubano de Amistad con los Pueblos** (Cuban Institute for People's Friendship, Calle 17 #301, e/ H y I) occupies a palatial beaux-arts villa. One block west, the equally magnificent Casa de Juan Gelats is another spectacular exemplar of beaux-arts style; built in 1920 it houses the **Unión Nacional de Escritores y Artistas de Cuba** (National Union of Cuban Writers and Artists, UNEAC, Calle 17 #351, esq. H, tel. 07/832-4551, www.uneac.org.cu).

West of Avenida de los Presidentes, the **Centro Hebreo Sefaradi** (Calle

17 #462, esq. E, tel. 07/832-6623) hosts a small Holocaust museum that is limited to visual displays. The **Museo de Artes Decorativas** (Museum of Decorative Arts, Calle 17 #502, e/ D y E, tel. 07/861-0241 or 07/832-0924, Tues.-Sat. 9:30am-5pm and Sun. 10am-2pm, CUC5 with guide, cameras CUC5, videos CUC10), housed in the former mansion of a Cuban countess, brims with lavish furniture, paintings, textiles, and chinoiserie from the 18th and 19th centuries.

Beyond Paseo, on the west side, to the left, is the **Casa de la Amistad** (Paseo #406, e/ 17 y 19, tel. 07/830-3114), an Italian Renaissance mansion built in 1926 with a surfeit of Carrara marble, silver-laminated banisters, decorative Lalique glass, and Baccarat crystal.

Two blocks west, Calle 17 opens onto **Parque Lennon** (Calle 6), where in 2000, on the 20th anniversary of John Lennon's death, a life-size bronze statue was unveiled in the presence of Fidel (who had previously banned Beatles music). Lennon sits on a cast-iron bench, with plenty of room for anyone who wants to join him. The sculpture is by Cuban artist José Villa, who inscribed the words "People say I'm a dreamer, but I'm not the only one," at Lennon's feet. A *custodio* is there 24/7; he takes care of Lennon's spectacles.

Stroll two blocks north and one block west to reach Calle 11 (bet. 10 and 12), where revolutionary heroine Celia Sánchez once lived. Fidel had an apartment here until his death, and the area was off-limits until 2017. MININT security still patrol the street, where the **Oficinas de Asuntos Históricos del Consejo del Estado** (Linea e/ 10 y 12, c/o tel. 07/832-9149) is located. It houses the official archives of the Cuban Revolution and boasts an astonishing art collection, but is closed to public view.

AVENIDA DE LOS PRESIDENTES

Avenida de los Presidentes (Calle G) runs perpendicular to Calle 23 and climbs from the Malecón toward Plaza de la Revolución. The avenue is

Beaux Arts Museo de Artes Decorativas, Vedado

named for the statues of Cuban and Latin American presidents that grace its length.

The **Monumento Calixto García** studs the Malecón. One block south, on your right, the **Casa de las Américas** (Presidentes, esq. 3ra, tel. 07/832-2706, www.casa.cult.cu, Mon.-Fri. 8am-4:45pm), formed in 1959 to study and promote the cultures of Latin America and the Caribbean, is housed in a cathedral-like art deco building. Fifty meters south is the Casa's **Galería Haydee Santamaría** (e/ 5ta and G).

The **Museo de la Danza** (Calle Línea #365, esq. Presidentes, tel. 07/831-2198, musdanza@cubarte.cult.cu, Tues.-Sat. 10am-5pm, CUC2, guide CUC1) occupies a restored mansion and has salons dedicated to Russian ballet, modern dance, and the Ballet Nacional de Cuba. Divert one block west along Linea to visit **Galería Habana** (Línea 460 e/ E y F, tel. 07/832-7101, www.galerihabana.com, Mon.-Fri. 10am-4pm, Sat. 10am-1pm, free), a superb art gallery showing works by leading contemporary and yester-year maestros.

Ascending the avenue, you'll pass statues to Ecuadorian president Eloy Alfaro (e/ 15 y 17; note the wall mural called *Wrinkles,* for self-evident reasons, on the southwest corner), Mexican president Benito Juárez (e/ 17 y 19), Venezuelan Simón Bolívar (e/ 19 y 21), Panamanian strongman president Omar Torrijos (e/ 19 y 21), and Chilean president Salvador Allende (e/ 21 y 23).

The tree-shaded boulevard climbs two blocks to the **Monumento a José Miguel Gómez** (Calle 29), designed by Italian sculptor Giovanni Nicolini and erected in 1936 in classical style to honor the vainglorious republican president (1909-1913). Beyond, the road drops through a canyon to the junction with Avenida Salvador Allende.

To the west, on the north side of the road, the once-graceful **Quinta de los Molinos** (e/ Infanta y Luaces, tel. 07/879-8850) was closed for restoration at last visit. Built between 1837 and 1840, it was a summer palace for the captains-general. In 1899, it was granted as the private residence of General Máximo Gómez, the Dominican-born commander in chief of the liberation army. The *molino* (mill) refers to a tobacco mill that operated 1800-1835, powered by the waters of the Zanja Real. The *quinta*'s 4.8-hectare grounds form the **Jardín Botánico** (Botanical Gardens, Tues.-Sun. 7am-7pm, free), featuring a *mariposario* (butterfly garden). Guided walks are offered.

★ Necrópolis Cristóbal Colón

The **Necrópolis Cristóbal Colón** (Columbus Cemetery, Zapata, esq. 12, tel. 07/830-4517, daily 8am-5pm, entrance CUC5 includes guide and right to photograph) covers 56 hectares and contains more than 500 major mausoleums, chapels, vaults, tombs, and galleries (in addition to countless gravestones) embellished with angels, griffins, cherubs, and other flamboyant ornamentation. You'll even find Greco-Roman temples in miniature, an Egyptian pyramid, and medieval castles, plus baroque, Romantic, Renaissance, art deco, and art nouveau monuments. The triple-arched

Necrópolis Cristóbal Colón

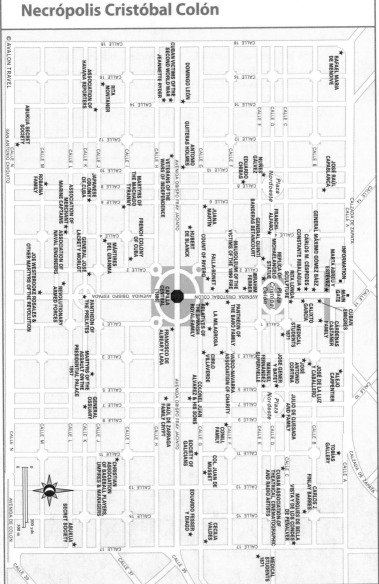

entrance gate has marble reliefs depicting the crucifixion and Lazarus rising from the grave and is topped by a marble coronation stone representing the theological virtues of faith, hope, and charity.

Today a national monument, the cemetery was laid out between 1871 and 1886 in 16 rectangular blocks, like a Roman military camp, divided by social status. Nobles competed to build the most elaborate tombs, with social standing dictating the size and location of plots.

Famous *criollo* patricians, colonial aristocrats, and war heroes such as Máximo Gómez are buried here alongside noted intellectuals and politicians. The list goes on and on: José Raúl Capablanca, the world chess champion 1921-1927 (his tomb is guarded by a marble queen chess piece); Alejo Carpentier, Cuba's most revered contemporary novelist; Celia Sánchez, Haydee Santamaría, and a plethora of other revolutionaries killed for the cause; and even some of the Revolution's enemies. The **Galería Tobias** is one of several massive underground ossuaries.

The major tombs line Avenida Cristóbal Colón, the main avenue, which leads south from the gate to an ocher-colored, octagonal neo-Byzantine church, the **Capilla Central,** containing a fresco of the Last Judgment.

The most visited grave is the flower-bedecked tomb of Amelia Goyri de Hoz, revered as **La Milagrosa** (The Miraculous One, Calles 3 y F) and to whom the superstitious ascribe miraculous healings. According to legend, she died during childbirth in 1901 and was buried with her stillborn child at her feet. When her sarcophagus was later opened, the baby was supposedly cradled in her arms. Ever since, believers have paid homage by knocking three times on the tombstone with one of its brass rings, before touching the tomb and requesting a favor (one must not turn one's back on the tomb when departing). Many childless women pray here in hopes of a pregnancy.

The Chinese built their own cemetery immediately southwest of Cementerio Colón, on the west side of Avenida 26 (e/ 28 y 33, tel.

Necrópolis Cristóbal Colón

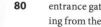

07/831-1645, daily 8am-4pm, free). Beyond the circular gateway, traditional lions stand guard over burial chapels with upward-curving roofs.

GALERÍA 23 Y 12

The northwest corner of Calles 23 and 12, one block north of Cementerio Colón, marks the spot where, on April 16, 1961 (the eve of the Bay of Pigs invasion), Castro announced that Cuba was henceforth socialist. The anniversary of the declaration of socialism is marked each April 16. A **bronze bas-relief** shows Fidel surrounded by soldiers, rifles held aloft. It honors citizens killed in the U.S.-sponsored strike on the airfield at Marianao that was a prelude to the invasion, repeating his words: "This is the socialist and democratic revolution of the humble, with the humble, for the humble." At last visit, the building (and memorial) were boarded up as unsafe.

Plaza de la Revolución

Havana's largest plaza, Plaza de la Revolución (Revolution Plaza), which occupies the Loma de los Catalanes (Hill of the Catalans), is an ugly tarred square. The trapezoidal complex spanning 11 acres was laid out during the Batista era, when it was known as the Plaza Cívica. It forms the administrative center for Cuba. All the major edifices date to the 1950s. Huge rallies are held here on May 1.

Among the important buildings are the monumentalist **Biblioteca Nacional** (National Library, tel. 07/855-5542, Mon. 8:15am-1pm, Tues.-Fri. 8:15am-6:30pm, Sat. 8am-4:30pm, guided tours offered), Cuba's largest library, built 1955-1957; the 21-story **Ministerio de Defensa,** originally built as the municipal seat of government on the plaza's southeast side; and the **Teatro Nacional** (National Theater, Paseo y Av. Carlos M. de Céspedes, tel. 07/878-5590, www.teatronacional.cu), one block to the northwest of the plaza, built 1954-1960 with a convex glazed facade. Paseo climbs northwest from the plaza to Zapata, where in the middle of the road rises the **Memorial a Ethel y Julius Rosenberg,** bearing cement doves and an inset sculpture of the U.S. couple executed in 1953 for passing nuclear secrets to the Soviet Union. An inscription reads, "Assassinated June 19, 1953." The Cuban government holds a memorial service here each June 19.

MEMORIAL Y MUSEO JOSÉ MARTÍ

The massive **Memorial José Martí** on the south side of the square sits atop a 30-meter-tall base that is shaped as a five-pointed star. It is made entirely of gray granite and marble and was designed by Enrique Luis Varela and completed in 1958. To each side, arching stairways lead to an 18-meter-tall (59-foot) gray-white marble statue of Martí sitting in a contemplative pose, like Rodin's *The Thinker*.

Behind looms a 109-meter-tall marble edifice stepped like a soaring ziggurat from a sci-fi movie. It's the highest point in Havana. The edifice houses the **Museo José Martí** (tel. 07/859-2347, Mon.-Sat. 9am-4:30pm, entrance CUC3, cameras CUC5, videos CUC10), dedicated to Martí's life, with maps, texts, paintings, and a multiscreen broadcast on independence and the Revolution. An elevator whisks you to the top of the tower for a 360-degree view over Havana (CUC2).

PALACIO DE LA REVOLUCIÓN

The center of government is the **Palacio de la Revolución** (Palace of the Revolution), immediately south of the José Martí monument. This imposing structure was inspired by the architecture then popular in Fascist Europe and was built 1954-1957 as the Palace of Justice. Today, it is where Raúl Castro and the Council of Ministers work out the policies of state. The labyrinthine, ocher-colored palace with gleaming black stone walls and checkered floors adjoins the buildings of the Central Committee of the Communist Party. Before the Revolution, the buildings served as the Cuban Supreme Court and national police headquarters. No visitors are allowed.

MINISTERIO DEL INTERIOR

Commanding the northwest side of the plaza is the seven-story Ministerio del Interior (Ministry of the Interior, MININT, in charge of national security), built in 1953 to be the Office of the Comptroller. On its east side is a windowless horizontal block that bears a soaring **"mural" of Che Guevara** and the words *Hasta la victoria siempre* ("Always toward victory"), erected in 1995 from steel railings donated by the French government. See it by day *and* by night, when it is illuminated.

MINISTERIO DE COMUNICACIONES

In October 2009, a visage of Comandante Camilo Cienfuegos (identical in style to that of Che) was erected on the facade of the **Ministerio de Comunicaciones** (Ministry of Communications), on the plaza's northeast corner. The 100-ton steel mural was raised for the 50th anniversary of Cienfuegos's death and is accompanied by the words *Vas bien, Fidel* ("You're doing fine, Fidel"). Cienfuegos's famous response was in reply to Fidel's question "Am I doing all right, Camilo?" at a rally on January 8, 1959. The ground-floor **Museo Postal Cubano** (Cuban Post Museum, Av. Rancho Boyeros, esq. 19 de Mayo, tel. 07/882-8255, Mon.-Fri. 8am-4pm, entrance CUC1) has a well-catalogued philatelic collection, including a complete range of Cuban postage stamps dating from 1855, plus stamps from almost 100 other countries.

Nuevo Vedado

Nuevo Vedado, which stretches southwest of Plaza de la Revolución, is a sprawling complex of mid-20th-century housing, including postrevolutionary high-rise apartment blocks. The most magnificent and prominent building is undoutedbly the **Coliseo de la Ciudad Deportiva** (Sports Coliseum, colloquially called "El Coliseo"), a giant Olympic stadium with a massive concrete dome. It was built in 1957 at Avenida 26, Avenida de la Independencia (Rancho Boyeros), and Vía Blanca.

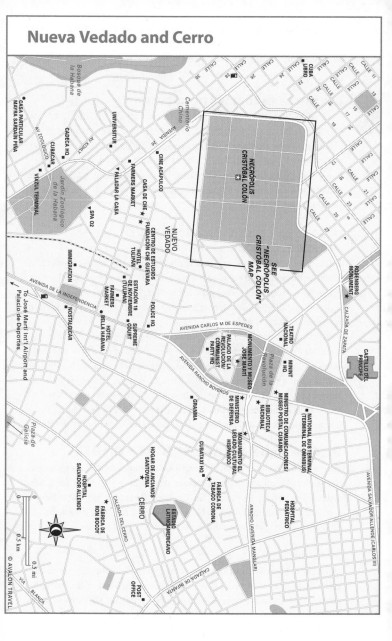

Nueva Vedado and Cerro

Note: Those with children in tow might be tempted to visit the poorly managed **Jardín Zoológico de la Habana** (Havana Zoological Garden, Av. 26 y Zoológico, tel. 07/881-8915, zoohabana@ch.gov.cu, Wed.-Sun. 9:30am-5pm, CUC2), but this depressing zoo is best avoided.

CENTRO DE ESTUDIOS CHE GUEVARA

Opened in 2014, the **Center for Che Guevara Studies** (Calle 47 #772 e/ Conill y Tulipán, tel. 07/814-1013, www.centroche.co.cu) is housed in a handsome contemporary building opposite Che's gorgeous former modernist home (Calle 47 #770), where he lived 1962-1964 and which now houses offices for the center. It has separate *salas* dedicated to Che, Camilo Cienfuegos, and Haydee Santamaría, plus a library, auditorium, and expositions on Che's life.

BOSQUE DE LA HABANA AND PARQUE METROPOLITANO DE LA HABANA

Follow Avenida Zoológica west to the bridge over the Río Almendares to enter the **Bosque de la Habana** (Havana Forest). This ribbon of wild, vine-draped woodland stretches alongside the river. There is no path—you must walk along Calle 49C, which parallels the river. Going alone is not advised; robberies have occurred.

North of Bosque de la Habana, and accessed from Avenida 47, the motley riverside **Parque Metropolitano de la Habana** has pony rides, rowboats, mini-golf, and a children's playground. To the south, the woods extend to **Los Jardines de la Tropical** (Calle Rizo, Tues.-Sun. 9am-6pm), a landscaped park built 1904-1910 on the grounds of a former brewery. The park found its inspiration in Antoni Gaudí's Parque Güell in Barcelona. Today it is near-derelict and looks like an abandoned set from *Lord of the Rings*.

PLAYA (MIRAMAR AND BEYOND)

West of Vedado and the Río Almendares, the *municipio* of Playa extends to the western boundary of Havana as far as the Río Quibu. Most areas were renamed following the Revolution. Gone are Country Club and Biltmore, replaced with politically acceptable names such as Atabey, Cubanacán, and Siboney, in honor of Cuba's indigenous past.

Miramar

Miramar is Havana's upscale residential district, laid out in an expansive grid of tree-shaded streets lined by fine mansions. Most of their original owners fled Cuba after the Revolution. Nonetheless, Miramar is at the forefront of Cuba's quasi-capitalist remake. The best-stocked stores are here, as are the foreign embassies and many of the city's top *paladares* and private nightclubs.

Primera Avenida (1st Avenue, 1ra Av.) runs along the shore. Time-worn *balnearios* (bathing areas) are found along Miramar's waterfront, cut into the shore. Of limited appeal to tourists, they draw Cubans on hot summer

Avenida, 5ta Avenida (the main thoroughfare), and 7ma Avenida.

Tunnels under the Río Almendares connect Miramar to Vedado. The Malecón connects with 5ta Avenida; Línea (Calle 9) connects with 7ma Avenida and Avenida 31, which leads to the Marianao district; Calle 11 connects with 7ma Avenida; and Calle 23 becomes Avenida 47, linking Vedado with Kohly and Marianao.

QUINTA AVENIDA

The wide, fig-tree-lined, eight-kilometer-long boulevard called 5th Avenue, or "Quinta," runs ruler-straight through the heart of Miramar. It is flanked by mansions, many now occupied by foreign embassies; Quinta Avenida (5ta Av.) is known as "Embassy Row."

At its eastern end, the **Casa de la Tejas Verdes** (House of Green Tiles, Calle 2 #318, Miramar, tel. 07/212-5282, tejasverde@patrimonio.ohc.cu, visits by appointment), or Edificio Fraxas, is a restored beaux-arts mansion on the north side of Quinta at Calle 2, immediately west of the tunnel. Built in 1926, after the Revolution it fell into utter decay. It has a sumptuous postmodern interior.

The junction at Calle 10 is pinned by **Reloj de Quinta Avenida,** a large clock erected in 1924 in the central median. At Calle 12, the **Memorial de la Denuncia** (Museum of Denouncement, 5ta Av., esq. 14, tel. 07/206-8802, ext. 108, www.cubadenuncia.cu) opened in 2016 and is dedicated to U.S.-Cuba relations. Six *salas* (rooms) are themed, including one dedicated to the CIA's efforts to dethrone Fidel and another to *el bloqueo* (the embargo). It's run by the Ministry of the Interior.

Parque de los Ahorcados (Park of the Hanged), aka Parque de la Quinta, spans Quinta between Calles 24 and 26. The park is shaded by massive jagüey trees and features a Greek-style rotunda, a bust of Gandhi (north side), and a statue of Emilio Zapata (south side). The park is best avoided on Sunday mornings, when the "Ladies in White" dissident group gathers to march, with no shortage of secret police present. Rising over the west side is **Iglesia de Santa Rita de Casia** (5ta, esq. Calle 26, tel. 07/204-2001). This exemplar of modernist church architecture dates from 1942; its main feature is a statue of Santa Rita by Rita Longa. Music lovers might head two blocks north to **Casa Museo Compay Segundo** (Calle 22 #103, e/ 1ra y 3ra, tel. 07/206-8629 or 202-5922, Mon.-Fri. 10am-noon and 2pm-4pm, free), where the crooner of *Buena Vista Social Club* fame is honored.

The modernist-style Romanesque **Iglesia San Antonio de Padua** (Calle 60 #316, esq. 5ta, tel. 07/203-5045) dates from 1951 and boasts a magnificent, albeit nonfunctional, organ. On the north side of Quinta, a monstrous Cubist tower can be seen virtually the length of the avenue. Formerly the Soviet Embassy, it is now the **Russian Embassy** (5ta, e/ 62 y 66), topped by an intelligence-gathering tower with a view over the horizon to Florida.

Playa

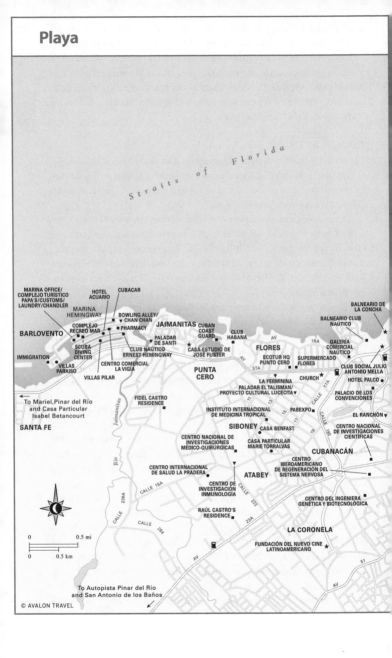

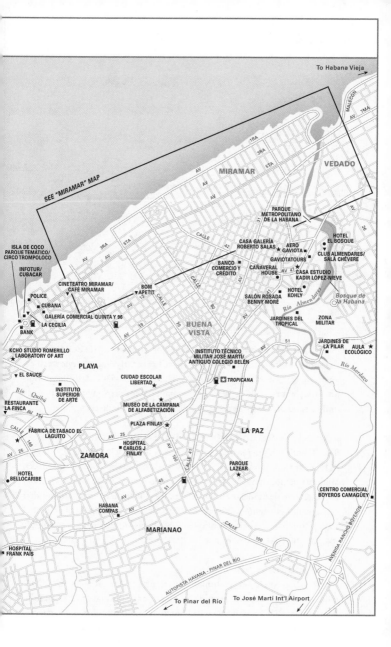

Miramar

At Calle 70 is the **Miramar Trade Center,** comprising six buildings. On the south side of Quinta rises the massive Roman-Byzantine-style **Basílica Jesús de Miramar** (5ta #8003, e/ 80 y 82, tel. 07/203-5301, daily 9am-noon and 4pm-6pm), built in 1953 with a magnificent organ with 5,000 pipes and 14 splendid oversize paintings of the stations of the cross.

PABELLÓN DE LA MAQUETA DE LA HABANA

The **Pabellón de la Maqueta de la Habana** (Model of Havana, Calle 28 #113, e/ 1ra y 3ra, tel. 07/202-7303, Mon.-Sat. 9:30am-5pm, adults CUC3, students, seniors, and children CUC1, guided tour CUC1, cameras CUC2) is a 1:1,000 scale model of the city. The 144-square-meter *maqueta* (model) represents 144 square kilometers of Havana and its environs. The model took more than 10 years to complete and shows Havana with every building present, color-coded by age.

ACUARIO NACIONAL

The **Acuario Nacional** (National Aquarium, 3ra Av., esq. 62, tel. 07/203-6401, www.acuarionacional.cu, Tues.-Sun. 10am-6pm and until 10pm July-Aug., adults CUC10, children CUC7, including shows) exhibits 450 species of sealife, including corals, exotic tropical fish, sharks, hawksbill turtles, sea lions, and dolphins. The displays are disappointing by international standards. Sea lion shows (Tues.-Sun. 11am and 4pm, Sat.-Sun. 11am, 2pm, and 4pm) and dolphin shows (daily noon, 3pm, and 5pm) are offered.

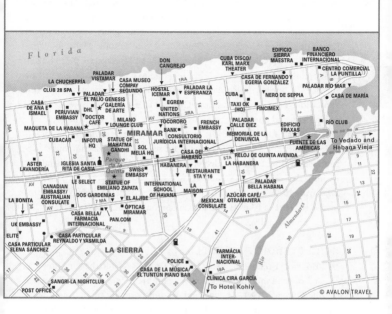

FUNDACIÓN NATURALEZA Y EL HOMBRE

The **Fundación Naturaleza y El Hombre** (Foundation of Man and Nature, Av. 5B #6611, e/ 66 y 70, tel. 07/204-2985, www.fanj.cult.cu, Mon.-Fri. 9am-4pm, CUC2) honors Cuban naturalist and explorer Antonio Nuñez Jiménez. Many of the eclectic exhibits in its **Museo de la Canoa** are dedicated to the 10,889-mile journey by a team of Cubans (led by Nuñez in 1996) that paddled from the source of the Amazon to the Bahamas in dugout canoes. There is a replica of the canoe along with indigenous artifacts, including pre-Columbian erotic ceramics.

Náutico and Jaimanitas

Beyond Miramar, 5ta Avenida curls around the half-moon Playa Marianao and passes through the Náutico district, a setting for Havana's elite prerevolutionary social clubs and *balnearios*. Following the Revolution, the area reopened to the hoi polloi and was rechristened. The beaches—collectively known as Playas del Oeste—are popular with Cubans on weekends. There was even an eponymous mini-version of New York's famous Coney Island theme park, re-created in 2008 as **Isla de Coco Parque Temático** (tel. 07/208-0330, Wed.-Fri. 4pm-10pm, Sat.-Sun. 10am-10pm).

Commanding the scene are the palatial Mudejar-style former **Balneario de la Concha** (5ta e/ 112 and 146) and, immediately west, the **Balneario Club Náutico** with its sweeping modernist entrance. Beyond the Río Quibu, 5ta Avenida passes into the Flores district. The Havana-Biltmore Yacht and Country Club was here, dating from 1928 and fronting Havana's most beautiful expanse of white sand. The "Yacht" was founded in 1886 and became the snootiest place in Havana (it was here that President Fulgencio Batista, mulatto, was famously refused entry for being too "black") until the Revolution, when it became the Club Social Julio Antonio Mella, for workers. Today, as the **Club Habana** (5ta Av., e/ 188 y 214, Playa, tel. 07/204-5700, yanis@clubhabana.palco.cu), it has reverted to its former role as a private club for the (mostly foreign) elite. Nonmembers are welcome (daily 9am-7pm, Mon.-Fri. CUC20, Sat.-Sun. CUC30) to use the beach, water sports equipment, and pool.

Fidel Castro's main domicile was here at **Punta Cero** in Jaimanitas, although you can't see it. The home is set in an expansive compound surrounded by pine trees and electrified fences and heavy security south of Avenida 5ta. All streets surrounding it are marked as one-way, heading away from the house, which is connected by a tunnel to the navy base immediately west of Club Havana. Avenida 5ta between Calles 188 and 230 is a no-photography zone.

KCHO ESTUDIO ROMERILLO

In 2014, world-renowned artist Alexis Leiva Machado, better known as "Kcho," opened this contemporary **art complex** (7ma, esq. 120, Playa, tel. 07/208-4750 or 5279-1844, www.kchoestudio.com, by appointment) with a library, theater, experimental graphic workshop, and galleries showing revolving exhibitions of leading artists worldwide. It also has a foundry and carpentry and pottery workshops. Enhancing the complex are the local parks that comprise **Museo Orgánico Romerillo,** which spans 20 blocks. Kcho finances the project himself.

CASA-ESTUDIO DE JOSÉ FUSTER

Artist José R. Fuster, a world-renowned painter and ceramist nicknamed the "Picasso of the Caribbean," has an open-air workshop-gallery at **his home** (Calle 226, esq. Av. 3ra, Jaimanitas, tel. 07/271-2932 or 5281-5421, www.josefuster.com, daily 9am-5pm; call ahead). You step through a giant doorway to discover a surreal world made of ceramics. Many of the naïve, childlike works are inspired by farmyard scenes and icons of *cubanidad,* such as *El Torre del Gallo* (Rooster's Tower), a four-meter-tall statement on male chauvinism. Fuster's creativity now graces the entryways, benches, roofs, and facades of houses throughout his local community.

Cubanacán and Siboney

Cubanacán is—or was—Havana's Beverly Hills, an exclusive area inland of Náutico and Flores. It was developed in the 1920s with winding tree-lined streets on which the most grandiose of Havana's mansions arose. The golf course at the Havana Country Club lent the name "Country Club Park" to what is now called Cubanacán, still the swankiest address in town. Following the Revolution, most of the area's homeowners fled Cuba. Many mansions were dispensed to Communist officials, who live in a manner that the majority of Cubans can only dream of and, of course, never see. The area is replete with military camps and security personnel. Other homes serve either as "protocol" houses—villas where foreign dignitaries and VIPs are housed during visits—or as foreign embassies and ambassadors' homes.

One of the swankiest mansions was built in 1910 for the Marqués de Pinar del Río; it was later adorned with 1930s art deco glass and chrome, a spiral staircase, and abstract floral designs. Today it is the **Fábrica El Laguito** (Av. 146 #2302, e/ 21 y 21A, tel. 07/208-0738, by appointment only), the nation's premier cigar factory, making Montecristos and the majority of Cohibas—*the* premium Havana cigar.

Havana's impressive convention center, the **Palacio de las Convenciones** (Convention Palace, Calle 146, e/ 11 y 13, tel. 07/202-6011, www.eventospalco.com), was built in 1979 for the Non-Aligned Conference. The main hall hosts twice-yearly meetings of the Cuban National Assembly. Two blocks west, **Pabexpo** (Av. 17 e/ 180 y 182, tel. 07/271-3670) has four exhibition halls for trade shows and is Cuba's main expo space.

Cuba's biotechnology industry is also centered here and extends westward into the districts of Atabey and Siboney (a residential area for MININT and military elite), earning the area the moniker "Scientific City." The **Centro de Ingeniería Genética y Biotecnología** (Center for Genetic Engineering and Biotechnology, Av. 31, e/ 158 y 190, Havana, tel. 07/271-8008, http://cigb.edu.cu) is Cuba's main research facility and perhaps the most sophisticated research facility in any developing nation.

INSTITUTO SUPERIOR DE ARTE

Following the Revolution, Fidel Castro and Che Guevara famously played a few rounds of golf at the exclusive Havana Country Club before tearing it up and converting the grounds to house Cuba's leading art academy, the **Instituto Superior de Arte** (Higher Art Institute, Calle 120 #1110, esq. 9na, tel. 07/208-9771, www.isa.cult.cu, appointment only through a tour agency; closed in summer), featuring the Escuela de Música (School of Music), Escuela de Ballet (Ballet School), Escuela de Baile Moderno (School of Modern Dance), and Escuela de Bellas Artes (School of Fine Arts). The school was designed by three young "rebel" architects: Italians Roberto Gottardi and Vittorio Garatti, and Cuban Ricardo Porro. As the five redbrick main buildings emerged, they were thought too avant-garde. The project was halted, though the school did open. Many buildings were never completed and fell into ruin. Calles 15 and 134 have the best views.

Marianao and La Coronela

This dilapidated *municipio*, on the heights south of Miramar, evolved since the mid-19th century along newly laid streets. During the 1920s, Marianao boasted the Marianao Country Club, the Oriental Park racetrack, and Grand Nacional Casino; it was given a boost on New Year's Eve 1939 when the Tropicana opened as Havana's ritziest nightclub. After the Revolution, the casinos, racetrack, and even Tropicana (briefly) were shut down.

Following the U.S. occupation of Cuba in 1898, the U.S. military governor, General Fitzhugh Lee, established his headquarters in Marianao and called it Camp Columbia. Campamento Columbia later became headquarters for Batista's army, and it was from here that the sergeant effected his *golpes* in 1933 and 1952. Camp Columbia was bombed on April 15, 1960, during the prelude to the CIA-run Bay of Pigs invasion.

Following the Revolution, Castro turned the barracks into **Ciudad Escolar Libertad,** a school complex that became the headquarters for Castro's national literacy campaign. The **Museo de la Campaña de Alfabetización** (Museum of the Literacy Campaign, Av. 29E, esq. 76, tel. 07/260-8054, Mon.-Fri. 8am-5pm, Sat. 8am-noon, free) is dedicated to the campaign initiated on January 1, 1960, when 120,632 uniformed *brigadistas,* mostly students, spread out across the country to teach illiterate peasantry to read and write. The blue building 100 meters west was Fulgencio Batista's former manse.

A tower in the center of the traffic circle—**Plaza Finlay**—outside the main entrance, at Avenida 31 and Avenida 100, was erected in 1944 as a beacon for the military airfield. In 1948 a needle was added so that today it is shaped like a syringe in honor of Carlos Finlay, the Cuban who in 1881 discovered the cause of yellow fever.

The Autopista a San Antonio links Havana with San Antonio de los Baños. Midway between the two cities, you'll pass the **Universidad de las Ciencias Informáticas** (Carretera de San Antonio de los Baños, Km 2, Torrens, tel. 07/837-2548, www.uci.cu), Cuba's university dedicated to making the country a world power in software technology. Immediately north is the gray marble **Memorial al Soldado Internacionalista Soviético,** with an eternal flame dedicated to Soviet military personnel who died in combat.

TROPICANA

The **Tropicana** (Calle 72 e/ 41 y 45, tel. 07/207-0110, www.cabaret-tropicana.com) is an astonishing exemplar of modernist architecture. Most of the structures date from 1951, when the nightclub was restored with a new showroom—the Salon Arcos de Cristal (Crystal Bows)—designed by Max Borges Recio with a roof of five arcing concrete vaults and curving bands of glass to fill the intervening space. Built in decreasing order of height, they produce a telescopic effect that channels the perspective toward the orchestra platform. Borges also added the famous geometric sculpture that still forms the backdrop to the main stage, in the outdoor Salón Bajo las Estrellas.

A ballet dancer pirouettes on the tips of her toes amid the lush foliage in front of the entrance. The statue, by the renowned Cuban sculptor Rita Longa, is surrounded by bacchantes performing a wild ritual dance to honor Dionysius.

The harbor channel and Bahía de la Habana (Havana Bay) separate Habana Vieja from the communities of Casablanca, Regla, and Guanabacoa. The communities can be reached through a tunnel under the channel (access is eastbound off Avenida del Puerto and the Prado) or along Vía Blanca, skirting the harbor. Little ferries bob their way across the water, connecting Casablanca and Regla with each other and with Habana Vieja.

★ Parque Histórico Militar Morro-Cabaña

Looming over Habana Vieja, on the north side of the harbor channel, the rugged cliff face is dominated by two great fortresses that constitute **Parque Histórico Militar Morro-Cabaña** (Morro-La Cabaña Historical Military Park, Carretera de la Cabaña, Habana del Este, tel. 07/862-4095). Together, the castles comprise the largest and most powerful defensive complex built by the Spanish in the Americas.

Visitors arriving by car reach the complex via the harbor tunnel (no pedestrians or motorcycles without sidecars are allowed) that descends beneath the Monumento al General Máximo Gómez off Avenida de Céspedes. Buses from Parque de la Fraternidad pass through the tunnel and stop by the fortress access road.

CASTILLO DE LOS TRES REYES DEL MORRO

The **Castillo de Los Tres Reyes del Morro** (Castle of the Three Kings of the Headland, tel. 07/863-7941, daily 8am-7pm, entrance CUC6, children under 12 free, guide CUC1) is built into the rocky palisades of Punta Barlovento at the entrance to Havana's narrow harbor channel. The fort—designed by Italian engineer Bautista Antonelli and initiated in 1589—forms an irregular polygon that follows the contours of the headland, with a sharp-angled bastion at the apex, stone walls 10 feet thick, and a series of batteries stepping down to the shore. Slaves toiled under the lash of whip and sun to cut the stone in situ, extracted from the void that forms the moats. El Morro took 40 years to complete and served its job well, repelling countless pirate attacks and withstanding for 44 days a siege by British cannons in 1762.

Enter via a drawbridge across a deep moat, leading through the **Túnel Aspillerado** (Tunnel of Loopholes) to vast wooden gates that open to the **Camino de Rondas,** a small parade ground (Plaza de Armas) containing a two-story building atop water cisterns that supplied the garrison of 1,000 men. To the right of the plaza, a narrow entrance leads to the **Baluarte de Austria** (Austrian Bastion), with cannon embrasures for firing down on the moat.

To the left of the Plaza de Armas, the **Sala de Historia del Faro y Castillo** profiles the various lighthouses and castles in Cuba. Beyond is the **Surtida de los Tinajones,** where giant earthenware vases are inset in stone. They once contained rapeseed oil as lantern fuel for the 25-meter-tall **Faro del Morro** (daily 10am-noon and 2pm-7pm, CUC2 extra), a lighthouse

Parque Histórico Militar Morro-Cabaña

To Havana
ENTRANCE GATE
To Playas del Este, Matanzas and Varadero

Bahía de la Habana

VÍA MONUMENTAL

BATERÍA DE VELASCO

ENTRANCE TO MORRO

Moat

PARKING
P

EL POLVORÍN
LOS DOCE APÓSTOLES

LIGHTHOUSE

BATERÍA DE LOS DOCE APÓSTOLES

0   100 yds
0   100 m

© AVALON TRAVEL

To Habana Vieja

constructed in 1844. Today an electric lantern still flashes twice every 15 seconds. You can climb to the top for a bird's-eye view.

All maritime traffic in and out of Havana harbor is controlled from the **Estación Semafórica,** the semaphore station atop the castle, accessed via the Baluarte de Tejeda. Below the castle, facing the city on the landward side and reached by a cobbled ramp, is the **Batería de los Doce Apóstoles** (Battery of the Twelve Apostles). It boasts massive cannons and El Polvorín (The Powderhouse) bar.

FORTALEZA DE SAN CARLOS DE LA CABAÑA

The massive **Fortaleza de San Carlos de la Cabaña** (Saint Charles of the Flock Fortress, Carretera de la Cabaña, tel. 07/862-4095, daily 10am-10pm, entrance CUC6 adults, children under 12 free, CUC8 for the *cañonazo* ceremony, guide CUC1), half a kilometer east of the Morro, enjoys a fantastic strategic position overlooking the city and harbor. It is the largest fort in the Americas, covering 10 hectares and stretching 700 meters in length. It was built 1763-1774 following the English invasion, and cost the staggering sum of 14 million pesos—when told the cost, the king after whom it is named reached for a telescope; surely, he said, it must be large enough to see from Madrid. The castle counted some 120 bronze cannons and mortars, plus a permanent garrison of 1,300 men. While never actually used in battle, it has been claimed that its dissuasive presence won all potential battles—a tribute to the French designer and engineer entrusted with its conception and construction.

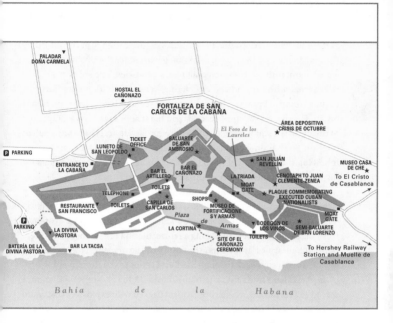

From the north, you pass through two defensive structures before reaching the monumental baroque portal flanked by great columns with a pediment etched with the escutcheon of Kings Charles III, followed by a massive drawbridge over a 12-meter-deep moat, one of several moats carved from solid rock and separating individual fortress components.

Beyond the entrance gate a paved alley leads to the **Plaza de Armas**, centered on a grassy, tree-shaded park fronted by a 400-meter-long curtain wall: **La Cortina** runs the length of the castle on its south side and formed

Castillo de los Tres Reyes del Morro

the main gun position overlooking Havana. It is lined with cannons. The *Ceremonía del Cañonazo* (cannon-firing ceremony, CUC6) is held nightly at 8:30pm, when troops dressed in 18th-century military garb and led by fife and drum light the fuse of a cannon to announce the closing of the city gates, maintaining a tradition going back centuries. The soldiers prepare the cannon with ramrod and live charge. When the soldier puts the torch to the cannon at 9pm, you have about three seconds before the thunderous boom. It's all over in a millisecond, and the troops march away. Opening to the plaza is a small **chapel** with a baroque facade and charming vaulted interior. The building opposite served as the headquarters for Che Guevara following the Triunfo del Revolución, when he oversaw the tribunals for "crimes against the security of the state."

Facing the plaza on its north side is the **Museo de Fortificaciones y Armas.** The museum (set in thick-walled, vaulted storage rooms, or *bovedas*) traces the castle's development and features uniforms and weaponry from the colonial epoch, including a representation of a former prison cell, plus suits of armor and weaponry that span the ancient Arab and Asian worlds and stretch back through medieval times to the Roman era.

A portal here leads into a garden—**Patio de los Jagüeyes**—that once served as a *cortadura,* a defensive element packed with explosives that could be ignited to foil the enemy's attempts to gain entry. The *bovedas* open to the north to cobbled **Calle de la Marina,** where converted barracks, armaments stores, and prisoners' cells now contain restaurants and the **Casa del Tabaco y Ron,** displaying the world's longest cigar (11 meters long).

Midway down Marina, a gate leads down to **El Foso de los Laureles,** a massive moat containing the execution wall where nationalist sympathizers were shot during the wars of independence. Following the Revolution, scores of Batista supporters and "counterrevolutionaries" met a similar fate.

ÁREA DEPÓSITO CRISIS DE OCTUBRE

Displayed atop the **San Julián Revellín** moat, on the north side of Fortaleza de San Carlos, are missiles and armaments from the Cuban Missile Crisis (called the October 1962 Crisis by Cubans). These include an SS-4 nuclear missile; English-language panels explain that it had a range of 2,100 kilometers and a one-megaton load. It was one of 36 such missiles installed at the time. Also here are a MiG fighter jet, various antiaircraft guns, and the remains of the U-2 piloted by Major Rudolf Anderson shot down over Cuba on October 27, 1962. You can view them from the road but it costs CUC1 to get up close and personal.

ESTATUA CRISTO DE LA HABANA

The **Estatua Cristo de la Habana** (Havana Christ Statue, Carretera del Asilo, daily 9am-8pm, entrance CUC1, children under 12 free) looms over Casablanca, dominating the cliff face immediately east of the *fortaleza.* The 15-meter-tall statue, unveiled on December 25, 1958, was hewn from Italian Carrara marble by Cuban sculptor Jilma Madera. From the *mirador* surrounding the statue, you have a bird's-eye view of the harbor. It is possible, with the sun gilding the waters, to imagine great galleons slipping in and out of the harbor laden with treasure en route to Spain.

The adjoining **Casa-Museo del Che** (tel. 07/866-4747, daily 9am-7pm, entrance CUC6, guide CUC1) is where Che Guevara lived immediately following the fall of Batista. Today it displays his M-1 rifle, submachine gun, radio, and rucksack, among other exhibits.

A ferry (10 centavos) runs to Casablanca every 20 minutes or so from the Emboque de Luz (Av. del Puerto y Calle Luz) in Habana Vieja. You can walk uphill from Casablanca.

Regla

Regla, a working-class barrio on the eastern shore of Havana harbor, evolved in the 16th century as a fishing village and eventually became Havana's foremost warehousing and slaving center. It developed into a smugglers' port in colonial days. Havana's main electricity-generating plant and petrochemical works are here, pouring bilious plumes over town.

Regla is a center of Santería; note the tiny shrines outside many houses. Calle Calixto García has many fine examples. Many *babalawos* (Santería priests) live here and will happily dispense advice for a fee.

The **Museo Municipal de Regla** (Martí #158, e/ Facciolo y La Piedra, tel. 07/797-6989, Tues.-Sat. 9am-8:45pm, Sun. 1pm-8:45pm, entrance CUC2, guide CUC1), two blocks east of the harborfront, tells the tale of the town's Santería associations. Other displays include colonial-era swords, slave shackles, and the like.

Calle Martí, the main street, leads southeast to the city cemetery; from there, turn east onto Avenida Rosario for two blocks, where steps ascend to **Colina Lenin** (Lenin Hill, Calle Vieja, e/ Enlase y Rosaria). A three-meter-tall bronze face of the Communist leader is carved into the cliff face; a dozen life-size figures (in cement) cheer him from below. A **museum** (tel. 07/797-6899, Tues.-Sat. 9am-5pm, free) atop the hill is dedicated to Lenin and various martyrs of the Cuban Revolution.

The Colina is more directly reached from Parque Guaycanamar (Calle Martí, six blocks east of the harborfront) via Calle Albuquerque and 24 de Febrero; you'll reach a metal staircase that leads to the park. Bus #29 will take you there from the Regla dock.

Ferries (10 centavos) run between Regla and the Emboque de Luz (Av. San Pedro y Luz) in Habana Vieja. Bus P15 departs the Capitolio for Regla.

IGLESIA DE NUESTRA SEÑORA DE REGLA

The **Iglesia de Nuestra Señora de Regla** (Church of Our Lady of Regla, Sanctuario #11, e/ Máximo Gómez y Litoral, tel. 07/797-6228, daily 7:30am-5:30pm), built in 1810 on the harborfront, is one of Havana's loveliest churches, highlighted by a gilt altar. Figurines of miscellaneous saints dwell in wall alcoves, including a statue of St. Anthony leading a wooden suckling pig. *Habaneros* flock to pay homage to the black Virgen de Regla,

Regla and Guanabacoa

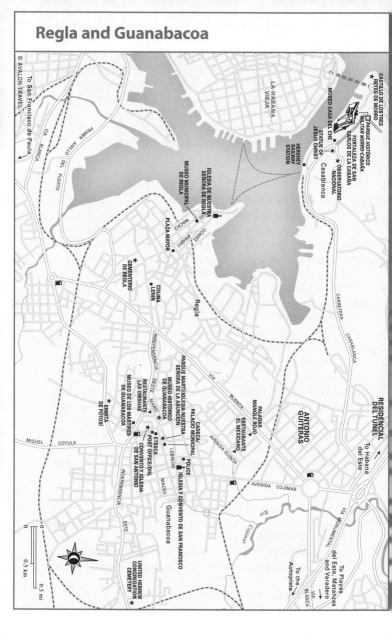

To San Francisco de Paula

To Habana del Este

To Playas del Este, Matanzas and Varadero

To the Autopista

© AVALON TRAVEL

LA HABANA VIEJA

CASTILLO DE LOS TRES REYES DEL MORRO

MUSEO CASA DEL CHE

PARQUE HISTÓRICO MILITAR MORRO-CABAÑA

FORTALEZA DE SAN CARLOS DE LA CABAÑA

STATUE OF JESUS CHRIST

OBSERVATORIO NACIONAL

Casablanca

HERSHEY RAILWAY STATION

MUSEO MUNICIPAL DE REGLA

IGLESIA DE NUESTRA SEÑORA DE REGLA

PLAZA MAYOR

CEMENTERIO DE REGLA

COLINA LENIN

MÁCEO

GÓMEZ

MARTÍ

Regla

PRIMER ANILLO DEL PUERTO

VÍA BLANCA

CARRETERA CASABLANCA

RESIDENCIAL DEL TÚNEL

ANTONIO GUITERAS

VÍA BLANCA

INDEPENDENCIA

OESTE MARTÍ

MIGUEL COYULA

ERMITA DE POTOSÍ

MUSEO DE LOS MÁRTIRES DE GUANABACOA

RESTAURANTE LAS ORISHAS

MUSEO HISTÓRICO DE GUANABACOA

PARQUE MARTÍ/IGLESIA NUESTRA SEÑORA DE LA ASUNCIÓN

PALACIO MUNICIPAL

CADECA

ETESCA

POST OFFICE/DHL

CONVENTO Y IGLESIA DE SAN ANTONIO

POLICE

IGLESIA Y CONVENTO DE SAN FRANCISCO

Guanabacoa

PALADAR MANGLE ROJO

RESTAURANTE EL MEXICANO

AVENIDA QUINTA

LEBREDO

MACEO

AVENIDA COJÍMAR

Río Cojímar

INDEPENDENCIA

ESTE

UNITED HEBREW CONGREGATION CEMETERY

VÍA MONUMENTAL

VÍA BLANCA

0   0.5 km

0   0.5 mi

patron saint of sailors and Catholic counterpart to Yemayá, the goddess of water in the Santería religion. Time your visit for the seventh of each month, when large masses are held, or for a pilgrimage each September 7, when the Virgin is paraded through town.

Outside, 20 meters to the east and presiding over her own private chapel, is a statue of the Virgen de la Caridad del Cobre, Cuba's patron saint. Syncretized as the *orisha* Ochún, she also draws adherents of Santería.

Guanabacoa

Guanabacoa, three kilometers east of Regla, was founded in 1607 and developed as the major trading center for slaves. An Afro-Cuban culture evolved here, expressed in a strong musical heritage. The **Casa de la Trova** (Martí #111, e/ San Antonio y Versalles, tel. 07/797-7687, hours vary, entrance one peso) hosts performances of Afro-Cuban music and dance, as does **Centro Cultural Recreativo Los Orishas** (Calle Martí, e/ Lamas y Cruz Verde, tel. 07/794-7878, daily noon-midnight), which hosts live rumba on weekends plus Friday 9pm shows; it doubles as a restaurant serving *criolla* dishes and pizzas (CUC2-10). Guanabacoa is also Cuba's most important center of Santería. So strong is the association that all over Cuba, folks facing extreme adversity will say "I'm going to have to go to Guanabacoa," implying that only the power of a *babalawo* can fix the problem.

Guanabacoa also boasts several religious sites (most are tumbledown and await restoration), including two Jewish cemeteries on the east side of town.

SIGHTS

The sprawling town is centered on the small tree-shaded **Parque Martí** (Calles Martí, División Pepe Antonio, y Adolfo del Castillo Cadenas), dominated by the **Iglesia Nuestra Señora de la Asunción** (División #331, e/ Martí y Cadenas, tel. 07/797-7368, Mon.-Fri. 8am-noon and 2pm-5pm, Sun. 8am-11am), commonly called the Parroquial Mayor. Completed in 1748, it features a lofty Mudejar-inspired wooden roof and baroque gilt altar dripping with gold, plus 14 stations of the cross. If the doors are locked, try the side entrance on Calle Enrique Güiral.

The **Museo Histórico de Guanabacoa** (Historical Museum of Guanabacoa, Martí #108, e/ Valenzuela y Quintín Bandera, tel. 07/797-9117, musgbcoa@cubarte.cult.cu, Tues.-Sat. 9:30am-5:30pm, entrance CUC2, guide CUC1), one block west of the plaza, tells of Guanabacoa's development and the evolution of Afro-Cuban culture.

One block southwest of the park, the **Convento y Iglesia de San Antonio** (Máximo Gómez, esq. San Antonio, tel. 07/797-7241), begun in 1720 and completed in 1806, is now a school. The *custodio* may let you in to admire the exquisite *alfarje* ceiling.

The **Convento de Santo Domingo** (Santo Domingo #407, esq. Rafael de Cadena, tel. 07/797-7376, Tues.-Fri. 9am-11:30am and 3:30pm-5pm but often closed) dates from 1728 and has an impressive neobaroque facade.

Its church, the **Iglesia de Nuestra Señora de la Candelaria,** boasts a magnificent blue-and-gilt baroque altar plus an intricate *alfarje.* The door is usually closed; ring the doorbell to the left of the entrance.

The only ecclesiastical edifice thus far restored is the tiny hilltop **Ermita de Potosí** (Potosí Hermitage, Calzada Vieja Guanabacoa, esq. Calle Potosí, tel. 07/797-9867, daily 8am-5pm). The simple hermitage dates to 1644 and is the oldest religious structure still standing in Cuba. It has an intriguing cemetery.

GETTING THERE

Bus #29 runs to Guanabacoa from the Regla dock. Bus P15 departs for Guanabacoa via Regla from in front of the Capitolio, on the south side of Parque de la Fraternidad; you can catch it in Vedado from G y 23.

Entertainment and Events

Yes, the city has lost the Barbary Coast spirit of prerevolutionary days, but *habaneros* love to paint the town red as much as their budgets allow. Many venues are seedier than they were in the 1950s—in some, the decor hasn't changed. Pricey entrance fees dissuade Cubans from attending the hottest new venues. Cubans are even priced out of most bars (one beer can cost the equivalent of a week's salary).

The great news is that private bars and nightclubs have sprouted like mushrooms on a damp log; all serve food to get around the legal licensing restrictions on bars. Havana now has some chic scenes reminiscent of L.A. or Miami.

For theater, classical concerts, and other live performances it's difficult to make a reservation by telephone. Instead, go to the venue and buy a ticket in advance or just before the performance. Call ahead to double-check dates, times, and venue.

Cartelera, a cultural magazine for tourists published monthly by Artex, has information on exhibitions, galleries, performances, and more. A fantastic Internet source is **La Habana** (www.lahabana.com), which publishes a monthly update of live concerts and other cultural events nationwide. **Havana Club** (www.havana-cultura.com) maintains a pretty cool website with hip profiles on cultural events. And both **Suena Cubano** (www.suenacubano.com) and **Vistar** (www.vistarmagazine.com), two Cuban start-ups, also have up-to-date listings of events.

Radio Taíno (1290 AM and 93.3 FM, daily 5pm-7pm) serves tourists with information on cultural happenings via nightly broadcasts.

Since so many young Cubans lack money for bars and clubs, thousands hang out on the Malecón (principally between Calle 23 and Calle 0) and along Avenida de los Presidentes (Calle G) on weekend nights. The latter chiefly draws *frikis* (Goths and punks), *roqueros,* and what Julia Cooke or rum and listening to music played on cell phones.

NIGHTLIFE
Bars and Lounges
HABANA VIEJA

Every tourist in town wants to sip a *mojito* at **La Bodeguita del Medio** (Empedrado #207, e/ Cuba y Tacón, tel. 07/867-1374, daily 10am-midnight). Go for the ambience, aided by troubadours, rather than the drinks: The *mojitos* are weak, perhaps explaining why Hemingway didn't sup here, contrary to legend. Instead, Hemingway preferred to tipple his mojitos at the **Dos Hermanos** (Av. San Pedro #304, esq. Sol, tel. 07/861-3514, 11am-11pm), a refurbished wharf-front saloon where he bent elbows with sailors and prostitutes at the long wooden bar. Tourists and a sprinkling of locals are today's clientele, but the mojitos are consistently good (CUC4). There's often live music.

Hemingway enjoyed his sugarless *papa doble* daiquiri (double shot of rum) at **El Floridita** (Obispo, esq. Monserrate, tel. 07/867-1301, bar open daily 11:30am-midnight). It may not quite live up to its 1950s aura, when *Esquire* magazine named it one of the great bars of the world, but to visit Havana without sipping a daiquiri here would be like visiting France without tasting wine. It gets packed; the only Cubans are the musicians and waitstaff.

Now that the de rigueur tourist bars have been addressed, find the real fun at the bi-level **O'Reilly 304** (Calle O'Reilly #304, e/ Habana y Aguiar, tel. 5264-4725, oreilly304@gmail.com, daily noon-midnight), one of the hippest and trendiest spots in town. Most folks come to dine, but you can hang at the bar and sample the mango daiquiri and killer watermelon mojitos while grooving to hip music played by a live band on the stairwell. Get there early for a seat.

Privately run, **Lamparilla Tapas y Cerveza** (Calle Lamparilla #361 e/ Aguacate y Villegas, tel. 5289-5324, daily 11:30am-11:30pm) is a chill place to hang, listen to cool sounds, and savor beer and tapas such as fish *croquetas* and *adobo* pork chops with zucchini tempura. Bare brick walls are festooned with hip art, and the eclectic furnishings add a note of the bohemian.

For chic, try **Sloppy Joe's** (Animas, esq. Zulueta, tel. 07/866-7157, daily noon-2am). This once-legendary bar—founded in 1918 by José Abel, who turned a dilapidated and messy grocery store into "Sloppy Joe's"—reopened in 2013 after decades in ruins. It's been remade as it was, with glossy wood paneling and a long mahogany bar with tall barstools and flat-screen TVs. The Sloppy Joe house drink is made of brandy, Cointreau, port, and pineapple juice (CUC5).

Just around the corner is the trendy **Bar Asturias** (Prado #309 esq. Virtudes, tel. 07/864-1447, 10pm-2am), a cool and colorful club to the rear of the ground floor of the Sociedad Cultural Asturiana. Go for the late-night jazz, jam sessions, and boleros.

Beer lovers should head to Plaza Vieja, where the Viennese-style brew-pub **Factoría Plaza Vieja** (San Ignacio #364, tel. 07/866-4453, daily 11am-1am) produces delicious Pilsen (light) and Munich (dark) beer. You can order half liters (CUC2), liters, or a whopping three-liter *dispensa*, a tall glass cylinder fitted with a tap and with beer kept chilled by a thin center tube filled with ice.

The penny-pinching *farandula* (in-crowd) heads to **Bar La Chanchullero** (Brasil, e/ Berraza y Cristo, tel. 07/861-0915, www.el-chanchullero.com, daily 1pm-midnight), a cool and down-to-earth hole-in-the-wall on Plaza del Cristo.

CENTRO HABANA

The suave, state-run **Adagio Barconcert** (Paseo de Martí esq. Neptuno, tel. 07/861-6575, daily 2pm-2am, no cover) combines chic styling with awesome classical music (think Andrea Boccelli), bolero, and jazz, including live performances.

Bohemian, eclectic, and offbeat sum up **Sia Kara** (Calle Industria #502 esq. Barcelona, tel. 07/867-4084, daily 1pm-2am), one of Havana's coolest bars. The brainchild of Cuban ballet dancer José Manuel Carreño and his partner, French-born artist Mateo Royar, it's a true artsy hangout, popular with locals (including Havana's cultural elite) who settle in on well-stuffed sofas and canoodle in the loft-style lounge. Tucked away behind the Capitolio, it's off the tourist radar, but not for long. It serves simple dishes (CUC5) and a full range of cocktails (CUC2.50), but the wine list is feeble. The mojitos are superb, as is the caipiroska—a caipirinha made of vodka.

To find out what happened to the Soviet influence, head to **Nazdarovie** (Malecón #24, e/ Prado y Carcel, tel. 07/860-2947, daily noon-midnight), located upstairs in a townhouse manse overlooking the Atlantic. You'll be greeted by a comrade in Soviet military cap. It's mainly a restaurant serving Slavic-inspired fare, but the bar adds a Russian twist to their cocktails.

For rumba, trova, and even jazz, join the locals at cubbyhole **El Jelengue de Areito** (Calle San Miguel #410, e/ Campanario y Lealtad, no tel). Friday nights are best.

VEDADO AND PLAZA DE LA REVOLUCIÓN

The Hotel Nacional's patio **Bar La Terraza** is a great place to laze in a rattan sofa chair with a cigar and cocktail while musicians entertain with live music. For superb sweeping views of the city, try the **Salón Turquino** (25th floor inside Hotel Habana Libre Tryp, Calle L, e/ 23 y 25, tel. 07/834-6100), or **La Torre** (Calle 17 #55, e/ M y N, tel. 07/838-3088), atop the Focsa building.

At **Esencia Habana** (Calle B #153, e/ Calzada y Línea, tel. 07/836-3031, www.esenciahabana.com, 1pm-3am), owner Juan (a Spaniard) and his Cuban partner have conjured a colonial-style mansion into a classic Cuban bar with quasi-European pretension. It's hugely popular with expats, perhaps because it feels slightly like an English pub. Go for happy hour Friday 5pm-8pm, and for tapas such as carpaccio (CUC6.50) and garlic shrimp (CUC5), best enjoyed on the patio terrace. Three blocks north, the **Corner Café** (Av. 1ra, esq. B, tel. 07/837-1220, daily 10am-close) has a hipper vibe thanks to DJs and live music.

La farandula (the in-crowd) hangs out atop **El Cocinero** (Calle 26, e/ 11 y 13, tel. 07/832-2355, www.elcocinerohabana.com), a former electricity station and fish warehouse turned open-air lounge club with a chic New York City vibe. Adjoining, the **Fábrica de Arte** (Calle 13 #61, esq. 26, tel. 07/838-2260, www.fac.cu, Thurs.-Sun. 8pm-3am, CUC2) is undisputably Havana's chicest bohemian nightspot—a complete cultural venue with theater, film, dance, fashion shows, art exhibitions, concerts, and DJ Iván Lejardi's experimental electronic raves. Alas, it's been taken over by the tourist crowd and is a party stop for visiting VIPs and tour groups. On last visit I had to ask "where are the Cubans?" It's housed in a former olive oil factory and fish warehouse and has multiple bars on two tiers. Drinks are on credit; you pay on check-out.

A great spot to mingle with Cuba's artsy bohemians, **Café Madrigal** (Calle 17 #809, e/ 2 y 4, tel. 07/831-2433, rafa@audiovisuales.icaic.cu, Tues.-Sun. 6pm-2am) is upstairs in the home of filmmaker Rafael Rosales. This is a spot for tapas and a brain-freezingly chilled daiquiri. Movie memorabilia festoons the redbrick walls, alongside art pieces by Rafael's pal Javier Garver. Relax over cocktails (from daiquiris to whiskey sours; CUC3) to laid-back tunes from Maxwell and Marvin Gaye.

For casual music and romantic ambience check out **Bar Bohemio** (Calle 21 #1065, e/ 12 y 14, tel. 07/833-6918, Tues.-Sun. 6pm-midnight, Fri.-Sat. 6pm-4am), housed in a spacious 1940s manse. Former ballet dancers run this private loungelike bar with an L-shaped terrace. Try the Moscow by Tang (a mojito made of vodka, with basil), best enjoyed on the planter-studded patio.

I love the bohemian ambience at **La Casa de la Bombilla Verde** (Calle 11 #905 e/ 6 y 8, tel. 5848-1331, daily noon-midnight), a chic, unpretentious art-filled lounge billed as a "café cultural."

PLAYA (MIRAMAR AND BEYOND)

This district is ground zero for the hip private lounge club craze sweeping Havana. Many clubs are frequented by high-class *jineteras*.

Risqué artwork is a head-twisting constant at **Espacios** (Calle 10 #513, e/ 5ta y 7ta, tel. 07/202-2921, daily 1pm-2am), catering to bohemian types and Havana's young monied crowd with several indoor lounges and an outdoor party space where live *trova* is played. It serves tapas.

Expats consider the Miami-style alfresco lounge bar at **La Fontana** (3ra Av. #305, esq. 46, tel. 07/202-8337, daily noon-2am) a second home for its cool blue-lit chic and great cocktails.

You're forgiven if you think you've landed in South Beach at **Melem**

Havana's Gay Scene

Gay life in Havana has loosened considerably from the traditional "scene" around hangout street locales and spontaneous private parties, usually featuring a drag show. Today, there are parties, known as *divino* parties or *fiestas de diez pesos,* at private venues that change nightly and are spread by word of mouth (entrance costs 10 pesos or CUC1-2). To find out where tonight's party is, head to the **Malecón,** opposite Fiat Café near the foot of La Rampa.

Discoteca Escaleras al Cielo (Zulueta #658 e/ Gloria y Apodaca, Habana Vieja, tel. 07/861-9198, Fri.-Sat. 10pm-4am) serves the LGBT crowd, with pole-dancing boys (and sometimes one or two token girls) in hot pants.

Havana's first dedicated, openly gay bar is **Humboldt 52** (Calle Humboldt #52 e/ Infanta y Hospitál, Centro Habana, tel. 5330-2898, www.facebook.com/Humboldt52), which features drag shows, karaoke, and disco. It's an odd mix of wrought-iron furnishings with gingham tablecloths beneath a revolving disco ball.

In Vedado, **Cabaret Las Vegas** (Infanta esq. 25, tel. 07/863-7939, daily 10pm-3am, CUC2-3) is popular for its nightly transvestite cabarets.

Aside from clubs, gay-friendly **Casa de Carlos** (Calle 2 #505 altos e/ 21 y 23, Vedado, tel. 07/833-1329 or 5295-4893, www.carlosincuba.com, CUC35-45 low season, CUC45-55 high season) offers accommodations in a beautifully decorated mansion.

(Av. 1ra e/ 58 y 60, tel. 07/203-0433, 8pm-3am), a chic and classy contemporary take on a cocktail club; it gets in the groove after midnight. It permits smoking.

Drawing monied young Cubans, the Hotel Meliá Habana's chic alfresco **Sport Bar** (3ra Av., e/ 76 y 80, tel. 07/204-8500, Mon.-Fri. noon-3am and Sat.-Sun. 9am-3am) has a hip vibe, with omnipresent TVs tuned to sports, a DJ, and occasional live music.

Cabarets Espectáculos

CENTRO HABANA AND CERRO

Cabaret Nacional (San Rafael, esq. Prado, tel. 07/863-2361, CUC5), in the dingy basement of the Gran Teatro, has a modest *espectáculo* nightly at 10pm. The campy show is followed by a disco, drawing Cubans on weekends for steamy dancing; ostensibly only couples are admitted.

VEDADO AND PLAZA DE LA REVOLUCIÓN

The most lavish show is the **Cabaret Parisien** (Calle O, esq. 21, tel. 07/836-3564, CUC30), in the Hotel Nacional. The Cubano Cubano show is offered Sunday-Friday at 10pm and is followed by a Latin dance school. The dinner special (CUC50-70) is best avoided. The place is cramped and fills with smoke, and while the show is nowhere near the scale of the Tropicana, it has plenty of color and titillation and allows patrons to avoid the long trek out to the Tropicana.

The **Cabaret Copa Room** (Paseo y Malecón, tel. 07/836-4051, CUC20), in the Hotel Habana Riviera, hosts a cabaret (Wed.-Mon. 10:30pm). The dated venue features the top names in live Cuban music, such as Los Van Van, and is one of Havana's top spots for serious salsa fans.

Catering to a tourist crowd, **Habana Café** (Paseo, e/ 1ra y 3ra, tel. 07/833-3636, ext. 147, nightly 8pm-3am), adjoining the Hotel Meliá Cohiba, offers cabaret at 8:30pm. A vintage Harley-Davidson, two 1950s classic cars, and an airplane suspended from the ceiling add dramatic chic. Entrance is CUC10, but a *consumo mínimo* applies (CUC30 for top bands such as Los Van Van and Charanga Habanera).

PLAYA (MIRAMAR AND BEYOND)

The small yet popular open-air cabaret at **La Cecilia** (5ta Av. #11010, e/ 110 y 112, tel. 07/204-1562, Fri.-Sat. 10pm-3am, Fri. CUC5, Sat. CUC10) has been running for decades. It still draws monied expats and Cuba's youthful hipsters for the disco that follows. Top bands often perform (CUC20-25).

Cuba's catwalk divas strut at **La Maison** (Calle 16 #701, esq. 7ma, Miramar, tel. 07/204-1543, Thurs.-Sun. 10pm, CUC5), renowned for its *desfiles de modas* (fashion shows) and *cabaret espectáculo* in the terrace garden of an elegant old mansion. A piano bar adjoins, and it has weekend matinees.

★ TROPICANA

Cuba's premier Las Vegas-style nightclub is the **Tropicana** (Calle 72 #4504 y Línea del Ferrocarril, Marianao, tel. 07/267-1717, www.cabaret-tropicana.com, nightly 10pm, entrance CUC75/85/95, cameras CUC5, videos CUC15), which has been in continuous operation since New Year's Eve 1939, when it was the most flamboyant nightclub in the world. In its early days, celebrities such as Nat "King" Cole, Josephine Baker, and Carmen Miranda headlined the show, which was so popular that a 50-passenger "Tropicana Special" flew nightly from Miami for an evening of entertainment. Today patrons watch mesmerized as a troupe of showgirls parades down the aisles wearing glowing chandeliers atop their heads, while searchlights sweep over more gaudily feathered showgirls promenade among the floodlit palm trees. The glitzy, high-octane show boasts more than 200 performers, a fabulous orchestra, and astonishing acrobatic feats. The two-hour cabaret takes place in the open-air Salón Bajo Las Estrellas; on rainy nights, it's held in the Salon Arcos de Cristal.

The entrance fee is outrageous, but includes a bottle of rum with cola, a glass of cheap champagne, and a cheap cigar. It's best to book in advance through your hotel tour desk, as the show often sells out. Beware rip-offs by the waiters, who often wait until the end of the show to bill you for any incidentals, then disappear without bringing your change.

Discos and Nightclubs

CENTRO HABANA AND CERRO

One of the city's most popular venues is **Casa de la Música** (Galiano #253, e/ Concordia y Neptuno, tel. 07/860-8296, Tues.-Sun. 10pm-4am, CUC10-20). A modern theater known as "Dos" (for Casa de la Música 2, or *dos*), it fills with a mostly Cuban crowd for some of the hottest salsa bands and dancing in town. It has a live salsa matinee Saturdays at 5pm.

VEDADO AND PLAZA DE LA REVOLUCIÓN

Salón Turquino (Calle L, e/ 23 y 25, tel. 07/834-6100, Fri.-Sat. 10:30pm-3am, CUC10 cover), atop the Hotel Habana Libre, offers a medley of entertainment that varies nightly, followed by salsa dancing. This expensive and chic hot spot has amazing views. The retractable roof opens at midnight for dancing beneath the stars. Top bands often perform.

The **Salón Rojo** (Calle 21, e/ N y O, tel. 07/833-3747, nightly 10pm-4am, CUC10-25), beside the Hotel Capri, hosts Havana's hottest acts, such as Los Van Van and Bandolero. It's perhaps *the* venue for searing salsa.

Check with locals as to when **Casa Fiesta Jardines del 1830** (Malecón y Calle 20, tel. 07/838-3092, Tues.-Sun. 10pm-2am, CUC3 cover) is happening, as this venue comes and goes in popularity. It's located in the gardens of a mansion overlooking the mouth of the Río Almendares and is known for its Friday night "House Party" with *rueda* (wheel), where circles of couples dance in concert then on cue switch partners.

Despite its lackluster setting, Cubans flock to the **Café Cantante** (Paseo, esq. 39, tel. 07/878-4273, Tues.-Sat. 8pm-3am, CUC10) in the basement of the Teatro Nacional. No hats, T-shirts, or shorts are permitted for men. The plusher **Piano Bar Delirio Habanero** (tel. 07/878-4275), on the third floor, has Saturday afternoon *peñas* (4pm) and live music (Thurs.-Fri. 10pm, CUC5). The mood is similar at the **Café Teatro Bertolt Brecht** (Calle 13,

Tropicana

Learn to Salsa

For one-on-one salsa lessons I recommend **Mairym Cuesta** (Calle Estrella #364, e/ Escobar y Lealtad, tel. 07/862-5720, mirianvc@infomed.sld.cu); **Asmara Nuñez** (tel. 5293-0862)—who used to perform as a Tropicana dancer—and her partner, **Yoel Letan Peña**; or **La Casa del Són** (Edpredado #411, e/ Aguacate y Villegas, Habana Vieja), which also teaches *rueda de casino* and rumba. **Club Salseando Chévere** (Calle 49 y Av. 28, Kohly, tel. 07/204-4990, www.salseandochevere.com) offers intensive classes.

esq. I, tel. 07/832-9359), a sleek low-ceilinged, nonsmoking venue that draws a young crowd.

Getting better all the time, **Submarino Amarillo** (Yellow Submarine, Calle 17 esq. Calle 6, tel. 07/830-6808, Mon. 9am-2am, Tues.-Sat. 1pm-7:30pm and 9pm-2am, CUC2 cover), on the corner of Parque Lennon, thrills Beatles fans. The decor plays up the Beatles theme, while live bands perform Fab Four tunes amid Cuban rock. It has weekend matinees at 2pm.

Sarao's Bar (Calle 17, esq. E, tel. 07/832-0433 or 5263-8037, daily noon-3am) epitomizes the emerging hip new Cuba, drawing the likes of Usher and Katy Perry to high-octane parties with a South Beach state of mind. This slickly designed venue is the brainchild of several techno DJs and hip-hop artists. With its modern motif and gorgeous staff, this neon-lit nightclub is *the* hot spot for the monied young.

KingBar (Calle 23 #667, e/ D y E, tel. 07/833-0556, daily 5pm-3am) is a homier version of Sarao's, with a pumped-up party scene and occasional live music (from hip hop to electronica). Smooth retro soul and R&B tunes are staples in the garden space decorated with erotic art. The club is hidden away to the rear of a large white mansion and doubles as an open-air restaurant with a charcoal grill.

PLAYA (MIRAMAR AND BEYOND)

Long considered a top salsa venue by monied locals, **Casa de la Música** (Av. 25, esq. 20, tel. 07/204-0447, Wed.-Sun. 5pm-9pm and 10pm-3am, CUC10-20) has sizzling-hot afternoon salsa sessions as well as nightly (Tues.-Sun.) salsa and reggaeton performances by such legends as Alexander Abreu, Bamboleo, and NG La Banda. The headliner normally doesn't come on until 1am. Above the Casa is **Disco Tun Tún Piano Bar** (Tues.-Sun. 11pm-6am, CUC10), which keeps in the groove until dawn.

While I don't get its appeal, **Don Cangrejo** (1ra Av., e/ 16 y 18, tel. 07/204-4169, daily noon-midnight, entrance CUC5-20) is the unlikely Friday and Saturday night hot spot for the Havana elite. The restaurant's open-air oceanfront pool complex hosts live music by some of Cuba's top performers (such as Buena Fe and Kelvis Ochoa).

The privately owned, neon-lit **Sangri-La** (Calle 42, esq. 21, Playa, tel. 5264-8343, daily noon-3am) is a chic lounge club with kick-ass cocktails, white leather banquettes, and flat-screen TVs showing music videos. A small dance floor is tucked in one corner, but after midnight everyone dances wherever. Get there early on weekends to get in.

Cubans find their fun at **Teatro Karl Marx** (1ra Av., e/ 8 y 10, tel. 07/203-0801, Fri.-Sun. 9pm-2am, CUC10-20), Cuba's largest theater. Buena Fe, Isaac Delgado, and other big names play here. The vast theater also plays host to many of the city's gala events.

Farther out, **Salón Rosado Benny Moré** (Av. 41, esq. 48, tel. 07/203-5322, Fri.-Mon. 7pm-2am for live groups, Tues.-Wed. for cabaret, CUC5-10) is a basic open-air concert arena better known as El Tropical. It's immensely popular on weekends when top-billed Cuban salsa bands perform. Drawing a relatively impecunious crowd, it features killer music and salacious dancing. Rum-induced fights do break out; it's best to go with a Cuban friend.

Traditional Music
HABANA VIEJA

The **Asociación Cultural Yoruba de Cuba** (Prado #615, e/ Dragones y Monte, tel. 07/863-5953) hosts the Peña de Obini Bata with traditional Afro-Cuban music and dance (Fri. 6pm-8pm), plus cultural activities (Sat. 6pm-8pm, Sun. 9am-1pm, CUC5).

Watch for **Gigantería Teatro Callejero,** a group of performing street artists who dress as outlandish living statues. The principal group strolls the streets and plazas on stilts; their coming is announced by wailing of cornets and beating of drums, like an ancient *cabildo.*

The Afro-Cuban All Stars pack in the tourist crowds at **Sociedad Cultural Rosalia de Castro** (Egido #504 e/ Monte y Dragones, tel. 5270-5271, daily 9:30am-11:30pm) for "Gran Concierto Buena Vista Social Club" nightly shows by old Cuban legends from the Buena Vista Social Club era (CUC30 including dinner). And Buena Vista Social Club-era crooners entertain the tour groups at **Café Taberna** (Mercaderes #531, esq. Brasil, tel. 07/861-1637, daily 9:30am-11pm, CUC25), on the northeast side of Plaza Vieja.

CENTRO HABANA AND CERRO

The place to be on Sunday is **Rumba del "Salvador's Alley"** (Callejón de Hamel, e/ Aramburo y Hospital, tel. 07/878-1661, eliasasef@yahoo.es), with Afro-Cuban music and dance (Sun. noon-3pm) and traditional music (9pm last Friday of each month).

VEDADO AND PLAZA DE LA REVOLUCIÓN

Decades old and still going strong, the cramped and moody 1950s-style **Café Concierto Gato Tuerto** (Calle O #14, e/ 17 y 19, tel. 07/838-2696, 10pm-4am, CUC5 cover) nightclub hosts *música filin, trova,* and *bolero* nightly. It gets packed with patrons jammed cheek-to-jowl against the postage stamp-size stage tucked into a corner. I've been hanging out here for two decades and it hasn't lost its edge.

The **Salón 1930** (in the Hotel Nacional, Calle O y 21, tel. 07/836-3663) hosts traditional Buena Vista Social Club-style shows (Tues. and Sun. 9:30pm, CUC25 cover). **El Hurón Azul** (UNEAC, Calle 17 #351, esq. H, tel. 07/832-4551, www.uneac.org.cu, daily 5pm-2am) hosts themed *peñas* (social gatherings) on Wednesday at 5pm (CUC5); the music varies weekly. This is ground zero for intellectual life in Havana.

The acclaimed **Conjunto Folklórico Nacional** (National Folklore Dance Group, Calle 4 #103, e/ Calzada y 5ta, tel. 07/833-4560, www.folkcuba. cult.cu, CUC5) performs *sábado de rumba* (Saturday rumba) alfresco each Saturday at 3pm. This is Afro-Cuban music and dance at its best.

Who'd have thought a spa would host *trova*? If you dig Cuban ballads, or jazz, visit **O2 Spa & Jardín** (Calle 26 #5 esq. 26B, Nuevo Vedado, tel. 07/883-1663, www.o2habana.com), where top artistes such as Frank Delgado, Abdón Alcarez, and Luna Manzanares perform. Check out the calendar; reservations are essential.

Jazz
HABANA VIEJA
A key jazz venue, **Bar Chico O'Farrill** (Cuba #102, esq. Chacón, tel. 07/860-5080), in the Hotel Palacio O'Farrill, hosts Cuba's top performers Friday-Sunday evenings.

VEDADO AND PLAZA DE LA REVOLUCIÓN
The **Jazz Café** (1ra at the base of Paseo, tel. 07/838-3302, daily 10pm-2am, CUC10 *consumo mínimo*), on the third floor of the Galería del Paseo, is a classy supper club with some of the best live jazz in town, including resident maestro Chucho Valdés. Get there early to snag a seat. In 2015, Cuban jazz musician Lazarito Valdés (leader of the popular band Bamboleo) opened the nonsmoking **Valdés Jazz Club** (Calle E #105, e/ 5ta y Calzada, tel. 07/830-5898, valdesjazz@gmail.com), which features a bar, restaurant, and patio. The all-white decor is a bit cold, but the vibe is hot. Local maestros Bobby Carcassés and Maraca are regulars.

An incongruous red London phone booth serves as the entrance to **La Zorra y el Cuervo** (Calle 23, e/ N y O, tel. 07/833-2402, 10pm-2am, CUC10 including two drinks), a dreary, cramped basement setting (supposedly nonsmoking, but don't count on it) where Cuban greats such as Roberto Fonseca, Alexis Bosch, and saxophonist Michel Herrera perform. It has blues music on Thursdays, plus a Saturday matinee at 2pm.

Richard Egües—grandson of the eponymous Charanga maestro and lead flautist of Orquesta Aragón—keeps his granddad's legacy alive at **La Flauta Mágica** (Calzada #101 e/ L y M, tel. 07/832-3195, noon-4am). The small and intimate restaurant/bar occupies the penthouse suite of a 1950s high-rise overlooking the U.S. Embassy and Malecón. The live jazz can be sensational, and you can lounge on sofas by the rooftop pool.

A jazz ensemble performs at the **Tocororo** (Calle 18 y 3ra Av., tel. 07/202-2209, Mon.-Sat. noon-midnight) restaurant, where the lively bar is favored by local expats. The über-chic private club **Privé** (Calle 88A #306, e/ 3ra y 3raA, Miramar, tel. 07/209-2719, Tues.-Sun. 5pm-6am) hosts jazz and *nueva trova* greats such as Frank Delgado and has an open bar (CUC10).

The state entity Artex did a great job refurbishing **Café Miramar** (Calle 5ta, esq. 94, tel. 07/204-6244, Tues.-Sun. noon-2am, CUC2-4) as a snazzy jazz venue where you can catch Pacheco, Aldito López Gavilán, and other hot artists. Music kicks in at 10:30pm, plus it has Sunday afternoon jams. The audience can be quite loud.

THE ARTS
Tango and Flamenco
HABANA VIEJA

The Irene Rodríguez Compañía performs amazing flamenco at **Centro Andaluz en Cuba** (Prado #104, e/ Genios y Refugio, tel. 07/5246-8426, www.irenerodriguezcompania.com, free) each Wednesday, Friday, and Saturday at 9pm. Lessons are offered (Tues.-Thurs. 9am-11am, CUC15 per hour).

El Mesón de la Flota (Mercaderes #257, e/ Amargura y Brasil, tel. 07/863-3838, free) hosts high-energy flamenco shows daily 1pm-3pm and 8pm-11pm; you can even watch through the bars from the street. **Patio Sevillano** at the Hotel Sevilla (Trocadero, esq. Prado, tel. 07/860-9046) has flamenco on Saturday at 9pm. And the renowned **Ballet Lizt Alfonso** (Compostela e/ Luz y Acosta, tel. 07/866-3688, www.liztalfonso.com) offers flamenco classes and courses.

CENTRO HABANA AND CERRO

Caserón del Tango (Neptuno #309, e/ Águila y Italia, tel. 07/863-0097) hosts tango *peñas* on Monday 5pm-7pm, drawing local aficionados in Argentinian-style garb. **Unión Arabe de Cuba** (Prado e/ Animas y Trocadero, tel. 07/861-0582, www.unionarabecuba.org) hosts occasional tango.

MIRAMAR AND PLAYA

Watch for performances by the incomparable **Habana Compas Dance** (Av. 51 #12202 e/ 122 y 124, Marianao, tel. 07/262-8949, habanacompas@cubarte.cult.cu), a troupe that combines Spanish flamenco with Afro-Cuban drumming.

Theater, Classical Music, and Ballet
HABANA VIEJA

The most important theater in Havana is the renovated **Gran Teatro de la Habana Alicia Alonso** (Paseo de Martí #458, e/ San Rafael y San Martín, Habana Vieja, tel. 07/861-3079, CUC25 for best orchestra seats), on the west side of Parque Central. It's the main stage for the acclaimed Ballet Nacional de Cuba and the national opera company. Performances are Thursday-Saturday at 8:30pm and Sunday at 5pm. A dress code applies.

The **Basílica de San Francisco de Asís** (Calle Oficios, e/ Amargura y Brasil, tel. 07/862-9683) hosts classical concerts at 6pm (CUC2-10) most Saturdays and some Thursdays.

Classical and ecclesiastical concerts are also featured in the **Iglesia de San Francisco de Paula** (Av. del Puerto, esq. Leonor Pérez, tel. 07/860-4210, free or CUC5) on Friday at 7pm, and in the **Oratorio San Felipe Neri** (Calle Aguiar, esq. Obrapía, tel. 07/862-3243) on Thursday at 7pm and Saturday at 4pm.

Check out the program at the **Museo Nacional de Bellas Artes** (tel. 07/863-9484, www.bellasartes.cult.cu), which hosts classical artists on Thursday and Saturday at 7pm (Cuban section, Trocadero e/ Zulueta y Monserrate) and on Saturday at 4pm (international section, San Rafael e/ Zulueta y Monserrate).

For more avant-garde fare, peruse the schedule at Danza-Teatro Retazos, a contemporary troupe that performs at the **Teatro Retazos** (Calle Amargura #61 e/ San Ignacio y Mercaderes, tel. 07/860-4341).

CENTRO HABANA
The **Palacio de Matrimonio** (Prado #306, esq. Ánimas, tel. 07/866-0661, Tues.-Fri. 8am-6pm) hosts live chamber and classical music.

VEDADO AND PLAZA DE LA REVOLUCIÓN
Performances of the Orquesta Sinfónica Nacional de Cuba (National Symphony) and Danza Contemporánea de Cuba are hosted at the **Teatro Nacional** (Av. Carlos M. de Céspedes, esq. Paseo, Vedado, tel. 07/878-5590, www.teatronacional.cu) every Friday-Saturday at 8:30pm and Sunday at 5pm (CUC1.80-8.90).

classical concert in Basílica de San Francisco de Asís, Habana Vieja

The Little Beehive

Unforgettable. Endearing. A tear-jerker. That's a performance by **La Colmenita** (tel. 07/860-7699, colmena@cubarte.cult.cu), an amazing children's musical theater group that has charmed audiences worldwide with high-octane repertoires that mix fairy tales and rock and roll with messages of justice and peace.

La Colmenita—the name means "Little Beehive"—was founded as a small community theater in 1994 by TV producer Carlos Alberto Cremata. His dad was the pilot of the Cubana flight 455 passenger airliner downed by a Cuban American terrorist bomb after it took off from Barbados on October 6, 1976. La Colmenita was begun as homage to Alberto's father (a lover of music and theater) to convey a message of love, humanity, and forgiveness. It has since grown into a worldwide cultural phenomenon, spawning more than two dozen similar "beehives" throughout Cuba and the Americas.

UNICEF has adopted La Colmenita as an official goodwill ambassador, working to help protect and promote the rights of, and improve the lives of, children and women worldwide. The productions, such as "Cinderella by the Beatles" and "The Little Roach Called Martina," are their own. Costumes are prepared by the kids' parents. And any child is welcome to join, even those with physical and mental impairments. The ensemble frequently tours the country to share a positive message with disadvantaged communities and children.

It principally performs at the Teatro de la Orden Tres (Obispo esq. Churrusco), in Habana Vieja.

The **Teatro Mella** (Línea #657, e/ A y B, Vedado, tel. 07/833-8696, box office Tues.-Sun. 2pm-6pm) is noted for contemporary dance, theater, and ballet (CUC5-10), and hosts the Conjunto Folklórico Nacional.

The last Thursday of each month, **UNEAC** (Calle 17 #351, e/ G y H, Vedado, tel. 07/832-4551, www.uneac.org.cu) hosts an open *peña* for chamber musicians at 6pm.

The **Teatro Amadeo Roldán** (Calzada y D, Vedado, tel. 07/832-1168, CUC5-10) hosts the Simfonia Nacional de Cuba and has two *salas*; it features classical concerts year-round. Nearby is the **Teatro Hubert de Blanck** (Calzada #657, e/ A y B, tel. 07/830-1011, CUC5), known for both modern and classical plays. Shows (in Spanish) are usually Friday-Saturday at 8:30pm and Sunday at 5pm.

The 150-seat **Teatro Buendía** (Calle Loma y 38, Nuevo Vedado, tel. 07/881-6689, five pesos), in a converted Greek Orthodox church, hosts performances by the eponymous theater company, considered to be Cuba's most innovative and accomplished. It performs here Friday-Sunday at 8:30pm.

Circuses

Named for a famed, late Cuban clown, Havana's **Circo Trompoloco** (Calle 112, esq. 5ta Av., Miramar, tel. 07/206-5609 or 07/206-5641, www.

Cinemas

Most of Havana's cinemas are mid-20th-century gems that have been allowed to deteriorate to the point of near-dilapidation. Movie houses on La Rampa, in Vedado, tend to be less run-down than those in Habana Vieja and Centro Habana. *Granma* and *Cartelera* (a cultural magazine available at many tourist hotels) list what's currently showing.

The **Sala Glauber Rocha** (Av. 212, esq. 31, La Coronela, tel. 07/271-8967, www.cinelatinoamericano.org), in the Fundación del Nuevo Cine Latinoamericano, shows mostly Latin American movies.

The most important cinemas are:

- **Cine Acapulco** (Av. 26, e/ 35 y 37, Vedado, tel. 07/833-9573).

- **Cine Charles Chaplin** (Calle 23 #1155, e/ 10 y 12, Vedado, tel. 07/831-1101).

- **Cine La Rampa** (Calle 23 #111, e/ O y P, Vedado, tel. 07/878-6146) mostly shows Cuban and Latin American films, plus the occasional obscure foreign movie.

- **Cine Payret** (Prado #503, esq. San José, Habana Vieja, tel. 07/863-3163) is Havana's largest cinema and has as many as six showings daily.

- **Cine Riviera** (Calles 23, e/ H y G, Vedado, tel. 07/832-9564).

- **Cine-Teatro Astral** (Calzada de Infanta #501, esq. San Martín, Centro Habana, tel. 07/878-1001) is the comfiest *cine* in Havana. It functions mostly as a theater for political features.

- **Cine Yara** (Calle 23 y Calle L, Vedado, tel. 07/832-9430) is Havana's "main" theater.

- **Multi-Cine Infanta** (Infanta, e/ Neptuno y San Miguel, tel. 07/878-9323) has four up-to-date auditoriums.

circonacionaldecuba.cu, Thurs.-Fri. 4pm, Sat.-Sun. 4pm and 7pm, CUC10) is the headquarters of the Circo Nacional de Cuba, which performs beneath a red-and-white-striped "big top."

FESTIVALS AND EVENTS

For a list of forthcoming festivals, conferences, and events, visit www.lahabana.com.

January

The **Cabildos** festival is held on January 6, when Habana Vieja resounds with festivities recalling the days when Afro-Cuban *comparsas* danced through the streets. Contact Agencia de Viajes San Cristóbal (Oficios #110, e/ Lamparilla y Amargura, tel. 07/861-9171).

February

The **Habanos Festival** (tel. 07/204-0510, www.habanos.com) celebrates Cuban cigars. It opens at the Tropicana with an elegant dinner and auction for big spenders.

The **Feria Internacional del Libro de la Habana** (Havana Book Fair, Calle 15 #602 e/ B y C, Vedado, tel. 07/832-9526, www.filcuba.cult.cu) is held in Fortaleza San Carlos de la Cabaña.

The **Festival Internacional de Tambor** (International Drum Festival, tel. 07/836-5381, www.fiestadeltambor.cult.cu) is held at various venues.

April

The prestigious **Bienal de la Habana** (Havana Biennial, tel. 07/209-6569, www.bienalhabana.cult.cu) features artists from more than 50 countries. It is hosted in even-numbered years by the Centro Wilfredo Lam (Calle San Ignacio #22, tel. 07/861-2096, www.cnap.cult.cu).

May

On May 1, head to the Plaza de la Revolución for the **Primero de Mayo** (May Day Parade) to honor workers. Intended to appear as a spontaneous demonstration of revolutionary loyalty, in reality it is carefully choreographed. Stooges use loudspeakers to work up the crowd of 500,000 people with chants of *"¡Viva Fidel!"* and *"¡Viva Raúl!"* Raúl has toned down the anti-United States flavor since taking over.

The **Festival Internacional de Guitarra** (International Guitar Festival and Contest) is held at the Teatro Roldán in even-numbered years.

June

The **Festival Internacional Boleros de Oro** (International Boleros Festival, UNEAC, Calle 17 #354, e/ G y H, Vedado, tel. 07/832-4571, www.uneac.org.cu) features traditional Latin American folk music.

July

The **Coloquio Internacional Hemingway** (International Hemingway Colloquium, tel. 07/691-0809, mushem@cubarte.cult.cu) takes place in early July every odd-numbered year.

August

The amateurish **Carnaval de la Habana** (Carnival in Havana, tel. 07/832-3742) is held the first or second week of August on the Malecón.

September

The 10-day biennial **Festival Habanarte**, sponsored by the Consejo Nacional de Las Artes (National Council of Arts, Calle 4 #257, Miramar, tel. 07/832-4126, www.habanarte.com), is held in odd-numbered years.

The **Festival Internacional de Ballet** (International Ballet Festival) features ballet corps from around the world, plus the acclaimed Ballet Nacional de Cuba (BNC, Calzada #510, e/ D y E, Vedado, Ciudad Habana, tel. 07/832-4625, www.balletcuba.cult.cu).

The annual **Festival de la Habana de Música Contemporánea** (Havana Festival of Contemporary Music, c/o UNEAC, Calle 17 #351, e/ G y H, Vedado, tel. 07/832-0194, www.musicacontemporanea.cult.cu) spans a week in early October, with performances ranging from choral to electro-acoustic.

November

Expo Canina (tel. 07/267-3156, cdc@enet.cu) is Havana's answer to the Crufts and Westminster dog shows.

December

The **Festival del Nuevo Cine Latinoamericano** (Festival of New Latin American Cinema, c/o the Instituto de Cinematografía, Calle 23 #1155, Vedado, tel. 07/838-2354, www.habanafilmfestival.com) is one of Cuba's most glittering events, attended by Cuban actors and directors and their Hollywood counterparts. Movies are shown at cinemas across the city, and the festival culminates with Cuba's own version of the Oscars, the Coral prizes. Buy your tickets well before the programming is announced; you can buy a pass (CUC25) good for the duration of the festival.

The star-studded **Festival Internacional de Jazz** (International Havana Jazz Festival, Calle 15, esq. F, Vedado, tel. 07/862-4938) is highlighted by the greats of Cuban jazz, such as Chucho Valdés and Irakere, and Juan Formell and Los Van Van. Concerts are held at various venues.

Shopping

The Cuban government bans the sale and export of antiques. Hence, there are no stores selling antiques to tourists.

ARTS AND CRAFTS
Habana Vieja

The city's largest market is the **Centro Cultural Almacenes de San José** (Av. Desamparados at San Ignacio, tel. 07/864-7793, daily 10am-6pm), on the waterfront side of the Alameda. Also known as the Feria de la Artesanía, it sells everything from little ceramic figurines, miniature bongo drums, and papier-mâché 1950s autos to banana-leaf hats, crocheted bikinis, straw hats, and paintings.

Habana Vieja contains dozens of *expo-ventas* (commercial galleries representing freelance artists) selling original art. They are concentrated along Calle Obispo. Try **Estudio-Taller Ribogerto Mena** (Calle San Ignacio

#154 e/ Obispo y Obrapía, tel. 07/867-5884) or **Taller La 6ta Puerta** (Calle Oficios #6 esq. Obispo, tel. 07/860-6866, www.amramirez.com), the gallery of Angel Ramírez. The **Asociación Cubana de Artesana Artistas** (Obispo #411, tel. 07/860-8577, www.acaa.cult.cu, Mon.-Sat. 10am-8pm, Sun. 10am-6pm) represents various artists.

One of the best galleries is **Galería Victor Manuel** (San Ignacio #46, e/ Callejón del Chorro y Empedrado, tel. 07/861-2955, daily 10am-9pm), on the west side of Plaza de la Catedral. Around the corner is the **Taller Experimental de la Gráfica** (Callejón del Chorro, tel. 07/867-7622, tgrafica@cubarte.cult.cu, Mon.-Fri. 9am-4pm), a cooperative that makes and sells exclusive lithographic prints. It's one of the more fascinating places to buy exceptional art.

You can buy handmade Spanish fans (*abanicos*) at the **Casa del Abanicos** (Obrapía #107, e/ Mercaderes y Oficios, tel. 07/863-4452, Mon.-Sat. 10am-7pm and Sun. 10am-1pm).

The **Tienda El Soldadito de Plomo** (Muralla #164, tel. 07/866-0232, Mon.-Fri. 9am-5pm, Sat. 9am-1:30pm) sells miniature lead (!) soldiers, including a 22-piece War of Independence collection, for CUC5.45 apiece. A large glass window lets you watch artists painting the pieces.

Centro Habana

This area doesn't abound with galleries. Two exceptions are **Galería Galiano** (Galiano #256 e/ Concordia y Neptuno, tel. 07/860-0224, Mon.-Fri. 10am-6pm, Sat. 10am-noon) and **Collage Habana** (San Rafael e/ Consulado y Industria, tel. 07/833-3826, Mon.-Fri. 10am-6pm, Sat. 10am-noon), both with works by top artists and pertaining to the Fondo be Bienes Culturales (www.fcbc.cu).

Vedado and Plaza de la Revolución

Vedado has an **artisans' market** on La Rampa (e/ M y N, daily 8am-6pm). The **Casa de las Américas** (Av. de los Presidentes, esq. 3ra, tel. 07/55-2706, www.casa.cult.cu, Mon.-Fri. 8am-4:45pm) hosts exhibitions with works for sale.

Servando Galería de Arte (Calle 23, esq. 10, tel. 07/830-6150, www.galeriaservando.com) represents some of the top artists in Cuba. The everfascinating **El Espacio Aglutinador** (Calle 6 #602 e/ 25 y 27, tel. 07/832-3531) offers avante-garde works.

Playa (Miramar and Beyond)

Two of my favorite art galleries are **Estudio-Galería Flora Fong** (Calle 11 #4212 e/ 42 y 44, Playa, tel. 07/204-9543) and **Lighthouse Studio** (Av. 47 #3430 e/ 34 y 41, Kohly, tel. 07/206-5772, www.kadirlopez.com), displaying the works of Kadir López-Nieves.

For one-of-a-kind prints signed by world-renowned photographer Roberto Salas, head to his **Galería Roberto Salas** (Calle 30 #3709 e/ 37 y 39, tel. 07/206-5213), where he sells iconic images of Cuba during the past 50 years.

A visit to **Casa-Estudio de José Fuster** (Calle 226, esq. Av. 3ra, tel. 07/271-2932 or 5281-5421, www.josefuster.com, daily 9am-5pm) is a *must* while in Havana, regardless of whether you buy or not. The "Picasso of the Caribbean" sells ceramics priced CUC25 and up, and main art pieces sell from CUC150 into the thousands.

BOOKS
Habana Vieja

The **Instituto Cubano del Libro** (Cuban Book Institute, Obispo, esq. Aguiar, tel. 07/862-8091, Mon.-Fri. 8am-4:30pm) has a bookshop; most books are in Spanish. To the southeast of Plaza de Armas, tucked off Calle Baratillo, is the setting Feria de Publicaciones y Curiosidades.

Librería La Internacional (Obispo #528, Habana Vieja, tel. 07/861-3238, daily 10am-5:30pm) stocks a limited selection of texts in English, plus a small selection of English-language novels. **La Moderna Poesía** (Obispo #527, esq. Bernaza, tel. 07/861-6983, Mon.-Sat. 10am-8pm) is Cuba's largest bookstore, although virtually the entire stock is in Spanish.

La Papelería (O'Reilly #102, esq. Tacón, Habana Vieja, tel. 07/863-4263, Mon.-Sat. 9am-6:30pm), catercorner to the Plaza de Armas, sells pens and other office supplies.

Vedado and Plaza de la Revolución

Librería Fernando Ortíz (Calle L, esq. 27, tel. 07/832-9653, Mon.-Sat. 10am-5:30pm) is your best bet for English-language books. Its meager collection spans a wide range. **Librería Centenario del Apóstol** (Calle 25 #164, e/ Infanta y O, tel. 07/835-0805, daily 9am-9pm) has used texts.

CIGARS AND RUM

Havana has about two dozen official La Casa del Habano cigar stores (daily 9am-5pm). Buy here; if you buy off the street, you're almost certainly going to be sold fakes, even if they look real.

Habana Vieja

The best cigar store is **La Casa del Habano** (Industria #520, e/ Barcelona y Dragones, tel. 07/866-8086, Mon.-Fri. 9am-7pm, Sat. 9am-5pm, Sun. 10am-4pm) in Fábrica de Tabaco Partagás. It has a massive walk-in humidor, plus a hidden lounge with a narrow humidified walk-in cigar showcase for serious smokers.

My other favorites are **La Casa del Habano** (Mercaderes #202, esq. Lamparilla, tel. 07/862-9682, daily 10:30am-7pm) in the **Hostal Conde de Villanueva** and **Salón Cuba** (Neptuno, e/ Prado y Zulueta, tel. 07/862-9293, daily 8:30am-9:15pm) in the Hotel Iberostar Parque Central. And the **Casa del Ron y Tabaco** (Obispo, e/ Monserrate y Bernaza, tel. 07/866-0911, daily

9am-5pm), above El Floridita, has knowledgeable staff. This store also lets you sample the rums before buying.

Taberna del Galeón (Baratillo, esq. Obispo, tel. 07/866-8476, Mon.-Sat. 9am-6pm, Sun. 9am-5pm), off the southeast corner of Plaza de Armas, is well stocked with rums.

Vedado and Plaza de la Revolución

The **Casa del Habano** stores in the **Hotel Nacional** (Calle O y 21, tel. 07/873-3564), **Hotel Habana Libre Tryp** (Calle L, e/ 23 y 25, tel. 07/834-6100), **Hotel Meliá Cohiba** (Paseo, e/ 1ra y 3ra, tel. 07/833-3636), and **Hotel Habana Riviera** (Malecón y Paseo, tel. 07/836-4051) are well stocked.

Playa (Miramar and Beyond)

Miramar has the best cigar store in town: **La Casa del Habano** (5ta Av., esq. 16, tel. 07/204-7974, Mon.-Sat. 10am-6pm), run by Carlos Robaina, son of the legendary tobacco farmer Alejandro Robaina. It boasts a vast humidor, executive rooms, private lockers, bar and lounge, and good service. Club Habana's **La Casa del Habano** (5ta Av. e/ 188 y 192, tel. 07/275-0366, daily 9am-5pm) is also excellent.

CLOTHING AND SHOES

Habana Vieja

Men seeking a classic *guayabera* shirt should head to the state's **El Quitrín** (Obispo #163, e/ San Ignacio y Mercaderes, tel. 07/862-0810, daily 9am-5pm) or **Guayabera Habana** (Calle Tacó #20, e/ O'Reilly y Empedrado, Mon.-Sat. 10am-7pm). El Quitrín also sells embroideries and lace for ladies, plus chic blouses and skirts. Most items are Cuban made and of merely average quality. For quality designer *guayaberas,* head to **PiscoLabis** (Calle San Ignacio #75, e/ Callejón del Chorro y O'Reilly, tel. 5843-3219, www.piscolabishabana.com, daily 9:30am-7:30pm). This private cooperative also sells one-of-a-kind sandals, purses, and adornments.

Nearby, **Sombreros Jipi Japa** (Obispo, esq. Compostela, tel. 07/861-5292, Mon.-Fri. 9am-5pm) is the place to go for hats of every shade. **La Habana** (Obispo, e/ Habana y Compostela, tel. 07/861-5292, and Obispo, esq. Aguacate, Mon.-Fri. 9am-5pm) offers a reasonable stock of shoes and leather goods. Designer shoes and handbags are the expensive name of the game at **Zapatería Obrapía** (Obrapía esq. Oficios). Catercorner, **Carpisa Italia** sells high-end Italian imports.

Jacqueline Fumero Café Boutique (Compostela #1, esq. Cuarteles, tel. 07/862-6562, www.jacquelinefumero.com, daily 10am-10pm) sells exquisite women's fashionwear by the internationally acclaimed designer.

Vedado and Plaza de la Revolución

Adidas and Nike have well-stocked branches selling sportswear in the **Galería Habana Libre** (Calle 25, e/ L y M, daily 8am-7pm).

The **Complejo Comercial Comodoro** (3ra Av., esq. 84, tel. 07/204-5551, daily 8am-7pm), adjoining the Hotel Comodoro, and **Miramar Trade Center** (Av. 3ra, e/ 76 y 80) have outlets for various name-brand European designers.

The boutiques at **La Maison** (Calle 16 #701, esq. 7ma, tel. 07/204-1543, Mon.-Sat. 10am-6:45pm) sell upscale imported clothing, shoes, and duty-free items. Likewise, **Le Select** (5ta Av., esq. 30, tel. 07/204-7410, Mon.-Sat. 10am-8pm, Sun. 10am-2pm), with its ritzy chandeliers and marble statues, is as close as you'll come to Bond Street or Rodeo Drive.

MUSIC AND FILM
Habana Vieja

Longina Música (Obispo #360, tel. 07/862-8371, Mon.-Sat. 10am-7pm, Sun. 10am-1pm) sells musical instruments and has a large CD collection.

Graphic artist Idania del Rio sells cool contemporary posters and cards at **Clandestina** (Villegas #403 e/ Brasil y Muralla, tel. 5381-4802, www.clandestinacuba.com).

Vedado and Plaza de la Revolución

The **Centro Cultural Cinematográfico** (Calle 23 #1155, e/ 10 y 12, tel. 07/833-6430, Mon.-Sat. 9am-5pm) sells posters and videos of Cuban films; it's on the fourth floor of the Cuban Film Institute (ICAIC). **La Habana Sí** (Calle L, esq. 23, tel. 07/832-3162, Mon.-Sat. 10am-9pm) has a large CD selection.

Playa (Miramar and Beyond)

For the widest CD selection in town, head to the **Casa de la Música** (Calle 10 #309, tel. 07/202-6900), the salesroom of Egrem, the state recording agency.

PERFUMES, TOILETRIES, AND JEWELRY
Habana Vieja

Havana 1791 (Mercaderes #156, esq. Obrapía, tel. 07/861-3525, Mon.-Sat. 10am-7pm, Sun. 10am-1pm) sells locally made scents (CUC6-18) in exquisitely engraved bottles with not entirely trustworthy cork tops, in an embossed linen bag. **Farmacia Taquechel** (Obispo #155, e/ Mercaderes y San Ignacio, tel. 07/862-9286, daily 9am-5pm) sells face creams, lotions, and other natural products made in Cuba.

Tienda Museo el Reloj (Oficios, esq. Muralla, tel. 07/864-9515, www.cuervoysobrinos.com, Mon.-Sat. 10am-7pm and Sun. 10am-1pm) will cause a double-take. At this deluxe store, gold-plated fountain pens (each in an elegant cedar humidor with five cigars) sell for CUC1,000 and the cheapest watch costs US$2,000. These are limited editions made in Switzerland and sold under the old Cuevos y Sobrinos label.

Vedado

You'll "ooh!" and "ahh!" over the fine handcrafted jewelry at **Rox 950** (Calle Linea #256 e/ I y J, tel. 07/209-1479 or 5281-7118, www.rox950.com), where silversmith artist Rosana Varga sells her stunning contemporary silver creations in a fittingly beautiful manse.

Playa (Miramar and Beyond)

Most upscale hotels have quality jewelry stores, as do **La Maison** (Calle 16 #701, esq. 7ma, Miramar, tel. 07/204-1543, daily 9am-5pm), **Le Select** (5ta Av., esq. 30, Miramar, tel. 07/204-7410, daily 9am-5pm), **Joyería La Habanera** (Calle 12 #505, e/ 5ta y 7ma, tel. 07/204-2546, Mon.-Sat. 10am-6pm), and the Club Habana's **Joyería Bella Cantando** (5ta Av. y 188, tel. 07/204-5700, daily 9am-5pm).

DEPARTMENT STORES AND SHOPPING CENTERS

Habana Vieja

Harris Brothers (Monserrate #305, e/ O'Reilly y Progreso, Habana Vieja, tel. 07/861-1644, daily 9am-7pm) has four stories of separate stores that sell everything from fashion and children's items to toiletries. The only photography store in town is in the **Gran Hotel Kempinski Manzana** (Agramonte esq. Neptuno). Opened in June 2017, it sells Canons, Leicas and Nikons at vastly inflated prices.

Centro Habana and Cerro

East of Avenida de Italia (Galiano) is Calle San Rafael—a pedestrian-only shopping zone, known colloquially as "El Bulevar." Havana's main shopping street retains many department stores from prerevolutionary days. **La Época** (Av. de Italia, esq. Neptuno, Centro Habana, tel. 07/866-9423, Mon.-Sat. 9:30am-7pm, Sun. 9:30am-2pm) is a good place for clothing, including kiddie items and designer fashions. The former Woolworth's, today called **Variedades Galiano** (Av. de Italia, esq. San Rafael, tel. 07/862-7717, Mon.-Sat. 9am-5pm), still has its original lunch counter.

Vedado and Plaza de la Revolución

Galerías de Paseo (1ra Calle, e/ Paseo y A, tel. 07/833-9888, Mon.-Sat. 9am-6pm, Sun. 9am-1pm), at the foot of Paseo, has more than two dozen stores of varying kinds.

Playa (Miramar and Beyond)

La Puntilla Centro Comercial (1ra Av., esq. 0, tel. 07/204-7240, daily 8am-8pm) has four floors of stores covering electronics, furniture, clothing, and more. Similarly, there's **Quinta y 42** (5ta Av. y 42, Miramar, tel. 07/204-7070, Mon.-Sat. 10am-6pm, Sun. 9am-1pm) and **Complejo Comercial Comodoro** (3ra Av., esq. 84, Miramar, tel. 07/204-5551, daily 8am-7pm).

The largest supermarket is **Supermercado 70** (3ra Av., e/ 62 y 70, foodstuffs. The best-stocked store for food items is **Palco** in the Miramar Trade Center (Av. 3ra e/ 76 y 80, Mon.-Sat. 10am-6pm and Sun. 10am-1pm).

Sports and Recreation

Havana has many *centros deportivos* (sports centers). The largest are the **Complejo Panamericano** (Vía Monumental, Km 1.5, Ciudad Panamericano, Habana del Este, tel. 07/795-4140), with an Olympic stadium, tennis courts, swimming pool, and even a velodrome for cycling; and **Ciudad Deportiva** (Vía Blanca, esq. Av. Rancho Boyeros, tel. 07/854-5022), or Sports City, colloquially called "El Coliseo," in Nuevo Vedado.

GOLF

The **Club Habana** (5ta Av., e/ 188 y 192, Rpto. Flores, tel. 07/204-5700) has a practice range. Nonmembers are welcome (entrance CUC20 Mon.-Fri.). **Club de Golf Habana** (Carretera de Vento, Km 8, Boyeros, tel. 07/649-8918, 8:30am-sunset) is about 20 kilometers south of Havana. The nine-hole "golfito" (as the locals know it) has 18 tees positioned for play on both sides of the fairway. It has a minimally stocked pro shop, five tennis courts, a swimming pool, and two restaurants. Membership costs CUC70 plus CUC45 monthly. Nine holes costs nonmembers CUC20 (CUC30 for 18 holes). Clubs can be rented for CUC15; caddies cost CUC6.

GYMS AND SPAS

Upscale hotels have tiny gyms and/or spas, though most are a letdown. The best are at the **Hotel Nacional** (Calle O y 21, tel. 07/873-3564, nonguests CUC15), **Hotel Meliá Cohiba** (Paseo, esq. 1ra, tel. 07/833-3636), and **Hotel Meliá Habana** (3ra Av., e/ 76 y 80, tel. 07/204-8500).

Gimnasio Biomerica (Calle E, esq. 17, Vedado, tel. 07/832-9087, Mon.-Fri. 8am-8pm), below the Centro Hebreo Sefaradi, charges CUC8 monthly. One of the best facilities is at **Club Habana** (5ta Av., e/ 188 y 192, Rpto. Flores, tel. 07/204-5700, Mon.-Fri. 7:30am-7pm, nonmembers CUC20).

Private spas have blossomed in Cuba. One top-notch option is **Spa O2** (Calle 26, esq. 26B, Nuevo Vedado, tel. 07/883-1663, www.o2habana.com, daily 9am-11:45pm), with a small gym, beauty treatments, and a café. In Habana Vieja, **Spasio** (San Ignacio #364, tel. 07/768-2602, carlos.fente@ nauta.cu), on Plaza Vieja, is recommended. And in Miramar, **Vida Spa** (Calle 34 #308 e/ 3ra y 5ta, tel. 07/209-2022 or 5483-3005) offers treatments from massage to skin peels.

SAILING AND SPORTFISHING

Club Habana (5ta Av., e/ 188 y 192, Playa, tel. 07/204-5700) has aqua-bikes and kayaks for rent. Full-size yachts and motor vessels can be rented at **Marina Hemingway** (5ta Av., esq. 248, Santa Fe, tel. 07/273-1867), which also offers sportfishing (from CUC275 for four hours; from CUC375 for eight hours, including skipper and tackle).

SCUBA DIVING

There's excellent diving offshore of Havana. The Gulf Stream and Atlantic Ocean currents meet west of the city, where many ships have been sunk through the centuries. The so-called "Blue Circuit," a series of dive sites, extends east from Bacuranao, about 10 kilometers east of Havana, to the Playas del Este.

Centro de Buceo La Aguja (Marina Hemingway, 5ta Av. y 248, Santa Fe, tel. 07/204-5088 or 07/271-5277, daily 8:30am-4:30pm) rents equipment and charges CUC30 for one dive, CUC50 for two dives, CUC60 for a "resort course," and CUC360 for an open-water certification. The **Centro Internacional Buceo Residencial Club Habana** (5ta Av., e/ 188 y 192, Rpto. Flores, tel. 07/204-5700, Mon.-Fri. 7:30am-7pm, nonmembers entrance CUC20) offers scuba certification.

SWIMMING

Most large tourist hotels have pools and permit use by nonguests. In Habana Vieja, head to **Piscina Hotel Mercure Sevilla** (Prado, esq. Ánimas, tel. 07/860-8560, daily 10am-6pm, entrance CUC20).

The **Hotel Nacional** (Calle O y 21, tel. 07/873-3564, CUC18) and **Hotel Habana Libre Tryp** (Calle L, e/ 23 y 25, tel. 07/834-6100, CUC15), in the Vedado and Plaza de la Revolución, have excellent pools.

In Playa, the best pools are at the **Memories Miramar** (5ta Av., e/ 72 y 76, tel. 07/204-8140) and **Hotel Meliá Habana** (3ra Av., e/ 76 y 80, tel. 07/204-8500). **Club Habana** (5ta Av., e/ 188 y 192, Playa, tel. 07/204-5700, Mon.-Fri. 9am-7pm, entrance CUC20) has a swimming pool. The pool at **Club Almendares** (Av. 49C, esq. 28A, Rpto. Kohly, tel. 07/204-4990, daily 10am-6pm, CUC5) gets mobbed by Cubans on weekends. Farther west, the pool at Papa's Complejo Turistico in **Marina Hemingway** (5ta Av., esq. 248, Santa Fe, tel. 07/209-7920) can get crowded with locals.

SPECTATOR SPORTS

Baseball

Havana's Industriales (colloquially called "Los Leones," or "The Lions") play at the 60,000-seat **Estadio Latinoamericano** (Consejero Aranjo y Pedro Pérez, Cerro, tel. 07/870-6526), the main baseball stadium. Games are played November-May, Tuesday-Thursday and Saturday at 8pm, and Sunday at 2pm (CUC3). Contact the **Federación Cubana de Béisbol** (tel. 07/879-7980, www.beisbolcubano.cu).

Basketball

Havana's Capitalinos play September-November at the **Coliseo de Deportes** (Ciudad Deportiva, Vía Blanca, esq. Av. Rancho Boyeros, Nuevo Vedado, tel. 07/854-5022) and at the **Sala Polivalente Ramón Fonst** (Av.

Contact the **Federación Cubana de Baloncesto** (tel. 07/648-7156).

Boxing

Championship matches are hosted at the **Coliseo de Deportes** (Vía Blanca, esq. Av. Rancho Boyeros, tel. 07/854-5022), base for the **Federación Cubana de Boxeo** (tel. 07/857-7047). You can watch boxing at the **Gimnasio de Boxeo Rafael Trejo** (Calle Cuba #815, Habana Vieja, tel. 07/862-0266, Mon.-Fri. 8am-5pm) and at **Sala Polivalente Kid Chocolate** (Prado, e/ San Martín y Brasil, Habana Vieja, tel. 07/862-8634).

Soccer

Cuba's soccer program is not well developed, although there *is* a national league. Havana's *fútbol* team is Ciudad Havana (nicknamed "Los Rojos"— "The Reds"). Games are played at the **Estadio Pedro Marrero** (Av. 41 #4409, e/ 44 y 50, Rpto. Kohly, tel. 07/203-4698).

Food

Havana is in the midst of a gastronomic revolution. Privately owned restaurants (*paladares*) have exploded in number, offering heapings of style and good food. It's hard to stay abreast of new openings. Few state restaurants can compete on ambience and flavorful fare, although many are improving as they convert into workers' cooperatives. Many state restaurants still attain true Soviet-class awfulness, especially the hotel buffets. The best *paladares* have been entirely taken over by U.S. tour groups; if you want to dine with locals opt for budget locales. When the U.S. cruise ships are in town, avoid lunch at popular venues.

HABANA VIEJA
Breakfast and Cafés

Most hotel restaurants are open to nonguests for breakfast. The buffet at the **Mediterráneo** (Neptuno, e/ Prado y Zulueta, tel. 07/866-6627, daily 7am-10am, CUC15) in the Hotel Iberostar Parque Central is the best in town.

If all you want is a croissant and coffee, head to **Pastelería Francesca** (Prado #410, e/ Neptuno y San Rafael, tel. 07/862-0739, daily 8am-noon), on the west side of Parque Central. The ★ **Café El Escorial** (Mercaderes #317, tel. 07/868-3545, daily 9am-10pm), on Plaza Vieja, is the closest in Havana you'll come to a European-style coffee shop. This atmospheric venue with a Tuscan mood sells croissants, truffle cream cakes, ice cream, and gourmet coffees and coffee liqueurs.

Bianchini Croissantería-Dulcería (Sol #12 e/ Av. del Puerto y Oficios, no tel., www.dulceria-bianchini.com, daily 9am-9pm) is a delightfully bohemian, pocket-sized hole-in-the-wall that is the brainchild of Katia, the Italian-Swiss owner who has created a piece of Europe transplanted. She serves quiches, croissants, buns, and tarts, plus coffees and teas. The place is usually packed. Katia has a second outlet—equally small and cozy—in Callejón del Chorro (tel. 07/862-8477), off Plaza de la Catedral.

Paladares

Hugely popular, the cozy ★ **Doña Eutimia** (Callejón del Chorro #60C, tel. 07/861-1332, daily noon-midnight), tucked off Plaza de la Catedral, transports you back two centuries with its antique clocks and quirky oddities. Delightful owner Leticia delivers delicious down-home creole cooking that includes a superb *ropa vieja* (braised lamb prepared with garlic, tomatoes, and spices, CUC7) with heaps of cumin-spiced black beans. Leave room for the chocolate torta (CUC2.50). Reservations are imperative.

Beyoncé and Jay-Z have lunched at **La Moneda Cubana** (Empedrado #152, esq. Mercaderes, tel. 07/861-5304, daily noon-midnight), a colonial military-themed restaurant off Plaza de la Catedral. The creative Cuban cuisine includes lamb in garlic and coffee. Start with ceviche and end with rice pudding with shredded coconut. Tour groups take up much of the space. The rooftop terrace has castle views, good for witnessing the *cañonazo* ceremony at 9pm.

Fidel's former private chef Tomás Erasmo Hernández prepares delicious Cuban dishes at ★ **Mama Inés** (Calle de la Obrapía #60, e/ Oficios y Baratillo, tel. 07/862-2669, Mon.-Sat. noon-10:30pm). The menu features filet mignon (CUC12), veal scallopini (CUC8), and a flavorful and piquant stewed lamb (CUC10), but the succulent *ropa vieja* (CUC12) gets my vote as the best in Havana. The octopus with garlic and pepper is to die for. Erasmo often makes the rounds to chat with guests.

Paladar Los Mercaderes (Mercaderes #207, e/ Lamparillos y Amargura, tel. 07/861-2437, daily noon-midnight) greets you with fresh rose petals on the marble staircase. Upstairs, this lovely colonial space has huge French doors open to the street below. Food is top-notch. I salivated over my octopus with pesto and onion sauce (CUC12), risotto with veggies and dried fruit (CUC8.50), and *ropa vieja* (CUC14).

Restaurante Chef Iván Justo (Calle Aguacate #9, esq. Chacón, tel. 07/863-9697, ivanchefsjusto.restaurant@yahoo.com, daily noon-midnight) rates highly, not least for the charming ambience in a restored and rambling two-story home dating from 1776. The kitchen dishes up such divine treats as cream of squash soup (CUC5), crab claw enchilada (CUC10), veggie and mushroom risotto (CUC12), and even roast pheasant (CUC18), although the *lechón* (suckling pig) and the seafood paella are the signature dishes. Warning: The upstairs restaurant is reached by a steep, narrow staircase. The same owner runs the adjoining **Al Carbón** (same details) downstairs. It specializes in Cuban dishes cooked over charcoal, but the paella is also available.

For something light, check out **Jacqueline Fumero Café Boutique** (Compostela #1, esq. Cuarteles, tel. 07/862-6562, www.jacquelinefumero.com, daily 10am-10pm). The eponymous Cuban fashion designer has conjured a sensational South Beach-style setting—walls of glass, electric-blue lighting, slate-gray tile floors, see-through plastic chairs—in one of Habana Vieja's quintessential colonial *plazuelas*. It's ideal for refueling on coffee, cappuccino, chocolate tarts, smoothies, or delicious sandwiches.

Consider Cinco Esquinas ground zero in the gentrification of Habana Vieja, with several great options. **Café de los Artistas** (Calle Aguilar #22 bajos, e/ Av. de los Misiones y Peña Pobre, tel. 07/866-2418, daily 10am-1am) offers excellent quality and value for a classic Cuban menu, including mouthwatering *tostones* and *ropa vieja*. Owner Luis Carlos is the stage manager for the Ballet Nacional de Cuba and photos of Cuba's elite dancers festoon the walls.

Motorcyclists will love the decor at **Chacón 162** (Chacón #162, esq. Callejón de Espada, tel. 07/860-1386, daily 11am-midnight), owned by Harley-Davidson enthusiasts and a hangout for local *harlistas* since opening in 2016. A motorcycle hangs over the bar, and the cocktails are cued to the theme: Street Bob, Bloody Mary V-Twin, and so forth. The fusion menu is well executed, too. I enjoyed a deliciously spicy *pulpo peruana*—octopus with veggies in tomato salsa (CUC9).

Intimate is an understatement for **Habana 61** (Calle Habana #6, e/ Cuarteles y Peña Pobre, tel. 07/861-9433, www.habana61.com, daily noon-midnight), a cubbyhole restaurant tucked off Cinco Esquinas. It dishes out some of the most creative cuisine in the city, served amid contemporary surrounds in a converted colonial townhouse.

Count your blessings to get a seat at ★ **O'Reilly 304** (Calle O'Reilly #304, e/ Habana y Aguiar, tel. 5264-4725, daily noon-midnight, CUC8-18). Cuba's monied *farandula* (in-crowd) and tourists in the know cram into what has become one of Habana Vieja's trendiest joints. The edgy art and high-energy buzz act like a gravitational force to passersby. Tiny it may be, but the *paladar* serves an imaginative menu of delicious dishes, from to-die-for ceviche to crab tacos.

I wish I could keep **Azúcar** (Mercaderes #315, tel. 07/801-1563, daily 11am-midnight) a secret—this is my favorite lunch spot in town. Owners Allison and Liset serve awesome tapas, tuna sandwiches, and even lobster in *criollo* sauce out of a contemporary colonial townhome that opens to the plaza. At night, the all-female Octava Nota performs.

Penny-pinching *farandulas* head to **Bar La Chanchullero** (Brasil e/ Berraza y Cristo, tel. 5276-0938, daily 1pm-midnight), a down-to-earth hole-in-the-wall on Plaza del Cristo. It serves tapas, plus garlic shrimp (CUC4), pork with parsley (CUC4), and chicken fricassee (CUC4).

Criolla

La Bodeguita del Medio (Empedrado #207, e/ San Ignacio y Cuba, tel. 07/862-1374, restaurant daily noon-midnight, bar 10:30am-midnight, CUC10-20), one block west of Plaza de la Catedral, specializes in traditional Cuban dishes—most famously its roast pork, steeped black beans, fried bananas, garlicky yucca, and sweet guava pudding. Troubadours entertain.

To dine with Cubans, you can't beat ★ **Los Nardos** (Paseo de Martí #563, e/ Teniente Rey y Dragones, tel. 07/863-2985, daily noon-midnight), in a run-down building opposite the Capitolio. The long lines at night hint how good this place is. It has restaurants on three levels; be sure to dine in the atmospheric Los Nardos, not the more ascetic El Trofeo or El Asturianito, on the upper levels. The huge meals include garlic shrimp, lobster in Catalan sauce, paella, and Cuban staples. House sangria is served in a pitcher. The place is run by Cuba's Spanish Asturian association.

The Sociedad Cultural Asturiana runs **La Terraza** (Prado #309, esq. Virtudes, tel. 07/862-3625, daily noon-midnight), a covered open-air rooftop space overlooking the Prado; get there early to snag a seat with a view. Master chef Jorge Falco Ochoa specializes in grilled meats and seafood. Try the grilled octopus with pesto and grilled potatoes, and perhaps a succulent leg of lamb, or grilled sausage in spicy mustard sauce. The food makes up for the ho-hum decor.

European

The modern **Restaurante Prado y Neptuno** (Prado, esq. Neptuno, tel. 07/860-9636, daily noon-midnight) is popular with expats for reasonable Italian fare and pizzas. The *bodega*-style **La Paella** (Oficios #53, esq. Obrapía, tel. 07/867-1037, daily noon-11pm), in the Hostal Valencia, serves paella for two people only (although one person could ostensibly eat a double serving) for CUC7-15. The *caldo* (soup) and bread is a meal in itself (CUC3). The kitchen also serves the **Bodegón Ouda** (Obrapía, esq. Baratillo, tel. 07/867-1037, Mon.-Sat. noon-7pm), a quaint tapas bar around the corner in the Hotel El Comendador.

Surf and Turf

The ritzy **Café del Oriente** (Oficios, esq. Amargura, tel. 07/860-6686, daily noon-midnight), on Plaza de San Francisco, is considered a showcase state restaurant and draws U.S. tour groups. It has tux-clad waiters and a jazz pianist downstairs in the Bar Café—heck, you could be in New York or San Francisco. The mostly steak and seafood dishes (CUC12-30), include calf's brains with mustard and brandy cream sauce and a divine filet mignon, but it can't hold a candle to the best *paladares*.

A merely adequate state-run restaurant is **Restaurante El Templete** (Av. del Puerto, esq. Narciso López, tel. 07/866-8807, daily noon-midnight), along with adjoining sibling **Restaurante La Barca.** Housed in a restored colonial mansion, this dual restaurant has a diverse menu ranging from delicious fried calamari (CUC5) to overpriced lobster (CUC28) and a chocolate brownie dessert. It's a great place to catch the firing of the cannon across the harbor at 9pm.

Self-Catering

The *agromercado* on Avenida de Bélgica (Egido, e/ Apodada y Corrales) is a great place to stock up on fresh produce. Imported meats are sold at **La**

Monserrate (Monserrate, e/ Brasil y Muralles), an air-conditioned butcher shop, and at **Harris Brothers** (Monserrate #305, e/ O'Reilly y Progreso, Habana Vieja, tel. 07/861-1644, daily 9am-6pm), a department store with various foodstuff sections.

CENTRO HABANA
Paladares

Centro Habana boasts the most acclaimed *paladar* in town: ★ **La Guarida** (Concordia #418, e/ Gervasio y Escobartel, tel. 07/866-9047, www.laguarida.com, daily noon-midnight), on the third floor of a dilapidated 19th-century townhouse turned crowded *ciudadela* (tenement). Don't let the near-derelict staircase put you off the world-class Parisian-style restaurant. The walls are festooned with period Cuban pieces and giant prints of famous personages who've dined here (from Jack Nicholson to Beyoncé, Rhianna, and Madonna) and fashion shoots on the crumbling stairways. (You may recognize it as the setting for the Oscar-nominated 1995 movie *Fresa y Chocolate*.) Owners Enrique Nuñez and Odeysis Baullosa serve such treats as gazpacho (CUC4) and *tartar de atún* (tuna tartare, CUC6) for starters and an out-of-this-world roast chicken in orange sauce and honey (CUC13), plus desserts such as lemon pie (CUC5). Despite the large wine list, only house wine is available by the glass (CUC4). There's also a chic rooftop tapas bar and cigar lounge. Reservations are essential.

Giving La Guarida a run for its money is ★ **San Cristóbal** (Calle San Rafael #469, e/ Campanario y Lealtad, tel. 07/860-1705, rashemarquez@yahoo.com, Mon.-Sat. noon-midnight), with an eclectic museum's worth of antiques, objets d'art, religious and musical icons, and armoires stuffed with old books. Ebullient owner-chef Carlos Cristóbal Márquez and his kitchen team deliver superbly flavorful traditional Cuban dishes, such as grilled lobster, succulent roast pork, and Cuban-style mezze plates. Beyoncé dined here and this was the *only* private restaurant where President Obama dined during his 2016 visit. Good luck booking a table! This is not a place for walking the streets alone late at night; take a taxi.

The homespun **Paladar Doña Blanquita** (Prado #158, e/ Colón y Refugio, tel. 07/867-4958, Tues.-Sun. noon-midnight) offers dining on a balcony overlooking the Prado. The *criolla* menu delivers large portions for CUC5-10. The place overflows with whimsical Woolworth's art, such as cheap *muñequitas* (dolls), plastic flowers, animals, and cuckoo clocks.

For a view over the Malecón, head to **Castropol** (Malecón #107, e/ Genios y Crespo, tel. 07/861-4864, daily 11am-midnight), run by the Sociedad Asturiano. The chef conjures up fusion dishes such as pork tenderloin medallions with honey and Dijon mustard, but I prefer the ceviche (CUC4.50) or delicious octopus Galician style with sweet-and-sour pepper and potatoes (CUC3.65). The downstairs restaurant serves Cuban dishes from the grill; call ahead to book an upstairs terrace table.

The inspiration of Swedish film director and owner Michel Miglis, ★ **Casa Miglis** (Calle Lealtad #120, e/ Animas y Lagunas, tel. 07/863-1486, www.casamiglis.com, daily noon-1am) offers the only Scandinavian cuisine in town, although I'd more accurately call it Cuban-meets-the-world. The menu includes couscous, Mexican chili, and Greek souvlaki. My pork with herb-fried potatoes in bean sauce, chopped shrimp, and balsamic cream induced a sigh of delight. As did a divine vanilla ice cream with raisins and *añejo* rum topped with cacao. Your setting is a centenary townhouse with classically elegant all-white furnishings and place settings from Sweden. The bar is a work of art: Aged seats hang suspended as if floating in air. Miglis hosts live theme nights Friday-Sunday.

Nearby, **Restaurant La California** (Calle Crespo #55 e/ San Lázaro y Refugio, tel. 07/869-7510, californiarestasurant@gmail.com, daily noon-midnight) is justifiably popular with tour groups. I like the four distinct and antique-filled *salas* (salons), including a redbrick terrace, and its clever use of former sewing machine pedestals for tables. The house speciality is oven-grilled pizza. I love the mushroom risotto with squid-ink rice (CUC12), and the chicken supreme in lemon caper sauce (CUC8) is sure to satisfy. Sated? Then climb the spiral staircase to the wine and cigar lounge.

Asian

Barrio Chino boasts a score of Chinese restaurants, concentrated along Calle Cuchillo. However, this isn't Hong Kong or San Francisco, so temper your expectations. ★ **Restaurante Tien-Tan** (Cuchillo #17, tel. 07/863-2081, daily 9am-midnight) is the best of a dozen options on Cuchillo. Chef Tao Qi hails from Shanghai. The extensive menu includes such tantalizing offerings as sweet-and-sour fried fish balls with vinegar and soy, and pot-stewed liver with seasoning. The budget-minded will find many options for around CUC2, but dishes run to CUC18. A 20 percent service fee is charged.

One of the best bargains in town is ★ **Flor de Loto** (Salud #313, e/ Gervasio y Escobar, tel. 07/860-8501, daily noon-midnight). Though the staff dress in Chinese robes, about the only Asian item on the menu is *mariposistas* (fried wontons). However, the *criolla* fare, such as spicy shrimp (CUC6.50) and grilled lobster (CUC7.50), is tasty and filling.

Self-Catering

For groceries, try the basement supermarket in **La Época** (Galiano, esq. Neptuno, Mon.-Sat. 9:30am-9:30pm, Sun. 9am-1pm). Milk is the hardest item to find in Cuba. Try **La Castillo del Lacteo** (Av. Simón Bolívar, esq. Galiano, daily 9am-8pm), selling ice cream, yogurt, and, hopefully, milk.

VEDADO AND PLAZA DE LA REVOLUCIÓN
Breakfast and Cafés

★ **Café La Rampa** (Calle 23, esq. L, tel. 07/834-6125, 24 hours), at the Hotel Habana Libre Tryp, serves American-style breakfasts, including a breakfast special of toast, eggs, bacon, coffee, and juice for CUC7. The burgers here

Ice-Cream Parlors

patrons at Coppelia ice cream parlor, Vedado

Street stalls sell ice-cream cones for about 2.50 pesos. However, hygiene is always questionable.

Habana Vieja: For penny-pinchers, the **Cremería el Naranjal** (Obispo, esq. Cuba) sells ice-cream sundaes, including a banana split (CUC1.50-3). Gourmands won't believe they're in Havana at **Helad'oro** (Calle Aguiar #206 e/ Empedrado y Tejadillo, tel. 5305-9131; daily 11am-10pm, CUC1), serving artesanal gelatos. Flavors include mojito, of course.

Vedado: An institution, **Coppelia** (Calle 23, esq. Calle L, tel. 07/832-6149, Tues.-Sun. 10am-9:30pm) serves ice cream of excellent quality. Tourists are often steered toward a special section that, though offering immediate service, charges CUC2.60 for an *ensalada* (three scoops), while the half-dozen communal peso sections (choose from indoor or outdoor dining) offer larger *ensaladas* (five scoops) for only five pesos, a *jimagua* (two scoops) for two pesos, and a *marquesita* (two scoops plus a sponge cake) for 2.50 pesos, all served in simple aluminum bowls. The fun is in waiting in line and dining communally with Cubans; you'll need *moneda nacional.* A kiosk on the west side (Calle K) sells cones. Be prepared for a *long* wait in summer.

Dulce Habana (Calle 25, tel. 07/836-6100, daily 10am-9pm), on the south side of the Hotel Habana Libre Tryp, is run along the lines of Baskin-Robbins and charges accordingly.

My fave spot is **Amore** (Calle 15 #111, esq. L, tel. 5536-5152, daily 10am-midnight), an Italian-owned newcomer in a restored beaux arts mansion serving about 16 flavors of gelatos ranging from mamey to peanut.

Playa (Miramar and Beyond): Yanetzi Anahares dishes up gelato in 16 flavors at her **Casa de Gelato** (1ra Av. esq. 44, tel. 07/202-7938, www. alpescatorehabana.com, daily noon-midnight, CUC1.50-5), in front of the Hotel Copacabana.

are surprisingly good (CUC5), as are the tuna and fried egg sandwiches (CUC5) and hot chocolate brownies (CUC3.50).

Paladares

Vedado abounds with great *paladares,* and every month at least one quality private restaurant opens to take advantage of the new legal space. Here's my pick of the ever-expanding litter.

I regularly dine at ★ **Le Chansonnier** (Calle J #259, e/ 15 y Línea, tel. 07/832-1576, daily 1pm-11pm), a gorgeous restaurant in a vast, venerable mansion with soaring ceilings, beige leather banquettes, and sensational art—a testament to owner Héctor Higüera Martínez's Parisian sensibility. Creative fare is highlighted by delicious sauces. The marinated octopus in garlic appetizer is to die for. Other winning dishes include spicy crab appetizer, duck with *salsa guayabana*, pork loin with eggplant, and roasted rabbit in mustard sauce. The menu is ever-changing. Most dishes cost less than CUC15.

Héctor's influence is also all over ★ **Atelier** (Calle 5 #511, e/ Paseo y 2, tel. 07/836-2025, www.atelier-cuba.com, daily noon-midnight), another chic conversion of a 19th-century Spanish Renaissance mansion—formerly owned by the president of the Senate—adorned with fine Cuban art and, coincidentally, run by Héctor's brother (Herdys Higueras Martínez) and sister (Niuris Higueras Martínez). Daily menus might include candied duck and red snapper ceviche or a superb squash soup (CUC5) and chicken with shrimp *a la crema* (CUC12). Try to snag a table on the rooftop terrace; tour groups fill up the place. Reservations are essential.

The chilled-out **Café Laurent** (Calle M #257, e/ 19 y 21, tel. 07/832-6890, www.cafelaurent.ueuo.com, daily noon-midnight) is in a fifth-floor penthouse of a 1950s modernist apartment block with veranda dining and white ostrich-leather seats. The three owners have imbued the place with fantastic retro decor and nouvelle Cuban dishes that wow diners. Try the carpaccio ahi tuna, tuna-stuffed peppers (CUC5), or oven-baked chateaubriand with wild mushrooms served in a clay casserole (CUC11.50). And leave room for the delicious chocolate brownie with vanilla ice cream.

What's not to rave about at ★ **El Cocinero** (Calle 26, e/ 11 y 13, tel. 07/832-2355, www.elcocinerohabana.cu, daily noon-midnight)? Visionary entrepreneurs Alexander "Sasha" Ramos and Rafael Muñoz have turned an old redbrick factory that once made cooking oil into a superb *paladar* and lounge club adjoining (and part of) Fábrica de Arte Cubano (FAC). You ascend a spiral staircase augering up the old chimney to a classy second-floor restaurant (grilled lobster with basmati rice, CUC18; chicken with *criolla* sauce, CUC5; pork ribs, CUC5) and, above, an open-air rooftop lounge club favored by *la farandula* (the in-crowd); the latter serves tapas such as whole octopus, gazpacho Andaluz (CUC3), and baguette with goat cheese (CUC5). Leave room for the artisanal ice cream. The lounge also hosts live jazz.

Inside FAC, restaurater siblings Niurys and Hector Higüera Mártinez run the sublime **Tierra** (Calle 26 esq. 11, tel. 5565-2621, Thurs.-Sun.

8pm-1:30am, by reservation only, CUC7-10), using old shipping containers with glass-paneled sides that open to a faux-garden patio. The menu roams the globe from tuna lasagna and lamb moussaka (unimpressive) to a divine fish-and-chips served in newspaper. Start with a mixto Arabe platter (CUC10). You pay the CUC2 entrance to FAC but don't have to wait in line.

Tucked at the end of a brick walkway to the rear of a 1930s mansion and festooned with a decorative arbor, **La Moraleja** (Calle 25 #454, e/ I y J, tel. 07/832-0963, www.lamoraleja-cuba.com, noon-midnight) combines a romantic ambience—choose air-conditioned or patio dining—with superb nouvelle Cuban dishes, prepared in an outdoor brasserie. Try the house octopus salad, roast rabbit with port flambée (CUC10), or divine grilled shrimp with anise and garlic served in an earthenware bowl. The space also hosts live jazz.

Serving some of the best Italian fare in town, **Mediterráneo Havana** (Calle 13 #406, e/ F y G, tel. 07/832-4894, www.medhavana.com, daily noon-midnight) truly evokes the Mediterranean with its white and, well, Mediterranean blues in this converted 1920s mansion. Sardinian chef Luigi Fiori achieves sublime heights with his superb homemade sausages and ravioli (CUC6.50), lasagna (CUC5.50), and lobster spaghetti (CUC9), plus pizzas (from CUC4.75). The braised goat with herbs and olive oil is delicious (CUC6.50). It has been discovered by American tour groups who frequently take over the place. Two blocks east is **El Idilio** (Cale G #351 esq. 15, tel. 07/831-8182, daily noon-midnight), an unpretentious open-air Italian restaurant with gingham tablecloths. The open kitchen specializes in barbecued meats.

On Saturday night, you'll likely find me at ★ **La Chuchería Café Sport Bar** (1ra esq. C, tel. 07/830-7908, daily 9am-midnight), a hip, straight-from-Miami demonstration of private know-how with its Philippe Starck translucent plastic chairs. There's usually a line to savor delicious thin-crust pizza in the air-conditioned retro-themed diner or on a patio facing the Malecón.

El Cocinero, Vedado

FOOD

It's also a great place to start the day with crêpes or a classic American breakfast (CUC3.50). Plus, it has reasonable burgers, great sandwiches, and creative salads. It even has pizza and shakes to go.

Guests at the Meliá Cohiba can step across the street to enjoy superb fusion fare at ★ **HM 7** (Paseo #7 e/ 1ra y 3ra, tel. 07/830-2287, www.ha-banamia7.com, daily noon-11pm), with an open kitchen upstairs. Chic, 21st-century decor includes sleek contemporary styling that extends to the menu. I like the mushroom risotto in squid ink or the spaghetti Bolognese; ceviche (CUC5.25), octopus carpaccio (CUC6.95), and grilled dishes also feature. Downstairs, the bar serves tapas until the wee hours.

On the Malecón seafront (hence the name) is **El Litoral** (Malecón e/ K y L, tel. 07/830-2201, www.ellitoralhabana.com, daily noon-midnight). This maritime-themed restaurant in a graciously restored neo-colonial manse is one of few *paladares* that draws a Cuban elite for the all-you-can-eat antipasto bar—a brilliant and unique idea by owner Alejandro Marcel and chef-partner Alain Rivas. A wide range of seafood dishes include salmon pasta with vodka sauce (CUC18), as well as creative meat dishes such as lamb sausage with sweet potato patties. There's a chic lounge bar with music videos, or hang out on the raised seafront terrace and watch the old cars go by. Next door, **Dolce Vita** (Malecón #159, tel. 07/836-0100 or 5291-1444, daily noon-midnight) raises the bar with its chic styling, glass-enclosed seafront terrace, and excellent Italian fare. Try the spinach ravioli with cream and peanut sauce (CUC12) or gnocchi with Italian sausage and tomato and basil sauce (CUC12), followed by profiteroles (CUC4).

For someplace unpretentious, try **Paladar Los Amigos** (Calle M #253, e/ 19 y 21, tel. 07/830-0880, daily noon-midnight), a cramped and popular little spot adorned with posters and photographs of famous Cuban musicians who've dined here. It serves huge plates of traditional Cuban dishes for about CUC10.

The tiny and cramped **Paladar Restaurante Monguito** (Calle L #408, e/ 23 y 25, tel. 07/831-2615, Fri.-Wed. noon-11pm), directly opposite the Hotel Habana Libre Tryp, is a bargain for simple but filling Cuban dishes such as *pollo asado*, grilled fish, and pork dishes (CUC3-6). Budget hounds are equally well served at **Paladar Mesón Sancho Panza** (Calle J #508, e/ 23 y 25, tel. 07/831-2862, daily noon-3am), on the south side of Parque Don Quijote. It has simple decor and fills with Cubans who come for its vast menu of tapas (such as fried garbanzos), shrimp cocktail (CUC3.30), stuffed eggs (CUC3.50), paellas (from CUC10), and *ropa vieja* (CUC6) at bargain prices.

Chef Osmany Cisnero's **StarBien** (Calle 29 #205, e/ B y C, tel. 07/830-0711 or 5386-2222, starbien.restaurante@gmail.com, Mon.-Sat. noon-midnight, Sun. 7pm-midnight), a fine-dining *paladar* in a restored 1938 building, has garnered a loyal expat clientele. It has a patio, plus an air-conditioned interior with a lofty ceiling and contemporary furnishings. Recommended dishes include the superb ceviche and ravioli with spinach and blue cheese. After dinner, head up to the chic and popular bar to smoke a cigar.

VIP Havana (Calle 9na #454, e/ E y F, tel. 07/832-0178, www.viphavana454.com, daily noon-midnight, CUC25-50) is a soaring and stylishly avant-garde space rehashed from a centenary mansion. Chaplin movies show on a giant screen and a pianist tickles the ivories as you dine on Spanish tapas, pizzas, pastas, paellas, meat, and seafood. The veranda is preferred for lunch on clement days.

Spanish owner Massimo has done a superb conversion of a huge, late-19th-century mansion into ★ **Versus 1900** (Linea #504 altos, e/ D y E, tel. 07/835-1852, versus1900lahabana@gmail.com, daily noon-3am). The ambience stresses antiques and colonial tile floors and floor-to-ceiling shuttered windows that open onto a dining terrace. My favorite dish: charcoal-baked pork in mojo *criollo* sauce with dried fruits (CUC16). The rooftop serves as a stylish neon-lit lounge space, good for postprandial cigars and rum cocktails.

In Nuevo Vedado, ★ **La Casa** (Calle 30 #865, e/ 26 y 41, tel. 07/881-7000, www.restaurantelacasacuba.com, daily noon-midnight) is worth the drive. This 1950s modernist house retains its original decor and is lush with tropical plantings. La Casa serves such delicious dishes as octopus with vinaigrette, tomatoes, and onions (CUC7), ham and spinach cannelloni (CUC75), pasta chicken curry (CUC10), and rabbit with mushroom sauce (CUC12). Actor Matt Dillon and soccer misfit Diego Maradona are among the famous clientele. Savvy owner Alejandro Robaina is usually on hand to fuss over guests. He has an elegant bar upstairs with hookahs and music videos, and hosts Thursday sushi nights.

One of only two dedicated sushi restaurants in town is **PP's Teppanyaki** (Calle 12 #104, e/ L y M, tel. 07/836-2530, ppsteppanyakihavana@yahoo.com, Mon.-Thurs. 6pm-11pm), upstairs in an apartment block. The owner, Pepe, spent eight years as a naval engineer in Japan and has done a good job of replicating Japanese decor, including a teppanyaki bar. He serves professionally presented dishes, such as an excellent octopus vinaigrette and a selection of maki (CUC9), including delicious Danish rolls.

Criolla

Popular with Cubans, the dark, chilly **La Roca** (Calle 21, esq. M, tel. 07/836-3219, daily noon-midnight) has bargain-priced garlic shrimp (CUC9), plus set meals from CUC5, including beer.

ArteChef (Calle 3ra, esq. A, tel. 07/831-1089, www.arteculinario.cu, daily noon-midnight) is operated by the Federación de Asociaciones Culinarias de la República de Cuba, a chefs association that offers professional cooking shows and classes. The space impresses with its classical elegance and wraparound walls of glass. The menu includes traditional dishes such as malanga fritters, plus paella (CUC5), rabbit in wine (CUC6), and lobster thermidor (CUC14).

La Torre (Calle 17 #155, e/ M y N, tel. 07/838-3088, daily noon-midnight), atop the Focsa building, offers amazing all-around views of the city. Its French-inspired nouvelle cuisine is of higher than usual standard: I recommend the prawns and mushrooms in olive oil and garlic starter (CUC10). I also enjoyed a fish fillet poached in white wine, butter, and cream, and roasted with cheese, served with mashed potatoes and crisp vegetables (CUC15). Order the mountainous and delicious profiteroles (CUC5) for dessert.

The Hotel Meliá Cohiba's baseball-themed **La Piazza Ristorante** (tel. 07/833-3636, daily 1pm-midnight) offers 17 types of pizza (CUC7-20) but also has minestrone (CUC7.50), gnocchi (CUC10), seafood (from CUC11), and an excellent risotto with mushrooms (tinned). Smoking is tolerated and fouls the place.

Self-Catering

There are *agromercados* at Calle 15 (esq. 10), Calle 17 (e/ K y L), Calle 19 (e/ F y Av. de los Presidentes), Calle 21 (esq. J), Calle 16 (e/ 11 y 13), and Pozos Dulces (e/ Av. Salvador Allende and Bruzón).

PLAYA (MIRAMAR AND BEYOND)

This is ground zero for the boom in quality *paladares*. The scene is evolving so quickly that it's truly dizzying.

Breakfast and Cafés

All the tourist hotels have buffet breakfasts. For freshly baked croissants and good coffee, I like **Pain de Paris** (Calle 26, e/ 5ta y 7ma, daily 8am-10pm). **Pan.Com** (Calle 26, esq. 7ma, Mon.-Fri. 8am-2am, Sat.-Sun. 10am-2am), pronounced "pahn POOHN-to com," makes every kind of sandwich. It also has omelets, burgers, and tortillas, all for less than CUC5, plus yogurts, fruit juices, *batidos,* and cappuccinos.

In the Miramar Trade Center, the small, modern, clean, and air-conditioned **Café Amelia** (no tel., daily 8am-10pm) sells simple sandwiches, empanadas, and pastries, all below CUC3.

Paladares

At the homey ★ **Corte de Principe** (Calle 9na, esq. 74, tel. 5255-9091, daily noon-3pm and 7pm-11pm), Italian owner-chef Sergio serves probably the finest Italian fare in town on a simple alfresco patio with a quasi-Italian motif. Go with Sergio's nightly recommendations (there's no written menu), such as a divine beef carpaccio with mozzarella and olive oil, eggplant parmesan, or garlic shrimp. Leave room for real Häagen-Dazs ice cream. Sergio over-chills the red wines, so call ahead to have him open a bottle ahead of time. And if only he wouldn't smoke in his own restaurant! Around the corner, and more elegant and avant-garde, is **Bom Apetíte** (Calle 11 #7210, e/ 72 y 74, Playa, tel. 07/203-3634, open daily 24 hours), an air-conditioned Italian restaurant serving divine pizza, ravioli, and gnocchi.

Gourmet Italian fare is the name of the game at **Nero di Seppia** (Cale 6 #122 e/ 1ra y 3ra, tel. 5478-7871, walterginevri@nauta.cu, Tues.-Sun noon-midnight). Wood-oven pizza, fettuccine with porcini and salsiccia—it's all here, and all beyond good. You'll dine on generous portions in a renovated mansion with various dining rooms and a terrace.

Moscatelli (Av. 7ma #6609 e/ 66 y 70, tel. 07/203-4507, Tues.-Sun. noon-4pm and 5pm-1am) is overseen by Marco, a dietician from Italy's Lazio region. He amazes with his ability to import ingredients from his home. This is classic Italian fare, such as eggplant parmigiana, and seafood fettucine (CUC14). Given its location, it's popular with local business folk and diplomats.

Boasting a one-of-a-kind riverside setting, ★ **Río Mar** (3ra y Final #11, La Puntilla, tel. 07/720-4838, riomarbargrill@gmail.com, daily noon-midnight) has a sensational locale and a ritzy modern aesthetic, thanks to a yearlong renovation of a 1950s modernist manse. Choose the alfresco waterfront deck over the snazzy air-conditioned interior, but bring a sweater in winter when a chill wind can kick in. The fusion *criolla* menu includes artfully presented ceviche (CUC5), beef carpaccio (CUC8), lamb with red wine and rosemary (CUC12), and chicken in blue cheese sauce with malanga purée (CUC15). Chef Alberto Álvarez is best known for his house dish: red snapper on a bed of potatoes.

Reservations are vital at the venerable **Cocina de Lilliam** (Calle 48 #1311, e/ 13 y 15, Miramar, tel. 07/209-6514, Sun.-Fri. noon-3pm and 7pm-10pm, CUC15-25), in the lush grounds of a 1930s-era mansion romantically lit at night. The brick-lined patio is shaded by trees and set with colonial lanterns and wrought-iron tables and chairs. Lilliam Domínguez conjures up tasty nouvelle Cuban. Her appetizers include tartlets of tuna and onion, and a savory dish of garbanzo beans and ham with onion and red and green peppers. Entrées include such Cuban classics as simmered lamb with onions and peppers; chicken breast with pineapple; and fresh fish dishes and oven-roasted meats served with creamy mashed potatoes.

By the shore, the suave, South Beach-style ★ **Paladar Vistamar** (1ra Av. #2206, e/ 22 y 24, tel. 07/203-8328, www.restaurantevistamar.com, daily noon-midnight) appeals for its ocean view with the Atlantic breakers crashing in front of an infinity pool. Owner Joel Arcu Otaño's modernist villa is popular for its high-quality seafood. It also serves continental fare as well as Cuban staples. Starters include mussels in white wine sauce (CUC8), while main dishes include swordfish fillet with parmesan sauce (CUC15) and Mediterranean-style seafood pasta (CUC13). I never fail to order the serrano stuffed with honey and fig paste; the lobster presentation is a work of art. Leave room for a thick slab of lemon pie topped with meringue.

Fresh from a makeover, **Paladar Ristorante El Palio** (1ra Av. #2402, esq. 24, tel. 5289-2410 or 5358-6690, daily noon-midnight) has lured Ernesto Cárdenas, former head chef at the Hotel Parque Central. The menu has expanded, but still focuses on Italian-*criolla* cuisine, such as garlic octopus (CUC4) and shrimp cocktail (CUC6), plus a shrimp and lobster casserole (CUC8). Dine in a shaded garden or in a chic air-conditioned room with white-and-bottle-green settings.

La Fontana (3ra Av. #305, esq. 46, tel. 07/202-8337, www.lafontanahavana.info, daily noon-midnight, CUC2-15) specializes in barbecued meats from an outdoor grill serving T-bone steak. Starters include salads, *escabeche* (ceviche), and onion soup; main dishes include flavorful chicken with rice, pepper, and onions served in an earthenware bowl. Rice and extras cost additional. Choose cellar or garden seating in a traditional country *bohío* setting.

Cuban-Spanish couple Amy Torralbas (an artist) and Álvaro Díez (a sommelier) combine their respective skills at ★ **Otra Manera** (Calle 35 #1810, e/ 20 y 41, tel. 07/203-8315, www.otramaneralahabana.com, Tues.-Sat. noon-3pm and 7pm-11pm). Their *paladar* re-creates Amy's grandma's restaurant. Its gorgeous 21st-century minimalist sophistication draws expats to savor the sublime Cuban-Spanish fusion fare such as Andalusian gazpacho, baked snapper with ginger and coconut vinaigrette, or a chicken casserole with candied potatoes. Otra Manera defines Cuba's *nueva cocina* fare.

The unpretentious **Mi Jardín** (Calle 66 #517, esq. 5ta Av. B, tel. 07/203-4627, daily noon-midnight, CUC15-20), in a beautiful 1950s home full of antiques, is run by an affable and conscientious Mexican and his Italian wife. They serve quasi-Mexican fare. The chicken *molé mexicano* and house special fish Veracruz are recommended. You'll also find enchiladas and *totopos* (nachos), plus Italian and *criolla* dishes. You can dine inside or on a patio beneath an arbor.

Doctor Café (Calle 28 #111, e/ 1ra y 3ra, tel. 07/203-4718, www.doctorcafehavana.com, Mon.-Fri. 11am-11pm, Sat. 12:30pm-10pm) has some of the most creative gourmet dishes in town, courtesy of chef Juan Carlos. Every dish I've eaten here has been sublime. Try the crab ceviche or shredded crab enchilada appetizers, lasagna bolognesa (CUC13), or maybe a "deluxe burger" (CUC16). Choose patio dining or the atmospheric air-conditioned interior. Reservations are required.

Savor the best pizza in town at **La Chuchería** (Av. 1ra esq. 28, tel. 07/212-5013, daily 8am-1am), an oceanfront edition of Vedado's eponymous pizzeria. This converted Spanish Renaissance manse has great ambience, and the bargain-priced pizzas are the best in town. Wash it all down with a milk shake.

Restaurante Habanera (Calle 16 #506, e/ 5ta y 7ma., tel. 07/202-9941 or 5511-8723, habnera506@gmail.com, daily noon-midnight) offers casual elegance in a converted 1930s mansion with faux-washed walls and a checkered floor. Curried shrimp in coconut cream, lobster with mango, and lamb with red wine sauce are highlights of the fusion cuisine menu. In clement weather, opt for the lovely garden terrace.

Out in Jaimanitas, ★ **Santy Pescador** (Calle 240A #3C23, e/ 3raC y best sashimi and nigiri you'll ever eat (CUC10-20). Each morning Carlos and Felix, the fishermen-hosts (Santy was their dad), bring in their own catch; they kill and gut the fish to serve minutes before you eat it, prepared with some olive oil, coriander, and soy. There are two private air-conditioned rooms and bi-level riverside dining overlooking the funky fishing boats tethered to even funkier wharves.

Criolla

I return time and again to ★ **El Aljibe** (7ma Av., e/ 24 y 26, tel. 07/204-1583, daily noon-midnight), my favorite state-run restaurant in Havana. It's popular with tour groups. You dine beneath a soaring thatch roof. The sole reason to be here is for the delicious house dish: *pollo asado el aljibe,* roast chicken glazed with a sweet orange sauce, then baked and served with fried plantain chips, rice, french fries, and black beans served until you can eat no more. It's a tremendous bargain at CUC12; desserts and beverages cost extra. Other *criolla* dishes are served (CUC10-20). You can even take away what you don't eat. A 10 percent service charge is also billed. The wine cellar is the city's largest.

Seafood

State-run **Don Cangrejo** (1ra Av., e/ 16 y 18, tel. 07/204-3837, daily noon-midnight) offers some of the finest seafood in town, served in a converted colonial mansion offering views out to sea. It's popular with the monied Cuban elite. The menu features crab cocktail (CUC6), crab claws (CUC18), and seafood mix (CUC25). The wine list runs to more than 150 labels.

Continental

Long a favorite of the Cuban elite, the overpriced **Tocororo** (Calle 18 #302, esq. 3ra, tel. 07/204-2209, Mon.-Sat. noon-midnight, CUC25-35), housed in a neoclassical mansion, has an antique-filled lobby extending into a garden patio with rattan furniture, Tiffany lamps, potted plants, and wooden parrots hanging from gilt perches, plus real parrots in cages. A pianist (by day) and jazz ensemble (by night) entertain. The merely average food is typical Cuban fare, although crocodile and ostrich occasionally feature. Even the bread will be charged, and a 10 percent service charge is automatic.

Self-Catering

Supermercado 70 (3ra Av., e/ 62 y 70, Miramar, tel. 07/204-2890, Mon.-Sat. 9am-6pm, Sun. 9am-1pm) is Cuba's largest supermarket selling imported foodstuffs. However, the best selection is at **Palco** (Mon.-Sat. 10am-6pm, Sun. 9am-1pm), in the Miramar Trade Center; aficionados know that if you can't find it here, it ain't to be found in Cuba. **Zona+** (Av. 7ma 3/ 66 y 68) is the nation's first wholesale store for private businesses, a kind of mini Cuban Costco.

ACROSS THE HARBOR

La Divina Pastora (tel. 07/860-8341, daily noon-midnight), below the Fortaleza de San Carlos de la Cabaña, offers average *criolla* fare in a harborfront setting; go for the setting. Its adjoining **La Tasca** bar-restaurant (tel. 07/860-8341, daily noon-11pm) offers an escape from the tour groups that descend on the main restaurant.

Paladar Doña Carmela (Calle B #10, tel. 07/867-7472, beatrizbarletta@ yahoo.com, daily 7pm-11pm) serves delicious *criolla* fare such as a sublime octopus in garlic in an outdoor setting. Competing with Doña Carmela, **El Cañonazo** (Casa #27, tel. 07/867-7476 or 5361-7503), opposite the entrance to Fortaleza de San Carlos, is almost identical. This re-creation of a farmstead with poultry running around underfoot packs in the tourists, brought for commissions by every other taxi driver in town. As such, you pay inflated prices for roast chicken (CUC14), lobster (CUC17), and other dishes.

In Guanabacoa, the best option is the casual **Mangle Rojo** (Av. 1ra #2, e/ 11 y 12, Rpto. Chibas, tel. 07/797-8613, manglerojo.havana@yahoo.es, daily noon-11pm), serving fresh salads, superb pizzas, and tasty *criolla* dishes, all less than CUC10. Opt for either air-conditioned dining or the patio. It's worth the detour to **El Mexicano** (Av. 3ra #6 e/ 2da y 3ra, Rpto. Chibás, Guanabacoa, tel. 5263-5413, daily noon-11pm) for its superb sandwiches and grilled meat dishes. Owner Jorge Luis Pérez has been running his cafécounter restaurant with aplomb for two decades.

Accommodations

All hotels have air-conditioned rooms with satellite TVs, telephones, and safes; most have Wi-Fi. With the U.S. tourism tsunami in full flood, tour groups take over the high-end hotels and push up prices astronomically. There is no longer a low season! You'll be wise to make reservations far in advance.

Casas particulares (private room rentals) have air-conditioning and private bathrooms, unless noted. New *casas* open weekly; Havana now has several thousand. The huge demand drives up standards (and prices). Since 2015, several deluxe privately owned "boutique" hotels have opened within the *casa particular* category.

With room availability at such a premium, keep your eyes on new hotels expected to open in the next two years: the 212-room **Sofitel So La Habana** (Prado esq. Malecón), Accor's 112-room **MGallery,** the 202-room **Ibis,** and the 82-room **Pancea Havana Cuba** (Dragones esq. Industriales). Habaguanex plans to open six hotels in 2017-2019: **Catedral** (Mercaderes esq. Empedrado; 24 rooms), **Cueto** (Plaza Vieja; 57 rooms), the **Marque de Cárdenas de Monte Hermoso** (21 rooms), and **Real Aduana** (in the current Customs building; 55 rooms) on Plaza San Francisco. Havana will get its first airport hotel when Canada's Wilton Properties builds the 363-room **Hotel Arte,** near José Martí Aeropuerto Internacional. And China's

Suntime International has partnered with Cubanacán to build the 600-room **Hemingway Hotel** at the Hemingway Marina.

139

Which District?

Location is important in choosing your hotel.

Habana Vieja puts you in the heart of the old city, within walking distance of Havana's main tourist sights. Two dozen colonial-era mansions previously administered by Habaguanex (the commercial branch of the Office of the City Historian) offer yesteryear ambience and modern bathrooms; at press time, these hotels were being transferred to the military's Gaviota tourism branch. There's also a full range of state-run hotels and a wide choice of private room rentals. In this neighborhood the term *hostal* merely refers to small size.

Centro Habana, although offering few sites of interest, has three budget-oriented hotels; Cuba's state tour agencies push the Hotel Deauville, used by many budget package-tour companies, but this gloomy cement tower is terrible and everyone who stays there has a complaint. This run-down residential district also has many *casas particulares,* but safety is a concern.

Vedado and Plaza de la Revolución offer mid-20th-century accommodations well situated for sightseeing, including several first-class modernist hotels with modest decor. Vedado also has dozens of superb *casas particulares*.

Playa (Miramar and Beyond) has moderate hotels popular with tour groups, modern deluxe hotels aimed at business travelers, and deluxe private villas. All are far from the main tourist sights; you'll need wheels or taxis to get around.

HABANA VIEJA
Casas Particulares

Hands-down the most sensational offering is ★ **Casa Vitrales** (Calle Habana #106, tel. 07/866-2607 or 5264-7673, www.cvitrales.com, CUC100 including breakfast). Owner Osmani Hernández bills his nine-bedroom guesthouse as a "boutique hotel" and has exquisitely restored and furnished his *casa particular* with a mix of antiques, '50s modernist pieces, and vibrant contemporary art. The only drawback is the narrow staircase, which winds up four flights to the rooftop breakfast terrace. Situated in the epicenter of Habana Vieja's gentrification, reservations here are essential.

The pricey ★ **Casa Pedro y María** (Calle Chacón #209, e/ Aguacate y Compostela, tel. 07/861-4641, www.boutiquehotelsincuba.com, CUC100 including breakfast) is in a gorgeously restored 18th-century townhouse. Behind the huge nail-studded door, colonial decor fuses with 21st-century touches; you'll love the rough stone walls. Three bedrooms and one junior suite open to a quiet patio where breakfast is served. (My room had a tiny but delightful en suite shower-bathroom in a space hidden by a curtain.)

Emblematic of the new boutique-type offerings is ★ **Loft Habana** (Calle Oficios #402 e/ Luz y Acosta, tel. 07/864-4685 or 5284-2256, www.

ACCOMMODATIONS

lofthabana.com, CUC120-350), with seven unique loft-like units inside a knocked-about building facing the harbor. These stylish air-conditioned units range from standard to deluxe; all have bare stone walls, mezzanine bedrooms, and en suite shower bathrooms. The rooms are kitted out to 21st-century standards and exhibit the good taste of Cuban designer José Antonio Choy. There is a two-night minimum stay.

Hundreds of budget *casas* offer humbler yet adequate lodging. For example, **Hostal del Ángel** (Cuarteles #118 e/ Monserrate y Habana, tel. 07/860-0771 or 5264-7686, www.pradocolonial.com, CUC30-35) offers a better bargain, although it doesn't have the chic of Casa Vitrales or Casa Pedro-María. Restored by German owner Kenia, this centenary town home is stuffed with gorgeous antique furnishings. A spiral staircase leads to a mezzanine library, and balconies hang over the plaza. Its two bedrooms have en suite bathrooms.

Casa de Raquel y Ricardo (Calle Cristo #12, e/ Brasil y Muralla, tel. 07/867-5026, kasarakel@gmail.com, CUC25-30) is a gracious upstairs home; the spacious, airy lounge has rockers and *mediopuntos.* There are two rooms with lofty ceilings; one is air-conditioned and has its own bathroom.

Gay-friendly **Casa de Eugenio Barral García** (San Ignacio #656, e/ Jesús María y Merced, tel. 07/862-9877, CUC30), in southern Habana Vieja, has seven air-conditioned bedrooms with fans and refrigerators; five have private modern bathrooms. The old home is graciously and eclectically appointed with antiques.

Casa de Pepe y Rafaela (San Ignacio #454, e/ Sol y Santa Clara, tel. 07/867-5551, CUC30-35), on the second floor of a colonial home, has a spacious lounge full of antiques and songbirds. The owners rent three rooms with tall ceilings, fridges, fans, antique beds and furniture, glass chandeliers, and heaps of light pouring in from the balcony windows. Modern bathrooms have large showers.

Hotels
CUC100-200

At press time, the historic **Hotel Inglaterra** (Prado #416, esq. San Rafael, tel. 07/860-8594, www.gran-caribe.cu, from CUC90 s, CUC142 d low season, CUC120 s, CUC175 d high season), on the west side of Parque Central, was in the midst of a much-needed redo and relaunch by U.S. hotel company Starwood. It will reopen as a luxury hotel. No doubt it will retain its extravagant lobby bar and restaurant that whisk you metaphorically to Morocco. Expect its 83 rooms to offer great comfort and furnishings.

I like the **Hotel del Tejadillo** (Tejadillo, esq. San Ignacio, tel. 07/863-7283, from CUC95 s, CUC150 d low season, from CUC120 s, CUC195 d high season), another converted colonial mansion. Beyond the huge doors is an airy marble-clad lobby with a quaint dining area. It offers 32 rooms around two courtyards with fountains. The cool, high-ceilinged rooms are graced by *mediopuntos* (stained glass half-moon windows) and modern furniture.

Playing on a monastic theme, the **Hostal Los Frailes** (Brasil, e/ Oficios y Mercaderes, tel. 07/862-9383, from CUC95 s, CUC145 d low season, from CUC120 s, CUC195 d high season) has staff dressed in monks' habits. It has 22 rooms around a patio with a fountain. The rooms have medieval-style heavy timbers and wrought iron, religious prints, period telephones, and spacious bathrooms. It has a bar, but no restaurant.

Just one block from Plaza Vieja, **Hotel Beltrán de Santa Cruz** (San Ignacio #411, e/ Muralla y Sol, tel. 07/860-8330, from CUC95 s, CUC150 d low season, from CUC120 s, CUC195 d high season) is a handsome conversion of a three-story 18th-century mansion with exquisite *mediopuntos*. Its 11 rooms and one junior suite have gracious antique reproductions.

The latest of Habaguanex's boutique properties is the delightful **Habana 1612 Hotel** (Calle Habana #612, e/ Brasil y Muralla, tel. 07/866-5035, from CUC95 s, CUC140 d low season, from CUC120 s, CUC195 d high season). The 17th-century townhouse mansion has undergone a gorgeous refurbishing, melding modern decor throughout. With only 12 rooms, it exudes intimacy; seven rooms face the courtyard. The immediate neighborhood awaits restoration, so you're in the heart of earthy Habana Vieja.

If you're struggling to find rooms, there are other properties to try. **El Mesón de la Flota** (Mercaderes #257, e/ Amargura y Brasil, tel. 07/863-3838, CUC80 s, CUC130 d low season, CUC100 s, CUC170 d high season, including breakfast) is a classic Spanish *bodega* bar-restaurant with five intimate rooms. **Hotel Park View** (Colón, esq. Morro, tel. 07/861-3293, CUC62 s, CUC100 d low season, CUC67 s, CUC110 d high season, including breakfast) has 55 lofty and nicely furnished rooms, but minimal facilities. The drab **Hotel Plaza** (Zulueta #267, esq. Neptuno, tel. 07/860-8583, www.gran-caribe.cu, from CUC84 s, CUC120 d low-season) was built in 1909 on the northeast corner of Parque Central. It has 188 rooms (some gloomy; others noisy) that feature antique reproductions.

OVER CUC200

The Moorish-inspired **Hotel Mercure Sevilla Havane** (Trocadero #55, e/ Prado y Zulueta, tel. 07/860-8560, www.accorhotels.com, from CUC132 s, CUC164 d low season, CUC255 s, CUC274 d high season) was built in 1924, with an exterior and lobby straight out of *1,001 Arabian Nights*. Its 178 refurbished rooms feature antique reproductions. There's a sumptuous top-floor restaurant, plus a swimming pool and assorted shops.

Hotel Santa Isabel (Baratillo #9, e/ Obispo y Narciso López, tel. 07/860-8201, from CUC175 s, CUC260 d low season, from CUC210 s, CUC295 d high season), a small and intimate hostelry in the former 18th-century palace of the Count of Santovenia, enjoys a fabulous setting overlooking Plaza de Armas. The hotel has 27 rooms furnished with four-poster beds, reproduction antique furniture, and leather recliners on wide balconies; suites have whirlpool tubs. At press time, it was taken over by U.S. hotel giant Starwood, with plans to upgrade and rebrand as a mega-luxury option.

Overpriced **Hostal Valencia** (Oficios #53, e/ Obrapía y Lamparilla, tel. 07/867-1037, from CUC115 s, CUC165 d low season, from CUC140 s, CUC230 d high season) might induce a flashback to the romantic *posadas* of Spain. The 18th-century mansion-turned-hotel exudes charm with its lobby of hefty oak beams, Spanish tiles, and wrought-iron chandeliers. The 12 spacious rooms and junior suites have cool marble floors. The La Paella restaurant is a bonus. Attached is the **Hotel El Comendador** (Oficios #53, e/ Obrapía y Lamparilla, tel. 07/857-1037, from CUC115 s, CUC165 d low season, from CUC140 s, CUC230 d high season), another endearingly restored colonial home with 14 exquisite rooms.

The **Hotel Ambos Mundos** (Obispo #153, e/ San Ignacio y Mercaderes, tel. 07/860-9530, from CUC115 s, CUC175 d low season, from CUC140 s, CUC230 d high season), one block west of Plaza de Armas, lets you rest your head where Ernest Hemingway found inspiration in the 1930s. The hotel offers 59 overpriced rooms and three junior suites arranged atrium style. Most are small, dark, and undistinguished. Those facing the interior courtyard are quieter. Avoid the fifth floor—a thoroughfare for sightseers.

On the harborfront, **Hotel Armadores de Santander** (Luz #4, esq. San Pedro, tel. 07/862-8000, from CUC115 s, CUC175 d low season, from CUC140 s, CUC230 d high season, CUC300 s/d suite year-round) has 39 spacious rooms with colonial tile floors and handsome furnishings. A contemporary suite boasts a whirlpool tub in the center of a mezzanine bedroom with a four-poster bed.

A fine colonial conversion, the romantic **Hotel Palacio O'Farrill** (Cuba #102, esq. Chacón, tel. 07/860-5080, from CUC115 s, CUC175 d low season, from CUC140 s, CUC230 d high season) is centered on a three-story atrium courtyard lit by a skylight. It has 38 graciously furnished rooms on three floors, with decor reflecting the 18th (mezzanine), 19th (3rd floor), and 20th (4th floor) centuries. Facilities include a cybercafé, an elegant restaurant, and a jazz café.

Dating to 1905, ★ **Hotel Raquel** (San Ignacio, esq. Amargura, tel. 07/860-8280, from CUC115 s, CUC175 d low season, from CUC145 s, CUC230 d high season, including breakfast) is a dramatic exemplar of art nouveau style. The lobby gleams with marble columns and period detailing such as Tiffany lamps and a mahogany bar. It has an elegant restaurant and a rooftop solarium and gym. Located on the edge of the old Jewish quarter, the Hotel Raquel is Jewish themed and the restaurant serves kosher food.

City slickers will love the urbane sophistication of the stylish, 27-room **Hotel Palacio del Marqués de San Felipe y Santiago de Bejucal** (Calle Oficios #152, esq. Mercaderes, tel. 07/864-9194, from CUC145 s, CUC230 d low season, from CUC170 s, CUC280 d high season), on Plaza de San Francisco. The converted 1771 mansion of Don Sebastián de Peñalver blends a chic 21st-century interior—including dark mahogany in a sleek reception area—with a baroque exterior. Rooms (including three suites) have Wi-Fi, DVDs, and flat-screen TVs, plus Jacuzzis.

Entered via giant brass-studded carriage doors, ★ **Hotel Conde de Villanueva** (Mercaderes #202, esq. Lamparilla, tel. 07/862-9293, from

CUC115 s, CUC175 d low season, from CUC140 s, CUC230 d high season) is an exquisite conversion of the mansion of the Conde de Villanueva. Doors open to an intimate courtyard with caged birds and tropical foliage. It has nine large and simply appointed rooms and one suite (with whirlpool tub) with 1920s reproduction furnishings. There's an excellent restaurant and bar. The hotel courts cigar smokers with a cigar store and smokers' lounge.

★ **Hotel Florida** (Obispo #252, esq. Cuba, tel. 07/862-4127, from CUC115 s, CUC175 d low season, from CUC140 s, CUC230 d high season) is built around an atrium courtyard with rattan lounge chairs, a stained glass skylight, and black-and-white checkered marble floors. Sumptuously furnished, its 25 rooms feature tasteful colonial decor. Immediately behind the hotel, and part of the same building, is the similarly priced **Hotel Marqués de Prado Ameno** (Obispo #252, esq. Cuba, tel. 07/862-4127). The restored 18th-century mansion has 16 stylishly furnished rooms. A *bodega* (colonial-style bar/restaurant) will whisk you back 200 years.

On Parque Central, **Hotel Telégrafo** (Paseo de Martí #408, esq. Neptuno, tel. 07/861-1010, from CUC115 s, CUC175 d low season, from CUC140 s, CUC230 d high season) melds its classical elements into an exciting contemporary vogue. It has 63 rooms with beautiful furnishings and trendy color schemes. The hip lobby bar is skylit within an atrium framed by colonial ruins.

Perhaps the best hotel in Havana for its combination of location, service, and sophistication, the ★ **Hotel Iberostar Parque Central** (Neptuno, e/ Prado y Zulueta, tel. 07/860-6627, www.iberostar.com, from CUC235 s, CUC295 d year-round) occupies the north side of Parque Central and fuses colonial and contemporary styles in its 281 spacious and tastefully furnished rooms. Ask for a room with a wooden floor, as some rooms with carpets smell mildewed. It has two restaurants, a cigar lounge-bar, a business center, a rooftop swimming pool, and a fitness room. A modern 150-room annex, the similarly priced **Iberostar Parque Central Torre,** offers far hipper decor and postmodern design. It also has a rooftop restaurant and pool.

The finest rooms in Havana are at the ★ **Hotel Saratoga** (Paseo de Martí #603, esq. Dragones, tel. 07/868-1000, www.hotel-saratoga.com, CUC284 s/d low season, from CUC506 s/d high season). European architects and designers have turned this colonial edifice into a visual stunner. Guest room decor varies from colonially inspired to thoroughly contemporary. Most rooms have king-size four-poster beds; all have halogen-lit bathrooms and 21st-century amenities. A rooftop pool, spa, and gym offer fabulous views. The bar and restaurant are New York-chic.

The ultra-deluxe ★ **Gran Hotel Kempinski Manzana** (Agramonte esq. Neptuno, www.kempinski.com, from CUC370 s/d low seasn, CUC499 s/d high season) is *the* place to bed down in town. Located in the reconstructed Edificio Manzana de Gómez (dating from 1918) on Parque Central, the 24-room hotel is managed by Swiss hotel group Kempinski and features a rooftop terrace with a swimming pool, plus three restaurants, a spa, and a business center.

The formerly grandiose building at the corner of Prado and Capdevila lay in ruins for two decades, its facade supported by scaffolding. In 2016, Cuba's Gaviota group began building a new hotel there integrated into the century-old facade. At press time, it was nearing completion as the 300-room deluxe **Hotel Packard** (www.gaviota-grupo.com).

CENTRO HABANA
Casas Particulares

In a townhouse overlooking the Malecón, **Casa de Martha y Leona** (Malecón #115, e/ Crespo y Genios, tel. 07/864-1582, leorangisbert@yahoo.es, CUC25) has a loft room that overlooks the family lounge with floor-to-ceiling windows with ocean views. Although simply furnished, the air-conditioned room has a modern bathroom, fridge, and fan.

For boutique chic, check into the appropriately named ★ **Casa Blanca** (Malecón #413 e/ Manrique y Perseverancia, tel. 07/862-3137, www.casa-blancacuba.net, CUC35-50), which has all-white decor and European furnishings. It has three rooms, each with a balcony overlooking the Atlantic.

Casa 1932 Habana (Campanario #63, e/ Lagunas y San Lázaro, tel. 07/863-6203, www.casahabana.net, CUC30-35) is an art deco wonder with an antique-filled lounge. There are three bedrooms, all with private bathrooms and hot water. Enjoy coffee or cocktails on the exquisite patio.

Party animals stumbling out of Casa de las Américas in the wee hours will appreciate bedding down at **Casa Elaine González López** (Galiano #257 Apt. 81, e/ Neptuno y Concordia, tel. 07/866-0910 or 5273-9295), on the 8th floor of Edificio América. Choose either a large single bedroom (CUC25-30) with modern bathroom or the entire floor as a two-bedroom apartment (CU50); the lounge has heaps of light and great views toward Vedado.

Perfect for families and small groups, the luxurious and self-contained ★ **Casa Concordia** (Concordia #151, Apt. B, esq. San Nicolás, tel. 5254-5240 or 5360-5300, www.casaconcordia.net, from CUC240 nightly) is furnished to boutique hotel standards. This gorgeous fifth-floor, three-bedroom apartment is adorned with fine-art ceramics and photography, a 32-inch flat-screen TV and other modern accoutrements, plus plush linens, including in the en suite bathrooms. The rate includes maid service, and breakfast and car transfers are offered. The same owners offer a homier one-room unit at the nearby **Tropicana Penthouse** (Galiano #60 Apt 101, e/ San Lázaro y Trocadero, www.tropicanapenthouse.com, CUC50), with modern furnishings, flat-screen TV, breakfast service, and a terrace atop a 10-story apartment block.

Bringing chic to a whole new level is the boutique ★ **Malecón 633** (Malecón #633 e/ Escobar y Lealtad, tel. 5840-5403, www.malecon663.com, CUC50). Its four rooms are individually themed: the Eclectic Room evokes sumptuous centenary art nouveau; fans of art deco get the bi-level Art Deco Room with mezzanine bedroom; the Modern Room is furnished in 1950s style; and the Contemporary Suite offers a 21st-century take. You even get a Jacuzzi in the rooftop solarium. If midnight hunger pangs strike, downstairs is the eponymous tapas bar-restaurant. (Hopefully the music won't disturb your sweet dreams.) Owners Orlandito (Cuban) and Sandra (French) also offer vintage car tours. A stone's throw away, the three-bedroom ★ **Malecón 215** (Malecón #215 esq. Escobar, tel. 5319-7569, CUC295) inspires oohs and aahs with its sumptuous remake. It has terrazo floors, gorgeous furnishings, and a to-die-for ocean view. It rents in entirety.

Hotels
CUC100-200

A stylish boutique option, the ultra-contemporary 14-room **Hotel Terral** (Malecón, esq. Lealtad, tel. 07/860-2100, comercial@hotelterral.co.cu, from CUC850 s, CUC130 d low season, CUC110 s, CUC175 d high season) opens onto the Malecón and features glass walls and heaps of travertine and stainless steel. Flat-screen TVs, minibars, and safes are standard, as are spa tubs. Some rooms have terraces. It has a bar, plus room service, but no restaurant.

VEDADO AND PLAZA DE LA REVOLUCIÓN
Casas Particulares

★ **Casa de Jorge Coalla Potts** (Calle I #456, Apto. 11, e/ 21 y 23, Vedado, tel. 07/832-9032 or 07/5283-1237, www.havanaroomrental.com, CUC30-35) is my favorite *casa particular* in Havana. This delightful home is run by Jorge and his wife, Marisel, who offer two large, well-lit, and well-furnished bedrooms to the rear of their spotless ground-floor apartment, only two blocks from the Hotel Habana Libre Tryp. Each room has a telephone, refrigerator, double bed with firm mattress, ceiling fan, and spacious bathroom with plentiful hot water. There's a TV lounge with rockers, plus secure parking nearby. The couple and their daughter Jessica (fluent in English) go out of their way to make you feel at home.

I've enjoyed stays with Jorge Praga and Amparo Sánchez at **Casa Fraga** (Calle 11 #452 alto, e/ E y F, tel. 07/832-7184, amparosanchezg@hotmail.com, CUC35), where you are treated like family. They rent four rooms (two share a bathroom). One has lovely antique furnishings. Plus you can use their computer with Internet. A sparsely furnished lounge looks onto the street.

The filling breakfasts—including crêpes with honey—are reason enough to choose **Casa de Eddy Gutiérrez** (Calle 21 #408, e/ F y G, tel. 07/832-5207 or 5281-0041, carmeddy2@yahoo.es, CUC35). Four independent apartments are to the rear of the owner's colonial mansion, including a lovely little cross-ventilated rooftop unit. All have fans and refrigerators. One apartment has its own small kitchen. There's secure parking.

A true standout, ★ **Casa Marta** (Av. de los Presidentes #301, e/ 17 y 19, tel. 07/832-6475, www.casamartainhavana.com, CUC40) is a sensational four-room apartment that takes up the entire 14th floor and boasts wraparound glass windows. The beautifully maintained and spacious rooms feature antique beds and modern bathrooms, and all have spectacular views. Martha is an engaging conversationalist who speaks fluent English. She also offers an impeccably maintained 10th-floor self-contained two-bedroom apartment nearby (Calle 9 #453 e/ F y G, CUC60-70).

One block away from Hotel Presidente, ★ **Casa Nieves** (Calle 9na #485 altos e/ F y F, tel. 07/832-2974, CUC175 s/d) offers boutique hotel ambience. Graced with a delightful hostess, this spacious and airy four-bedroom upstairs manse opens to a lovely courtyard where delicious meals are served. It has been thoroughly renovated with modern bathrooms and consistent hot water.

A delightful hostess adds to your stay at **Casa Elaine Colonial Guesthouse** (Av. de los Presidentes esq. 13, tel. 07/832-4108 or 5275-1876, travelcuba73@yahoo.com, CUC35), a huge centenary home with lofty ceilings and twin lounges with eclectic furnishings. Elaine rents five large rooms, each different in style.

Casa Blanca (Calle 13 #917, e/ 6 y 8, tel. 07/833-5697, cb1917@hotmail.com, CUC30), in the heart of western Vedado, is a gracious colonial home with a front garden riotous with bougainvillea. Your host, Jorge, rents two antique-filled rooms with clean, modern bathrooms. It has parking.

"Palatial" sums up the 1915 ★ **Palacete de Vedado** (Calle D #154 e/ Linea y Calzada, www.palacetedelvedado.com, CUC400), a fully restored, two-story, four-bedroom manse tastefully furnished in white with cutting-edge art and boutique-hotel-standard bathrooms. There's even a pool table! The owners offer airport pickup in an old Chevy. It rents in entirety. A stone's throw away, ★ **Hostal Boutique Maraby** (Calle 11 #513, tel. 07/833-6276, www.mariby.com, from CUC230 suites, CUC500 entire house) taps the high-end market with uniformed staff and stunning and vibrant period decor. This romantic time warp is run to professional standards as a five-bedroom boutique B&B. There's a reason haute couture designer Jean Paul Gaultier stayed here.

For a room with a view, you can't beat the sensational (albeit pricey) ★ **Habana Vista Penthouse** (Calle 13 #51 es. N, tel. 5388-7866, www.habanavista.com, CUC115-135). It occupies two floors atop a 16-story 1950s high-rise and is accessed by elevator. Three bedrooms have views, retro-themed furnishings fit for a fashion shoot, and modern marble-clad bathrooms and tubs. It even boasts a private rooftop swimming pool and dining terrace for meals prepared by the kitchen staff. Two-night minimum.

Setting an even higher bar is ★ **Artedel Luxury Penthouse** (Calle 17 #260 e/ I y J, tel. 5295-5700, www.cubaguesthouse.com, CUC120), a three-room high-rise owned by Ydalgo Martínez. The eclectic furnishings are its real charm and include original 1950s lamps and Murano glass items. The suite with a blood-red wall is simply gorgeous. A rooftop wraparound terrace with 360 views will have you blessing your fortune.

Could *this* be the nicest place in Vedado? ★ **Solinos y Yo** (Calle 16 #2, e/ Calzada y Linea, tel. 07/329-9933, www.solinosyyo.com, CUC90), overlooking the Malecón at the far west end of Veado, combines jaw-dropping white-and-salmon decor with superb ocean vistas. With six air-conditioned and sparse yet lovingly furnished bedrooms, it's perfect for families or small groups. The highlight is the huge lounge with an all-glass wall opening onto a seafront balcony. It's staffed and operates like a B&B.

Want to know what $1,000 a night buys you in Havana's new deluxe private property stakes? Then rent the rooftop apartment in the sleek 10-story high-rise at **Atlantic Penthouse** (Calle D, e/ 1ra y 2ra, tel. 5281-7751, renta.atlantic@gmail.com, from CUC200 s/d), with its chic and luxurious all-white interiors and wall-of-glass vistas over the city and Atlantic. You even get your own rooftop swimming pool with butler service.

Hotels
CUC50-100
Hotel Complejo Vedado St. John's (Calle O #206, e/ 23 y 25, tel. 07/833-3740, www.gran-caribe.cu, CUC48 s, CUC70 d low season, CUC56 s, CUC82 d high season) is a dour and gloomy 14-story property with 87 rooms, plus 203 rooms in the adjoining Hotel Vedado. Facilities include a nightclub, rooftop swimming pool, and the Steak House Toro.

A better option for budget hounds is Islazul's **Hotel Paseo Habana** (Calle 17 #618, esq. A, tel. 07/836-0810, CUC34 s, CUC45 d low season; CUC42 s, CUC55 d high season), in a restored former private mansion in a peaceful section of Vedado. It has delightfully decorated rooms with modern bathrooms at bargain prices.

CUC100-200
The art deco high-rise **Hotel Roc Presidente** (Calzada #110, esq. Av. de los Presidentes, tel. 07/855-1801, www.roc-hotels.com, from UC80 s, CUC130 d low season, CUC98 s, CUC150 d high season) was inaugurated in 1927 and retains its maroon and pink interior, with sumptuous Louis XIV-style furnishings. Now Spanish run, it has 160 spacious rooms with tasteful contemporary furnishings, including marble bathrooms. Amenities include an elegant restaurant, swimming pool, gym, and sauna.

Mobster Meyer Lansky's 23-story **Hotel Habana Riviera** (Malecón y Paseo, tel. 07/836-4051, www.gran-caribe.cu, from CUC80 s, CU125 d low season, from CUC95 s, CUC158 d high season) long ago lost its 1950s luxe but still retains its original lobby decor, with acres of marble and glass and original furnishings. The 352 spacious rooms are one by one being upgraded to modern standards; ensure you get a renovated room. It has two restaurants, a 24-hour snack bar, a swimming pool, gym, cigar store, and the Copa Room nightclub. It was being renovated at press time and will be managed by Spain's Iberostar hotel group.

The **Hotel Capri** (Calle 21, esq. M, tel. 07/839-7200 or 07/839-7257, from CUC120 s, CUC150 d low season; CUC135 s, CUC180 d high season) reopened in February 2014 after a 10-year closure. This 1950s classic has been stylishly refurbished with a retro look in classy brown and pistachio tones.

Closer inspection reveals many faults, including shoddy workmanship and pathetic lighting in guest rooms.

Almost boutique in style, the well-positioned **Hotel Victoria** (Calle 19 #101, esq. M, tel. 07/833-3510, www.gran-caribe.cu, CUC62 s, CUC85 d low season; CUC90 s, CUC133 d high season) offers 31 small rooms with antique reproduction furnishings and Internet modems. It has a small swimming pool, an intimate lobby bar, and an elegant restaurant.

OVER CUC200

Hotel Tryp Habana Libre (Calle L, e/ 23 y 25, tel. 07/834-6100, www.meliacuba.com, from CUC222 s, CUC280 d low season; from CUC288 s, CUC372 d high season), managed by Spain's Meliá, is Havana's landmark high-rise hotel. It was built in the 1950s by the Hilton chain and became a favorite of mobsters. The modernist atrium lobby with glass dome exudes a 1950s retro feel. The 533 rooms are decorated in a handsome contemporary vogue. The hotel is loaded with facilities, including a 24-hour café, four restaurants, an open-air swimming pool, a business center, underground parking, and one of Havana's best nightclubs.

The deluxe 22-story ★ **Hotel Meliá Cohiba** (Paseo, esq. 1ra, tel. 07/833-3636, www.meliacuba.com, from CUC221 s, CUC230 d low season; from CUC235 s, CUC280 d high season) has 462 spacious and elegant rooms featuring contemporary furnishings. It boasts first-rate executive services, and the magnificent swimming pool, gym, squash court, solarium, boutiques, five top-ranked restaurants, four bars, and the Habana Café nightclub combine to make this one of the city's finest hotels.

The overpriced, state-run **Hotel Nacional** (Calle O y 21, tel. 07/836-3564, www.hotelnacionaldecuba.com, from CUC338 s, CUC468 d year-round) is Havana's flagship hotel and where celebrities flock. A restoration revived much of the majesty of this eclectic 1930s gem, perched overlooking the Malecón. However, furnishings in the 475 large rooms remain dowdy;

Hotel Habana Riviera, Vedado

even the Executive Floor, with 63 specially appointed rooms and suites, has threadbare carpets and other faults. Dining is a letdown except at La Barranca, the open-air garden restaurant serving *criolla* fare. The Cabaret Parisien, the top-floor cocktail lounge, and the open-air terrace bar—perfect for enjoying a cigar and rum—are high points. Features include two swimming pools, upscale boutiques, a beauty salon, spa, tennis courts, a bank, and a business center.

PLAYA (MIRAMAR AND BEYOND)
Casas Particulares

Casa de Fernando y Egeria González (1ra #205, e/ 2 y 4, Miramar, tel. 07/203-3866, martell@alba.co.cu, CUC50) is a superb property. This gracious family home offers two spacious and airy rooms with huge and exquisite tiled bathrooms. Secure parking is available and there's a patio to the rear.

Many homes in Miramar rent out in entirety, including ★ **Casa de Elena Sánchez** (Calle 34 #714, e/ 7ma y 17, tel. 07/202-8969, gerardo@ enet.cu, CUC100), one of the nicest 1950s-style rentals in town. It has two rooms, each with TV, fridge, private hot-water bathroom, and a mix of antiques, 1950s modernist pieces, and contemporary furniture. A large TV lounge opens to a shaded garden patio with rockers. There's secure parking.

For a complete apartment, I like ★ **Casa de Reynaldo y Yasmina** (Calle 17 #3401 e/ 34 y 36, tel. 07/209-2958 or 5241-6794, CUC120), whose ground floor apartment in a lovely 1950s home has three bedrooms, two bathrooms, and a full modern kitchen. Meals can be prepared and served on a shaded rooftop terrace. Reynaldo is a fixer and even rents his chauffeured Audi A4.

The three-bedroom ★ **Cañaveral House** (Calle 39A #4402 e/ 44 y 46, tel. 07/206-5338 or 5295-5700, www.cubaguesthouse.com, CUC120) astounds with its tasteful furnishings. Designer Ydalgo Martínez brought artistic sensibility to this gorgeous Spanish-style hacienda villa, furnished with effusive art, antiques, and contemporary pieces, including the state-of-the-art bathrooms. Rented in entirety, you get what you pay for in spades.

If you want to know how Cuba's elite lives, check out **Casa María Torralbas** (Calle 17 #20606, e/ 206 y 214, Siboney, tel. 07/217-2248 or 5258-5025, mariatorralbas@yahoo.es, CUC55), a gorgeous 1950s modernist bungalow in an area occupied by privileged MININT families. Two beautifully furnished rooms include use of a swimming pool in a lush garden.

Exemplary of the deluxe new breed of villas on the market, ★ **Villa Miller Benfast** (Calle 13 #2017 esq. 204, Siboney, tel. 07/2721-5314 or 5280-7636, CUC850 nightly) is a refurbished 1950s modernist gem with six bedrooms in two wings spanning a huge lounge and state-of-the-art kitchen. A lap pool graces the garden. You even get a well-equipped gym and a poolside lounge bar. It comes fully staffed.

A stunner worthy of *Vogue,* ★ **VIP Le Blanc** (Calle 92 #508 e/ 5ta y 5taA, Miramar, tel. 07/212-5436, www.espacios-de-lujo.com, CUC175 s/d) serves travelers with a taste for high living. Run as a deluxe boutique hotel, this six-bedroom villa is fully staffed with a concierge. Rooms include updated, en-suite baths and Wi-Fi. There's a pool with lounge chairs and a staffed bar plus an on-site chef. Children under age 12 are not permitted.

Out in Santa Fe, **Casa Isabel Betancourt** (Calle 1ra #29628 e/ 296 y 298, tel. 07/208-5070 or 5270-4042, CUC20-40) offers a beachfront location in a beautiful coral stone house with a TV lounge and two lovely rooms. For something more upscale, **Villa Yanin** (Av. 3ra A, www.airbnb.com/rooms/11453585, CUC500), in Cayito de Jaimanitas, offers an oceanfront swimming pool with *ranchón* bar, Jacuzzi, and sundeck. The four-bedroom villa is owned by an Italian-Cuban couple (Marco and Yanin) and has been upgraded with gorgeous terrazzo tile bathrooms. It's steps from Fusterlandia and Marina Hemingway and rents in entirety.

Though out of the way in southern La Vibora, the hilltop ★ **La Rosa de Ortega** (Patrocino #252 esq. Juan Bruno Zayas, tel. 07/641-4329 or 5246-4574, www.larosadeortega.com, CUC60-150) is irresistible for its magical ambience. Exposed brick abounds in this rambling Tuscan-like villa with romantic furnishings, city views, a swimming pool, and a Ford Model A in the driveway. One of the three sumptuously appointed rooms is a suite.

Hotels
CUC50-100

Hotel Kohly (Av. 49 y 36A, Rpto. Kohly, Playa, tel. 07/204-0240, www.gaviota-grupo.com, CUC48 s, CUC66 d low season, CUC58 s, CUC86 d) is a 1970s-style property used by budget tour groups, despite its out-of-the-way location. The 136 rooms have tasteful albeit simple furniture. Facilities include a 10-pin bowling alley.

The lonesome **Hotel Chateau Miramar** (1ra Av., e/ 60 y 62, tel. 07/204-1952, www.hotelescubanacan.com, from CUC72 s, CUC94 d year-round), on the shorefront, aims at business clientele. The handsome five-story hotel has 50 nicely furnished rooms (suites have whirlpool tubs), a pool, an elegant restaurant, and a business center. It's a 20-minute walk to several fine *paladares*.

CUC100-200

The Spanish-managed **Memories Miramar** (5ta Av., e/ 72 y 76, tel. 07/204-3584, www.memoriesresorts.com, from CUC120 s, CUC150 d low season, from CUC170 s, CUC200 d high season) lives up to its deluxe billing. This vast modern property features a mix of neoclassical wrought-iron furniture and hip contemporary pieces in the marble-clad lobby. Its 427 cavernous rooms include five wheelchair-accessible rooms. It has a beauty salon, squash court, health center, tennis courts, a business center, three restaurants, and a huge swimming pool.

Used principally by package-tour groups, the mid-priced oceanfront **Hotel Copacabana** (1ra Av., e/ 34 y 36, tel. 07/204-1037, www.hotelescubanacan.com, CUC90 s, CU110 d low season, CUC128 s, CUC150 d high season) has 168 rooms with a quasi-colonial and slightly dated look; however, its modern bathrooms gleam. Its strong suit is its swimming pool (popular with locals on weekends; day pass CUC15) and a disco.

The 1950s-era beachfront **Hotel Comodoro** (1ra Av. y Calle 84, tel. 07/204-5551, www.hotelescubanacan.com, from CUC60 s, CUC92 d low season, from CUC80 s, CUC130 d high season) has 134 spacious rooms, including 15 suites, with modern furnishings. Some rooms have a balcony. The contemporary lobby lounge opens to four restaurants, several bars, and a meager bathing area. A shuttle runs to Habana Vieja five times daily. The Comodoro's **Bungalows Pleamar** are the closest thing to a beach resort in the city. The 320 two-story villas (one-, two-, and three-bedroom) are built around two sinuous swimming pools.

OVER CUC200
Facing the Miramar Trade Center, **Hotel Meliá Habana** (3ra Av., e/ 76 y 80, tel. 07/204-8500, www.meliacuba.com, from CUC344 s, CUC361 d low season, from CUC475 s, CUC513 d high season), with its huge atrium lobby, is a superb hotel that aims at a business clientele. The 397 marble-clad rooms and four suites are suitably deluxe; the executive floor offers more personalized service plus data ports. Facilities include five restaurants, a cigar lounge, a swimming pool, tennis courts, a gym, and a business center.

With a blue-tinted glass exterior, the contemporary **H10 Panorama** (Calle 70, esq. 3ra, tel. 07/204-0100, www.10hotels.com, from CUC148 s, CUC211 d low season, from CUC204 s, CUC208 d high season) high-rise boasts an impressive black-and-gray marble and slate atrium lobby. I like the sophisticated decor in its 317 rooms, all with Internet modems. The executive rooms and suites get their own top-floor restaurant, and floors 7-11 have Wi-Fi. Other facilities include a piano bar, squash court, an Internet room, Italian- and German-themed restaurants, a swimming pool, and a top-floor piano bar with live jazz.

U.S. hospitality company Starwood took over management of the former Hotel Quinta Avenida in 2016, rebranding it the **Four Points by Sheraton** (5ta Av. e/ 76 y 78, tel. 07/214-1470, from CUC196 s, CUC246 d low season, from CUC333 s, CUC384 high season). It's a pleasant enough place and offers plenty of facilities plus 186 rooms, including six suites, but is hugely overpriced.

ACROSS THE HARBOR
★ **Casa Blanca** (Casa #29, tel. 5294-5397, www.havanacasablanca.com, CUC250) is a great *casa particular* near the El Morro Cabaña complex. This restored, two-bedroom 19th-century villa rents in entirety. It has a pool, shady terraces opening to lovely gardens, and maid service, including for meals.

Information and Services

MONEY

Banks and Exchange Agencies

The **Banco Financiero Internacional** (Mon.-Fri. 8am-3pm, 8am-noon only on the last working day of each month) is the main bank, with eight branches throughout Havana, including one in Edificio Jerusalem in the **Miramar Trade Center** (3ra Av., e/ 70 y 82, Miramar). Its main outlet, in the **Hotel Tryp Habana Libre** (Calle L, e/ 23 y 25, tel. 07/838-4429), has a desk handling credit card advances for foreigners. The Banco de Crédito y Comercio (Bandec), Banco Internacional de Comercio, Banco Popular, and Banco Metropolitano also serve foreigners.

The foreign exchange agency **Cadeca** (Obispo, e/ Cuba y Aguiar, Habana Vieja, tel. 07/866-4152, daily 8am-10pm) has outlets throughout the city, including most hotels.

ATMs

ATMs allowing cash advances of Cuban convertible pesos from Visa cards (but not MasterCard or U.S.-issued Visa cards) are located at **Cadeca** (Obispo, e/ Cuba y Aguiar, Habana Vieja, tel. 07/866-4152, daily 8am-10pm) and major banks.

COMMUNICATIONS

Post Offices and Mail Service

Most major tourist hotels have small post offices and will accept your mail for delivery. In Habana Vieja, there are post offices on the east side of Plaza de la Catedral; at Obispo #102, on the west side of Plaza de San Francisco (Mon.-Fri. 8am-6pm); at Obispo #518; and next to the Gran Teatro on Parque Central.

In Vedado, there's a 24-hour post office in the lobby of the **Hotel Tryp Habana Libre** (Calle L, e/ 23 y 25). Havana's main post office is **Correos de Cuba** (tel. 07/879-6824, 24 hours) on Avenida Rancho Boyeros, one block north of the Plaza de la Revolución.

Servi-Postal (Havana Trade Center, 3ra Av., e/ 76 y 80, Miramar, tel. 07/204-5122, Mon.-Sat. 10am-6pm) has a copy center and Western Union agency.

DHL (1ra Av. y Calle 26, Miramar, tel. 07/204-1578, commercial@dhl.cutisa.cu, Mon.-Fri. 8am-8pm, Sat. 8:30am-4pm) is headquartered at Edificio Habana in the Miramar Trade Center (3ra Av., e/ 76 y 80, Miramar).

Telephone and Fax Service

Etecsa is headquartered on the east side of Edificio Barcelona at **Miramar Trade Center** (3ra Av., e/ 76 y 80, Miramar). The main international telephone exchange is in the lobby of the **Hotel Habana Libre Tryp** (Calle L, e/ 23 y 25, tel. 07/834-6100, 24 hours).

You can rent or buy cellular phones from **Cubacel** (Calle 28 #510, e/ 5
y 7, Miramar, tel. 05/264-2266 or 07/880-2222, www.cubacel.com, Mon.-
Fri. 8:30am-7:30pm, Sat. 8am-noon); they can also activate your own cell
phone for CUC40. The main Havana office is in Edificio Santa Clara in the
Miramar Trade Center (3ra Av., e/ 70 y 82).

Internet Access
Internet access has expanded markedly since 2015. Wi-Fi is installed in
most tourist hotels and public Wi-Fi zones are along Paseo de Martí and
Parque Central (Habana Vieja); Parque Trillo (Centro Habana); La Rampa,
Linea y L, and Parque John Lennon (Vedado); and Av. 1ra y 42 and Parque
13 y 76 (Miramar). In 2016, the government announced that it will create
the world's largest Wi-Fi zone the length of the Malecón. In 2017, another
47 public Wi-Fi zones were added. Users must buy a prepaid "Nauta" card
(CUC2.50 or CUC6-10 for one hour at some deluxe hotels).

The main **Etecsa** outlets are in Habana Vieja (Obispo, esq. Habana, tel.
07/866-0089, daily 8:30am-9pm); at Calle 17 (e/ B y C) and Edificio Focsa
(Calle M, e/ 17 y 19), in Vedado; and on the west side of Edificio Barcelona,
at the Miramar Trade Center.

The **Hotel Nacional** (Calle O y 21, tel. 07/836-3564, daily 8am-8pm)
and **Hotel Habana Libre Tryp** (Calle L, e/ 23 y 25, tel. 07/834-6100, daily
7am-11pm) charge CUC10 for Wi-Fi access.

Students at the Universidad de la Habana have free Internet service in
the **Biblioteca Central** (San Lázaro, esq. Ronda, tel. 07/878-5573), at the
faculty of Artes y Letras (you need to sign up the day before), and at the
faculty of Filosofía y Historia, with long lines for use.

GOVERNMENT OFFICES
Immigration and Customs
Requests for visa extensions (*prórrogas*) and other immigration issues relating to foreigners are handled by **Inmigración** (Calle 17 e/ J y K, Vedado,
tel. 07/836-7832 or 07/861-3462, Mon.-Wed. and Fri. 8:30am-4pm, Thurs.
and Sat. 8:30am-11am); you need CUC25 of stamps purchased at any bank,
plus proof of medical insurance and airline reservation to exit. Journalists
and others requiring special treatment are handled by the **Ministerio de
Relaciones Exteriores** (Ministry of Foreign Relations, Calzada #360, e/ G
y H, Vedado, tel. 07/830-9775, www.cubaminrex.cu).

The main customs office is on Avenida del Puerto, opposite Plaza de
San Francisco.

Consulates and Embassies
The following nations have embassies/consulates in Havana. Those of other
countries can be found in the local telephone directory under *Embajadas*.

- **Australia:** c/o Canadian Embassy
- **Canada:** Calle 30 #518, esq. 7ma, Miramar, tel. 07/204-2516

- **United Kingdom:** Calle 34 #702, e/ 7ma y 17-A, Miramar, tel. 07/204-1771

- **United States:** Calzada, e/ L y M, Vedado, tel. 07/833-3551 or 07/833-3559, emergency/after hours tel. 07/833-3026, http://havana.usembassy.gov

MAPS AND TOURIST INFORMATION
Information Bureaus

Infotur (tel. 07/204-0624, www.infotur.cu), the government tourist information bureau, has nine outlets in Havana, including in the arrivals lounges at José Martí International Airport (Terminal Three, tel. 07/266-4094, 24 hours) and at the Terminal de Cruceros (Cruise Terminal), plus the following outlets in Havana (daily 8:30am-8:30pm):

- Calle Obispo, e/ Bernazas y Villegas, Habana Vieja, tel. 07/866-3333

- Calle Obispo, esq. San Ignacio, Habana Vieja, tel. 07/863-6884

- Calle 23 e/ L y M, Vedado, tel. 07/832-9288

- 5ta Avenida, esq. Calle 112, Miramar, tel. 07/204-3977

MEDICAL SERVICES

Most large tourist hotels have nurses on duty. Other hotels will be able to request a doctor for in-house diagnosis.

Hospitals

Tourists needing medical assistance are steered to the **Clínica Internacional Cira García** (Calle 20 #4101, esq. Av. 41, Miramar, tel. 07/204-2811, www.cirag.cu, 24 hours), a full-service hospital dedicated to serving foreigners. It's the finest facility in Cuba.

The **Centro Internacional Oftalmológica Camilo Cienfuegos** (Calle L, e/ Línea y 13, Vedado, tel. 07/832-5554) specializes in eye disorders but also offers a range of medical services.

Pharmacies

Local pharmacies serving Cubans are meagerly stocked. For homeopathic remedies try **Farmacia Ciren** (Calle 216, esq. 11B, Playa, tel. 07/271-5044).

Your best bets are the *farmacias internacionales,* stocked with imported medicines. They're located at the **Hotel Sevilla** (Prado esq Zulueta, tel. 07/861-5703, daily 8:30am-7:30pm), **Hospital Camilo Cienfuegos** (Calle L, e/ Línea y 13, Vedado, tel. 07/832-5554, cirpcc@infomed.sid.cu, daily 8am-8pm), the **Galería Comercial Habana Libre** (Calle 25 y L, Vedado, Mon.-Sat. 10am-7:30pm), the **Clínica Internacional Cira García** (Calle 20 #4101, esq. Av. 41, Miramar, tel. 07/204-2880, 24 hours), the **Farmacia Internacional** (Av. 41, esq. 20, Miramar, tel. 07/204-2051, daily 8:30am-8:30pm), and in the Edificio Habana at the **Miramar Trade Center** (3ra Av., e/ 76 y 80, Miramar, tel. 07/204-4515, Mon.-Fri. 8am-6pm).

Ópticas Miramar (Neptuno #411, e/ San Nicolás y Manrique, Centro Habana, tel. 07/863-2161, and 7ma Av., e/ Calle 24 y 26, Miramar, tel. 07/204-2990) provides services.

SAFETY

Havana is amazingly safe, and tourist zones are patrolled by police officers 24/7. Still, Havana is not entirely safe. Most crime is opportunistic, and thieves seek easy targets. Centro Habana is a center for street crime against tourists.

Avoid *all* dark back streets at night, especially those in southern Habana Vieja and Centro Habana, and anywhere in the Cerro district and other slum districts or wherever police are not present (these areas can be unsafe by day). I was mugged on a main street in Centro in broad daylight.

Beyond Habana Vieja, most parks should be avoided at night. Be cautious and circumspect of all *jineteros*.

PRACTICALITIES
Haircuts

For a clean cut, head to **ArteCorte** (Calle Aguiar #10, e/ Peña Pobre y Avenida de los Misiones, Habana Vieja, tel. 07/861-0202), on "Hairdressers' Alley." The fun, offbeat setting full of amazingly eclectic art and barber-related miscellany is unique. Or try **Salón Correo Barbería** (Brasil, e/ Oficios y Mercaderes, Habana Vieja, Mon.-Sat. 8am-6pm), an old-style barbershop. I use **Olimpo Salón** (tel. 07/860-6627, ext. 1960, or 5273-1371), in the basement of the Hotel Parque Central Torre.

Laundry

In Miramar, **Aster Lavandería** (Calle 34 #314, e/ 3ra y 5ta, Miramar, tel. 07/204-1622, Mon.-Fri. 8am-5pm, Sat. 8am-noon) has a wash-and-dry service (CUC3 per load) and dry cleaning (CUC2 for pants, CUC1.50 for shirts for three-day service; more for same-day service). There's also a laundry in the **Complejo Comercial Comodoro** (3ra Av., esq. 84, tel. 07/204-5551).

Legal Services

Consultoría Jurídica Internacional (CJI, International Judicial Consultative Bureau, Calle 16 #314, e/ 3ra y 5ta, Miramar, tel. 07/204-2490) provides legal services, as does the **Bufete Internacional** (5ta Av. esq. 40, Miramar, tel. 07/204-436, bufete@bufeteinternacional.cu).

Libraries

The **Biblioteca Nacional** (National Library, Av. de la Independencia, esq. 20 de Mayo, tel. 07/881-5442, www.bnjm.cu, Mon.-Fri. 8:15am-6pm, Sat. 8:15am-4pm), on the east side of Plaza de la Revolución, has about 500,000 texts. Getting access, however, is another matter. Five categories of individuals are permitted to use the library, including students and professionals, but not lay citizens. Foreigners can obtain a library card valid for one year (CUC3) if they have a letter from a sponsoring Cuban government agency and/or ID establishing academic credentials, plus two photographs and a passport, which you need to hand over whenever you wish to consult books. The antiquated, dilapidated file system makes research a Kafkaesque experience. There is no open access to books. Instead, individuals must request a specific work, which is then brought to you; your passport or (for Cubans) personal ID is recorded along with the purpose of your request.

The Universidad de la Habana, in Vedado, has several libraries, including the **Biblioteca Central** (San Lázaro, esq. Ronda, tel. 07/878-5573 or 07/878-3951).

The **Biblioteca Provincial de la Habana** (Obispo, Plaza de Armas, tel. 07/862-9035, Mon.-Fri. 8:15am-7pm, Sat. 8:15am-4:30pm) is a meagerly stocked affair. It's closed the first Monday of each month.

Cuba Libro (Calle 24, esq. 19, Vedado, tel. 07/830-5205, Mon.-Sat. 10am-8pm), a small English-language bookstore, café, and literary salon, has a shaded patio to enjoy the company of expat literati.

Toilets

The only modern public toilet to Western standards is on the ground floor of the Lonja del Comercio, **Plaza de Armas.** Most hotels and restaurants will let you use their facilities. An attendant usually sits outside the door dispensing a few sheets of toilet paper for pocket change (also note the bowl with a few coins, which is meant to invite a tip).

Transportation

GETTING THERE AND AWAY

Air

José Martí International Airport (switchboard tel. 07/266-4644) is 25 kilometers southwest of downtown Havana, in the Wajay district. It has five terminals spaced well apart and accessed by different roads (nor are they linked by a connecting bus service).

Terminal One: This terminal (tel. 07/275-1200) serves domestic flights.

Terminal Two: Charter flights and other select flights from the Caribbean, South America, and Europe arrive at Terminal Two. Occasionally other flights pull in here, although outbound flights will invariably depart Terminal Three.

Terminal Three: All international flights, including United States-Havana flights, arrive at Terminal Three (tel. 07/642-6225 or 07/266-4133 for arrivals and departures) on the north side of the airport. Immigration proceedings are slow. Beware porters who grab your bags outside; they'll expect a tip for hauling your bag the few meters to a taxi. A 24-hour Infotur (tel. 07/266-4094) tourist information office is outside the customs lounge.

Check in here if you have prepaid vouchers for transfers into town. A foreign exchange counter is also outside the customs lounge.

Terminal Four: This terminal is for cargo.

Terminal Five: Aero Caribbean flights arrive here, as do private planes. It has taxi service and car rental offices.

In 2016, the Cuban government granted a French company the right to upgrade, expand, and ultimately manage the airport. A military airfield at San Antonio de los Baños is to be converted into a new terminal to handle private planes and possibly all U.S. flights (or cargo). It's one hour from downtown Havana.

DEPARTING CUBA

Since 2015 a CUC25 departure tax is included in your airline ticket price. Make sure you arrive at the correct terminal for your departure. Terminals Two and Three have **VIP lounges** (tel. 07/642-0247 or 07/642-6225, salonvip@hav.ecasa.avianet.cu, CUC25 including drinks and snacks).

Bus

There's no bus service from either of the international terminals. A public bus marked *Aeropuerto* departs from Terminal One (domestic flights) for Vedado and the east side of Parque Central in Habana Vieja. The bus is intended for Cubans, and foreigners may be refused. It runs about once every two hours. When heading to the airport, the *cola* (line) begins near the José Martí statue at Parque Central. There are two lines: one for people wishing to be seated (*sentados*) and one for those willing to stand (*de pie*). The journey costs one peso, takes about one hour, and is very unreliable.

Alternatively, you can catch **Metrobus P12** (originating in Santiago de las Vegas) or Ómnibus #480 from the east side of Avenida de la Independencia, about a 10-minute walk east of the terminal—no fun with baggage. The bus goes to Parque de la Fraternidad on the edge of Habana Vieja (20 pesos). The journey takes about one hour, but the wait can be just as long. When heading to the airport, you can catch Ómnibus #480 or Metrobus P12 from the west side of Parque de la Fraternidad (you can also get on the P12 near the Universidad de la Habana on Avenida Salvador Allende). Both go to Santiago de las Vegas via the domestic terminal (Terminal One), but they will let you off about 400 meters east of Terminal Two. Do not use this bus for the international terminal.

Taxi

Cubataxi taxis wait outside the arrivals lounges. Official rates are CUC20-25 to downtown hotels, but most drivers will not use their meter. Avoid private (illegal) taxis, as several foreigners have been robbed.

Car Rental

These companies have booths at Terminal Three: **Cubacar** (tel.

International Airline Offices in Havana

Avianca (tel. 07/833-3114, www.avianca.com) has an office in the Hotel Habana Libre Tryp (Calle L, e/ 23 y 25, Vedado). **Cayman Airways** (tel. 07/649-7644, www.caymanairways.com) is based at Terminal Two, at José Martí International Airport.

The following airlines have offices at Calle 23 #64 (e/ P y Infanta, Vedado):

- **Aerocaribbean** (tel. 07/879-7525, www.fly-aerocaribbean.com)

- **Air Canada** (tel. 07/836-3226, www.aircanada.com)

- **Air Jamaica** (tel. 07/833-2447, www.airjamaica.com)

- **Blue Panorama** (tel. 07/833-2248, www.blue-panorama.com)

- **Condor** (tel. 07/833-3859, www.condor.com)

- **Cubana** (tel. 07/834-4446/7/8/9 or 07/834-4449, www.cubana.cu)

- **Havanatur** (tel. 07/201-9800, for U.S. flights only)

- **LanChile** (tel. 07/831-6186 or 266-4990, www.lanchile.com)

- **LTU** (tel. 07/833-3524, www.ltu.com)

- **Mexicana** (tel. 07/830-9528, www.mexicana.com)

07/649-9800), **Havanautos** (tel. 07/649-5197), and **Rex** (tel. 07/266-6074). These have booths at Terminal Two: **Cubacar** (tel. 07/649-5546), **Havanautos** (tel. 07/649-5215), and **Rex** (tel. 07/649-0306).

Cruise Ship

Havana's **Terminal Sierra Maestra** (Av. del Puerto, tel. 07/862-1925) is a natty conversion of the old customs building. Passengers step through the doorways directly onto Plaza de San Francisco, in the heart of Havana.

Private Vessel

Private yachts berth at **Marina Hemingway** (Av. 5ta y Calle 248, Santa Fe, tel. 07/273-7972, www.nauticamarlin.tur.cu), 15 kilometers west of downtown. The harbor coordinates are 23° 5'N and 82° 29'W. You should announce your arrival on VHF Channel 16, HF Channel 68, and SSB 2790.

Visas are not required for stays of less than 72 hours. For longer stays you'll need a tourist card (CUC25), issued at the harbormaster's office (tel. 07/204-1150, ext. 2884) at the end of channel B. Docking fees (CUC0.35 per foot per day) include water and electricity. Gasoline and diesel are available 8am-7pm (tel. 07/204-1150, ext. 450).

The following have offices at the Miramar Trade Center (5ta Av. y 76, Miramar):

- **Aero Caribe** (Edificio Barcelona, tel. 07/873-3621)

- **Aeroflot** (tel. 07/204-3200, www.aeroflot.com)

- **Air Europa** (Edificio Santiago, tel. 07/204-6904, www.aireuropa.com)

- **Air France** (Edificio Santiago, tel. 07/206-4444, www.airfrance.com/cu)

- **American Airlines** (www.aa.com)

- **COPA** (Edificio Barcelona, tel. 07/204-1111, www.copa.com)

- **Delta** (www.delta.com)

- **Iberia** (Edificio Santiago, tel. 07/204-3460, www.iberia.com)

- **JetBlue** (www.jetblue.com)

- **KLM** (Edificio Santiago, tel. 07/206-4444, www.klm.com)

- **Virgin Atlantic** (Edificio Santa Clara, tel. 07/204-0747, www.virgin-atlantic.com)

Exploring Beyond Havana
AIR

Cubana (Calle 23 #64, e/ P y Infanta, Vedado, tel. 07/870-9430, www.cubana.cu, Mon.-Fri. 8:30am-4pm, Sat. 8am-1pm) offers service to all major Cuban cities. Most domestic flights leave from José Martí International Airport's **Terminal One** (Av. Van Troi, off Av. Rancho Boyeros, tel. 07/275-1200).

AeroGaviota (Av. 47 #2814, e/ 28 y 34, Rpto. Kohly, tel. 07/204-2621 or 07/203-0668, www.aerogaviota.com) flights depart from Aeropuerto Baracao, about three kilometers west of Marina Hemingway.

BUS

Modern **Víazul** buses (Av. 26, esq. Zoológico, Nuevo Vedado, tel. 07/881-1413 or 07/883-6092, www.viazul.com, daily 7am-9:30pm) serve provincial capitals and major tourist destinations nationwide. They depart Terminal Víazul, which has a café and free luggage storage. It does not accept reservations by telephone; you must go in person or make a reservation on the website.

Ómnibus Nacionales buses to destinations throughout the country

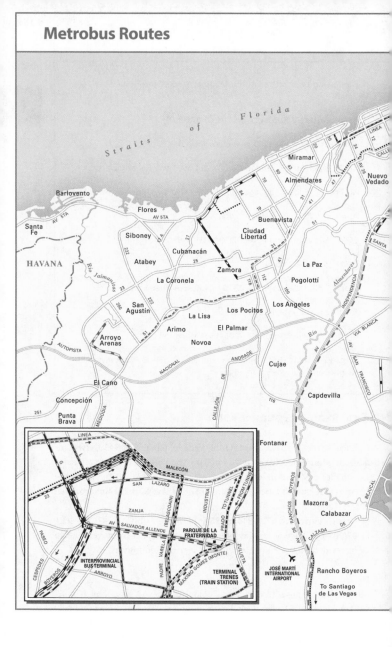

Metrobus Routes

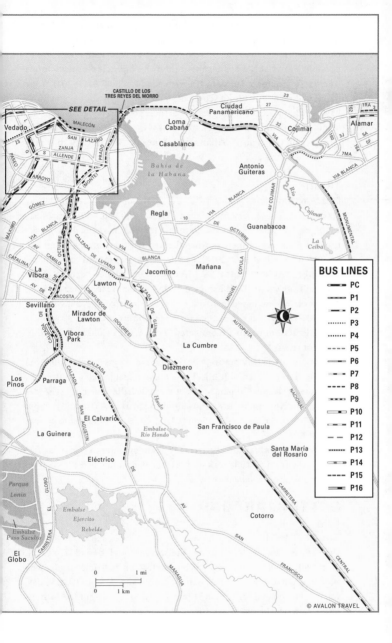

BUS LINES

- ▬ PC
- ▬ P1
- ▬ P2
- ⋯ P3
- ⋯ P4
- --- P5
- ▬ P6
- ▬ P7
- --- P8
- ▭▭ P9
- ▭▭ P10
- ▭▭ P11
- — P12
- ▭▭ P13
- ▭▭ P14
- --- P15
- ▬ P16

© AVALON TRAVEL

leave from the Terminal de Ómnibuses Nacionales. However, they do not accept foreigners, except for students with appropriate ID, who can travel like Cubans for pesos. Make your reservation as early as possible, either at the bus terminal or at the **Agencia Reservaciones de Pasaje** (Factor y Tulipán, Nuevo Vedado, tel. 07/870-9401). Your name will be added to the scores of names ahead of you. If you don't have a reservation or miss your departure, you can try getting on the standby list (*lista de espera,* tel. 07/862-4341) at **Terminal de la Última Hora** (Calle Gancedo e/ Villanueva y Linea de Ferrocarril), in southwest Habana Vieja.

TRAIN

Estación Central de Ferrocarril: The main station is the Central Railway Station (Egido, esq. Arsenal, Habana Vieja, tel. 07/861-2959 or 07/862-1920), or Terminal de Trenes. Unfortunately, Cuba's already dysfunctional system became more so when the station closed for lengthy repairs in 2015 (through at least 2018), and services were moved to **Terminal La Coubre** (Av. del Puerto, tel. 07/860-0700), 400 meters south of the main railway station (and Estación 19 de Noviembre for Pinar del Río). Tickets can be purchased up to one hour prior to departure, but you must purchase your ticket before 8pm for a nighttime departure. As soon as the main station repair is completed, Terminal La Coubre is slated to close for repair.

Estación 19 de Noviembre: Local commuter trains (*ferro-ómnibuses*) operate from this station (Calle Tulipán and Hidalgo, tel. 07/881-4431), also called Estación Tulipán, south of Plaza de la Revolución. Trains depart to San Antonio de los Baños and Rincón at 10:05am and 4:25pm (CUC1.70); to Artemisa at 5:45pm (CUC2.20); and to Batabanó at 5pm (CUC1.80).

Estación Casablanca: The Hershey Train operates to Matanzas five times daily from Casablanca's harborfront station (tel. 07/862-4888) on the north side of Havana harbor.

GETTING AROUND
Bus
TOURIST BUS

Havana has a double-decker tourist bus service, the **HabanaBusTour** (tel. 07/261-9017, daily 9am-9pm), which is perfect for first-time visitors who want to get their bearings and catch the main sights. For just CUC5 a day, you can hop on and off as many times as you wish at any of the 44 stops served by a fleet of buses covering 95 miles of route.

The T1 route (double-decker) begins on the west side of Parque Central and does a figure eight around the perimeter of Habana Vieja, and then heads through Vedado and Miramar. The T3 minibus is a great way to get out to the Playas del Este.

Havana is served by often crowded public buses, or *guaguas* (pronounced WAH-wahs). No buses operate within Habana Vieja except along the major peripheral thoroughfares.

Most buses run at least hourly during the day but on reduced schedules 11pm-5am. The standard fare for any journey throughout the city is 20 centavos, or 40 centavos on smaller buses called *ómnibuses ruteros,* which have the benefit of being uncrowded. *Taxibuses*—buses that ply a fixed, nonstop route to the airport and bus and train stations—charge one peso.

Many buses follow a loop route, traveling to and from destinations along different streets. Few routes are in a circle. (If you find yourself going in the wrong direction, don't assume that you'll eventually come around to where you want to be.) Most buses display the bus number and destination above the front window. Many buses arrive and depart from Parque Central and Parque de la Fraternidad in Habana Vieja and La Rampa (Calle 23) in Vedado, especially at Calle L and at Calzada de Infanta.

Taxi

Modern taxis serve the tourist trade while locals make do with wheezing jalopies. Hundreds of *cuentaspropistas* now offer private taxi service, and on almost any street you'll be solicited.

CUC TAXIS

The scene has been flipped on its head since 2013, when Transtur operated all *turistaxis* as **Cubataxi** (tel. 07/855-5555). Cubataxi still exists, but the taxi drivers are now self-employed and lease the vehicles, which can be hailed outside hotels or by calling for radio dispatch. Taxis range from modern Mercedes to beat-up Ladas. Only the most modern vehicles have functioning seat belts.

Some taxis are metered (CUC1 at flag drop, then CUC0.50 a kilometer);

HabanaBusTour in Habana Vieja

few drivers will use the meter, but will instead ask how much you want to pay. Alas, the U.S. tourist tsunami has inflated taxi rates. Expect to pay CUC10 between Habana Vieja and the Hotel Habana Libre Tryp, and minimum CUC12 to Miramar. Bargain the price before setting off! A light above the cab signifies if the taxi is *libre* (free).

Need a minivan? Gerardo Rojas (tel. 5273-3398) has served me well in a 13-seat Hyundai.

CLASSIC CARS

Fancy tooling around in a 1950 Studebaker or a 1959 Buick Invicta convertible? Private cars can be rented outside most major tourist hotels (CUC40-60 per hour, depending on car). **Nostalgicar** (tel 07/641-4053 or 5295-3842, www.nostalgicarcuba.com) can supply a fleet of hard-top Chevys to meet you at the airport and drive you around. **Vintage Tours** (tel. 5840-5403, www.vintagetour-cuba.com) offers tours (from CUC70 for two hours), as does **OldCarTours** (tel. 07/289-9155, www.oldcartours.com).

The state agency **Gran Car** (Calle Marino, esq. Santa María, Nuevo Vedado, tel. 07/855-5567, grancardp@transnet.cu) rents classic-car taxis for CUC30 per hour (20-km limit the first hour, with shorter limits per extra hour).

PESO TAXIS

Privately owned 1950s-era *colectivos* or *máquinas* run along fixed routes, much like buses, and charge 50 pesos for a ride anywhere along the route. Parque de las Agrimensores, on the north side of the railway station, is the official starting point for most routes. It's fun, so hop in—but don't slam the door!

colectivo taxi

Hundreds of homespun tricycle taxis with shade canopies ply the streets of Habana Vieja and Centro. The minimum fare is usually CUC2. You can go the full length of the Malecón, from Habana Vieja to Vedado, for CUC5. Always agree to a fare before setting off. These jalopies are barred from certain streets and areas, so you might end up taking a zigzag route to your destination.

COCO-TAXIS

These cutesy three-wheeled eggshells on wheels whiz around the touristed areas of Havana and charge the same as taxis. However, they are inherently unsafe.

COCHES

Horse-drawn coaches are a popular way of exploring the Malecón and Old Havana, although the buggies are barred from entering the pedestrian-only quarter. They're operated by **San Cristóbal Agencia de Viajes** (tel. 07/861-9171). Their official starting point is the junction of Empedrado and Tacón, but you can hail them wherever you see them. Others can be hailed on Parque Central, and at Plaza de la Revolución. They charge CUC10 per person for one hour.

Car

The narrow one-way streets in Habana Vieja are purgatory for vehicles. The main plazas and streets between them are barred to traffic.

A treacherously potholed four-lane freeway—the Autopista Circular (route Calle 100 or *circunvalación*)—encircles southern and eastern Havana, linking the arterial highways and separating the core from suburban Havana. The intersections are dangerous.

PARKING

A capital city without parking meters? Imagine. Parking meters were detested during the Batista era, mostly because they were a source of *botellas* (skimming) for corrupt officials. After the triumph of the Revolution, *habaneros* smashed the meters. However, the state employs *custodios* in red vests to collect fees around many parks and major streets.

Avoid No Parking zones like the plague, especially if it's an officials-only zone. Havana has an efficient towing system.

Never leave your car parked unguarded. In central Vedado, the Hotel Habana Libre Tryp has an underground car park (CUC0.60 for one hour, CUC6 max. for 24 hours).

CAR RENTAL

All hotels have car rental booths, and there are scores of outlets citywide.

Transtur (Calle L #456, e/ 25 y 27, Vedado, tel. 07/835-0000) operates the two main car rental agencies: **Cubacar** (Calle 21, e/ N y O, Vedado, Havana, tel. 07/836-4038) and **Havanautos** (tel. 07/285-0703).

Rex (tel. 07/273-9166 or 07/835-6830, www.rex.cu) employs Hyundais, VWs, and Audis and has offices at the airport; in Vedado (Malecón y Línea, tel. 07/835-7788); in Miramar at Hotel Neptuno-Triton (tel. 07/204-2213) and 5ta Av. y 92 (tel. 07/209-2207); the cruise terminal (tel. 07/862-6343); and in the Hotel Parque Central Torre (Zulueta esq. Virtudes, tel. 07/860-0096).

Bicycle

Bicycling offers a chance to explore the city alongside Cubans, although very few *habaneros* cycle and the city has no bicycle culture.

Specially converted buses—the *ciclobuses*—ferry cyclists and their *bicis* through the tunnel beneath Havana harbor (10 centavos). Buses depart from Parque de la Fraternidad and Calle Tacón at the corner of Aguiar (Habana Vieja).

Tito, of **Bike Rentals & Tours** (Av. de los Presidentes #359 Apto. 11A e/ 15 y 17, tel. 5841-4839 or 5463-7103, www.bikerentalhavana.com), rents cruiser-type bikes (CUC15 daily) and offers three-hour guided tours (CUC25). He also has bikes equipped for longer journeys beyond Havana (CUC17 per day). **Roma Rent Bike & City Tour** (Compostela #255 e/ Obispo y O'Reilly, tel. 5436-4243 and 5501-3562) charges similar rates for its 18-speed rental bikes.

Ferry

Tiny ferries (standing room only) bob across the harbor between the Havana waterfront and Regla (on the east side of the bay) and Casablanca (on the north side of the bay). The ferries, which operate 24 hours, leave irregularly from Emboque de Luz wharf on Avenida San Pedro at the foot of Calle Luz in Habana Vieja (tel. 07/797-7473 in Regla); the ride costs 10 centavos and takes five minutes.

Organized Excursions

Havanatur (Calle 23, esq. M, Vedado, tel. 07/830-3107 or 07/201-9800, www.havanatur.cu, daily 8am-8pm) offers a city tour, including walking tour, plus excursions to key sights in the suburbs and farther afield.

Agencia de Viajes San Cristóbal (Oficios #110, e/ Lamparilla y Amargura, tel. 07/861-9171, daily 8:30am-5pm) offers city excursions—from a walking tour of Habana Vieja (daily 10am) to modern Havana for architecture buffs. However, at press time it had been taken over the the military economic division, GAESA, and its status was in flux.

Paradiso (Calle 82 #8202 esq. 5ta, Miramar, tel. 07/204-0601, contacto@paradiso.artex.cu, and Calle 23 y P, tel. 07/836-5381) offers cultural programs.

Curated Cuba Tours (www.curatedcubatours.com) arranges personalized multiday itineraries for groups of four people or more, with private guides. **Tours by Locals** (www.toursbylocals.com) offers guiding services with Havana-born guides.

Jineteros (street hustlers) will offer to be your guide. They're usually useless as sightseeing guides, and most will pull a scam.

Havana Suburbs

SANTIAGO DE LAS VEGAS

This rural colonial-era town is 20 kilometers south of Havana. It is accessed via Avenida de la Independencia.

Mausoleo de General Antonio Maceo Grajales

Avenida de los Mártires rises south of Santiago de las Vegas and deposits you at **El Cacahual.** Here, Antonio Maceo Grajales (1845-1896), general and hero of the independence movement, slumbers in a mausoleum engraved in the style of Mexican artist Diego Rivera. The mausoleum also contains the tomb of Capitán Ayudante (Captain-Adjutant) Francisco Gómez Toro (1876-1896), General Máximo Gómez's son, who gave his life alongside Maceo at the Battle of San Pedro on December 7, 1896.

Santuario de San Lázaro

Cuba's most important pilgrimage site is the **Sanctuary of San Lázaro** (Carretera de San Antonio de los Baños, tel. 047/683-2396, daily 7am-7pm, free), on the west side of Rincón, a hamlet about four kilometers southwest of Santiago de las Vegas. The church, **Iglesia de San Lázaro,** is busy with mendicants who have come to have their children baptized. Behind the church is the **Parque de la Fuente de Agua,** where believers bathe their hands and feet in a fountain to give thanks to Babalu Ayé, while others fill bottles with what they consider holy water. The Los Cocos sanatorium, behind the garden, houses leprosy and AIDS patients.

San Lázaro is the patron saint of the sick (in Santería, his avatar is Babalú Ayé). His symbol is the crutch, his stooped figure is covered in sores, and in effigy he goes about attended by his two dogs. Limbless beggars and other unfortunates crowd at the gates and plead for a charitable donation.

A procession to the sanctuary takes place the 17th of each month. The annual **Procesión de los Milagros** (Procession of the Miracles) takes place December 17, drawing thousands of pilgrims to beseech or give thanks to the saint for miracles they imagine he has the power to grant. The villagers of Rincón do a thriving business selling votive candles and flowers. Penitents crawl on their hands and knees as others sweep the road ahead with palm fronds.

Buses P12 (from Parque de la Fraternidad) and P16 (from outside Hospital Hermanos Ameijeiras, in Centro Habana) link Havana to Santiago de las Vegas. Ómnibus #480 also serves Santiago de las Vegas from Havana's main bus terminal (Av. Independencia #101, Plaza de la Revolución, tel. 07/870-9401). The **Terminal de Ómnibus** (Calle al Rincón #43, tel. 07/683-3159) is on the southwest side of town, on the road to Rincón.

A three-car train departs Havana's Estación 19 de Noviembre (Tulipán) at 10:05am and 4:25pm, stopping at Rincón (CUC1). Trains run continuously on December 17. If driving, follow Carretera al Rincón, which begins at the bus station on the southwest edge of Santiago de las Vegas; bus #476 also runs from here.

ARROYO NARANJO

This *municipio* lies east of Boyeros and due south of Havana.

Parque Zoológico Nacional

On Avenida Zoo-Lenin, Cuba's **national zoo** (Av. 8, esq. Av. Soto, tel. 07/644-7618 or 643-8063, comercial@pzn.cubazoo.cu, Wed.-Sun. 9:30am-3:15pm, adults CUC3, children CUC2), southeast of the village of Arroyo Naranjo, about 16 kilometers south of central Havana, contains about 1,000 animals, but the cages are small and bare, and many of the animals look woefully neglected.

Tour buses (CUC2) depart the parking lot about every 30 minutes and run through a wildlife park (*pradera africana*) resembling the African savanna, including a *foso de leones* (lion pit).

To get to the main entrance, take Avenida de la Independencia to Avenida San Francisco (the *parque* is signed at the junction), which merges with the *circunvalación*. Take the first exit to the right and follow Calzada de Bejucal south. Turn right onto Avenida Zoo-Lenin (signed).

Metrobus P12 operates from Parque de la Fraternidad, in Habana Vieja.

Parque Lenin

Lenin Park (Calle 100 y Carretera de la Presa, tel. 07/647-1533, Tues.-Sun. 9am-5pm), east of the zoo, was created from a former hacienda and landscaped mostly by volunteer labor. The vast complex features wide rolling pastures and small lakes surrounded by forests. What Lenin Park lacks in grandeur and stateliness (it is badly deteriorated), it makes up for in scale.

The park is bounded by the *circunvalación* to the north and Calzada de Bejucal to the west; there is an entrance off Calzada de Bejucal. A second road—Calle Cortina de la Presa—enters from the *circunvalación*, runs down the center of the park, and is linked to Calzada de Bejucal by a loop road; an **information bureau** (tel. 07/647-1165) is midway down Calle Cortina de la Presa.

The **Galería del Arte Amelia Peláez,** at the south end of Cortina, displays works by the eponymous Cuban ceramist. A short distance to the west is the **Monumento Lenin,** a huge granite visage of the Communist leader and thinker in Soviet-realist style, carved by Soviet sculptor I. E. Kerbel. Farther west, you'll pass an **aquarium** (entrance CUC1) displaying freshwater fish, turtles, and Cuban crocodiles. About 400 meters west of the aquarium is the **Monumento a Celia Sánchez.** Here, a trail follows a wide apse to a small museum fronting a bronze figure of the revolutionary heroine.

On the north side, the **Palacio de Pioneros Che Guevara** displays stainless steel sculptures of Che, plus a full-scale replica of the *Granma* (the vessel that brought Castro and his revolutionaries from Mexico).

An equestrian center, **Centro Ecuestre** (tel. 07/647-2436, daily 9am-5pm), also called Club Hípico, immediately east of the entrance off Calzada de Bejucal, offers one-hour trips (CUC15) plus free riding lessons for children, and has show-jumping exhibitions on Saturday morning, plus an annual show-jumping event (Subasta Elite de Caballos de Salto) in January. Horseback riding is also offered on weekends at **El Rodeo,** the national rodeo arena, in the southeast corner of the park. El Rodeo has rodeo every Sunday, with *rodeo pionero* (for youth) at noon and competitive adult rodeo at 3pm. The Feria de Rodeo (the national championship) is held each August 25.

A narrow-gauge railway circles the park, stopping at four stages. The old steam train (Sat.-Sun. 10am-4pm, four pesos), dating from 1870, departs from the information bureau in winter only and takes 25 minutes to circle the park. Another old steam train—**El Trencito**—is preserved in front of the disused Terminal Inglesa.

A *parque de diversiones* (theme park) in the northwest quarter includes carousels, a Ferris wheel, and pony rides.

Bus P13 operates between La Víbora and the park. Buses #88 and #113 leave from the north side of Havana's main railway station and continue to ExpoCuba.

ExpoCuba

ExpoCuba, on the Carretera del Globo (official address Carretera del Rocío, Km 3.5, Arroyo Naranjo, tel. 07/697-9111, Wed.-Sun. 10am-5pm, closed Sept.-Dec., CUC1), three kilometers south of Parque Lenin, houses a permanent exhibition of Cuban industry, technology, sports, and culture touting the achievements of socialism. The facility covers 588,000 square meters and is a museum, trade expo, world's fair, and entertainment hall rolled into one. It has 34 pavilions, including booths that display the crafts, products, music, and dance of each of Cuba's provinces. Pabellones Central and 14 have Wi-Fi.

Jardín Botánico Nacional

This 600-hectare **botanical garden** (tel. 07/697-9364, daily 8am-4pm, CUC1, or CUC4 including guide), directly opposite ExpoCuba, doesn't have the fine-trimmed herbaceous borders of Kew or Butchart but nonetheless is worth the drive for enthusiasts. Thirty-five kilometers of roads lead

Arroyo Naranjo

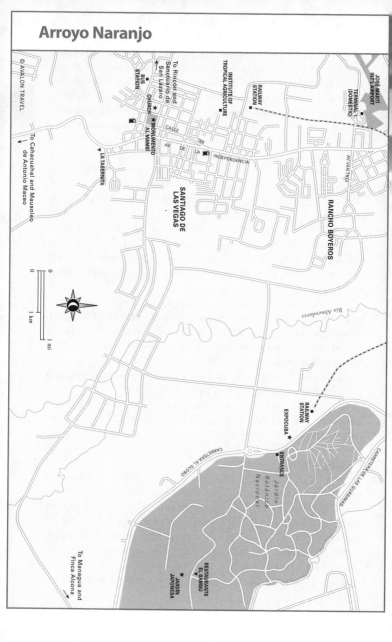

JOSÉ MARTÍ INT'L AIRPORT

TERMINAL 1 (DOMESTIC)

To Rincón and Santuario de San Lázaro

BUS STATION

CHURCH ★

★ MONUMENTO AL MAMBÍ

INSTITUTE OF TROPICAL AGRICULTURE

RAILWAY STATION

CALLE 188

AV. DE LA INDEPENDENCIA

AV. VAN TROI

RANCHO BOYEROS

SANTIAGO DE LAS VEGAS

LA TABERNITA ▼

To Cabacuahal and Mausoleo de Antonio Maceo

Río Almendares

0   1 km
0   1 mi

RAILWAY STATION

EXPOCUBA ★

ENTRANCE ★

Jardín Botánico Nacional

CARRETERA EL GLOBO

CARRETERA DE LAS GUASIMAS

RESTAURANTE EL BAMBÚ ★

JARDÍN JAPONESA ★

To Managua and Finca Alcona

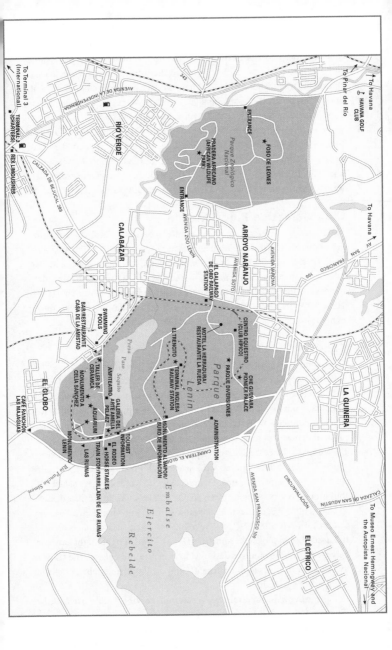

through the park, which was laid out between 1969 and 1984. You can drive your own vehicle with a guide, or take a guided tour aboard a tractor-trailer.

The garden consists mostly of wide pastures planted with copses divided by Cuban ecosystems and by regions of the tropical world (from coastal thicket to Oriental humid forest). There is even a permanent bonsai exhibit, and an "archaic forest" contains species such as *Microcyca calocom,* Cuba's cork palm. The highlight is the **Jardín Japonés** (Japanese Garden), landscaped with tiered cascades, fountains, and a jade-green lake full of koi. The **Invernáculo Rincón Eckman** is a massive greenhouse named after Erik Leonard Eckman (1883-1931), who documented Cuban flora between 1914 and 1924. It is laid out as a triptych with greenhouses for cactus, epiphytes, ferns, insectivorous plants, and tropical mountain plants.

Club Gallístico Finca Alcona

Fascinated by cockfighting or aviculture? The state-run **Club Gallístico Finca Alcona** (Calzada de Managua, Km 17.5, tel. 07/644-9398 or 07/643-1217, Tues.-Sun. 9am-7pm, tours 10am-3pm, CUC10 including lunch), two kilometers northeast of Managua, on the east side of the botanical garden, raises *gallo fino* gamecocks for export. It displays the cocks in a ring (8am-11am Sat.-Sun. Dec.-June, Sat. only July-Nov.) and has brief cockfighting exhibitions, but not to the death. It has two thatched restaurants.

Food

One of Havana's most sensational *paladares,* ★ **Il Divino** (Calle Raquel #50 e/ Esperanza y Lindero, Rpto. Castillo de Averhoff, Mantilla, tel. 07/643-7743 or 5812-7164, www.cubarestanredivino.com, daily 11am-midnight), four kilometers northeast of Parque Lenin, feels like a piece of Tuscany transplanted, complete with Italianate furnishings. That's because the owners are Italian businessman Marco DeLuca and his Cuban wife, Yoandra. Try the pumpkin soup (CUC3), stuffed peppers (CUC4), fish fillet in strawberry sauce (CUC8), or lamb in red wine sauce (C7). Pizzas and pastas are also served. It has a superb basement wine cellar with bar. It can get packed with tour groups; reservations are essential. On Sundays, Cuban families descend to enjoy cultural activities in the organic garden, known as Finca Yoandra.

Las Ruinas (Calle 100 y Cortina, tel. 07/643-8527, Tues.-Sun. noon-5pm), in Parque Lenin, looks like something Frank Lloyd Wright might have conceived. The restaurant was designed in concrete and encases the ruins of an old sugar mill. It serves continental and *criolla* cuisine (lobster Bellevue is a specialty, CUC20).

Parque Lenin has several basic restaurants serving simple *criolla* dishes for pesos.

The **Restaurante El Bambú** (tel. 07/697-9159, Tues.-Sun. noon-5pm), overlooking the Japanese Garden in the Jardín Botánico Nacional, bills itself as an *eco-restorán* and serves vegetables—beetroot, cassava, pumpkin, spinach, taro, and more—grown right there in the garden. It offers an all-you-can eat buffet (CUC1).

The *municipio* of San Miguel del Padrón, southeast of Habana Vieja, is mostly residential, with factory areas by the harbor and timeworn colonial housing on the hills south of town. The region is accessed from the Vía Blanca or (parallel to it) Calzada de Luyano via the Carretera Central (Calzada de Güines), which ascends to the village of San Francisco de Paula, 12.5 kilometers south of Habana Vieja.

★ Museo Ernest Hemingway

In 1939, Hemingway's third wife, Martha Gellhorn, saw and was struck by **Finca Vigía** (Vigía y Steinhart, tel. 07/691-0809, mushem@cubart.cult.cu, Mon.-Sat. 10am-5pm, entrance CUC5, guided tours CUC5), a one-story Spanish-colonial house built in 1887 and boasting a wonderful view of Havana. They rented Lookout Farm for US$100 a month. When Hemingway's first royalty check from *For Whom the Bell Tolls* arrived in 1940, he bought the house for US$18,500. In August 1961, his widow, Mary Welsh, was forced to sign papers handing over the home to the Castro government, along with its contents. On July 21, 1994, on the 95th anniversary of Papa's birth, Finca Vigía reopened its doors as a museum, just the way the great writer left it.

Bougainvilleas frame the gateway to the eight-hectare hilltop estate—today the most visited museum in Cuba. Mango trees and jacarandas line the driveway leading up to the house. No one is allowed inside—reasonably so, since every room can be viewed through the wide-open windows, and the temptation to pilfer priceless trinkets is thus reduced. Through the large windows, you can see trophies, firearms, bottles of spirits, old issues of *The Field, Spectator,* and *Sports Afield* strewn about, and more than 9,000 books, arranged in his fashion, with no concern for authors or subjects.

It is eerie being followed by countless eyes—those of the guides (one to each room) and of the beasts that found themselves in the crosshairs of Hemingway's hunting scope. "Don't know how a writer could write surrounded by so many dead animals," Graham Greene commented when he visited. There are bulls, too, including paintings by Paul Klee; photographs and posters of bullfighting scenes; and a chalk plate of a bull's head, a gift from Picasso.

Here Hemingway wrote *Islands in the Stream, Across the River and into the Trees, A Moveable Feast,* and *The Old Man and the Sea*. The four-story tower next to the house was built at his fourth wife's prompting so that he could write undisturbed. Hemingway disliked the tower and continued writing amid the comings and goings of the house, surrounded by papers, shirtless, in Bermuda shorts. Today, the tower contains exhibitions with floors dedicated to Hemingway's sportfishing and films.

The former garage is to be restored to display Hemingway's last car—a 1955 Chrysler New Yorker convertible, which was recovered in 2011 in destitute shape and at press time was being restored.

Hemingway's legendary cabin cruiser, the *Pilar,* is poised beneath a wooden pavilion on the former tennis court, shaded by bamboo and royal

Ernest Hemingway and Cuba

Ernest Hemingway first set out from Key West to wrestle marlin in the wide streaming currents off the Cuban coast in April 1932. The blue waters of the Gulf Stream, chock-full of billfish, brought him closer and closer until eventually he settled on this island of sensual charm. Hemingway loved Cuba and lived for 20 years at Finca Vigía, his home in the suburb of San Francisco de Paula, 12.5 kilometers southeast of Havana.

The Cult of Hemingway

Havana's marina is named for the prize-winning novelist. Hemingway's room in the Hotel Ambos Mundos and his home (Finca Vigía) are preserved as museums. And his likeness adorns T-shirts and billboards. The Cuban understanding of Hemingway's "Cuban novels" is that they support a core tenet of Communist ideology—that humans are only fulfilled acting in a "socialist" context for a moral purpose, not individualistically. "All the works of Hemingway are a defense of human rights," said Castro, who claimed that *For Whom the Bell Tolls,* Hemingway's fictional account of the Spanish Civil War, inspired his guerrilla tactics. The two headstrong fellows met only once, during the 10th Annual Ernest Hemingway Billfish Tournament in May 1960. Hemingway invited Cuba's youthful new leader as his guest of honor. Castro was to present the winner's trophy; instead, he hooked the biggest marlin and won the prize for himself.

With the Cold War and the United States' break with Cuba, Hemingway had to choose. Not being able to return to Cuba contributed to Hemingway's depression, said his son Patrick.

Papa and the Revolution

There has been a great deal of speculation about Hemingway's attitude toward the Cuban Revolution. Cuba attempts to portray him as sympathetic, not least because Hemingway's Cuban novels are full of images of

palms. Nearby are the swimming pool (where guests such as Ava Gardner swam naked) and the graves of four of Hemingway's dogs.

Several bus lines service the museum. The P7 Metrobus departs from Industria, between Dragones and Avenida Simón Bolívar, Parque de la Fraternidad, in Habana Vieja. P1 runs from La Rampa; the P2 runs from Paseo, in Vedado.

SANTA MARÍA DEL ROSARIO

The charming colonial village of Santa María del Rosario, 20 kilometers south of Parque Central, is in the *municipio* of Cotorro, about five kilometers southeast of San Francisco de Paula. The village was founded in 1732 by José Bayona y Chacón, the Conde (Count) de Casa Bayona, and was an important spa in colonial days.

Venerable 18th- and 19th-century buildings surround **Plaza Mayor,** the main square. **Casa del Conde Bayona** (Calle 33 #2404, esq. 24, tel. 07/682-3510, daily noon-10pm), the count's former home, includes a coach house. The **Casa de la Cultura** (Calle 33 #202, esq. 24, tel. 07/682-4259), prerevolutionary terror and destitution. "There is an absolutely murderous tyranny that extends over every little village in the country," he wrote in *Islands in the Stream*.

Hemingway's widow, Mary Welsh, told the journalist Luis Báez that "Hemingway was always in favor of the Revolution." Another writer, Lisandro Otero, records Hemingway as saying, "Had I been a few years younger, I would have climbed the Sierra Maestra with Fidel Castro."

Hemingway's enigmatic farewell comment as he departed the island in 1960 is illuminating: "*Vamos a ganar. Nosotros los cubanos vamos a ganar.* [We are going to win. We Cubans are going to win.] I'm not a Yankee, you know." Prophetically, in *Islands in the Stream*, a character says: "The Cubans...double-cross each other. They sell each other out. They got what they deserve. The hell with their revolutions."

Finca Vigía's Fate

After Hemingway's death, Finca Vigía was seized by the Castro government (along with all other U.S.-owned property), though the writer had willed the property to his fourth wife, Mary Welsh. The Cuban government allowed her to remove 200 pounds of papers but insisted that most of their home's contents remain untouched.

In his will, the author left his sportfishing vessel, the *Pilar*, to Gregorio Fuentes (the former skipper couldn't afford its upkeep, and it, too, became the property of the government). Hemingway's sleek red-and-white 1955 Chrysler New Yorker was left to his doctor but soon disappeared. In 2011, it was found in derelict condition and at press time was being restored, thanks to the efforts of actor/director David Soul (most famously Hutch from the 1970s cult detective series *Starsky & Hutch*), with whom I am partnered in a cinematic production about the car and its restoration: www.christopherp-baker.com/cuba-soul-documentary.

on the west side, features a patio mural by world-renowned Cuban artist Manuel Mendive.

The main reason to visit is to view the baroque **Iglesia de Santa María del Rosario** (Calle 24, e/ 31 y 33, tel. 07/682-2183, Tues.-Sat. 8am-noon, Sun. 3:30pm-6pm), dominating the plaza. One of the nation's finest churches, this national monument features a spectacular baroque altar of cedar dripping with gold leaf, a resplendent carved ceiling, plus four priceless art pieces by José Nicolás de Escalera.

Getting There

From Havana, take the P1 from La Rampa, P2 from Paseo in Vedado, or the P7 from Parque de la Fraternidad to Cotorro, then catch the #97.

CIUDAD PANAMERICANO AND COJÍMAR

Beyond the tunnel under Havana harbor, you travel the six-lane Vía Monumental freeway to modern **Ciudad Panamericano**, three kilometers east of Havana. It dates from the 1991 Pan-American Games, when a

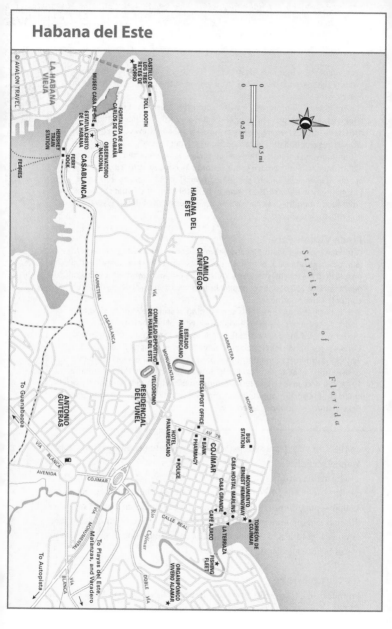

Habana del Este

© AVALON TRAVEL

LA HABANA VIEJA

HERSHEY TRAIN STATION

FERRIES

CASTILLO DE LOS TRES REYES DEL MORRO

TOLL BOOTH

FORTALEZA DE SAN CARLOS DE LA HABANA

MUSEO CASA DE CHE

ESTATUA CRISTO DE LA HABANA

OBSERVATORIO NACIONAL

FERRY DOCK

CASABLANCA

CARRETERA CASABLANCA

HABANA DEL ESTE

CAMILO CIENFUEGOS

To Guanabacoa

ANTONIO GUITERAS

VIA BLANCA

AVENIDA

COJIMAR

VIA MONUMENTAL

To Playas del Este, Matanzas, and Varadero

To Autopista

VIA BLANCA

DOBLE VIA

Río Cojímar

CALLE REAL

RESIDENCIAL DEL TUNEL

VELODROMO

COMPLEJO DEPORTIVO DEL HABANA DEL ESTE

ESTADIO PANAMERICANO

VIA MONUMENTAL

CARRETERA DEL MORRO

ETECSA/POST OFFICE

AV. 78

HOTEL PANAMERICANO

BANK

PHARMACY

POLICE

COJIMAR

CASA GRANDE

CAFÉ AJIACO

LA TERRAZA

BUS STATION

MONUMENTO ERNEST HEMINGWAY

CASA HOSTAL MARLINS

TORREÓN DE COJIMAR

FISHING FLEET

ORGANIPÓNICO VIVERO ALAMAR

Straits of Florida

0   0
0.5 mi
0.5 km

Alamar

Organipónico Vivero Alamar

Immediately east of Cojímar, you'll pass a dormitory city long prized by Fidel Castro as an example of the achievements of socialism. In April 1959, Alamar (pop. 100,000) emerged on the drawing board as the first housing scheme in postrevolutionary Cuba, featuring 4- to 11-story prefabricated concrete apartment blocks. The sea of concrete complexes was built with shoddy materials by microbrigades of untrained "volunteer" workers borrowed from their normal jobs.

Despite its overwhelming deficiencies (the plumbing came from the Soviet Union, the wiring from China, the stoves from North Korea), Alamar was vastly expanded beginning in 1976 and now covers 10 square kilometers. Today it is a virtual slum. Refuse litters the potholed roads, and the roadside parks are untended. There are no jobs here, either, and few stores, no proper transportation, and no logic to the maze of streets or to the addresses of buildings, so that finding your way around is maddening.

Much of Alamar's trash, from rusty old bottles to cash registers, has been recycled as street art at the surreal open-air **Jardin de los Afectos** (Edificio 11-C, Micro-X, tel. 07/765-6270), by local artist Héctor Gallo Portieles.

Well worth a visit is **Organipónico Vivero Alamar** (tel. 5253-6175, ubpc-alamar@minag.cu), an organic produce farm cooperative covering 11 hectares on land leased from the state.

One of the top nightspots in Havana is the **EnGuayabera** (Calle 7ma y 171, Zona 10, Alamar, tel. 07/763-3569, 9pm-3am, free but CUP50-250 for concerts), located in an old textile factory. It replicates the non-touristy Fábrica de Arte, in Vedado, as a multidimensional art and entertainment complex (but without the tourists). It even has a disco, 3-D theater, Wi-Fi, and an ice-cream store.

high-rise village was built in hurried, jerry-rigged style. Sports stadiums rise to each side of the Vía Monumental, most significantly the now-disused **Estadio Panamericano** (Vía Monumental, Km 4, Ciudad Panamericano). The desultory town has fallen to ruin.

Ciudad Panamericano is contiguous with **Cojímar,** a forlorn fishing village with a waterfront lined with weather-beaten cottages. Whitecaps are often whipped up in the bay, making the Cuban flag flutter above **Fuerte** de Cojímar (locally called El Torreón), a pocket-size fortress guarding the cove. It was here in 1762 that the English put ashore and marched on Havana to capture Cuba for King George III. It is slated to be restored as a museum.

Ernest Hemingway berthed his sportfishing boat, the *Pilar,* in Cojímar. When he died, every angler in the village donated a brass fitting from his boat. The collection was melted down to create a bust—**Monumento Ernest Hemingway**—that stares out to sea from within a columned rotunda at the base of El Torreón. A plaque reads: "Parque Ernest Hemingway. In grateful memory from the population of Cojímar to the immortal author of *Old Man and the Sea,* inaugurated July 21, 1962, on the 63rd anniversary of his birth."

Cojímar was most famous as the residence of Gregorio Fuentes, Hemingway's former skipper and friend, and the model for "Antonio" in *Islands in the Stream.* Fuentes died in 2002 at the grand old age of 104. The old man (who lived at Calle 98 #209, esq. 3D) could often be found regaling travelers in **La Terraza** (Calle 152 #161, esq. Candelaria, tel. 07/766-5151), where you can toast to his memory with a turquoise cocktail—Coctel Fuentes. You sense that Papa could stroll in at any moment. His favorite corner table is still there. He is there, too, patinated in bronze atop a pedestal, and adorning the walls in black and white, sharing a laugh with Fidel.

The funky fishing fleet shelters among the mangroves on the southeast bayshore. You might talk your way past the guard, but a footbridge gives you a birds-eye view of fishers bringing in and harvesting sharks (alas) and other fish.

Food and Accommodations

Islazul's **Hotel Panamericano** (Calle A y Av. Central, tel. 07/766-1000), in Ciudad Panermicano, is popular with budget-tour operators. Despite a swimming pool, it offers nothing but regret for tourists.

In Cojímar, the shorefront **Casa Hostal Marlins** (Calle Real #128A, e/ Santo Domingo y Chacón, tel. 07/766-6154, CUC30-35) has a nice air-conditioned apartment upstairs with kitchenette, TV, an enclosed dining patio, and modern bathroom, plus parking.

After exploring, appease your hunger with soup and paella at Hemingway's favorite restaurant, **La Terraza** (Calle 152 #161, esq. Candelaria, tel. 07/766-5151, daily 10:30am-10:30pm), with a gleaming mahogany bar at the front. The wide-ranging menu includes paella (CUC6-12), pickled shrimp (CUC6), oyster cocktail (CUC2), and sautéed calamari (CUC8).

★ **Café Ajiaco** (Calle 92 #267 e/ 3ra y 5ta, tel. 07/765-0514, cafeajiaco@ gmail.com, daily noon-midnight) serves delicious Cuban dishes alfresco under thatch. It packs in the tour groups; call ahead.

A steep, winding staircase delivers you to the second floor, open-air and breeze-swept **Casa Grande** (Calle Puezuela #86 esq. Foxa, tel. 07/766-6784, daily noon-midnight), where owner-chef Jorge Falcón cooks up a mean seafood grill (lobster, octopus, shrimp, and whitefish, CUC5-10),

served with the usual trimmings. His pork ribs, the house special, earn
raves. Reserve ahead.

Getting There and Around

Heading east from Havana on the Vía Monumental, take the first exit marked Cojímar and cross over the freeway to reach Ciudad Panamericano. For Cojímar, take the *second* exit. Metrobus P11 departs Paseo de Martí, opposite the Capitolio Nacional, in Habana Vieja, and runs along the Vía Monumental to Ciudad Panamericano. You can also catch it at the corner of Avenida de los Presidentes y 27 in Vedado.

PLAYAS DEL ESTE

On hot summer weekends all of Havana seems to come to Playas del Este to tan their bodies and flirt. The beaches stretch unbroken for six kilometers east-west, divided by name. A nearly constant breeze is usually strong enough to conjure surf from the warm turquoise seas—a perfect scenario for lazing, with occasional breaks for grilled fish from thatch-roofed *ranchitas* where you can eat practically with your feet in the water. Playas del Este is pushed as a hot destination for foreigners, bringing tourists and Cubans together for rendezvous under *palapas* and palms. It's a nonstarter other than for a day visit.

When driving from Havana via the Vía Monumental, it's easy to miss the turnoff, one kilometer east of the second (easternmost) turnoff for Cojímar, where the Vía Monumental splits awkwardly. Take the narrow Vía Blanca exit to the left to reach Playas del Este; the main Vía Monumental swings south (you'll end up circling Havana on the *circunvalación*).

Tarará

Beyond the Río Tarará you pass **Residencial Tarará** (reception tel. 07/798-2937), a tourist resort at the far western end of Playas del Este, at Vía Blanca (Km 19). Before 1990 it was the Campamento de Pioneros José Martí, used by Cuban schoolchildren who combined study with beachside pleasures. Here, too, victims of the 1986 Chernobyl nuclear disaster in Ukraine were treated free of charge. It was here also that Castro operated his secret government that usurped that of President Manuel Urrutia Lleó after Batista was ousted. Che Guevara was convalescing here after his debilitating years of guerrilla warfare in the Sierra Maestra; **Museo de Che** (Calle 14, esq. 17) recalls his stay.

To the west is a delightful pocket beach that forms a spit at the river mouth; it has a volleyball court and shady *palapas,* plus a restaurant and marina with water sports. Bring snorkel gear: The river mouth channel has corals. The main beach, **Playa Mégano,** to the east, has a sand volleyball court and is served by the **Casa Club** complex (tel. 07/798-3242), with a swimming pool with grill and restaurant.

Entry costs CUC15 including CUC10 *consumo mínimo;* you must show your passport.

Playas del Este

© AVALON TRAVEL

Santa María del Mar

Playa Mégano extends east from Tarará and merges into **Playa Santa María del Mar,** the broadest and most beautiful swathe, with golden sand shelving into turquoise waters. The beaches are palm-shaded and studded with umbrellas. Most of Playas del Este's tourist facilities are here, including bars and water sports.

Playa Santa María runs east for about three kilometers to the mouth of the Río Itabo—a popular bathing spot for Cuban families. A large mangrove swamp centered on **Laguna Itabo** extends inland from the mouth of the river, where waterfowl can be admired.

Boca Ciega and Guanabo

Playa Boca Ciega begins east of the Río Itabo estuary and is popular with Cuban families. Moving eastward, Playa Boca Ciega merges into **Playa Guanabo,** the least-attractive beach, running for several kilometers along the shorefront of Guanabo, a Cuban village with plantation-style wooden homes and a vibrant touristic scene. (In 2015, a Chinese company signed a deal to build a $462 million hotel-golf course-condo project here.)

For grand views up and down the beaches, head inland of Guanabo to **Mirador de Bellomonte** (Vía Blanca, Km 24.5, tel. 07/796-3431, daily noon-10pm), a restaurant above the highway; it's signed.

Recreation

Outlets on the beach rent watercraft (CUC15 for 15 minutes), Hobie Cats

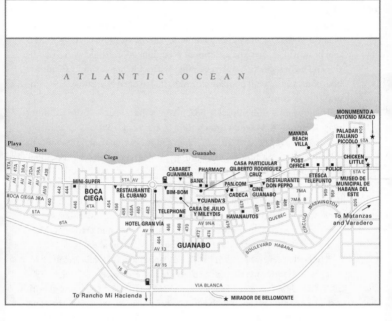

(CUC20 per hour), and beach chairs (CUC2 per day). **Restaurante Mi Cayito** (Av. las Terrazas, tel. 07/797-1339) rents kayaks and water bikes on the lagoon. **Havana Kiteboarding Club** (Calle Cobre e/ 12 y 14, tel. 5804-9656, www.havanakite.com) offers kiteboarding and stand-up paddleboarding at Tarará. **Yuniel Valderrama** (tel. 5284-4830, yunielvm80@ nauta.cu) offers surfing and kitesurfing lessons at the west end of Playa Mégano.

Food

Almost a dozen beach grills line the shore and serve *criolla* fare and seafood, including grilled fish and lobster, as does **Restaurante Mi Cayito** (Av. las Terrazas, tel. 07/797-1339, daily 10am-6pm), overhanging the mangroves of Laguna Itabo.

In Guanabo, the best place is ★ **Paladar Italiano Piccolo** (5ta Av., e/ 502 y 504, tel. 07/796-4300, noon-midnight daily), a spacious private restaurant with river-stone walls adorned with Greek murals. Run by Greek owners, it offers surprisingly tasty Mediterranean fare, including wood-fired pizzas, served with hearty salads at low prices (CUC5-10). The private **Restaurant Don Peppo** (Calle 482 #503 e/ 5 y 7, noon-midnight) serves Italian dishes on a shaded terrace with suitably Italian ambience. Try the Hawaiian pizza (CUC5.80), fresh garlic octopus (CUC6), or mixed seafood plate (CUC9).

Air-conditioned **Bim-Bom** (5ta Av., esq. 464, tel. 07/796-6205) serves 32 flavors of ice cream along the lines of Baskin-Robbins.

Accommodations

One of the best *casas particulares* options is ★ **Casa de Julio y Mileydis** (Calle 468 #512, e/ 5ta y 7ma, Guanabo, tel. 07/796-0100, CUC30-35). Set in a beautiful garden, the apartment is equipped for people with disabilities and has a security box, large lounge with a kitchen, a simply furnished bedroom, and a small pool for children. It also has a bungalow. The owners are a pleasure.

If you want a more upscale beachfront villa, check out the stunning two-bedroom ★ **Mayada Beach Villa** (Calle 1ra e/ 490 y 492, Guanabo, www.villamayada.com, CUC267), adorned to boutique hotel standards in all whites. It has a sundeck, swimming pool, and a garden with outdoor shower and an opening to the beach.

Villas Armonia Tarará (Calle 9na, esq. 14, Villa Tarará, tel. 07/796-0242, www.cubanacan.cu, from CUC27 low season, CUC30 high season for a two-bedroom villa) offers 94 two- to five-bedroom villas—*casas confort*—many with swimming pools. All have a kitchen and private parking. A grocery, laundry, restaurants, and pharmacy are on-site.

The best of several desultory state-run beach hotels is Cubanacán's five-story **Hotel Horizontes Tropicoco** (Av. de las Terrazas, e/ 5 y 7, tel. 07/797-1371, CUC58 s, CUC87 d low season, CUC66 s, CUC95 d high season), with 188 air-conditioned rooms with bamboo furniture plus modern bathrooms.

Gran Caribe's **Villas los Pinos** (Av. 4ta, tel. 07/797-1361, CUC120-220 low season, CUC160-250 high season) is the most elegant option, with 27 two-, three-, and four-bedroom villas; some have private pools. Cuban visitors are prohibited. **Islazul** (www.islazul.cu/es/houses) also rents former private homes.

Services

Infotur (Av. Las Terrazas, e/ 10 y 11, Santa María, tel. 07/796-1261; Av. 5ta esq. 468, Guanabo, tel. 07/796-6868; Mon.-Fri. 8:15am-4:45pm, Sat. 8:15am-12:15pm) provides tourist information.

There are two **post offices** (Edificio Los Corales at Av. de las Terrazas, e/ 10 y 11; in Guanabo, at 5ta-C Av. y 492). The **bank** (tel. 07/796-3320) is at 5ta Avenida (e/ 468 y 470).

Transportation

Tarará (Vía Blanca Km 17), 27 kilometers east of Havana, is signed off the Vía Blanca, as is Playas del Este, with three exits farther east. A taxi will cost about CUC35. Beware the *punto de control* (police control) near Bacuranao; keep to the posted speed limit!

The T3 **HabanaBusTour** (tel. 07/261-0917, daily 9am-9pm) charges CUC5 from Parque Central to Playas del Este.

Cubacar has car rental outlets at Tarará (tel. 07/796-4161) and in the parking lot of Hotel Horizontes Tropicoco (tel. 07/797-1535). There's also **Vía Rent-a-Car** (5ta Av., esq. 11, tel. 07/797-1494). A scooter is the perfect vehicle—rent one from Vía (CUC25 daily).

Cubataxi (tel. 07/796-6666) has taxis at the Hotel Horizontes Tropicoco.

Essentials

U.S. Law and Travel to Cuba

Moon Cuba provides complete travel information for all travelers, regardless of origin. Cuba has no restrictions on international travel. However, the U.S. government does. Most *yanquis* harbor the false impression that it's illegal for U.S. citizens to visit Cuba; it's not. The Supreme Court determined in the 1950s that U.S. citizens have a right to unrestricted travel under the Fifth Amendment. However, for decades, it has been illegal to spend money in Cuba, or to do so in pursuit of travel, without a license. The U.S. government invokes the 1916 Trading with the Enemy Act to prohibit travelers from *trading* with Cuba.

Except as specifically licensed by the Office of Foreign Assets Control (OFAC), payments of any kind in connection with travel to Cuba are prohibited, including prepaid tours to companies in third countries. The regulations change frequently and are open to interpretation by OFAC staff.

The regulations apply to U.S. citizens and permanent residents wherever they are located: all people and organizations physically in the United States (including airline passengers in transit) and all branches and subsidiaries of U.S. companies and organizations throughout the world. Now the good news…

New Regulations

On December 17, 2014, President Obama liberalized travel to Cuba. However, he did *not* end travel restrictions. That's the prerogative of Congress. Tourism (recreational travel) is not among the travel exemptions listed by the White House. These are changes made since December 2014:

- All 12 existing categories of licensed travel are covered by a general license. Previously, most categories (freelance journalists, humanitarians, athletes, etc.) had to request a specific license (i.e., written authorization) from OFAC, which could deny such requests. Now, under a general license all such individuals are *pre-authorized* to travel to Cuba.

- U.S. citizens are represented in Cuba by an embassy in Havana that opened in August 2015.

- U.S. travelers will be able to use their U.S. debit and credit cards in Cuba.

- U.S. travelers will be permitted to import Cuban goods up to $800 per trip, including $100 in cigars and rum.

Since July 2016, *all* U.S. citizens can travel to Cuba with any tour company or other entity licensed to operate "people-to-people educational exchange" group programs. The new regulations also permit any tour company, educational institution, or other entity that wishes to operate such educational exchange programs to do so without written authority.

Previous: *Bici-taxis;* U.S. cruise ship berthed in Havana harbor.

U.S. students wishing to study in Cuba may also now simply travel to Cuba with pre-authorization using the general license, so long as it's for a formal program of study. Plus, all licensed travelers are permitted to travel to Cuba by any means.

Tourism is still banned, which means no beach vacation! The truth is, since 2011, the U.S. government more or less stopped policing the regulations, and the people-to-people license (under which the majority of U.S. citizens now travel) ostensibly permits "disguised tourism" because the regulations are now unenforceable.

However, in June 2017 President Trump rescinded President Obama's provision permitting independent travel by individuals for "self-directed" people-to-people exchange. At press time, the only permissible way for all U.S. travelers to legally visit Cuba is on organized people-to-people programs.

The regulations are overseen by the Licensing Division, **Office of Foreign Assets Control** (U.S. Department of the Treasury, 1500 Pennsylvania Ave. NW, Washington, DC 20200, tel. 202/622-2480, www.treas.gov).

The U.S. government recommends that its citizens arriving in Cuba register at the U.S. Embassy in Havana.

General Licenses

The following categories of travelers are permitted to spend money for Cuban travel without the need to obtain special permission from OFAC on a case-by-case basis. They are not required to inform OFAC in advance of their visit to Cuba. *However, they must maintain a full-time schedule of activities relating to their license category; be able to document that their travel qualifies under a general license; and keep a written record of their activities in Cuba as relates to the authorized travel transactions for five years.*

Official government travelers, including representatives of international organizations of which the United States is a member, traveling on official business.

Journalists and supporting broadcasting or technical personnel regularly employed in that capacity by a news reporting organization and traveling for journalistic activities. (The Cuban government requires that you be issued a journalist's visa, not a tourist card.) The new regulations now permit freelance journalists with a suitable record of publication who are traveling to do research for a freelance article to do so under a general license.

Full-time professionals whose travel is directly related to "noncommercial, academic research" in their professional field and whose research will comprise a full work schedule in Cuba and has a likelihood of public dissemination; or whose travel is directly related to attendance at professional meetings or conferences that do not promote tourism or other commercial activity involving Cuba or the production of biotechnological products, so long as such meetings are organized by "qualifying international bodies."

Persons visiting Cuban family (or persons visiting "close relatives" who are U.S. government employees assigned to the U.S. Embassy in Havana) may visit them as often as desired and for an unlimited period.

Faculty, staff, and students of accredited U.S. graduate and undergraduate degree-granting academic institutions traveling for educational activities. University students may travel to Cuba for purposes of study toward their graduate or undergraduate degree for any length of time, provided that they have authorization from their university and a letter verifying that credit toward their degree will be granted for their study in Cuba.

Religious activities under the auspices of a religious organization located in the United States.

Humanitarian projects designed to directly benefit the Cuban people.

Activities intended to provide support for the Cuban people including but not limited to (1) activities of recognized human rights organizations; (2) activities of independent organizations designed to promote a rapid, peaceful transition to democracy; and (3) activities of individuals and nongovernmental organizations that promote independent activity intended to strengthen civil society in Cuba.

Professional research, conferences, and meetings so long as such activities do not include touristic activities, and conferences and meetings do not promote tourism in Cuba.

Academic educational activities for accredited U.S. graduate or undergraduate degree-granting academic institutions.

Educational exchanges not involving academic study pursuant to a degree program and that promotes people-to-people contact.

Academic seminars, conferences, and workshops related to Cuba or global issues involving Cuba and sponsored or cosponsored by the traveler's accredited U.S. graduate or undergraduate academic institution.

Athletic competitions by amateur or semiprofessional athletes or teams selected by the relevant U.S. federation.

Participation in a **public performance, clinic, workshop, competition, or exhibition** in Cuba.

Activities by **private foundations or research or educational institutes** that have an established interest in international relations to collect information related to Cuba for noncommercial purposes.

Persons traveling to engage in exportation, importation, or transmission of **informational materials.**

Marketing, sales negotiation, accompanied delivery, or servicing of exports consistent with the **export or re-export licensing policy** of the Department of Commerce.

Marketing, sales negotiation, accompanied delivery, or servicing of **medicine, medical supplies, or certain telecommunications equipment** by a U.S.-owned or -controlled firm in a third country.

Individuals traveling to conduct business in the field of **agricultural and medicinal product sales** (including marketing, negotiation, delivery, or servicing of exports), and in **telecommunications,** including conferences and meetings.

Spending Limits

Authorized travelers are now permitted to spend any amount of money "for transactions directly related to the activities for which they received a license." Money may be spent only for purchases of items directly related to licensed travel, such as hotel accommodations, meals, and goods personally used by the traveler in Cuba.

Also, as of January 2015, U.S. citizens are allowed to use debit and credit cards in Cuba (although only one U.S. bank had a functioning relationship at press time). Plus, the new regulations allow U.S. citizens to return to the United States with up to $800 of Cuban commercial purchases, including cigars and rum, and an unlimited amount of informational material, which includes art, CDs, and films.

U.S. regulations apply even to foreigners in transit through U.S. airports. Since the United States has no transit entry, *all* passengers in transit, say, from Mexico to Europe, must pass through U.S. Immigration and Customs; any Cuban items beyond the $800 limit may be confiscated, whether bought in Cuba or not.

Qualified Travel Service Providers

Any U.S. travel agent can now provide travel services involving travel-related transactions regarding Cuba. Moreover, persons subject to U.S. jurisdiction are now authorized to provide carrier service by aircraft to, from, and within Cuba. The first scheduled service to Cuba since 1961 was initiated on August 31, 2016, by JetBlue. The first U.S. cruise ships began service in 2015. Such entities are required to maintain certificates from each traveler for five years, demonstrating that they are legally authorized to travel to Cuba.

"Illegal" Travel

Individuals who choose to circumvent U.S. law do so at their own risk and the author and publisher accept no responsibility for any consequences that may result from such travel.

Thousands of U.S. citizens have slipped into Cuba through Canada, Mexico, and other third countries. Since 2012, Cuban immigration officials have been stamping all passports of arriving visitors. Persons subject to U.S. jurisdiction who travel to Cuba without a license bear a "presumption of guilt" and may be required to show documentation that all expenses incurred were paid by a third party not subject to U.S. law.

To my knowledge no one has been issued a "pre-penalty notice" since 2011. However, on paper trading with Cuba illegally is grounds for a fine up to US$55,000 under provisions of the Helms-Burton Bill, plus up to US$250,000 under the Trading with the Enemy Act, but most demands for fines have been US$7,500.

ESSENTIALS U.S. LAW AND TRAVEL TO CUBA

AIR

About 40 airlines service Cuba. Most flights arrive at Havana's José Martí International Airport or Varadero's Juan Gualberto Gómez International Airport. Cuba has eight additional international airports: Camagüey, Cayo Coco, Cayo Largo del Sur, Ciego de Ávila, Cienfuegos, Holguín, Santa Clara, and Santiago de Cuba.

Cuba's national airline, **Cubana de Aviación** (www.cubana.cu), generally offers lower fares than competing airlines. Cubana has DC-10s and Airbus A-320s that serve Europe and Mexico. The workhorses in the stable remain Soviet-made aircraft, including modern Antonovs.

Fares quoted in this book are based on rates advertised at press time. They are subject to change and should be used only as a guideline.

To get the cheapest fares, make your reservations as early as possible, especially during peak season, as flights often sell out. Low-season and midweek travel is often cheaper, as are stays of more than 30 days.

Most scheduled airlines permit two pieces of checked baggage, although a fee may apply; most charter airlines permit 20 kilos of baggage and charge extra for overweight bags. Cubana (20-40 kilograms, depending on class) charges extortionate rates for each kilo over your limit. Keep any valuable items, such as laptop computers, in your carry-on luggage. Always reconfirm your reservation and return flight within 72 hours of your departure (reservations are frequently canceled if not reconfirmed; Cubana is particularly bad), and arrive at the airport with plenty of time to spare. Always keep a photocopy of your ticket separate from your ticket and other documents as a safeguard in the event of loss or theft.

Online Bookings

Scheduled flights from the United States were authorized in 2016. Licensed travelers can legally book and pay by credit card for flights via U.S. websites such as www.orbitz.com and www.travelocity.com, as well as direct with any airline servicing Cuba. Travelers must sign a form affirming that they are traveling under one of the 12 approved categories of licensable travel. However, since June 2017 independent travel for people-to-people educational exchange is no longer permitted.

From the United States

Scheduled commercial flights between the United States and Cuba were authorized in 2016. At press time, seven airlines—Alaska Airlines, American Airlines, Frontier Airlines, JetBlue, Southwest Airlines, and Sun Country Airlines—had service to Cuba's provincial airports, solely for licensed passengers as permitted by the U.S. Treasury Department. A total of 110 weekly flights have been approved in a joint U.S.-Cuban accord. Havana will receive 20 flights daily: 14 will be from Florida, and the remainder

Private Aircraft

Private pilots must contact the **Instituto de Aeronáutica Civil de Cuba** (Calle 23 #64, e/ Infanta y P, Vedado, tel. 07/834-4949, www.iacc.gob. cu) at least 10 days before arrival in Cuba and at least 48 hours before an overflight.

U.S. owners of private aircraft, including air ambulance services, who intend to land in Cuba must obtain a temporary export permit for the aircraft from the U.S. Department of Commerce before departure.

Air Journey (tel. 561/841-1551, www.airjourney.com) offers group tours for private pilots who fly their own planes to Cuba.

from Atlanta, Charlotte, Houston, Los Angeles, Newark, and New York. (However, early demand was less than expected, and by mid-2017 several airlines had already reduced flights.) The average cost round-trip from Miami is about $150, including tourist visa and mandatory travel insurance.

Additionally, about two dozen companies—called Carrier Service Providers (CSPs)—are authorized to fly direct charters to Cuba from the United States. Charters use aircraft operated by American Airlines (www. aa.com), Eastern Airlines (www.easternairlines.aero), JetBlue (www.jetblue.com), World Airways (www.flywaa.com), and United Airlines (www. united.com). However, none was operating at press time.

From Canada

Most flights from Canada land at Varadero and other beach destinations. You can find cheap airfares—about C$400 round-trip—through **Travel Cuts** (tel. 800/667-2887, www.travelcuts.com).

A. Nash Travel Inc. (5865 McLaughlin Rd., Unit 2B, Mississauga, ON L5R 1B8, tel. 905/755-0647 or 800/818-2005, www.nashtravel.com) is a recommended Cuba specialist.

Air Canada (tel. 800/247-2262, www.aircanada.com) serves various destinations in Cuba from Canada. **Cubana** (675 King St. W. #206, Toronto, tel. 416/967-2822 or 866/428-2262, www.cubana.cu) flies from Montreal to Camagüey, Cayo Largo, Cienfuegos, and Havana; and from Toronto to Camagüey, Cayo Largo, Cienfuegos, Havana, Holguín, Santa Clara, and Santiago de Cuba.

Most charter flights are designed as beach vacation packages, but charter operators also sell "air-only" tickets. Try **Air Canada Vacations** (tel. 866/529-2079, www.vacations.aircanada.com); **Air Transat** (tel. 866/847-1112, www.airtransat.com); **SunWing** (tel. 877/786-9464, www.sunwing.ca); and **Westjet** (tel. 888/937-8538, www.westjet.com).

From Europe

From France: Havana is served by **Air France** (tel. 09-69-39-02, www.

Humanitarian Couriers

You can make tax-deductible donations to relief organizations licensed by OFAC to run food, medicine, and other humanitarian aid to Cuba using ordinary U.S. citizens as volunteer couriers. However, since 2011, OFAC has denied most humanitarian organizations a license. Currently, **Global Health Partners** (39 Broadway, Suite 1540, New York, NY 10006, tel. 212/353-9800, www.ghpartners.org) sends medical supplies to Cuba via its people-to-people humanitarian program.

airfrance.com), with daily flights from Paris's Charles de Gaulle Airport (from about €605 round-trip). **Cubana** (41 Blvd. du Montparnasse, 75006 Paris, tel. 01/53-63-23-38) flies from Paris Orly airport to Havana via Santiago de Cuba, and via Santa Clara (from about €950 round-trip). **Air Europa** (tel. 971/080-235 in Spain, www.aireuropa.com) flies between Charles de Gaulle and Havana via Madrid (from about €1,200).

From Germany: Charter company **Condor** (tel. 0180/6-76-77-76, www.condor.com) flies from Frankfurt and Munich to Havana and Holguín. **AirBerlin** (tel. 917/26-13-165, www.airberlin.com) flies from Berlin to Varadero.

From Italy: You can use **Alitalia** (tel. 89-20-10, www.alitalia.it) to connect with Air France, Iberia, or Virgin Atlantic flights. **Blue Panorama** (tel. 06/9895-6666, www.blue-panorama.com) carries the bulk of Italian tourists to Cuba with flights to Cayo Largo, Havana, Holguín, Santa Clara, and Santiago de Cuba.

From the Netherlands: Havana is served by **KLM** (tel. 20/474-7747, www.klm.com) from Amsterdam (from about €1,100 round-trip).

From Russia: Russia's **Aeroflot** (tel. 095/223-5555 or 800/444-5555, www.aeroflot.ru/cms/en) flies from Moscow to Havana. **Cubana** (tel. 095/238-4343, www.cubana.ru) operates once a week from Moscow.

From Spain: Havana is served by **Iberia** (tel. 800/772-4642, www.iberia.com) from Madrid daily, as well as by **Air Europa** (tel. 902/401-501, www.air-europa.com). **Cubana** (tel. 091/758-9750, www.cubana.cu) flies from Madrid to Havana and Santiago de Cuba.

From the United Kingdom: Virgin Atlantic (tel. 0344/874-7747, www.virgin-atlantic.com) flies from Gatwick to Havana (from £539 round-trip) twice weekly. Good online resources for discount tickets include www.ebookers.com, www.cheapflights.co.uk, and www.travelsupermarket.com; for charter flights, there's **Charter Flight Centre** (tel. 0845/045-0153, www.charterflights.co.uk).

From the Caribbean

From the Bahamas: Bahamasair (tel. 242/377-5505, http://up.bahamasair.com) has Nassau-Havana flights three times weekly.

(tel. 345/949-2311, www.caymanairways.com) from Grand Cayman.

From the Dominican Republic and Haiti: Cubana (tel. 809/227-2040, www.cubana.cu) serves Havana from Santo Domingo and Fort-de-France, twice weekly.

From Central America

Copa (tel. 507/217-2672 or 800/359-2672 in the U.S., www.copaair.com) flies to Havana from Panama City six times daily. **Avianca** (www.avianca.com) has daily flights from El Salvador and Costa Rica to Havana with connecting flights from the United States.

Cubana (tel. 52-55/52-506355 in Mexico City, tel. 52-9988/87-7210 in Cancún, www.cubana.cu) flies from Mexico City five times weekly and daily from Cancún.

From South America

Latam Airlines (tel. 866/435-9526, www.latam.com), formerly Lan Chile, flies to Havana from Santiago de Chile twice weekly.

Cubana (www.cubana.cu) flies to Havana from Quito, Ecuador; Buenos Aires, Argentina; Sao Paulo, Brazil; Bogota, Colombia; and Caracas, Venezuela.

From Asia

In 2016, **Air China** (tel. +86-10-95583, www.airchina.com) has twice-weekly flights from Beijing to Havana, with a stop in Montreal. You can also fly to Paris, London, Madrid, or Canada and connect with flights to Cuba. Eastbound, flying nonstop to Los Angeles or Miami, is perhaps the easiest route.

From Australia and New Zealand

The best bet is to fly to either Los Angeles or San Francisco and then direct to Havana or via Miami. **Air New Zealand** (Australia tel. 132-476, New Zealand tel. 0800/737-000, www.airnewzealand.com), **Qantas** (Australia tel. 13-13-13, New Zealand tel. 0800/808-767, www.qantas.com.au), and **United Airlines** (Australia tel. 131-777, New Zealand tel. 0800/747-400, www.united.com) offer direct service between Australia, New Zealand, and North America. A route via Santiago de Chile and then to Havana is also possible.

Specialists in discount fares include **STA Travel** (Australia tel. 134-782, www.statravel.com.au; New Zealand tel. 0800/474-400, www.statravel.co.nz). A good online resource for discount airfares is **Flight Centre** (Australia tel. 133-133, www.flightcentre.com.au).

SEA

As yet, no ferry service between Florida and Havana has been approved by Cuba (although as of 2014 President Obama approved such services).

Since 1961, the U.S. embargo restricted the cruise industry's access to Cuba (no vessel of any nation could berth in U.S. ports within 180 days of visiting Cuba). In April 2016, President Obama relaxed these regulations and the first U.S. cruise ship—**Fathom's** (tel. 855/932-8466, www.fathom. org) 700-passenger MV *Adonia*—arrived, initiating a regular schedule of so-called "people-to-people" cruises. In January 2017 **Pearl Sea Cruises'** 100-passenger *Pearl Mist* initiated three-times per-month 10-day cruises (Nov.-Mar., from US$7,810). **Royal Caribbean Lines** (tel. 866/562-7625, www.royalcaribbean.com) and **Norwegian Cruise Line** (tel. 866/234-7350, www.ncl.com) have also initiated cruises from Florida using much larger vessels. Carnival Corporation has requested permission to initiate "people-to-people" cruises for its Holland-America, P&O, Princess, and Seabourn lines. At press time, **Victory Cruise Lines** (tel. 888/907-2636, www.victorycruiselines.com) was awaiting Cuban authorization for its 202-passenger *M/V Victory*.

Lindblad Expeditions (tel. 800/397-3348, www.expeditions.com) offers 11-day "Land-Sea" programs aboard the 46-passenger *Harmony V* (Nov.-Mar.); **Variety Cruises** (tel. 800/833-2111, www.groupist.com) offers small-group sailings aboard the M/Y *Callisto* and *Sea Voyager*.

England's **Noble Caledonia** (tel. 020/7752-0000, www.noble-caledonia.co.uk) includes Cuba on its Caribbean itineraries using the M/S *Serenissima*. **Thomson Holidays** (tel. 0871/231-4691, www.thomson.co.uk) offers Caribbean itineraries featuring Cuba aboard the 1,500-passenger *Thomson Dream*.

Sea Cloud Cruises (www.seacloud.com) offers deluxe cruises aboard its legendary windjammers, *Sea Cloud* and *Sea Cloud II*.

Private Vessel

No advance permission is required to arrive by sea. However, it's wise to give at least 72 hours notice by faxing details of your boat, crew, and passengers to the six official entry ports operated by Cuba's **Marlin Náutica y Marinas** (tel. 07/273-7912, www.nauticamarlin.com). Cuba has 15 marinas, including one of the largest marinas in the Caribbean, at Varadero. Most offer fresh water, 110-volt electrical hookups, plus diesel and gasoline. Expansion and modernization at key marinas is underway.

For cruising, you'll need to register your boat upon arrival and receive a *permiso especial de navegación* (from CUC50, depending on the length of your boat). You'll need an official clearance (a *despacho*) to depart for your next, and every, stop. Authorities will usually ask for a planned itinerary, but insist on flexibility to cruise at random toward your final destination. A *permiso de salida* will be issued listing your final destination and possible stops en route.

As of 2016, all U.S. boaters are pre-authorized to sail to Cuba. All persons subject to U.S. law aboard vessels, including the owner, must be licensed travelers and have a valid reason for travel. (Since June 2017, U.S. citizens are no longer authorized for "people-to-people" travel except with an organized group through a licensed entity).

The United States and Cuba do not have a Coast Guard agreement (however, the U.S. Embassy *has* arranged such assistance to U.S. yachters). There are many reports of Cuban authorities being indifferent to yachters in distress, some of whom have had their vessels impounded; in several cases, foreign yachters have lost their vessels to corrupt officials. In case of emergencies requiring financial transactions, such as repair of vessels, travelers should contact OFAC (tel. 202/622-2480) for authorization.

Haut Insurance (tel. 978/475-0367, www.johngalden.com) handles insurance coverage for yachters cruising in Cuban waters.

ORGANIZED TOURS

Joining an organized tour offers certain advantages over traveling independently. Cuba isn't easy to fathom, so choosing a tour with an acclaimed Cuba expert is a major advantage. Check the tour inclusions to identify any hidden costs, such as airport taxes, tips, service charges, or extra meals. Most tours are priced according to quality of accommodations.

From the United States
PEOPLE-TO-PEOPLE PROGRAMS

People-to-people (P2P) educational programs are offered by U.S. entities such as National Geographic Expeditions. By law, they must provide a full schedule of "educational exchanges" with Cubans. The rationale is that by meeting with Cubans, participants become ambassadors for democratic values.

These organizations are among the best offering P2P programs:

- Cross Cultural Journeys (tel. 800/353-2276, http://crossculturaljourneys.com) offers a wide range of special-interest tours in Cuba.
- Cuba Motorcycle Tours (tel. 760/327-9879, www.cubamotorcycletours.com) offers 8-, 12-, and 14-day motorcycle trips using BMWs and Harley-Davidsons.
- Cuba Unbound (tel. 208/770-3359, http://www.cubaunbound.com) offers special-interest trips, from biking to kayaking.
- National Geographic Expeditions (tel. 888/966-8687, www.nationalgeographicexpeditions.com) offers a fun and highly educational eight-day "Cuba: Discovering Its People & Culture."
- Plaza Cuba (tel. 510/848-0911, www.plazacuba.com) specializes in music and dance workshops.

The following can arrange trips for academic and cultural organizations and business groups:

- Curated Cuba Tours (tel. 760/285-9827, www.curatedcubatours.com) specializes in customized tours for small groups.
- Marazul Tours (tel. 305/559-7114 or 800/993-9667, www.marazulcharters.com).

Tours from Canada

Cuba Education Tours (tel. 888/965-5647, www.cubaeducationaltravel.ca) offers "solidarity" and special-interest tours.

Real Cuba (tel. 306/205-0977, www.realcubaonline.com) offers special themed trips, including bicycling, walking, and bird-watching trips, as well as photography workshops and volunteer programs.

WowCuba (tel. 902/368-2453, www.wowcuba.com) specializes in bicycle tours of Cuba but has other programs, including scuba diving.

Tours from the United Kingdom

Captivating Cuba (tel. 44/01438-310099, www.captivatingcuba.com) offers a wide range of trips.

Cuba Direct (tel. 020/3811-1987, www.cubadirect.co.uk) offers tailor-made itineraries.

Journey Latin America (tel. 020/3811-5828, www.journeylatinamerica.co.uk) offers trips from a "Havana Weekend Break" to self-drive packages.

GETTING AWAY

A CUC25 departure tax is built into the cost of international flights.

Customs

Cuba prohibits the export of valuable antiques and art without a license.

Returning to the United States: U.S. citizens are now allowed to bring back $800 of Cuban purchases, plus an unlimited value of informational materials (art, music, literature). This includes the two bottles of liquor and up to 100 loose cigars or two boxes of cigars. For details, contact the **U.S. Customs Service** (1300 Pennsylvania Ave. NW, Washington DC 20229, tel. 703/526-4200, www.cbp.gov/travel).

Returning to Canada: Canadian citizens are allowed an "exemption" of C$800 for goods purchased abroad, plus 1.14 liters of spirits, 200 cigarettes, and 50 cigars. See www.cbsa-asfc.gc.ca.

Returning to the United Kingdom: U.K. citizens may import goods worth up to £390, plus 200 cigarettes, 50 cigars, and one liter of spirits. See www.hmrc.gov.uk/customs/arriving.

Getting Around

AIR

Most major Cuban cities have an airport. Cuba's state-owned airlines have a monopoly. Their safety records do not inspire confidence, although many old Soviet planes have been replaced by modern aircraft. Flights are often booked up weeks in advance, especially in peak season. Tickets are normally nonrefundable. If you reserve before arriving in Cuba, you'll be given a voucher to exchange for a ticket upon arrival in Cuba. Arrive on time for check-in; otherwise your seat will be given away. Delays, cancellations, and schedule changes are common. You can book at hotel tour desks.

Cubana (Calle 23, e/ 0 y P, Havana, tel. 07/834-4446, www.cubana.cu) serves most airports. Fares are 25 percent cheaper if booked in conjunction with an international Cubana flight. **Aerocaribbean** (Calle 23 #64, Vedado, tel. 07/879-7524) and **Aerogaviota** (Av. 47 #2814, e/ 28 y 34, Rpto. Kohly, Havana, tel. 07/203-0668, www.aerogaviota.com) also operate flights.

Since they're all state-owned, don't be surprised to find yourself flying Aerogaviota even if you booked with Cubana.

BUS
Tourist Buses
Víazul (Av. 26, esq. Zoológico, Nuevo Vedado, Havana, tel. 07/881-1413, www.viazul.com, daily 7am-9pm) operates bus services for foreigners to key places on the tourist circuit using modern air-conditioned buses. Children travel at half price. Bookings can only be made via the website (six days in advance) or at a Víazul ticket office. A 10 percent fee applies for cancellations made more than 24 hours before departure; a 25 percent fee applies if you cancel within 24 hours. A 20-kilo baggage limit applies. Excess baggage is charged 1 percent of your ticket cost per kilo.

Transtur (tel. 07/831-7333, www.transtur.tur.cu) operates tourist bus excursions within Havana and Varadero by open-top double-decker bus, and in Matanzas, Viñales, Playa Girón, Trinidad, Cayo Coco, Holguín, Guardalavaca, and Baracoa by minibus.

Public Buses
There are two classes of buses for long-distance travel: *Especiales* are faster (and often more comfortable) than crowded and slow *regulares,* which in many areas are still old and rickety with butt-numbing seats.

Most towns have *two* bus stations for out-of-town service: a Terminal de Ómnibus Intermunicipales (for local and municipal service) and a Terminal de Ómnibus Interprovinciales (for service between provinces). Often they're far apart.

Caution: Pickpockets plague the buses and often work in pairs; foreigners are their first targets.

INTERPROVINCIAL SERVICES
The state agency **Ómnibus Nacionales** (Av. Independencia #101, Havana, tel. 07/870-9401, ext. 100) operates all interprovincial services linking cities throughout the island. However, it is off-limits to foreigners except for students registered at Cuban institutions.

INTERMUNICIPAL SERVICES
You may or may not be denied service; it's a crapshoot. No reservations are available for short-distance services between towns within specific provinces. You'll have to join the queue.

Víazul Bus Schedule

Route	Departure Times	Duration	One-Way Fare
Havana-Santiago	6am, 3:15pm, and 8pm	13 hours	CUC51
Santiago-Havana	6am, 3:15pm, and 8pm	13 hours	CUC51

Stops are made at Entronque de Jagüey (CUC12), Santa Clara (CUC18), Sancti Spíritus (CUC23), Ciego de Ávila (CUC27), Camagüey (CUC33), Las Tunas (CUC39), Holguín (3:15pm departure only, CUC44), and Bayamo (CUC44).

Route	Departure Times	Duration	One-Way Fare
Havana-Trinidad	7am and 10:45am	5.75 hours	CUC25
Trinidad-Havana	7:45am and 2:30pm	5.75 hours	CUC25

Stops are made at Entronque de Jagüey (CUC12), Playa Larga and Playa Girón (8:15am departure only, CUC13), Aguada de Pasajeros (1pm departure only, CUC13), Yaguarama (CUC14), Rodas (CUC15), and Cienfuegos (CUC20).

Route	Departure Times	Duration	One-Way Fare
Havana-Varadero	8am, 10am, 1pm, and 5pm	3 hours	CUC10
Varadero-Havana	Noon, 2pm, 4pm, and 6pm	3 hours	CUC10

Stops are made at Playas del Este (8am departure only, CUC6), Matanzas (CUC7), and Aeropuerto de Varadero (by request).

CAMIONES

The staple of travel between towns is a truck, or *camión*. Most travel only to the nearest major town, so you'll need to change *camiones* frequently for long-distance travel. Some are open-sided flatbeds with canvas roofs. Sometimes it's a truck with a container of makeshift windows cut out of the metal sides and basic wooden seats welded to the floor. They depart from designated transportation hubs (often adjacent to bus or railway stations). You pay in pesos (1-10 pesos), depending on distance. Officially, foreigners are banned, so expect to be turned away by the drivers.

WITHIN TOWNS

Provincial capitals have intracity bus service, which can mean *camiones* or makeshift horse-drawn *coches*. Buses—*guaguas* (pronounced WAH-wahs)—are often secondhand Yankee school buses or uncomfortable

Route	Departure Times	Duration	One-Way Fare
Havana-Viñales	9am and 2:30pm	3.25 hours	CUC12
Viñales-Havana	8am and 2pm	3.25 hours	CUC12

Stops are made at Las Terrazas (9am departure only, CUC6) and Entronque de Candelaria (9am departure only, CUC6), and in Pinar del Río (CUC11).

Santiago-Baracoa	8am	5 hours	CUC15
Baracoa-Santiago	2pm	5 hours	CUC15
Trinidad-Santiago	8am	12 hours	CUC33
Santiago-Trinidad	7:30pm	12 hours	CUC33
Varadero-Trinidad	7:25am and 2pm	6 hours	CUC20
Trinidad-Varadero	7am and 1:55pm	6 hours	CUC20
Varadero-Santiago	9pm	15 hours	CUC49
Santiago-Varadero	8pm	15 hours	CUC49

Hungarian or Cuban models. They're usually overcrowded and cost 10-50 centavos. Many cities use *camellos,* uncomfortable and crowded homemade articulated bodies hauled by trucks.

Bus stops—*paradas*—are usually well marked. To stop the bus, shout *¡pare!* (stop!), or bash the box above the door in Cuban fashion. You'll need to elbow your way to the door well in advance (don't stand near the door, however, as you may literally be popped out onto your face; exiting has been compared to being birthed). Don't dally, as the bus driver is likely to hit the gas when you're only halfway out.

TRAIN

The nightmarishly dysfunctional **Ünion de Ferrocarriles de Cuba** operates rail service. One main line spans the country connecting major cities, with secondary cities linked by branch lines. Commuter trains called *ferro-óm-nibus* provide suburban rail service in and between many provincial towns.

Published schedules change frequently: Check departure and arrival times and plan accordingly, as many trains arrive (and depart) in the wee hours of the morning. The carriages haven't been cleaned in years (windows are usually so dirty you can barely see out), and most are derelict in all manner of ways. Few trains run on time, departures are frequently canceled, and safety is an issue. At last visit, an upgrade of tracks, signals, and communications was underway, and a fleet of brand-new Chinese locomotives was operating.

Bicycles are allowed in the baggage compartment (*coche de equipaje*). You usually pay (in pesos) at the end of the journey.

U.K.-based train enthusiast Mark Smith maintains "The Man in Seat 61" website (www.seat61.com/cuba.htm) with the latest info on Cuba train travel.

Reservations

The state agency **FerroCuba** (tel. 07/861-9389 or 07/861-8540, ferrotur@ceniai.cu) handles ticket sales and reservations for all national train service. Foreigners pay in CUC, for which you get a guaranteed first-class seat (when available). In Havana, tickets for foreigners are sold at the dysfunctional Terminal La Coubre (tel. 07/862-1000, Mon.-Fri. 9am-3pm), 100 meters south of the main railway station (Av. de Bélgica, esq. Arsenal, Habana Vieja, tel. 07/862-1920). Elsewhere you can normally walk up to the FerroCuba office at the station, buy your ticket, and take a seat on board within an hour. Buy your ticket as far in advance as possible. You should also buy your ticket for the next leg of your journey upon arrival in each destination. Reservations can sometimes be made through Infotur offices (tel. 07/866-3333, www.infotur.cu) and other regional tour agencies. You'll need your passport.

Reservations for local commuter services can't be made.

Service

Service has been reduced considerably since 2014, when trains #1, #2, #3, and #4 were taken out of service. The fast and generally reliable *especial* (train #11, also known as the Tren Francés [French train]), operates between Havana (departs Terminal Le Coubre at 6:15pm) and Santiago de Cuba (with stops in Matanzas, Santa Clara, and Camagüey) every fourth day and takes 13.5 hours for the 860-kilometer journey, arriving in Santiago de Cuba at 11:40am. The return train (#12) departs Santiago de Cuba at 11:45pm and arrives at Havana at 3:41pm. At press time, the following service also operated from Havana: train #7 to Sancti Spíritus (departs 9:21pm every second day) via Matanzas and Santa Clara; train #13 to Manzanillo (departs 7:25pm every fourth day) with five stops en route; train #15 to Guantánao (departs 6:53pm every fourth day) with five stops en route; train #71 to Pinar del Río (departs 6:10am every second day); and train #73 to Cienfuegos (departs 7:15am).

Expect bone-chilling air-conditioning, TVs showing movies (loudly),

Last in Line

Cuban lines (*colas*), or queues, can be confusing to foreign travelers. Cubans don't line up in order in the English fashion. Lines are always fluid, whether in a shop, bank, or bus station. Follow the Cubans' example and identify the last person ahead of you by asking *¿el último?* ("who's last?"). It's like a game of tag. You're now *el último* until the next person arrives. Thus you don't have to stand in line, but can wander off to find some shade and then simply follow the person ahead of you onto the bus.

a poorly stocked *cafetería* car, and *ferromoza* (rail hostess) meal service. Regardless, take snacks and drinks. Relieve yourself before boarding as toilets are grim (and some have no doors); bring toilet paper!

Fares

At press time, the following fares applied between Havana and: Santiago de Cuba, CUC30; Matanzas, CUC10; Sancti Spíritus, CUC14; Ciego de Ávila, CUC20; Morón, CUC24; Camagüey, CUC24; Cacocum (Holguín), CUC26; Bayamo/Manzanillo, CUC26; Guantánamo, CUC32. Children aged 5-11 are charged half price; children under 5 travel free.

TAXI

Tourist Taxis

Cubataxi operates radio-dispatched *turistaxis,* also found outside tourist hotels nationwide, and at *piqueras* (taxi stands) around the main squares. Since 2011, taxi drivers have leased the vehicles from the state. Few taxi drivers use their meters, and most now negotiate a fare (which have shot up in Havana due to U.S. travelers' willingness to overpay and overtip).

In tourist venues, modern Japanese or European cars are used. Beyond tourist areas, Cubataxi's vehicles are often beat-up Ladas. Few have seatbelts.

Peso Taxis

Havana and most provincial capitals have peso taxis serving locals and charging in pesos. Since 2009, peso-only taxis have been permitted to carry foreigners.

The workhorses are the *colectivos,* shared cabs that pick up anyone who flags them down (they also hang outside railway and bus terminals), often until they're packed to the gills. Sometimes called *máquinas* (machines) or *almendros* (almonds), they run along fixed routes much like buses and charge similar fares. Most are old Yankee jalopies. They usually take as many passengers as they can cram in.

Private Cabs

Private taxis were legalized in 2009; your vehicle could be anything from a clapped-out Lada to a ritzy Audi. Freelance driver-guides hang outside tourist hotels, restaurants, and discos. Your fare is negotiable. Educate yourself about *turistaxi* fares to your destination beforehand, as many drivers attempt to gouge you and you may end up paying more than you would in a tourist taxi. Agree on the fare *before* getting in. Make sure you know whether it is one-way or round-trip.

Coco-Taxis

These bright yellow fiberglass motorized tricycles look like scooped-out Easter eggs on wheels. You'll find them outside major hotels and cruising the tourist zones in large cities. They charge about the same as tourist taxis. However, they have no safety features, and several accidents involving tourists have been reported.

Bici-Taxis

Bici-taxis—the Cuban equivalent of rickshaws—patrol the main streets of most Cuban cities. These tricycles have been cobbled together with welding torches, with car-like seats and shade canopies. They offer a cheap (albeit bumpy) way of sightseeing and getting around if you're in no hurry. Some *ciclo-taxis* are only licensed to take Cubans (who pay pesos). Always negotiate a fare before setting off.

Coches

These horse-drawn cabs are a staple of local transport. In Havana, Varadero, and other beach resorts, antique carriages with leather seats are touted for sightseeing. Elsewhere they're a utility vehicle for the hoi polloi and are often decrepit, with basic bench seats. They operate along fixed routes and usually charge one to three pesos, depending on distance.

CAR

Cuba is a great place to drive if you can handle the often perilous conditions. There are no restrictions on where you can go. Cuba has 31,000 kilometers of roads (15,500 kilometers are paved), though even major highways are deteriorated to the point of being dangerous.

The main highway, the Carretera Central (Central Highway), runs along the island's spine for 1,200 kilometers from one end of the country to the other. This two-laner leads through sleepy rural towns. For maximum speed take the A-1, or Autopista Nacional (National Expressway), the country's only freeway—eight (unmarked) lanes wide but much deteriorated in recent years. About 650 kilometers have been completed, from Pinar del Río to a point just east of Sancti Spíritus, and from Santiago de Cuba about 30 kilometers northwestward.

Only a few highways are well signed, although things are improving. You can buy the excellent *Guía de Carreteras* road atlas at tour desks and souvenir outlets. It's extraordinary how little Cubans know of regions outside their own locale. Rather than asking, "Does this road go to so-and-so?"

("Where does this route go?").

Traffic Regulations and Safety

To drive in Cuba, you must be 21 years or older and hold either a valid national driver's license or an international driver's license (IDL), obtainable through automobile associations worldwide (www.aaa.com, United States; www.caa.ca, Canada; www.theaa.com, U.K.; www.aaa.asn.au, Australia; or www.aa.co.nz, New Zealand).

Traffic drives on the right. The speed limit is 100 kph (kilometers per hour) on the Autopista, 90 kph on highways, 60 kph on rural roads, 50 kph on urban roads, and 40 kph in children's zones. Speed limits are vigorously enforced. Ubiquitous, overzealous traffic police (*tránsitos* or *tráficos*) patrol the highways. Oncoming cars will flash their lights to indicate the presence of police ahead. Major highways have *puntos de control*—police control points, for which you must slow. If you receive a traffic fine, the policeman will note this on your car rental contract, to be deducted from your deposit. The *tráfico* cannot request a fine on the spot, although Cuban police occasionally attempt to extract a subtle bribe. If so, ask for the policeman's name and where you can fight the ticket (this usually results in you being waved on your way).

Seatbelt use is mandatory in front seats; motorcyclists are required to wear helmets. Note that it's illegal to: 1) enter an intersection unless you can exit; 2) make a right turn on a red light unless indicated by a white arrow or traffic signal (*derecha con luz roja*); or 3) overtake on the right. You must stop at *all* railway crossings before crossing. Headlights by day are illegal, except for emergency vehicles, but you should use yours and be seen.

Road conditions often deteriorate without warning, and obstacles are numerous and comprise everything from wayward livestock to mammoth potholes. Driving at night is perilous, not least because few roads are lit. Sticks jutting up in the road usually indicate a dangerous hole. *Keep your speed down!*

Accidents and Breakdowns

Rental car agencies have a clause to protect against damage to the car from unwarranted repairs. Call the rental agency; it will arrange a tow or send a mechanic.

In the event of an accident, *never* move the vehicles until the police arrive. Get the names, license plate numbers, and *cédulas* (legal identification numbers) of any witnesses. Make a sketch of the accident. Then call the **transit police** (tel. 07/882-0116 in Havana; tel. 116 outside Havana) and your rental agency. In case of injury, call for an **ambulance** (tel. 104 nationwide). Do not leave the accident scene; the other party may tamper with your car and the evidence. Don't let honking traffic pressure you into moving the cars. If you suspect the other driver has been drinking, ask the police officer to administer a Breathalyzer test—an *alcolemia*.

Cuba's Vintage American Cars

Automotive sentimentality is reason enough to visit Cuba, the greatest living car museum in the world. American cars flooded into Cuba for 50 years, culminating in the Batista era. Then came the Cuban Revolution and the U.S. trade embargo. In terms of American automobiles, time stopped when Castro took power.

Today, Cuba possesses about 600,000 cars, of which about one-sixth are prerevolutionary American autos. In certain areas, one rarely sees a vehicle that is *not* a venerable, usually decrepit, classic of yesteryear.

Lacking proper tools and replacement parts, Cubans adeptly cajole one more year out of their battered hulks. Their intestinally reconstituted engines are monuments to ingenuity—decades of improvised repairs have melded parts from Detroit and Moscow. One occasionally spots a shining example of museum quality. The majority, though, have long ago been touched up with house paint. That said, more cars today look better than ever thanks to the new accessibility of real car paint and replica car parts from the States.

Owners of prerevolutionary cars can sell them freely to anyone with money to buy, but the chances of owning a more modern car are slim. Virtually all cars imported since 1959—Ladas (a Russian-made Fiat described by Martha Gellhorn as "tough as a Land Rover, with iron-hard upholstery and, judging by sensation, no springs"), Soviet UAZs, jeep-like Romanian AROs, and more recently Mercedes-Benzes, Nissans, Citroëns, and Chinese Geelys—are owned by the state. New such cars were leased out to Communist bigwigs, high-level workers, and state executives. Sports stars and top artists were also gifted or allowed to buy cars. Since 2011, Cubans have been permitted to buy and sell cars freely, regardless of vintage. Cuba's new breed of middle class is finally flaunting its wealth with imported BMWs and Audis, although the state still controls sales of all imported vehicles, charges a fortune, and restricts who can buy (the self-employed, farmers, and foreign company employees, for example, must make do with the higher-priced private used car market).

Cuba Classics: A Celebration of Vintage American Automobiles (http://christopherpbaker.com/cuba-classics-2) is an illustrated coffee-table book that offers a paean to the cars and their owners.

Accidents that result in death or injury are treated like crimes, and the onus is on the driver to prove innocence. Prison sentences can range 1-10 years. If you are involved in an accident in which someone is injured or killed, you will not be allowed to leave Cuba until the trial has taken place, which can take up to a year. Contact your embassy for legal assistance.

Gasoline

Gasoline (*petróleo*) and diesel (*gasolina*) are sold at Cupet and Oro Negro stations (*servicentros*) nationwide. Most are open 24 hours. Gas stations are supposed to sell only *especial* (usually about CUC1.40 per liter—about CUC5.60 a gallon) to tourists in rental cars, and you may be refused cheaper *regular* (CUC1.20 per liter), even if that's all that's available. (Local gas

Making Sense of Addresses

In most Cuban cities, addresses are given as locations. Thus, the Havanatur office is at Calle 6, e/ 1ra y 3ra, Miramar, Havana, meaning it is on Calle 6 between (e/ for *entre*—between) 1st and 3rd Avenues (Avenidas 1ra y 3ra).

Street numbers are occasionally used. Thus, the Hotel Inglaterra is at Prado #416, esq. San Rafael, Habana Vieja; at the corner (esq. for *esquina*—corner) of Prado and Calle San Rafael, in Old Havana (Habana Vieja).

Reparto (abbreviated to Rpto.) is a district. *Final* refers to the end of a street, or a cul-de-sac.

Piso refers to the floor level (thus, an office on *piso 3ro* is on the third floor). *Altos* refers to "upstairs," and *bajos* refers to "downstairs."

Most cities are laid out on a grid pattern centered on a main square or plaza, with parallel streets (*calles*) running perpendicular to avenues (*avenidas*).

Many streets have at least two names: one predating the Revolution (and usually the most commonly used colloquially) and the other a postrevolutionary name. On maps, the modern name takes precedence, with the old name often shown in parentheses.

stations, *bombas,* serve *regular* to Cubans only.) Electricity blackouts often shut the pumps down. Few stations accept credit cards.

Insurance

If you have your own vehicle, the state-run organization **ESEN** (Calle 5ta #306, e/ C y D, Vedado, Havana, tel. 07/832-2508, www.esen.cu) insures automobiles and has special packages for foreigners. However, this does not include "liability" insurance similar to the United States or United Kingdom.

Rental

Don't rent a car at the airport; relax for a day or two first.

Demand exceeds supply. During Christmas and New Year's, you'll need reservations, which can only be made within 15 days of your arrival; it's no guarantee that your reservation will be honored (ask for a copy of the reservation to be faxed to you and take this with you). If one office tells you there are no cars, go to another office (even of the same company). In a worst-case scenario, head to the next town (cars are always in short supply in Havana but are often available in Matanzas).

Expect to pay CUC50-185 per day with unlimited mileage, depending on vehicle; a two-day minimum applies for unlimited mileage. Added charges apply for one-way rentals, for drivers under 25 years of age, and for second drivers (CUC15). Discounts apply for rentals over seven days. The companies accept cash or credit cards (except those issued by U.S. banks). You must pay a deposit of CUC200-500; the agency will run off a credit card authorization that you will receive back once you return the car, assuming it has no damage. You must pay in cash for the first tank of gas before you drive away, although your contract states that you must return the tank empty (an outrageous state-run rip-off). Gaviota's Vía is preferred—its gasoline policy is the international norm: You return the car with the same amount as when rented. Check the fuel level *before* setting off; if it doesn't look full to the brim, point this out to the rental agent and demand a refund, or that it be topped off (but good luck getting that). Clarify any late-return penalties, and that the time recorded on your contract is that for your *departure with the car,* not the time you entered into negotiation.

Rental cars are poorly serviced and often not roadworthy, although in 2014 Transtur (www.transtur.tur.cu), the parent company of Cubatur, Havanautos, and Rex, purchased several thousand new Audi, MG, Peugeot, Volkswagen, and other European and Asian sedans. Inspect your car thoroughly before setting off; otherwise, you may be charged for the slightest dent when you return. Don't forget the inside, plus radio antenna, spare tire, the jack, and wrench. Don't assume the car rental agency has taken care of tire pressure or fluids. Note the *Aviso Próximo Mantenimiento* column on the rental contract. This indicates the kilometer reading by which you—*the renter*—are required to take the car to an agency office for scheduled servicing; you're granted only 100 kilometers leeway. If you fail to honor the clause, you'll be charged CUC50. This scam is a disgrace, as you may have to drive miles out of your way to an agency and then wait hours, or even overnight, for the car to be serviced.

Most agencies offer a chauffeur service (CUC50-120 a day). A four-wheel-drive vehicle is recommended only for exploring mountain areas.

RENTAL COMPANIES

Only state-owned car rental agencies operate. **Transtur** (Calle L #456, e/ 25 y 27, Vedado, www.transtur.tur.cu) operates **Cubacar** (tel. 07/835-0000), **Havanautos** (tel. 07/273-2277), and **Rex** (tel. 07/835-6830, www.rex.cu). There are scores of offices nationwide. There's no difference between the companies, although rates vary. For example, Havanautos offers 20 types of vehicles—from the tiny Geely CK (about CUC325 weekly) to an eight-passenger VK Transporter minivan (CUC1,400 weekly) and BMW 5-series and Audi A6 (CUC1,450 weekly). Rex has nine models—from the Seat Ibiza (from CUC65 daily low season, CUC80 high season) to the Mercedes #200 (CUC225 daily). Rates may vary between agencies but typically include 150 kilometers daily (unlimited on rentals of three days or more).

Gaviota's **Vía Rent-a-Car** (tel. 07/206-9935, www.gaviota-grupo.com) mostly rents Peugeots and Chinese-made Geelys, plus the tiny Suzuki Jimny jeep.

INSURANCE

Be sure to purchase insurance offered by the rental agency. You have two choices: CDW (Collision Damage Waiver, CUC15-20 daily, with a deductible of CUC200-500) covers accidents but not theft. Super CDW

Travel Distances in Havana

Distances in Kilometers

	Havana
Baracoa	1,168
Bayamo	819
Camagüey	546
Ciego de Ávila	438
Cienfuegos	243
Guantánamo	1,026
Guardalavaca	802
Holguín	748
Las Tunas	670
Matanzas	102
Pinar del Río	176
Sancti Spíritus	362
Santa Clara	276
Santa Lucía	658
Santiago de Cuba	944
Soroa	86
Trinidad	321
Varadero	144
Viñales	193

(CUC20-40) offers fully comprehensive coverage, except for the radio and spare tire. The insurance must be paid in cash. If you decline, you'll be required to put down a huge cash deposit. If your car is broken into or otherwise damaged, you must get a police statement (a *denuncia*), otherwise you will be charged for the damage. You can also name any licensed Cuban driver on your rental policy. However, there is no comprehensive liability coverage in Cuban insurance packages: If you (or anyone else driving your rented vehicle) are deemed at fault in an accident, rental agencies will nullify coverage and seek damages to cover the cost of repairs. You may be prevented from leaving the country until payment is obtained.

SAFETY

Theft, including of car parts, is a huge problem. Always park in *parqueos,* designated parking lots with a *custodio* (guard). Alternatively, tip the hotel security staff or hire someone to guard your car.

Your car rental contract states that picking up hitchhikers is not allowed. Foreign embassies report that many tourists have been robbed, and I do not endorse picking up hitchhikers.

Motorcycles and Scooters

You cannot rent motorcycles in Cuba (except, perhaps, from private individuals). Scooters can be rented in Havana and at resort hotels. California-based **Cuba Motorcycle Tours** (tel. 760/327-9879, www.cubamotorcycletours.com) offers 8-, 12-, and 14-day "people-to-people" programs by motorcycle, but does not rent bikes. It can customize tours for small groups.

BICYCLE

Bike rental is increasingly available in Cuba from private entrepreneurs; feeble beach cruisers can be rented at resort hotels. You'll need to bring your own bike. A sturdy lock is essential.

HITCHHIKING

Roadways are lined with thousands of hitchers, many of them so desperate that they wave peso bills at passing vehicles—be it a tractor, a truck, or a motorcycle. If it moves, in Cuba it's fair game. The state has even set up *botellas* (hitchhiking posts) where officials wearing mustard-colored uniforms (and therefore termed *coges amarillas,* or yellow-jackets) wave down state vehicles, which must stop to pick up hitchers.

It can be excruciatingly slow going, and there are never any guarantees for your safety. Hence, I don't recommend or endorse hitchhiking. If you receive a ride in a private car, politeness dictates that you offer to pay for your ride: *"¿Cuánto le debo?"* after you're safely delivered.

Visas and Officialdom

DOCUMENTS AND REQUIREMENTS
Cuban Tourist Visas

A passport valid for six months from date of entry is required. Every visitor needs a Cuban visa or tourist card (*tarjeta de turista*) valid for a single trip of 30 days (90 days for Canadians); for most visitors, including U.S. citizens, a tourist card will suffice. No tourist card is required for transit passengers continuing their journey to a third country within 72 hours. Tourist cards are issued outside Cuba by tour agencies or the airline providing travel to Cuba. They cost US$85 (£30-40 in the U.K., or £15 if you go in person to the Cuban consulate; flights from Canada include the fee). In some cases, tourist cards can be obtained at the airport upon arrival within Cuba (CUC100 in Miami and other U.S. airports).

Journalists require a journalist visa; students and academics entering to take classes or engage in research need a student or academic visa. U.S. citizens entering under the general license category for professional research need a Cuban visa to that effect, including an invitation from a formal Cuban entity.

Don't list your occupation as journalist, police, military personnel, or government employee, as the Cuban government is highly suspicious of anyone with these occupations.

EXTENSIONS

You can request up to two 30-day tourist visa extensions (*prórroga,* CUC25, payable in stamps—*sellos*—purchased at Cuban banks) in Havana at **Inmigración** (Calle 17, e/ J y K, Vedado, tel. 07/861-3462, Mon.-Wed. and Fri. 8:30am-4pm, Thurs. and Sat. 8:30am-11am), or at immigration offices in major cities. Dress conservatively; short shorts and flip-flops are not allowed. You need CUC25 of stamps purchased at any bank, plus proof of medical insurance and airline reservation to exit; if you're staying in a *casa particular* you also need a receipt for the house.

Visitors who overstay their visas may be held in custody until reports are received on their activities in the country. In such an event, you are billed daily! Do not overextend your stay.

CUBAN ÉMIGRÉS

Cuban-born individuals who permanently left Cuba after December 31, 1970, must have a valid Cuban passport to enter and leave Cuba (you will also need your U.S. passport to depart and enter the United States). Cuban passports can be obtained from the **Cuban Embassy** (2630 16th St. NW, Washington DC 20009, tel. 202/797-8515, www.cubadiplomatica.cu) or any Cuban consulate in other countries. Cuban émigrés holding Cuban passports do not need to apply for a visa to travel to Cuba. Cuba does not recognize dual citizenship for Cuban citizens who are also U.S. citizens; Cuban-born citizens are thereby denied representation through the U.S. Embassy in the event of arrest.

Non-Tourist Visas

If you enter using a tourist visa and then wish to change your visa status, contact the **Ministerio de Relaciones Exteriores** (Ministry of Foreign Affairs; MINREX, Calle Calzada #360, e/ G y H, Vedado, tel. 07/835-7421

Regional Immigration Offices

The following regional offices have varying hours for handling requests for visa extensions (*prórrogas*) and other immigration issues:

- **Baracoa:** Maceo #48

- **Bayamo:** Carretera Central y 7ma, Rpto. Las Caobas, tel. 023/48-6148

- **Camagüey:** Calle 3ra #156, e/ 8 y 10, Rpto. Vista Hermosa, tel. 032/27-5201

- **Ciego de Ávila:** Independencia Este #14, tel. 033/27-3387

- **Cienfuegos:** Av. 48, e/ 29 y 31, tel. 043/52-1017

- **Guantánamo:** Calle 1 Oeste, e/ 14 y 15 Norte, tel. 024/43-0027, one block north of the Hotel Guantánamo

- **Holguín:** General Vásquez y General Marrero, tel. 024/40-2323

- **Las Tunas:** Av. Camilo Cienfuegos, esq. Jorge Rodríguez Nápoles, Rpto. Buena Vista

- **Manzanillo:** Martí, esq. Masó, tel. 023/57-2584

- **Matanzas:** Calle 85 #29408, e/ 2 de Mayo y Manzaneda

- **Nueva Gerona:** Calle 35 #3216, esq. 34, tel. 046/30-3284

- **Pinar del Río:** Gerardo Medina, esq. Isabel Rubio, tel. 048/77-1404

- **Sancti Spíritus:** Independencia Norte #107, tel. 041/32-4729

- **Santa Clara:** Av. Sandino, esq. 6ta, three blocks east of Estadio Sandino, tel. 042/20-5868

- **Santiago de Cuba:** Centro Negocios, Av. Jesús Menéndez, esq. José Saco, tel. 022/65-7507 (There's also an office outside the airport.)

- **Trinidad:** Concordia #20, off Paseo Agramonte, tel. 041/99-6950

- **Varadero:** Calle 39 y 1ra, tel. 045/61-3494

or 07/832-3279, www.cubaminrex.cu). Journalists must enter on a journalist's D-6 visa. Ostensibly these should be obtained in advance from Cuban embassies, and in the United States from the **Cuban Embassy** (2639 16th St. NW, Washington, DC 20009, tel. 202/797-8518, recepcion@usadc.embacuba.cu). However, processing can take months. If you enter on a tourist visa and intend to exercise your profession, you must register for a D-6 visa at the **Centro de Prensa Internacional** (International Press Center, Calle cu, Mon.-Fri. 8:30am-5pm). Ask for an Acreditación de Prensa Extranjera (Foreign Journalist's Accreditation). You'll need passport photos. Here, a journalist's visa (CUC70) can be got in a day, but you might not get your passport back for a week.

A commercial visa is required for individuals traveling to Cuba for business. These must also be obtained in advance from Cuban embassies.

Other Documentation

Visitors need a return ticket and adequate finances for their stay. The law requires that you carry your passport and tourist card with you at all times. Make photocopies of all your important documents and keep them separate from the originals, which you can keep in your hotel safe.

Cuban Embassies and Consulates

Cuba has Cuban embassies and representation in many nations. For a complete list, visit www.misiones.minrex.gob.cu.

- **Australia:** 1 Gregory Place, O'Malley, ACT 2606, tel. 02/6286-8770, asicuba@cubaus.net.
- **Canada:** 388 Main St., Ottawa, ON K1S 1E3, tel. 613/563-0141, consulcuba@embacubacanada.net (embassy and consulate); 4542 Decarie Blvd., Montreal, QC H4A 3P2, tel. 514/843-8897, seconcgc@bellnet.ca (consulate); 5353 Dundas St. W. #401, Toronto, ON M9B 6H8, tel. 416/234-8181, toronto@embacubacanada.net (consulate).
- **United Kingdom:** 167 High Holborn, London WC1V 6PA, tel. 020/7240-7463, consulcuba@uk.embacuba.cu.
- **United States:** 2630 16th St. NW, Washington DC 20009, tel. 202/797-8515, recepcion@usadc.embacuba.cu.

CUSTOMS

Visitors to Cuba are permitted 20 kilos of personal effects plus "other articles and equipment depending on their profession," all of which must be re-exported. An additional 2 kilos of gifts are permitted, if packed separately. Visitors are also allowed 10 kilos of medicines. An additional US$51 of "objects and articles for noncommercial use" can be imported free; thereafter, items up to $501 are subject to a tax equal to 100 percent of the declared value, and items $501-1,000 to a tax 200 percent of declared value, but this applies mostly to Cubans and returning foreign residents. Both the Obama and Raúl Castro administrations have lifted restrictions on many goods, such as computers, DVD players, and TVs. "Obscene and pornographic" literature is banned—the definition includes politically unacceptable tracts. (If you must leave items with customs authorities, obtain a signed receipt to enable you to reclaim the items upon departure.)

For further information, contact **Aduana** (Customs, Calle 6, esq. 39, Plaza de la Revolución, Havana, tel. 07/883-8282, www.aduana.gob.cu).

The following nations have embassies and consulates in Havana. Those of other countries can be found at www.embassypages.com/cuba.

- **Australia:** c/o Canadian Embassy.

- **Canada:** Calle 30 #518, esq. 7ma, Miramar, tel. 07/204-2516, www.la-habana.gc.ca.

- **United Kingdom:** Calle 34 #702, e/ 7ma y 17-A, Miramar, tel. 07/214-2200, embrit@ceniai.inf.cu.

- **United States:** Calzada, e/ L y M, Vedado, Havana, tel. 07/839-4100, https://cu.usembassy.gov. Readers report that it has been helpful to U.S. citizens in distress, and that staff are not overly concerned about policing infractions of travel restrictions.

Recreation

BICYCLING AND MOTORCYCLING

Bicycle touring offers a chance to explore the island alongside the Cubans themselves. Roads are little trafficked yet full of hazards. Wear a helmet! Most airlines treat bicycles as a piece of luggage and require that bicycles be boxed; Cubana does not. Bring essential spares, plus locks.

If planning an all-Cuba trip, touring is best done in a westerly direction to take advantage of prevailing winds. A good resource is *Bicycling Cuba,* by Barbara and Wally Smith.

In Cuba, **WowCuba** (Centro de Negocios Kohly, Calle 34 e/ 49 y 49A, Kohly, Havana, tel. 07/796-7655, www.wowcuba.com) offers bicycle tours, as do U.K.-based **Cubania Travel** (tel. 0208-355-7608, www.cubaniatravel.com) and Canada's **Exodus** (tel. 800/267-3347, www.exodustravels.com).

Motorcycling is big business, and four fleets of imported BMWs, Harley-Davidsons, and Suzukis serve foreigners. **Cross Cultural Journeys** (tel. 800/353-2276, http://www.crossculturaljourneys.com); **Cuba Motorcycle Tours** (tel. 760/327-9879, www.cubamotorcycletours.com); and **RTW Moto Tours** (tel. 480/328-3039, www.rtwmototours.com) serve the U.S. market. **Edelweiss** (tel. +43 5264-5690, www.edelweissbike.com) serves Europeans.

BIRD-WATCHING

The Península de Zapata is one of the best bird-watching areas in the Caribbean (its 203 species include 18 of the nation's 21 endemics), as are Cayo Coco (more than 200 species, including flamingos), Isla de la Juventud (for cranes and endemic parrots), and mountain zones such as the Reserva de la Biosfera Sierra del Rosario, Reserva de la Biosfera Baconao, and Reserva de la Biosfera Cuchillas de Toa.

U.S. company **Naturalist Journeys** (tel. 520/558-1146 or 866/900-1146, www.naturalistjourneys.com) has birding trips in Cuba, as does **Quest**

Nature Tours (491 King St., Toronto, ON M5A 1L9, tel. 416/633-5666 or 800/387-1483, www.questnaturetours.com).

ECOTOURISM AND HIKING

Cuba has the potential to be a hiking and ecotourism paradise. Both activities are relatively undeveloped. Notable exceptions are the trails in the Reserva de la Biosfera Sierra del Rosario and Parque Nacional Península de Guanahacabibes, in Pinar del Río; and Parque Nacional Pico Turquino and Cuchillas de Toa, in Oriente.

Guides are compulsory in national parks. Pinares de Mayarí (in Holguín Province), El Saltón (in Santiago Province), and Hotel Moka (in Pinar del Río) are Cuba's three so-called "eco-lodges," although they are really lodges merely set in wilderness areas.

EcoTur, S.A. (tel. 07/649-1055, www.ecoturcuba.tur.cu) offers eco-oriented tours—that include hunting and Jet Skiing!

FISHING
Freshwater and Inshore Fishing

Cuba's freshwater lakes and lagoons boil with tarpon, bonefish, snook, and bass. The star of the show is largemouth bass, which is best at Embalse Hanabanilla in the Sierra Escambray; Embalse Zaza in Sancti Spíritus Province; and Lago La Redonda, near Morón in Ciego de Ávila Province. As for bonefish and tarpon, few (if any) destinations can compare. This feisty shallow-water game fish is abundant off Cayo Largo and the Cayos de Villa Clara; in the Jardines de la Reina archipelago south of Ciego de Ávila Province; and in the coastal lagoons of Península de Zapata. In Cuba, EcoTur (tel. 07/649-1055, www.ecoturcuba.tur.cu) also offers fishing trips.

Italian company Avalon (http://cubanfishingcenters.com) has a monopoly for fishing in the Jardines de la Reina.

U.S. tour operator Orvis (tel. 800/547-4322, www.orvis.com) offers fly-fishing trips in Cuba, as does U.K.-based CubaWelcome (in Cuba tel. 5344-8888, U.K. tel. 020/7731-6871, www.cubawelcome.com), which has an office in Havana.

Deep-Sea Fishing

So many game fish travel through the Gulf Stream—Ernest Hemingway's "great blue river"—that hardly a season goes by without some IGFA record being broken. The marlin run begins in May, when the sailfish swim against the current close to the Cuban shore. The Cubans aren't yet into tag-and-release, preferring to let you sauté the trophy (for a cut of the steak).

Fishing expeditions are offered from Marlin Náutica y Marinas (www.nauticamarlin.com) nationwide.

GOLF

Before the Revolution, Cuba had several golf courses. After 1959, they were closed and fell into ruin. The only courses currently open are the 9-hole

Havana Golf Club and an 18-hole championship course in Varadero. For years, Cuba has been talking about investing in its future as a golfing destination. Ten new golf course projects are on the books. In 2010, Cuba announced it would finally approve financing the resorts through residential real estate sales to foreigners—a prerequisite for foreign investors. In 2015, Cuba created CubaGolf, a division of the state entity Palmares, to manage the planned golf courses.

ROCK CLIMBING AND SPELUNKING

Cuba is riddled with caverns, and caving (spelunking) is growing in popularity, organized through the **Sociedad Espeleológica de Cuba** (Calle 9na #8402, esq. 84, Havana, tel. 07/202-5025, funatss@enet.cu), which also has a climbing division (c/o Anibal Fernández, Calle Águila #367, e/ Neptuno y San Miguel, Centro Habana, tel. 07/862-0401, anibalpiaz@yahoo.com). Many climbing routes have been established in Viñales. Climbing routes are open and no permission is necessary. Cuban American climber Armando Menocal (U.S. tel. 307/734-6034) is a good resource. Fernández and Menocal's superb *Cuba Climbing* (www.quickdrawpublications.com) guidebook is indispensable.

SAILING AND KAYAKING

Most all-inclusive resort hotels have Hobie Cats for hourly rental. Some also have kayaks. Yachts and catamarans can be rented at most marinas; try **Marlin Náutica y Marinas** (tel. 07/273-7912, www.nauticamarlin.com). You can also charter through Germany-based **Plattensail** (www.platten-sailing.de), which offers yacht charters out of Cienfuegos. However, they must be reserved *before* arrival in Cuba.

Cuba Unbound (tel. 208/770-3359, www.cubaunbound.com) and **Cuba Adventure Company** (tel. 902/759-9096, www.cubaadventurecompany.com) offer kayaking trips for U.S. citizens.

SCUBA DIVING

Cuba is a diver's paradise. There are dozens of sunken Spanish galleons and modern vessels and aircraft, and the coral formations astound. Visibility ranges from 15 to 35 meters. Water temperatures average 27-29°C.

Cuba has almost 40 dive centers. Most large resort hotels have scuba outlets. Certification courses are usually for the American and Canadian Underwater Certification (ACUC), not PADI. Cuban dive masters are generally well trained, but equipment is often not up to Western standards, and dive shops are meagerly equipped. Spearfishing is strictly controlled. Spearguns and gigs are *not* allowed through customs.

Cuba has four principal dive areas: the Archipiélago de Las Colorados, off the north coast of Pinar del Río; the Jardines de la Rey archipelago, off the north coast of Ciego de Ávila and Camagüey Provinces; the Jardines de la Reina archipelago off the southern coast of Ciego de Ávila and Camagüey Provinces; and Isla de la Juventud and

Cayo Largo. The so-called Blue Circuit east of Havana also has prime sites, as do the waters off the tip of Cabo de Corrientes, at the western-most point of Cuba (good for whale sharks). Isla de la Juventud, with many of the best wrecks and walls, is primarily for experienced divers. Varadero is of only modest interest for experienced divers, although it has caves and wrecks.

For U.S. Citizens: Yes, you can finally dive in Cuba legally. Dr. David E. Guggenheim leads "people-to-people" trips through **Ocean Doctor** (tel. 202/695-2550, www.oceandoctor.org) to the "Garden of the Queens."

Entertainment and Events

Cuba pulsates with the Afro-Latin spirit, be it energy-charged Las Vegas-style cabarets or someone's home-based celebration (called *cumbanchas,* or rumbas), where drummers beat out thumping rhythms and partners dance overtly sexual *changüí* numbers. And *noches cubanas* take place in most towns on Saturday nights, when bars and discos are set up alfresco and the street is cleared for dancing.

Havana is now throbbing to a new breed of sizzling nightclubs, many privately owned, that rival the best of New York and South Beach. That said, Cuba's nocturnal entertainment scene is a far cry from days of yore, and in many locales you are hard-pressed to find any signs of life.

LaHabana (www.lahabana.com) is the best source for information on artistic and cultural events, festivals, courses, and workshops.

NIGHTLIFE
Bars and Discos

Cuba's bar scene is anemic. Cuban cities are relatively devoid of the kind of lively sidewalk bars that make Rio de Janeiro buzz and South Beach hum, although Havana has gained several sensational new bars in recent years. Tourist-only hotel bars are with few exceptions pretty dead, while those serving locals are run-down to the point of dilapidation (and often serving beer or rum in sawn-off beer bottles).

The dance scene is much livelier. Most towns have at least one disco or *centro nocturno* (nightclub or open-air disco) hosting live music from salsa bands to folkloric trios. Romantic crooners are a staple, wooing local crowds with dead-on deliveries of Benny Moré classics. Foreign males can expect to be solicited outside the entrance to a disco: Cuban women beg to be escorted in because the cover charge is beyond their means and/or because the venue only permits couples to enter. Drink prices can give you sticker shock: It's cheaper to buy a bottle of rum and a Coca-Cola. Few discos get their groove on before midnight.

Many clubs apply a *consumo mínimo* (minimum charge) policy that covers entry plus a certain value of drinks.

Consumo Mínimo

You'll come across this term everywhere for entry to nightclubs and many other facilities. The term means "minimum consumption." Basically, it means that patrons have a right to consume up to a specified amount of food and/or beverage with a cover charge. For example, entry to the swimming pool at the Hotel Sevilla costs CUC20 but includes a *consumo mínimo* of up to CUC16 of food and beverage. There are no refunds for unused portions of the fee. The system is rife with *estafas* (swindles).

Folkloric Music Venues

Every town has a *casa de la trova* and a *casa de la cultura* where you can hear traditional *música folklórica* (folkloric music), including ballad-style *trova* (love songs rendered with the aid of guitar and drum), often blended with revolutionary themes. UNEAC (National Union of Cuban Writers and Artists, www.uneac.org.cu) also has regional outlets hosting cultural events.

Cabarets

One of the first acts of the revolutionary government was to kick out the Mafia and close down the casinos and brothels. "It was as if the Amish had taken over Las Vegas," wrote Kenneth Tynan in a 1961 edition of *Holiday*. Not quite! Sure, the strip clubs and live sex shows are gone. But sexy Las Vegas-style cabarets (called *espectáculos,* or shows) remain a staple of Cuban entertainment; every town has at least one. They're highlighted by long-legged dancers wearing high heels and G-strings, with lots of feathers and frills. Singers, magicians, acrobats, and comedians are often featured.

Outshining all other venues is the Tropicana, with outlets in Havana, Matanzas, and Santiago de Cuba.

THE ARTS

Theater is the least developed of Cuba's cultural media. Theater was usurped by the Revolution as a medium for mass-consciousness-raising. As such it became heavily politicized. In recent years, however, an avant-garde theater scene has evolved. The run-down theaters are used mostly for operatic, symphonic, and comic theater. However, you'll need to be fluent in Spanish to get many giggles out of the comedy shows, full of burlesque and references to politically sensitive third-rail issues.

CINEMA

Cubans are passionate moviegoers, although most cinemas are extremely run-down. Entrance usually costs a peso, and the menu is surprisingly varied and hip. Movies are often subtitled in Spanish (others are dubbed; you'll need to be fluent in Spanish). No children under 16 are admitted;

Major Festivals

Festival/Event	Month	Location
Habanos Festival (Cigar Festival)	February	Havana
Festival Internacional de Jazz (International Jazz Festival)	February	Havana
Festival de Semana Santa (Easter)	April	Trinidad
Festival Internacional de Percusión (International Percussion Festival)	April	Havana
Festival Internacional de Cine Pobre (International Low-Budget Film Festival)	April	Gibara
Carnaval de la Habana	August	Havana
Fiesta del Caribe (Carnaval)	July	Santiago de Cuba
Festival de la Habana de Música Contemporánea (Havana Festival of Contemporary Music)	October	Havana
Fiesta Iberoamericana de la Cultura (Festival of Latin American Culture)	October	Holguín
Festival Internacional de Ballet (International Ballet Festival)	October	Havana
Festival del Nuevo Cine Latinoamericano (Festival of New Latin American Cinema)	November	Havana
Festival Internacional de Música Benny Moré (Benny Moré International Music Festival)	December	Cienfuegos

most towns have special children's screenings. Many cinemas also have *salas de videos*—tiny screening rooms.

FESTIVALS AND EVENTS

The annual calendar is filled with cultural events ranging from "high culture," such as the Festival Internacional de Ballet, to purely local affairs, such as the year-end *parrandas* of Villa Clara Province, where the townsfolk indulge in massive fireworks battles. A highlight is Carnaval, held in Havana (August) and Santiago (July). Religious parades include the Procession of the Miracles (December 17), when pilgrims descend on the Santuario de San Lázaro, at Rincón, on the outskirts of Santiago de las Vegas in suburban Havana. The old Spanish holiday El Día de los Reyes Magos (Three Kings' Day), on January 6, is the most important religious observance.

For a list of events, check out **LaHabana** (www.lahabana.com).

SPECTATOR SPORTS

Cuba is a world superstar in sports and athletics, as it was even before the Revolution, especially in baseball and boxing. Following the Revolution, professional sports were abolished and the state took over all sports under the **Instituto Nacional del Deportivo y Recreo** (National Institute for Sport, Physical Education, and Recreation, INDER, www.inder.cu).

The Cuban calendar is replete with sporting events. **Cubadeportes** (Calle 20 #706, e/ 7 y 9, Miramar, tel. 07/204-0946, www.cubadeportes. cu) specializes in sports tourism and arranges visits to sporting events and training facilities.

Shopping

Department stores and shopping malls can be found in Havana. These, and smaller outlets in every town, sell Western goods from toiletries, Levi's, and Reeboks to Chinese toys and Japanese electronics sold for CUC at vastly inflated prices. If you see something you want, *buy it!* If you dally, it most likely will disappear. Most stores selling to tourists accept foreign credit cards except those issued by U.S. banks, but an 11 percent surcharge applies. Peso stores are meagerly stocked with second-rate local produce.

ARTS AND CRAFTS

For quality arts and crafts, Cuba is unrivaled in the Caribbean. Arts and crafts are sold by artisans at street stalls and in state agency stores such as the Fondo Cubano de Bienes Culturales and Artex. The best stuff is sold in upscale hotels, which inflate prices accordingly. Tourist venues are overflowing with kitschy paintings, busty cigar-chomping ceramic mulattas, erotic carvings, and papier-mâché vintage Yankee cars. There is also plenty of true-quality art, ranging from paintings to hand-worked leather goods. You'll also see *muñequitas* (dolls) representing the goddesses of the Santería religion.

Most open-air markets offer silver-plated jewelry at bargain prices (a favorite form is old cutlery shaped into bracelets), while most upscale hotels have *joyerías* (jewelry stores) selling international-quality silver jewelry, much of it in a distinctly Cuban contemporary style. *Avoid buying black coral, turtle shell jewelry, and other animal "craft" items.* The Cuban government doesn't seem conscientious in this regard, but European and North American customs officials may seize these illegal items.

Turning Out Champions

Tiny Cuba is one of the world's sports powers, excelling in baseball, volleyball, boxing, and track and field. Cuba is by far the strongest Olympic power in Latin America.

Cuba's international success is credited to its splendid sports training system. When the Revolution triumphed, sports became a priority alongside land reform, education, and health care. In 1964 the Castro government opened a network of sports schools—Escuelas de Iniciación Deportiva (EIDE)—as part of the primary and secondary education system, with the job of preparing young talent for sports achievement. There are 15 EIDE schools throughout Cuba. The island also has 76 sports academies and an athletic "finishing" school in Havana, the Escuela Superior de Perfeccionamiento Atlético.

Sports training is incorporated into every school curriculum. School Games are held islandwide every year and help identify talent to be selected for specialized coaching. For example, María Colón Rueñes was identified as a potential javelin champion when she was only seven years old; she went on to win the gold medal at the Moscow Olympics. Many of Cuba's sports greats have passed through these schools—track-and-field stars such as world-record-holding high jumper Javier Sotomayor, world-record sprinters Leroy Burrel and Ana Fidelia Quirot, and volleyball legends such as Jel Despaigne and Mireya Luis. The system has been so successful that little Cuba was fifth in medal totals at the 1992 Summer Olympics in Barcelona.

Sports figures are considered workers and "part of the society's productive efforts." As such, sports stars are paid a salary on par with other workers, although most national team members also receive special perks, such as new cars. Not surprisingly, almost every international competition outside Cuba results in at least one defection.

A limited amount of bargaining is normal at street markets. However, most prices are very low to begin with. If the quoted price seems fair, pay up and feel blessed that you already have a bargain.

Exporting Arts and Antiques

Antiques may not be exported, including antiquarian books, stamp collections, furniture, and porcelain. An export permit is required for all quality artwork; the regulation doesn't apply to kitschy tourist art. State-run commercial galleries and *expo-ventas* (galleries representing freelance artists) will issue an export permit or arrange authorization for any items you buy.

Export permits for items for which you have not received an official receipt may be obtained from the **Registro Nacional de Bienes Culturales** (National Registry of Cultural Goods, Calle 17 #1009, e/ 10 y 12, Vedado, Havana, tel. 07/831-3362, Mon.-Fri. 9am-noon), in the Centro de Patrimonio Cultural, or at regional offices in provincial capitals. A single work costs CUC10, but CUC30 is good for up to 50 works of art. You must bring the object for inspection, or a photo if the object is too large. Allow up to two days for processing.

Cuba produces the world's best cigars (*habanos, tabacos,* or *puros*) at perhaps one-half the price of similar cigars in London.

Since 1985, handmade Cuban cigars have carried the Cubatabaco stamp plus a factory mark and, since 1989, the legend *"Hecho en Cuba. Totalmente a Mano."* (Made in Cuba. Completely by Hand.). If it reads *"Hecho a Mano,"* the cigars are most likely hand *finished* (i.e., the wrapper was put on by hand) rather than hand *made*. If it states only *"Hecho en Cuba,"* the cigars are assuredly machine made. All boxes feature a holographic seal (any other boxes are subject to seizure by Cuban customs).

There are about 40 brands, each in various sizes and even shapes; sizes are given specific names, such as Corona (142mm) and Julieta (178mm). Fatter cigars—the choice of connoisseurs—are more fully flavored and smoke more smoothly and slowly than those with smaller ring gauges. As a rule, darker cigars are also more full-bodied and sweeter.

All cigar factories produce various brands. Some factories specialize in particular flavors, others in particular sizes. Several factories might be producing any one brand simultaneously, so quality can vary markedly even though the label is the same. Experts consider cigars produced in Havana's El Laguito factory to be the best. As with fine wines, the quality of cigars varies from year to year. The source and year of production are marked in code on the underside of the box. The code tells you a lot about the cigars inside. Even novices can determine the provenance and date of cigars if they know the codes. However, the code system keeps changing to throw buyers off, so that cigars of different ages have different codes. The first three letters usually refer to the factory where the cigars were made, followed by four letters that give the date of manufacture.

The expertise and care expressed in the factory determine how well a cigar burns and tastes. Cigars, when properly stored, continue to ferment and mature in their boxes—an aging process similar to that of good wines. Rules on when to smoke a cigar don't exist, but many experts claim that the prime cigars are those aged for 6-8 years. Everyone agrees that a cigar should be smoked either within three months of manufacture or not for at least a year; the interim is known as a "period of sickness." Cigars should be slightly soft when gently squeezed; have a fresh, robust smell; be smooth and silky in texture; and free of any protuberances or air pockets. The cigars should be of near identical color and shape.

You may leave Cuba with up to CUC5,000 worth of cigars with purchase receipts (or 90 without receipts). You can buy additional cigars in the airport duty-free lounge after passing through customs controls. Cigars can be bought at virtually every tourist hotel and store, or at dedicated *casas del habano* or *casas del tabaco* nationwide. Most shop clerks know little about cigars. Prices can vary up to 20 percent from store to store. If one store doesn't have what you desire, another surely will. Inspect your cigars before committing to a purchase.

In cities, *jineteros* (street hustlers) will offer you cigars at what seems the

The *Guayabera*

The traditional *guayabera,* Cuba's all-purpose gift to menswear, was created in central Cuba (or Mexico, no one is certain) more than 200 years ago and is the quintessential symbol of Latin masculinity. In 2010, the Cuban government anointed it Cuba's "official formal dress garment."

Despite the infusion of New York fashion, this four-pocket, straight-bottom shirt remains the essence of sartorial style. The *guayabera,* thought Kimberley Cihlar, "is possessed of all the sex appeal any Latin peacock could want." Nonetheless, younger Cubans shun the shirt as a symbol of someone who works for the government.

The *guayabera,* which comes short sleeved or long, is made of light cotton perfect for weathering the tropical heat. In shape, it resembles a short-sleeved jacket or extended shirt and is worn draped outside the pants, usually as an outer garment with a T-shirt beneath. Thus it fulfills the needs of summertime dressing with the elegance of a jacket and the comfort of, well, a shirt. It is embellished with patterned embroidery running in parallel stripes *(alforzas)* down the front and is usually outfitted with pockets—with buttons—to stow enough *habanos* for a small shop.

deal of the century. Forget it! The vast majority are low-quality or defect cigars sold falsely as top-line cigars to unsuspecting travelers. The hustlers use empty boxes and seals stolen by colleagues who work in the cigar factories, so the unknowing buyer is easily convinced that this is the real McCoy.

LITERATURE

Books are severely restricted by the government, which maintains firm control over what may be read. There are few newsstands or newsagents and no foreign periodicals.

Most tourist outlets sell a limited range of English-language coffee-table books, travel-related books, and political treatises that have been approved by the censors. Otherwise the few bookstores that exist stock mostly Spanish-language texts, mainly socialist texts glorifying the Revolution.

Food and Drink

A standing joke in Cuba is: What are the three biggest failures of the Revolution? Breakfast, lunch, and dinner. The poor quality of food has long been a source of exasperation. Before the Revolution, Cuba boasted many world-class restaurants. After 1959 many of the middle- and upper-class clientele fled Cuba along with the restaurateurs and chefs, taking their knowledge and entrepreneurship with them. In 1967 all remaining restaurants were taken over by the state. It was downhill from there.

The blasé socialist attitude to dining, tough economic times, and general inefficiencies of the system became reflected in boring (usually identical) menus, abysmal standards (tablecloths rarely get washed), and lack of availability. Some of the lousiest service and dishes can be had for the most outrageous prices. And don't assume that a restaurant serving good dishes one day will do so the next. Restaurants have traditionally relied upon the dysfunctional state distribution system to deliver daily supplies.

In the provinces trying to find somewhere with palatable food can *still* be a challenge. Shortages are everywhere. Plan ahead. Stock up on sodas, biscuits, and other packaged snacks at CUC-only stores before setting out each day.

Now the good news! Since 2011, restrictions on private restaurants have been lifted, leading to a boom in quality dining options. Havana is now blessed with dozens of world-class *paladares* (private restaurants). And many state restaurants have vastly improved, as the government has invested in culinary (and management) training and turned most such restaurants over to the workers to run as cooperatives. In general, the best meals are served in *paladares* (which outside Havana mostly serve *criolla*, or Cuban fare) and in the upscale hotels, which tend toward "continental" cuisine. Few places other than hotel restaurants serve breakfast; most offer variations on the same dreary buffets.

Sometimes service is swift and friendly, sometimes protracted and surly. You're likely to be serenaded by musicians, who usually hit up any available tourists for a tip (or to sell a CD or cassette recording). Eating in Cuba doesn't present the health problems associated with many other destinations in Latin America. However, hygiene at streetside stalls is often questionable.

Peso Eateries

Pesos-only restaurants are for Cubans. Food availability tends to be hit or miss and the cuisine undistinguished at best. Many restaurants offer an *oferta especial* (special offer), usually a set meal of the day. Some sell *cajitas,* bargain-priced boxed take-out meals for a few pesos.

State-run *merenderos* and private roadside snack stalls—the staple for local dining—display their meager offerings in glass cases. A signboard indicates what's available, with items noted on strips that can be removed as particular items sell out. These stalls are an incredibly cheap way of appeasing your stomach with snacks. The "$" sign at peso eateries refers to Cuban pesos, not U.S. dollars.

The staple of street stalls is basic *pizzeta* (pizza), usually five pesos per slice. Pizzas are dismal by North American standards—usually a bland doughy base covered with a thin layer of tomato paste and a smattering of cheese and ham. Other staples are fatty pork *bocaditos, pan con queso* (basic but tasty cheese sandwich), *fritura de maíz* (corn fritters), and *pay de coco* (coconut flan).

Eating at street stalls poses a serious health risk.

Restaurant Scams

The creativity that Cubans apply to wheedle dollars from foreigners has been turned into an art form in restaurants. Here are a few tricks:

Added Items: Bread and butter is often served without asking, but you are charged extra. Mineral water and other items often appear on your bill, even though you didn't ask for them, or they never arrived.

Á la Carte Be Damned: The restaurant has a fixed price for a set menu but your bill charges separately for itemized dishes, which add up to considerably more. Beware menus that don't list prices.

Bait and Switch: You ask for a cola and are brought an imported Coca-Cola (CUC2) instead of Tropicola (CUC0.50), a perfectly adequate Cuban equivalent.

Commissions: The *jinetero* who leads you to a recommended *paladar* gets his commission added to your bill, even if he's merely picked you up outside the *paladar* you've already chosen.

Dollars or Pesos? The dollar sign ($) is used for both dollars and pesos. In a peso restaurant you may be told that the $ prices are in dollars. Sometimes this is true. Even so, change may be given in pesos.

¡No Hay! You're dying for a Hatuey beer but are told ¡no hay! (there is none). The waiter brings you a Bucanero. Then you notice that Cubans are drinking Hatuey. You're then told that the Hatueys aren't cold, or that Bucanero (which is more expensive) is better.

Overpricing: Compare prices on your bill against those on the menu. One or two items on your bill may be inflated.

Variable Pricing: Always ask for a printed menu with prices. Some places charge according to how much they think you are worth. If you're dressed in Gucci, expect to pay accordingly.

PALADARES

Private restaurants—*paladares*—have been permitted since September 1994. The word means "palate" and comes from the name of the restaurant of the character Raquel, a poor woman who makes her fortune cooking, in the popular Brazilian TV soap opera *Vale Todo*. Here you can fill up for CUC5-35, depending on snazziness of the restaurant—from simple, albeit huge *criolla* meals to creative fusion fare in joints that would do London and New York proud. Some are open 24 hours. Not all owners are honorable, however; lack of a written menu listing prices can be a warning sign: Don't order food without seeing the menu, or the price is likely to be jacked up.

Taxi drivers and *jineteros* may offer recommendations. Their commission will be added to your bill.

FOOD CHAINS

There are as yet no McDonald's or KFCs in Cuba (except at the U.S. military base at Guantánamo). However, the Cuban government has established a chain of tacky equivalents, including KFC-style fried-chicken joints called El Rápido. Food often runs out or is severely limited, and the quality is usually awful. Cuba's answer to McDonald's is Burgui, open 24 hours.

The government has done a better job with seafood. The Dimar chain has roadside restaurants in major cities selling seafood at fair prices. The Baturro chain of Spanish-style *bodegas* has outlets in major cities, with charming ambience and *criolla* fare of acceptable standard.

SELF-CATERING

There are scant groceries and no roadside 7-Eleven equivalents. The state-run groceries, called *puestos,* where fresh produce often of questionable quality is sold, can make Westerners cringe. Cuba's best fruits and vegetables are exported for hard currency or turned into juices. Cheese and milk are precious scarcities. As a result, most Cubans rely on the black market or private produce markets called *mercados agropecuarios* (or *agros* for short). Every town has at least one *agro.* Carrots, cucumbers, chard, and pole beans are about the only vegetables available year-round; tomatoes disappear about May and reappear around November, when beets, eggplants, cabbages, and onions are also in season. Chicken and pork are sold at *agros,* but not beef. The government-run *pescaderías especiales* sell fish and other seafood.

You can buy imported packaged and canned goods (at inflated prices) at CUC-only stores.

CAFÉS AND BAKERIES

Cuba has few sidewalk cafés, and most of the prerevolutionary *cafeterías* (coffee stands) and tea shops (*casas de té* or *casas de infusiones*) have vanished. Still, cafés in the purist Parisian tradition have begun to sprout, notably in Havana.

Most towns have bakeries serving sugary confections and bread (served as buns or twisted rolls). The situation has improved following the arrival of French expertise to run the Pain de Paris bakery chain. Doña Neli bakeries and the Pan.Com snack restaurant chain, in most large cities, offer quality baked goods and sandwiches, respectively. In Havana, several private *dulcerías* offer baked goods of international quality.

WHAT TO EAT
Cuban Dishes

Cuban food is mostly peasant fare, usually lacking in sauces and spices. *Cerdo* (pork) and *pollo* (chicken) are the two main protein staples, usually served with *arroz y frijoles negros* (rice and black beans) and *plátanos* (fried banana or plantain). *Cerdo asado* (succulent roast pork), *moros y cristianos* (Moors and Christians—rice and black beans), and *arroz congrí* (rice with red beans) are the most popular dishes. *Congrí oriental* is rice and red beans cooked together. *Frijoles negros dormidos* are black beans cooked and allowed to stand till the next day. Another national dish is *ajiaco* (hotchpotch), a stew of meats and vegetables.

Cubans like *pollo frito* (fried chicken) and *pollo asado* (grilled chicken), but above all love roast pork, the most ubiquitous dish along with ham.

Beef is virtually unknown outside the tourist restaurants, where filet mignon and prime rib are often on the menu, alongside *ropa vieja* (a braised shredded beef dish). Meat is used in snacks such as *empanadas de carne,* pies or flat pancakes enclosing meat morsels; and *picadillo,* a snack of spiced beef, onion, and tomato. Crumbled pork rinds are an ingredient in *fufu,* mixed with cooked plantain, a popular dish in Oriente. And ham and cheese find their way into fish and are stuffed inside steaks as *bistec uruguayo.*

Corvina (sea bass), *filet de emperador* (swordfish), and *pargo* (red snapper) are the most common fish, and lobster and shrimp are widely available.

Vegetables

Few Cubans understand the concept of vegetarianism. Since colonial days meat has been at the very center of Cuban cooking. Cubans disdain greens, preferring a sugar- and starch-heavy diet. Only a few restaurants serve vegetarian dishes, and servers in restaurants may tell you that a particular dish is vegetarian, even though it contains chunks of meat. Most beans are cooked in pork fat, and most *congrí* (rice with red beans) dishes contain meat. *"Protein vegetal"* translates as "soy product."

Ensaladas mixtas (mixed salads) usually consist of a plate of lettuce or *pepinos* (cucumbers) and tomatoes (often served green, yet sweet) with oil and vinaigrette dressing. *Palmito,* the succulent heart of palm, is also common. Often you'll receive canned vegetables. Sometimes you'll receive shredded *col* (cabbage), often alone.

Plátano (plantain), a relative of the banana, is a staple and almost always served fried, including as *tostones,* fried green plantains eaten as a snack. Yucca (manioc) is also popular: It resembles a stringy potato in look, taste, and texture and is prepared and served like a potato in any number of ways. *Boniato* (sweet potato) and *malanga* (taro), a bland root crop rich in starch, are used in many dishes.

Fruits

Until recently you could pass field after field of pineapples, melons, oranges, and grapefruits but not see any for sale along the road. Virtually the entire state fruit harvest goes to produce fruit juice. But these days private farmers can freely sell their produce, resulting in an explosion of roadside stalls and *mercado agropecuarios* selling well-known fruits such as papayas (which should be referred to as *fruta bomba;* in Cuba, "papaya" is a slang term for vagina), plus such lesser-known types as the furry *mamey colorado,* an oval, chocolate-brown fruit with a custardy texture and taste; the cylindrical, orange-colored *marañon,* or cashew-apple; the oval, coarse-skinned *zapote,* a sweet granular fruit most commonly found in Oriente; and the large, irregular-shaped *guanábana,* whose pulp is sweet and "soupy," with a hint of vanilla.

Coconuts are rare, except in sweets and around Baracoa, where coconut forms a base for the nation's only real regional cuisine.

Desserts

Cubans have a sweet tooth, as befits the land of sugar. They're especially fond of sickly sweet sponge cakes (*kek* or *ke*) covered in soft "shaving-foam" icing and sold for a few centavos at *panaderías* (bakeries). *Flan,* a caramel custard, is also popular (a variant is a delicious pudding called *natilla*), as is marmalade and cheese. Also try *tatianoff,* chocolate cake smothered with cream; *chu,* bite-size puff pastries stuffed with an almost-bitter cheesy meringue; and *churrizo,* deep-fried doughnut rings sold at every bakery and streetside stalls, where you can also buy *galletas,* sweet biscuits sold loose.

Coconut-based desserts include *coco quemado* (coconut pudding), *coco rallado y queso* (grated coconut with cheese in syrup), and the *cucurucho,* a regional specialty of Baracoa made of pressed coconut and sugar or honey.

Cubans are lovers of ice cream, sold at *heladerías* (ice-cream stores) and street stalls. Cubans use specific terms for different kinds of scoops. *Helado,* which means "ice cream," also means a single large scoop; two large scoops are called *jimagua;* several small scoops is an *ensalada;* and *sundae* is ice cream served with fruit.

DRINKING
Nonalcoholic Drinks

Water is not always reliable, and many water pipes are contaminated through decay. Stick to bottled mineral water, readily available carbonated (*con gas*) or non-carbonated (*sin gas*). Coca-Cola and Pepsi (or their Cuban-made equivalent, Tropicola), Fanta (or Cuban-made Najita), and other soft drinks are widely available. Malta is a popular nonalcoholic drink that resembles a dark English stout but tastes like root beer.

Far more thirst-quenching and energy-giving, however, are *guarapo,* fresh-squeezed sugarcane juice sold at roadside *guaraperías; prú,* a refreshing soft drink concocted from fruit, herbs, roots, and sugar; *batidos,* fruit shakes blended with milk and ice; and *refrescos naturales,* chilled fruit juices (avoid the sickly sweet water-based *refrescos*); and *limonadas* (lemonade).

No home visit is complete without being offered a *cafecito.* Cubans love their coffee espresso-style, thick and strong, served black in tiny cups and heavily sweetened. Much of Cuban domestic coffee has been adulterated— *café mezclado*—with other roasted products. Stick with export brands sold vacuum packed. *Café con leche* (coffee with milk) is served in tourist restaurants, usually at a 1:1 coffee-to-hot milk ratio. Don't confuse this with *café americano,* diluted Cuban coffee.

Alcoholic Drinks

Cuba makes several excellent German-style beers, usually served chilled, although only two are usually available: Bucanero, a heavy-bodied lager that comes light or dark; and lighter Cristal. Imported Heineken and Canadian and Mexican brands are sold in CUC stores and hotel bars. Clara is a rough-brewed beer for domestic consumption (typically one peso) sold

Cuba's Cocktails

Cuba Libre

Who can resist the killer kick of a rum and Coke? Supposedly, the simple concoction was named more than a century ago after the war cry of the independence army: "Free Cuba!"

The Perfect Cuba Libre: Place ice cubes in a tall glass, then pour in 2 ounces of seven-year-old Havana Club *añejo* rum. Fill with Coca-Cola, topped off with 1 ounce of lemon juice. Decorate the rim with a slice of lemon. Serve with a stirrer.

Daiquiri

The daiquiri is named for a Cuban hamlet 16 miles east of Santiago de Cuba, near a copper mine where the mining firm's chief engineer, Jennings S. Cox, created the now world-famous cocktail that Hemingway immortalized in his novels. It is still associated with El Floridita bar and Hemingway's immortal words: *"Mi mojito en La Bodeguita, mi daiquirí en El Floridita."*

Shaved ice, which gave the drink its final touch of enchantment, was added by Constante Ribailagua, El Floridita's bartender, in the 1920s. The "Papa Special," which Constante made for Hemingway, contained a double dose of rum, no sugar, and a half ounce of grapefruit juice.

The Perfect Daiquiri: In an electric blender, pour half a tablespoon of sugar, the juice of half a lemon, and 1.5 ounces of white rum. Serve semi-frozen blended with ice (or on the rocks) in a tall martini glass with a maraschino cherry.

Mojito

The *mojito* is considered the classic drink of Cuba.

The Perfect *Mojito*: With a stirrer, mix half a tablespoon of sugar and the juice of half a lime in an eight-inch highball glass. Add a sprig of yerba buena (mint), crushing the stalk to release the juice; two ice cubes; and 1.5 ounces of Havana Club Light Dry Cuban rum. Fill with soda water, add a small splash of angostura, then dress with a mint sprig. *¡Salud!*

at *cervecerías* (beer dispensaries) for the hoi polloi; often these are roadside dispensers on wheels where you can buy beer in paper cups or bottles sawed in half for a few centavos.

About one dozen Cuban rum distilleries produce some 60 brands of rum. They vary widely—the worst can taste like paint thinner. Cuban rums resemble Bacardi rums, not surprisingly, as the company was based in Santiago de Cuba. Each brand generally has three types of rum: clear "white rum," labeled *carta blanca*, which is aged three years (about CUC5 a 0.75-liter bottle); the more assertive "golden rum," labeled *dorado* or *carta oro*, aged five years (about CUC6); and *añejo*, aged seven years or longer (CUC10 or more). The best in all categories are Havana Club's rums, topped only by Matusalem Añejo Superior. A few limited-production rums, such as the 50-year-old Havana Club Máximo (from CUC1,300 per bottle) and Ron Santiago 500 Aniversario (CUC3,000) exceed the harmony and finesse of fine cognacs.

Golden and aged rums are best enjoyed straight. White rum is ideal for cocktails such as a piña colada (rum, pineapple juice, coconut cream, and crushed ice) and, most notably, the daiquiri and the *mojito*—favorites of Ernest Hemingway, who helped launch both drinks to world fame.

Impecunious Cubans drink *tragos* (shots) of *aguardiente*—cheap, over-proof white rum.

Cuba's rum manufacturers also make liqueurs, including from coffee, crème de menthe, cocoa, guava, lemon, pineapple, and other fruits. Certain regions are known for unique liqueurs, such as *guayabita,* a drink made from rum and guava exclusive to Pinar del Río.

Imported South American, French, and Californian wines (*vinos*) are widely available. Avoid the local and truly terrible Soroa brand, made of unsophisticated Italian wine blended with local grapes from Soroa, Pinar del Río.

Accommodations

RESERVATIONS

Cuba is in the midst of a tourism boom and accommodations are at a premium. It's wise to prebook rooms for at least your first few nights.

Christmas and New Year's are particularly busy, as are major festivals. And these days, many all-inclusive beach hotels offer deep discounts to Cubans in summer low season. Book well ahead; call direct, send an email, or have a tour operator abroad make your reservation (the latter are sometimes cheaper thanks to wholesalers' discounts). Insist on written confirmation and take copies with you, as Cuban hotels are notorious for not honoring reservations. Pay in advance for all nights you intend to stay; otherwise you might be asked to check out to make room for someone else.

Charter package tours with airfare and hotel included may offer the cheapest rates, although the less notable hotels are often used.

If you are a journalist or in a similar sensitive occupation, expect your assigned hotel room to be bugged. (Don't believe me? Read *The Double Life of Fidel Castro*, by Juan Reinaldo Sánchez.)

Private room rentals, *casas particulares,* offer by far the best bargains and permit you to experience *real* Cuban life alongside the Cubans themselves.

PRICES

The Cuban government has a monopoly on hotels, and it jacks up and reduces prices nationwide according to market trends; since 2015 rates in Havana have doubled to outrageous levels. Rates also vary for low (May-June and Sept.-Nov.) and high season (Dec.-Apr. and July-Aug.). Cuba has no room tax or service charge.

Often it's cheaper to pay as you go rather than prepaying. The same goes for meals. A "modified American plan" (MAP; room rate that includes breakfast and dinner) can be a bargain at beach resorts, where ordering meals individually can be a lot more expensive. In Havana, you're better off with a European plan (EP; room with breakfast only). If you're not intent on exploring beyond your resort, consider an all-inclusive property, where the cost of all meals, drinks, and activities is included in the room rate.

TYPES OF ACCOMMODATION

Camping

Cuba is not geared for camping. Tent sites don't exist and you need permission to camp "wild." While urbanites are savvy about the rules, rural folks may not be; you potentially expose farmers to ruinous fines merely for having you on their land. The system assumes guilt unless the farmer can prove that he or she has not, or was not going to, accept money.

Cuba has dozens of *campismos,* simple holiday camps with basic cabins and facilities operated by **Campismo Popular** (Calle 13 #857, e/ 4 y 6, Vedado, Havana, tel. 07/835-2502, www.campismopopular.cu), which has booking offices islandwide. Often camps are closed Monday-Thursday and in the off-season; in summer they're often full with Cubans.

Hotels

In 2016, Cuba claimed more than 65,000 hotel rooms (with a goal of 130,000 by 2030), of which 60 percent were declared to be four- or five-star. All hotels in Cuba are owned by four state-run entities that ostensibly compete for business, some in cooperative management agreements with foreign (mostly Spanish) hotel groups. However, hotels frequently juggle between the following entities:

- **Cubanacán** (www.cubanacan.cu) has more than 50 hotels. Its Hoteles Brisas and Hoteles Club Amigo are (supposedly) four-star and three-star all-inclusive beach resorts. Its Hoteles Horizontes are urban hotels (usually lackluster two- or three-star ones). Hoteles E are small boutique hotels. It also has modest Hoteles Cubanacán.

- **Gaviota** (www.gaviota-grupo.com), a branch of the military, owns ecolodges, deluxe city hotels, and all-inclusive beach resorts.

- **Gran Caribe** (www.gran-caribe.cu) once managed deluxe hotels; today it has some three dozen hotels ranging from two to five stars.

- **Islazul** (www.islazul.cu) operates inexpensive hotels catering primarily to Cubans (who pay in pesos). Some of its properties are splendid bargains.

Habaguanex, the commercial division of the Oficina del Historiador de la Habana, has controlled some 20 boutique hotels in Habana Vieja. It was being disbanded at press time and Gaviota is expected to assume responsibility for the properties.

The ratings Cuba gives its hotels are far too generous; most fall one or two categories below their international equivalents. Most towns have one or two historic hotels around the central park and a concrete Soviet-era hotel on the outskirts. Hotels built in recent years are constructed to international standards, although even the best suffer from poor design, shoddy construction, and (often) poor management. The top-line hotels run by foreign management groups are usually up to international par.

Many hotels use both 220-volt and 110-volt outlets (usually marked), often in the same room. Check before plugging in any electrical appliances, or you could blow a fuse. Note that "minibars" in most hotel guest rooms are actually small (and empty) refrigerators.

Upon registering, you'll be issued a *tarjeta de huésped* (guest card) at each hotel, identifying you as a hotel guest. Depending on your hotel, the card may have to be presented when ordering and signing for meals and drinks, changing money, and often when entering the elevator to your room.

Many hotels open their swimming pools to Cuban locals; most all-inclusive hotels sell day passes to nonguests wishing to use the facilities.

ALL-INCLUSIVE RESORTS

Most beach resorts are run as all-inclusives: cash-free, self-contained properties where your room rate theoretically includes all meals and beverages, entertainment, and water sports at no additional fee. Standards vary. Properties managed by international name-brand hotel chains are preferred to the purely Cuban-run affairs.

APARTHOTELS AND *PROTOCOLOS*

Aparthotels offer rooms with kitchens or kitchenettes. Most are characterless. Many are linked to regular hotels, giving you access to broader facilities.

Cubanacán and Gran Caribe handle reservations for *protocolos*—special houses reserved for foreign dignitaries. Most are in mansions in the Cubanacán and Siboney regions of Havana (they include Frank Sinatra's former home), but most other towns have at least one.

NATURE LODGES

About half a dozen quasi-"ecotourism" properties can be found in mountain areas or close to nature reserves. Cuba has no eco-lodges to international standards. The most prominent is Hotel Moka (Pinar del Río), though it's an eco-lodge only in name; others include Villa Pinares de Mayarí (Holguín) and Villa El Saltón (Santiago de Cuba).

SECURITY

All tourist hotel lobbies have security staff, posted following the spate of bombs planted in Havana's hotels in 1997 by Cuban American terrorists. They serve to prevent a repeat performance, but also do double duty to keep out unsavory characters and unregistered Cubans slipping upstairs with foreign guests.

Theft is an issue in hotels. If your hotel has a safe deposit box, use it.

Before accepting a room, ensure that the door is secure and that someone
can't climb in through the window. *Always* lock your door. Keep your suit-
case locked when you're not in your room, as maids frequently make off
with clothing and other items.

Casas Particulares

My recommendation is to stay wherever possible in a *casa particular* (private house)—a room in a family home, granting you a chance to gain a
perspective on Cuban life. This can be anything from a single room with
a live-in family to a self-sufficient apartment. Increasingly, foreign money
is being invested to turn larger properties into boutique hotels, such that
the term *casa particular* is morphing to mean any privately owned property—from a single room to a 10-bedroom "hotel."

The going room rate in Havana is CUC25-40 (but up to CUC1,000 for
entire houses), and CUC15-35 outside Havana, but boutique properties may
charge CUC100-300 per room.

Legally licensed houses post a blue Arrendador Divisa sign, like an in-
verted anchor, on the front door (those with a red sign are licensed to rent
only to Cubans, in pesos). Avoid illegal, unlicensed *casas particulares.*

Check to see if hot water is available 24 hours, or only at specific times.
Avoid rooms facing streets, although even rooms tucked at the backs of
buildings can hold an unpleasant surprise in predawn hours, when all manner of noises can intrude on your slumber.

Reservations are recommended during high season (since 2012, state
tourism agencies are allowed to make reservations for *casas particulares*).
If you arrive in a town without a reservation, owners of *casas particulares*
are happy to call around on your behalf. Touts do a brisk business trying
to steer travelers to specific *casas,* and are not above telling independent
travelers lies, such as that a particular house you might be seeking has
closed. The tout's commission will be added to your rent. Many touts
pose as hitchhikers on roads into major cities; others chase you around
by bicycle.

Spell out all the prices involved before settling on a place to stay.
Remember, most homeowners have cut their rates to the bare bones while
facing punitive taxes. Most serve meals: breakfasts usually cost CUC3-5,
dinners typically cost CUC5-10. Many homes have shower units with electric heater elements, which you switch on for the duration of your shower.
Beware: It's easy to give yourself a shock.

Your host must record your passport details, to be presented to the
Ministry of the Interior within 24 hours (hence, MININT is always abreast
of every foreigner's whereabouts). Honor regulations and avoid attracting
undue attention to your host's home, as the legal repercussions of even the
hint of an infraction can be serious.

Many *casa particular* owners maintain their own websites, but you
can also book online via AirBnB (www.airbnb.com) and similar booking agencies.

Unauthorized Accommodations

Tourists must receive written permission from immigration authorities to stay anywhere other than a hotel or licensed *casa particular*. If you wish to stay with Cuban friends, you must go to an immigration office within 24 hours to convert from a tourist visa to an A2 visa (CUC25). You must be accompanied by the person you wish to stay with. If an unregistered foreigner is found staying in a house (or camping), the Cuban host must prove that the foreigner is not a paying guest—an almost impossible situation. Thus, the Cuban is automatically found guilty of renting illegally. The regulations are strictly enforced, and fines are ruinous.

Cuban Guests

Since 2008, Cubans have been allowed to room in hotels. The new rulings also permit foreigners and Cubans to share a hotel room. Foreigners staying in *casas particulares* are also permitted to share their room with Cubans of either gender; in all cases, your host must record your guest's *cédula* (ID) details for presentation to MININT within 24 hours. MININT runs the Cuban guest's name through a computer database; if the name of a woman appears three times with a different man, she is arrested as a "prostitute" and gets a mandatory jail term; no equivalent exists for Cuban male "prostitutes."

The rules keep changing. A foreigner is permitted to host only one Cuban partner during his or her stay in a hotel or *casa particular*. Woe betide any *casa particular* owner whose guest is discovered with an unrecorded Cuban in his or her room, let alone underage. In such cases, the owner of the *casa particular* can lose his or her license and receive a jail term.

Health and Safety

BEFORE YOU GO

Dental and medical checkups are advisable before departing home. Take along any medications; keep prescription drugs in their original bottles to avoid suspicion at customs. I had my spectacles stolen in Cuba—a reminder to take a spare pair (or at least a prescription for eyewear). If you suffer from a debilitating health problem, wear a medical alert bracelet.

A basic health kit should include alcohol swabs and medicinal alcohol, antiseptic cream, Band-Aids, aspirin, diarrhea medication, sunburn remedy, antifungal foot powder, antihistamine, surgical tape, bandages and gauze, and scissors. Most important? A bottle of hand sanitizer: Use it frequently!

Information on health concerns can be answered in advance of travel by the **Department of State Citizens Emergency Center** (tel. 888/407-4747 or 202/501-4444 from overseas, http://travel.state.gov), the **Centers for** the **International Association for Medical Assistance to Travellers** (tel. 716/754-4883, www.iamat.org), with offices worldwide.

Travel and Health Insurance

Travel insurance is recommended. Travel agencies can sell you travelers' health, baggage, and trip cancellation insurance. Check to see if policies cover expenses in Cuba, which now requires that all arriving travelers demonstrate that they have health insurance. If you can't show proof of insurance, you will be required to purchase an insurance package from **Asistur** (Prado #212, e/ Trocadero y Colón, Habana Vieja, tel. 07/866-4499, 07/866-8527, or 5280-3563 and 5805-6292, www.asistur.cu, Mon.-Fri. 8:30am-5pm), which represents about 160 insurance companies in 40 countries. It has offices at all international airports. Rates vary from CUC3 daily (for CUC7,000 medical and CUC15,000 evacuation coverage) to CUC4.50 daily (CUC25,000 medical and CUC15,000 evacuation).

Vaccinations

No vaccinations are required to enter Cuba unless you are arriving from areas of cholera and yellow fever infection. Epidemic diseases have mostly been eradicated throughout the country. However, viral meningitis and dengue fever occasionally break out. Consult your physician for recommended vaccinations. Consider vaccinations against tetanus and infectious hepatitis.

MEDICAL SERVICES

Sanitary standards in Cuba are a mixed bag. As long as you take appropriate precautions and use common sense, you're not likely to incur a serious illness or disease. Cuba's vaunted public health system faces severe shortages of medicines and equipment; with few exceptions, facilities and standards are not up to those of North America or northern Europe. In many local hospitals, hygiene conditions are appalling, facilities rudimentary, and medical know-how often lacking. Local pharmacies are mostly well stocked. *Turnos regulares* pharmacies are open 8am-5pm; *turnos permanentes* are open 24 hours.

Facilities for Foreigners

Foreigners receive special treatment through **Servios Médicos Cubanos** (tel. 07/204-4811, www.servimedcuba.com), a division of Cubanacán that promotes health tourism, from "stress breaks" to advanced treatments such as eye, open-heart, and plastic surgery.

Most major cities and resort destinations have 24-hour international clinics (*clínicas internacionales*) staffed by English-speaking doctors and nurses, plus foreigners-only international pharmacies (*farmacias internacionales*) stocked with Western pharmaceuticals. Larger tourist hotels also have nurses on duty and doctors on call, and some have pharmacies. **Óptica**

Miramar (7ma Av., e/ 24 y 26, Miramar, tel. 07/204-2269, direccion@opticam.cha.cyt.cu) provides optician services and sells contact lenses and eyeglasses. It has outlets nationwide.

Pay in CUC or by credit card (unless issued by a U.S. bank). Get a receipt with which to make an insurance claim once you return home. You can call your insurance company in advance of medical treatment. If approved, the company can pay direct to Asistur (Prado #208, Havana, tel. 07/866-4499, or 5280-3563 and 5805-6292, www.asistur.cu), which then pays the Cuban clinic. However, U.S. citizens should note that even if visiting Cuba legally, payment for "nonemergency medical services" is prohibited.

Medical Evacuation

Uncle Sam has deemed that even U.S. emergency evacuation services cannot fly to Cuba to evacuate U.S. citizens without a license from the Treasury Department. The rules keep changing, so it's worth checking the latest situation with such companies as **Traveler's Emergency Network** (tel. 800/275-4836, www.tenweb.com), **International SOS Assistance** (tel. 215/942-8226, www.internationalsos.com), and **MedJet Assist** (tel. 800/527-7478, www.medjetassist.com), which provide worldwide ground and air evacuation.

HEALTH PROBLEMS

Cuba is a tropical country and the health hazards are many: filthy public fixtures, garbage rotting in the streets, polluted watercourses, broken sewer pipes, holes in sidewalks, dilapidated buildings, and so on. In addition, molds, fungus, and bacteria thrive. The slightest scratch can fester quickly. Treat promptly with antiseptic and keep any wounds clean.

Intestinal Problems

Cuba's tap water is questionable. Drink bottled water, which is widely available. Don't brush your teeth using suspect water. Milk is pasteurized, and dairy products in Cuba are usually safe.

Diarrhea: The change in diet may briefly cause diarrhea or constipation. Most cases of diarrhea are caused by microbial bowel infections resulting from contaminated food. Don't eat uncooked fish or shellfish, uncooked vegetables, unwashed salads, or unpeeled fruit. Diarrhea is usually temporary, and many doctors recommend letting it run its course. If that's not preferable, medicate with Lomotil or similar antidiarrheal product. Drink lots of liquids. Avoid alcohol and milk. If conditions don't improve after three days, seek medical help.

Dysentery: Diarrhea accompanied by severe abdominal pain, blood in your stool, and fever requires immediate medical diagnosis. Tetracycline or ampicillin is normally used to cure bacillary dysentery. More complex treatment is required for amoebic dysentery.

Cholera: Symptoms of this potential killer include extreme diarrhea resulting in dehydration and drowsiness. Urgent medical care and quarantine are required. Cholera can be caused by infected water, seafood, and vegetables. Follow good hygiene at all times. In 2012 a cholera outbreak (the first since the Revolution) swept eastern Cuba, causing at least three deaths. It was soon eradicated.

Other Infections: Giardiasis, acquired from infected water, causes diarrhea, bloating, persistent indigestion, and weight loss. Intestinal worms can be contracted by walking barefoot on infested beaches, grass, or ground. Hepatitis A can be contracted through unhygienic foods or contaminated water (salads and unpeeled fruits are major culprits). The main symptoms are stomach pains, loss of appetite, yellowing skin and eyes, and extreme tiredness. The much rarer hepatitis B is usually contracted through unclean needles, blood transfusions, or unprotected sex.

Sunburn and Skin Problems

The tropical sun can burn even through light clothing or shade. Use a suncream or sunblock of at least SPF 15. Bring sunscreen; it's not readily available beyond beach resorts in Cuba. Wear a wide-brimmed hat.

Sun glare can cause conjunctivitis; wear sunglasses. Prickly heat is an itchy rash, normally caused by clothing that is too tight or in need of washing; this and athlete's foot (a fungal infection) are best treated by airing the skin and washing your clothes. Ringworm, another fungal infection, shows up as a ring, most commonly on the scalp and groin; it's treated with over-the-counter ointments.

Dehydration and Heat Problems

The tropical humidity and heat can sap your body fluids like blotting paper. Leg cramps, exhaustion, dizziness, and headaches are signs of dehydration. Drink lots of water. Avoid alcohol.

Excessive exposure to too much heat can cause potentially fatal heat stroke. Excessive sweating, extreme headaches, and disorientation leading to possible convulsions and delirium are symptoms. Emergency medical care is essential.

The common cold (*gripe,* pronounced GREE-pay, or *catarro cubano*) is a pandemic among Cubans.

Critters

Snakes (*culebras*) are common in Cuba; they're nonvenomous. Scorpions (*alacranes*) also exist; their venom can cause nausea and fever but is not usually serious. In the wild, watch where you're treading or putting your hands. Crocodiles are a serious threat in swampy coastal areas and estuaries; don't swim in rivers! Most areas inhabited by crocodiles, such as the Zapata swamps, are off-limits to foreigners without guides.

Mosquitoes abound. Repellent sprays and lotions are a must by day for many areas. Citronella candles, electric fans, and mosquito coils (*espirales,* which are rarely sold in Cuba) help keep mosquitoes at bay at night. Bites can easily become infected in the tropics; avoid scratching! Treat with antiseptics or antibiotics. Antihistamines and hydrocortisone can help relieve itching.

Malaria isn't present in Cuba. However, mosquitoes *do* transmit **dengue fever,** which *is* present. Its symptoms are similar to those for malaria, with severe headaches and high fever and, unlike malaria, additional severe pain in the joints, for which it is sometimes called "breaking bones disease." It is not recurring. There is no cure; dengue fever must run its course. The illness can be fatal (death usually results from internal hemorrhaging).

Chiggers (*coloradillas*) inhabit tall grasslands. Their bites itch like hell. Nail polish apparently works (over the bites, not on the nails) by suffocating the beasts.

Tiny, irritating *jejenes* (known worldwide as "no-see-ums"), sand flies about the size of a pinpoint, inhabit beaches and marshy coastal areas. This nuisance is active only around dawn and dusk, when you should avoid the beach. They are not fazed by bug repellent, but Avon's Skin-So-Soft supposedly works.

Jellyfish (*agua mala*) are common along the Atlantic shore, especially in winter and spring. They can give a painful, even dangerous, welt that leaves a permanent scar. Dousing in vinegar can help neutralize the stingers, while calamine and antihistamines should be used to soothe the pain. In Caribbean waters, a microscopic mollusk that locals call *caribe* can induce all manner of illnesses, from diarrhea and severe fever to itching. It, too, is more frequent in winter.

Sea urchins (*erizos*) are common beneath the inshore waterline and around coral reefs. These softball-size creatures are surrounded by long spines that will pierce your skin and break off if you touch or step on them. This is excruciatingly painful. You'll have to extract the spines.

Rabies, though rare in Cuba, can be contracted through the bite of an infected animal. It's always fatal unless treated.

Sexually Transmitted Diseases

Cubans are promiscuous, and sexually transmitted diseases are common, although the risk of contracting AIDS in Cuba is extremely low (the rate of infection is among the world's lowest). Use condoms (*preservativos*), widely available in Cuba.

SAFETY

Crime and Hustling

All the negative media hype sponsored by Washington has left many people with a false impression that Cuba is unsafe. Far from it. In rural areas many residents still say they can hardly remember the last time a crime was committed. Sexual assault is rare. However, the material hardships of Cubans combined with the influx of wealthy tourists *has* fostered crime. Pickpockets (*carteristas*) and purse slashers work the streets and buses. Chambermaids pilfer items from guests' luggage. Theft from luggage occurs at the airport, where bogus tour operators and taxi drivers also prey

Cuba's War on AIDS

Cuba has one of the world's most aggressive and successful campaigns against AIDS. The World Health Organization (WHO) and the Pan-American Health Organization have praised as exemplary Cuba's AIDS surveillance system and prevention program. The program has stemmed an epidemic that rages only 50 miles away in Haiti and has kept the spread of the disease to a level that no other country in the Americas can equal. According to UN-AIDS (www.unaids.org), as of 2015 fewer than 500 people had died of AIDS in Cuba, which has an adult HIV prevalence rate of 0.3 percent, the lowest in the Americas and on a par with Finland and Singapore. Although in Cuba in the early years it was predominantly a heterosexual disease, today 81 percent of HIV sufferers are gay men.

Cuba's unique response to the worldwide epidemic that began in the early 1980s was to initiate mass testing of the population and a "mandatory quarantine" of everyone testing positive. Twelve AIDS sanatoriums were developed throughout the island. By 1994, when the policies of mandatory testing and confinement were ended, about 98 percent of the adult population had been tested. Voluntary testing continues. An outpatient program was implemented so that sufferers could continue to lead a normal life; residents live in small houses or apartments, alone or as couples.

Cuba's biogenetic engineering industry has been at the forefront of research for an AIDS vaccine and cure. Plus, the government distributes more than 100 million free condoms a year.

on tourists (the British embassy also reports attempted robberies from vehicles on the Havana airport road). Muggings have escalated. Car-related crime is on the increase, notably by bogus hitchhikers and staged punctures (if you get a puncture, drive several kilometers, preferably to a town, before stopping).

There have even been several unreported murders of tourists in recent years. Most, but not all, have involved sexual relations between foreigners and Cubans. *Never* go to a *casa clandestina* (an illegal room rental, usually rented by the hour), and *always* check a Cuban partner's *carnet* (ID) and leave a copy with someone you trust if possible.

Most crime is opportunistic snatch-and-grab. Caution is required when walking city streets (especially at night) and in crowded places. If you sense yourself being squeezed or jostled, elbow your way out of there immediately.

The **U.S. State Department** (tel. 888/407-4747, from overseas tel. 202/501-4444, www.travel.state.gov) and **British Foreign and Commonwealth Office** (tel. 020/7008-1500, from overseas tel. 020/7008-0210, www.fco.gov.uk) publish travel advisories.

HUSTLING AND SCAMS

Your biggest problem will probably be hustling by *jineteros* (street hustlers), plus scams pulled by restaurants, hotels, and other tourist entities.

Jineterismo

Jineteros (male hustlers) and *jineteras* (females who trade sex for money) are a persistent presence in tourist zones, where they pester foreigners like flies around fish.

Jineteros try to sell you cigars, tout places to stay or eat, or even suggest a good time with their sisters. In provincial cities, touts on bicycles descend on tourists at traffic lights and will trail you through town, sometimes merely in the hope that you'll give them money to go away. If you're a female tourist, expect to be hustled by Cuban males ingratiating themselves as potential boyfriends.

The best defense is to completely ignore them. Don't say a word. Don't look them in the eye. Don't even acknowledge their presence. Just keep walking.

And the *consumo mínimo* charge in many bars and nightclubs is an invitation to fleece you. Be prepared for charges for things you didn't consume or which didn't materialize, and for higher charges than you were quoted. Insist on an itemized bill at restaurants, add it up diligently, and count your change. *Always* ask for a receipt at Cadeca exchange bureaus; staff regularly scam tourists.

Car rental companies and tour agencies (and their employees) are adept at scams. You pay for a deluxe hotel, say, on a package to Cayo Largo, but are told when you arrive that the hotel in question doesn't honor such packages. You're then fobbed off to the cheapest hotel. When you return to Havana to request a refund, the documents relating to your trip can't be found. Rarely is there a manager available, and usually they say there's nothing that can be done. If the scam amounts to outright theft, take the staffer's name and threaten to report him or her to the head office and police. Don't pay cash in such conditions. Pay with a credit card and challenge the bill. Or simply refuse to pay. Once it has your money, the Cuban government is not about to give refunds under virtually any condition.

COMMONSENSE PRECAUTIONS

Make photocopies of all important documents. Carry the photocopies with you, and leave the originals along with your other valuables in the hotel safe. Prepare an "emergency kit" to tide you over if your wallet gets stolen.

Never carry more cash than you need for the day. Never carry your wallet in your back pocket; wear a secure money belt. Spread your money around your person. Thread fanny pack straps through the belt loops of your pants, and never wear your purse or camera loosely slung over your shoulder. Wear an inexpensive watch. Don't flaunt jewelry. Be wary when cashing money at a bank. Do *not* deal with *jineteros*. Insist that credit card imprints are made in your presence. And make sure any imprints incorrectly completed are torn up; destroy the carbons yourself.

public transportation. Don't carry more luggage than you can adequately manage. And have a lock for each luggage item. Always keep purses fully zipped and luggage locked, even in your hotel room. Don't leave *anything* within reach of an open window or in your car, which should always be parked in a secure area overnight.

Drugs

Few countries are so drug-free. You may occasionally come across home-grown marijuana, but serious drug use is unknown in Cuba. Nonetheless, drug use has increased in recent years with the blossoming of tourism and as Colombian and Jamaican drug lords take advantage of Cuba's remote, scattered cays to make transshipments en route to the United States. Draconian laws are strictly enforced and foreigners receive no special favors. Sentences in excess of 20 years are the norm.

Traffic and Pedestrians

Be wary when crossing streets. Stand well away from the curb—especially on corners, where buses often mount the sidewalk. *Watch your step!* Sidewalks are full of gaping potholes and tilted curbstones. And drive with extreme caution. Driving in Cuba presents unique dangers, from treacherous potholes and wayward bicyclists to cattle and ox-drawn carts wandering across four-lane freeways. Use extra caution when passing tractors and trucks, which without warning tend to make sweeping turns across the road.

Racial Discrimination

Despite all the hype about Cuba being a color-blind society, racial discrimination still exists (although it pales in comparison to the U.S.). Nonwhite tourists can expect to be mistaken for Cubans and hassled on the streets by police requesting ID. Likewise, tourists of non-European descent are more likely to be stopped at the entrances to hotel lobbies and other tourist venues. Mixed-race couples can expect to draw unwanted attention from the police.

Officialdom

Cuba has an insufferable bureaucracy, and working with government entities can be a perplexing and frustrating endeavor. Very few people have the power to say "Yes," but everyone can say "No!" Finding the person who can say "Yes" is the key. Logic and ranting get you nowhere. Charm, *piropos* (witty compliments), or a gift of chocolate works better.

The Policía Revolucionario Nacional (National Revolutionary Police, or PNR) is a branch of the Ministry of the Interior (MININT) and its major task is to enforce revolutionary purity. Uniformed police officers also perform the same functions as in Western countries, although with far less professionalism than you may be used to in the United States or Europe.

Bite Your Tongue!

Cubans are a paranoid people, never sure who might be a *chivato*, a finger pointer for the CDR or MININT, the much-loathed Ministry of the Interior. In this regard, Cuba doesn't seem to have changed much since the 1930s, when Hemingway told Arnold Samuelson, "Don't trust anybody. That fellow might have been a government spy trying to get you in bad. You can never tell who they are."

Since Raúl took over from Fidel, things have eased. These days, Cubans aren't so frightened to voice their frustrations verbally on the street. Still, no one in his or her right mind would dare to *overly* criticize the government or the Castros in public. Sometimes a diatribe against the government (usually offered in hushed tones) will end in midstream as the speaker taps his two forefingers on his opposite shoulder, signifying the presence of a member of State Security. Hence, Cubans have developed a cryptic, elliptical way of talking where nuance and meaning are hidden from casual tourists.

Even foreigners are not above surreptitious surveillance by the General Directorate for State Security (G2). Foreign journalists may even be assigned specific hotel rooms that may be bugged. The Cuban government looks with suspicion on U.S. travelers entering on religious or humanitarian licenses, and U.S. "people-to-people" programs are handled exclusively by Celimar, a division of Havanatur that is said to report to MININT and is heavily laden with ex-MININT staffers.

Tourists are free to roam wherever they wish without hindrance or a need to look over their shoulders, but nay-saying the Revolution in public can swiftly land you in trouble.

Cuban police officers are trained to be paranoid about foreigners. Never attempt to photograph police or military without their permission.

If a police officer wants to search you, insist on it being done in front of a neutral witness—*"solamente con testigos."* Do *not* allow an official to confiscate your passport. Tell as little as circumspection dictates—unlike priests, policemen rarely offer absolution for confessions. If a police officer asks for money, get his name and badge number and file a complaint with the Ministry of Foreign Relations.

If Trouble Strikes

In emergencies, call:

- 104 for an ambulance
- 105 for fire
- 106 for police

If things turn dire, contact **Asistur** (Prado #212, e/ Trocadero y Colón, Habana Vieja, tel. 07/866-4499, 07/866-8527, 5280-3563, or 5805-6292, www.asistur.cu, Mon.-Fri. 8:30am-5pm), which assists tourists in trouble. It has a 24-hour "alarm center," plus outlets in Camagüey, Ciego de Ávila, Cienfuegos, Guardalavaca, Santiago de Cuba, and Varadero. You should also contact your embassy or consulate. It can't get you out of jail, but it can help locate a lawyer or arrange for funds (U.S. citizens in Cuba can request help in an emergency).

If you're robbed, immediately file a police report with the **Policía Revolucionaria Nacional** (PNR, in Havana, Calle Picota, e/ Leonor Pérez y San Isidro, tel. 07/867-0496 or 07/862-0116). You'll receive a statement (*denuncia*) for insurance purposes. Proceedings can take hours (readers report Kafkaesque experiences). If you're involved in a car accident, call the *tránsitos* (transit police, tel. 07/862-0116 in Havana, 106 outside Havana).

If you're charged with a crime, request that a representative of your embassy be present, and that any deposition be made in front of an independent witness (*testigo*).

There are reports of Cuban police jailing victims of passport theft while the crime and victim are investigated. Report to your embassy *before* reporting ID theft to the police.

HELP FOR U.S. CITIZENS

Travelers report that the **U.S. Embassy** (Calzada, e/ L y M, Vedado, tel. 07/839-4100, emergency/after-hours tel. 07/839-4100 +1, https:// cu.usembassy.gov, Mon.-Fri. 8am-4:30pm) has a good record in helping U.S. citizens in need in Cuba. The U.S. Department of State has a **Hotline for American Travelers** (tel. 202/647-5225), and you can call the **Overseas Citizen Service** (tel. 888/407-4747, from overseas tel. 202/501-4444 for after-hours emergencies, http://travel.state.gov, Mon.-Fri. 8am-8pm) if things go awry. If arrested, U.S. citizens should ask Cuban authorities to notify the U.S. Embassy. A U.S. consular officer will then try to arrange regular visits. Cuba does not recognize dual citizenship for Cuban citizens who are also U.S. citizens; Cuban-born citizens are denied representation through the U.S. Embassy.

LEGAL ASSISTANCE

Consultoría Jurídica Internacional (CJI, International Judicial Consultative Bureau, Calle 16 #314, e/ 3ra y 5ta, Miramar, tel. 07/204-2490, www.cji.co.cu) provides legal advice and services. It can assist travelers, including those who lose their passports or have them stolen.

Travel Tips

WHAT TO PACK

Dress for a tropical climate. Pack a **warm sweater** and a **windbreaker** for winter visits. In summer, the weather is hot and humid; you'll want **light, loose-fitting shirts and shorts.** Ideally, everything should be drip-dry, wash-and-wear. Cubans dress informally, though neatly, for all occasions.

A comfortable, well-fitting pair of **sneakers** will work for most occasions. Pack a pair of **dress shoes** for your evening ensemble. Take all the **toiletries** you think you'll need, including toilet paper and face cloth. Medicines are rarely available except in Havana and other key tourist venues; come prepared with aspirin and other essentials. Hand sanitizer is a must—use it regularly!

International credit cards are accepted throughout Cuba, although the system is dysfunctional and unreliable. At press time, most U.S. citizens need to operate on a **cash-only** basis.

MONEY
Currency

Cuba has two currencies. At press time, the government's announced intention to unify the currencies was far from fruition.

CONVERTIBLE PESOS

All prices in this book are quoted in Cuban convertible pesos (*pesos convertibles*), denominated by "CUC" (pronounced "say-ooh-say" and colloquially called *kooks*) and often, within Cuba, by "$." Foreigners must exchange their foreign currency for convertible pesos (at press time the CUC is at parity with the U.S. dollar), issued in the following denominations: 1-, 3-, 5-, 10-, 20-, 50-, and 100-peso notes, along with 1-, 5-, 10-, 25-, and 50-centavo coins plus CUC1 and CUC5 coins. Euros are acceptable tender in Varadero, Cayo Coco, and Havana.

Always carry a wad of small bills; change for larger bills is often hard to come by.

CUBAN PESOS

The Cuban currency (*moneda nacional*), in which state salaries are paid, is the peso, which is worth about US$0.05 (the exchange rate at press time was 25 pesos to the dollar). It is also designated "$" and should not be confused with the CUC or US$ (to make matters worse, the dollar is sometimes called the peso). The peso is divided into 100 centavos.

There is very little that you will need pesos for. Exceptions are if you want to travel on local buses or buy ice cream at Coppelia.

EXCHANGING CURRENCY

Foreign currency can be changed for CUC at tourist hotels, banks, and official *burós de cambios* (exchange bureaus) operated by **Cadeca** (tel. 07/855-5701), which has outlets throughout Cuba; a 3 percent commission is charged for all exchanges. They can also change CUC or foreign currency for *moneda nacional*. Cadeca charges a 3 percent commission plus an additional 10 percent commission for exchanging U.S. dollars. To avoid the surcharge, U.S. visitors should bring Canadian dollars or euros. Check the current exchange rates at the **Banco Central de Cuba** website (www.bc.gob. cu). Always ask for a receipt before changing your money, as Cadeca clerks often shortchange tourists.

Jineteros may offer to change currency on the streets. Many tourists are ripped off, and muggings have been reported. One scam is for *jineteros*

to tell you that the banks are closed and that they can help. *Never* change money on the street. It's also illegal; tourists who have been scammed and have reported it to the police have been fined.

Banks

All banks in Cuba are state entities. No foreign banks are present. The most important of the banks catering to foreigners is the **Banco Financiero Internacional,** which offers a full range of services. Branches nationwide are open Monday-Saturday 8am-3pm (but 8am-noon only on the last working day of each month). **Banco de Crédito y Comercio** (Bandec) is the main commercial bank, with outlets islandwide (most are open weekdays 8:30am-3pm). **Banco Popular** and **Banco Metropolitano** also provide foreign transaction services.

Cuban banks have been known to pass off counterfeit CUC50 and CUC100 bills to foreigners. When receiving such bills, always check for watermarks.

Credit Cards and ATMs

Most hotels, larger restaurants, and major shops accept credit cards, as long as they are not issued or processed by U.S. banks (other nationalities should check that their cards can be used; for example, about 20 percent of British-issued cards are outsourced to U.S. companies). Credit card transactions are charged 11 percent commission (comprising an 8 percent levy on currency exchange, plus a 3 percent conversion fee).

Automated teller machines (ATMs) at major banks dispense CUC to Cubans with cash cards. Many ATMs are linked to international systems such as Cirrus (non-U.S. Visa-designated cards work, but not MasterCard). Use them only during bank hours, as they often eat your card. You can use your non-U.S. credit card to obtain a cash advance up to CUC500 (CUC100 minimum).

Although use of U.S. credit cards was legalized in 2016, at press time only cards issued by **Stonegate Bank** (www.stonegatebank.com) functioned in Cuba. The bureaucratic financial system was still treating Cuba as pariah. Plan on needing to travel on a cash-only basis.

Problem with your card? Contact **Fincimex** (Calle 8 #319, e/ 3ra y 5ta, Miramar, Havana, tel. 07/224-3191), which has branches in major cities.

U.S. citizens should avoid checking their bank statements online while in Cuba, which can result in an instant block on your account when the financial infrastructure identifies the Cuban IPC address.

Travelers Checks

Travelers checks (unless issued by U.S. banks) are accepted in some tourist restaurants, hotels, and foreign-goods stores. They can also be cashed at most hotel cashier desks, as well as at banks. You should *not* enter the date or the place when signing your checks—a quirky Cuban requirement.

241

ESSENTIALS
TRAVEL TIPS

Studying in Cuba

Thousands of people every year choose to study in Cuba, be it for a month-long dance course or six years of medical training. Be prepared for basic living conditions if signing up for a long-term residential course. Restrictions for U.S. students apply.

UniversiTUR (Calle 30 #768, e/ Kohly y 41, Nuevo Vedado, tel. 07/261-4939 or 07/855-5978) arranges study at centers of higher learning. For study at the **Universidad de la Habana** (Calle J #556, e/ 25 y 27, Vedado, www.uh.cu), contact Isabel Milán Licea (tel. 07/832-1692, imilan@rect.uh.cu).

Study Abroad (www.studyabroad.com/in-cuba) is a clearinghouse for institutions offering study opportunities in Cuba.

Student Visas

You can study in Cuba using a tourist visa only if you travel via UniversiTUR. All others require a student visa (CUC80), which can be requested in advance from the Director of Graduate Degrees of the relevant university 20 days prior to your intended arrival date. Visas are good for 30 days but can be extended upon arrival in Cuba for CUC25.

You can *arrive* in Cuba with a tourist visa, however. You then have 48 hours to register for your university program and request a change of visa status (CUC65). You'll need six passport photos, your passport and tourist card, and a license certificate for the *casa particular* where you'll be staying.

Arts, Music, and Dance

The **Cátedra de Danza** (Calzada #510, e/ D y E, Vedado, tel. 07/832-4625, www.balletcuba.cult.cu) offers monthlong ballet courses for intermediate- and advanced-level professionals and students.

The **Centro Nacional de Conservación, Restauración y**

Money Transfers

In 2011 President Obama lifted restrictions on how much money Cuban Americans can send to Cuba. And *any* U.S. citizen can now send up to $500 every three months to any Cuban (but no Communist Party member) to "support private economic activity."

Western Union (U.S. tel. 800/325-6000, www.westernunion.com) is licensed to handle wire transfers to Cuba. Senders must fill out an electronic affidavit.

For foreigners, Cuba's **TransCard** (Canada tel. 800/724-5685, www.smart-transfer.com) operates much like a debit card. The user deposits funds into a secure account abroad (you can do so online), then uses that account to withdraw cash at ATMs, banks, and Cadeca, or to pay for goods and services at locations in Cuba.

Costs

Prices rise and fall like a yo-yo, according to the Cuban government's whim. If you use public transport, rent *casas particulares,* and dine on the street and at peso snack bars, you may be able to survive on as little as CUC40 a

Museología (Calle Oficios, e/ Jústiz y Obrapía, Habana Vieja, tel. 07/861-5846) offers courses for urban planners, conservationists, and architects.

The **Instituto Superior de Arte** (Calle 120 #1110, e/ 9na y 13, Cubanacán, tel. 07/208-8075, www.isa.cult.cu) offers courses in music, dance, theater, and visual arts.

The **Taller Experimental de Gráfica** (Callejón del Chorro #6, Plaza de la Catedral, Habana Vieja, tel. 07/864-6013, tgrafica@cubarte.cult.cu) offers courses in engraving and lithography.

Medical Training

Cuba offers scholarships for disadvantaged and minority students from the United States and developing nations to attend the **Escuela Latinoamericana de Medicina** (Latin American School of Medical Sciences, ELACM, Carretera Panamericana Km 3.5, Playa, Havana, tel. 07/210-4644, www.elacm.sld.cu). Courses last six years and graduates are full-fledged doctors.

Spanish-Language Courses

The **Universidad de la Habana** (Dirección de Posgrado, Calle J #556, e/ 25 y 27, Vedado, tel. 07/832-4245, www.uh.cu) and provincial universities throughout Cuba offer Spanish-language courses of 20-80 hours (CUC100-300), plus "Spanish and Cuban Culture" courses of 320-480 hours (CUC960-1,392). Courses begin the first Monday of the month, year-round.

The **Centro de Idiomas y Computación José Martí** (José Martí Language and Computer Center, Calle 90 #531, e/ 5ta B y 5ta C, Miramar, Havana, tel. 07/209-6692, cice@ceniai.inf.cu) offers Spanish-language courses of 20-80 hours (CUC130-330).

day (more in Havana). For a modicum of comforts, budget at least CUC75 a day.

TIPPING

Cubans receive slave-rate wages (although fixed living costs are virtually zero). Your waiter or chambermaid probably lives in a slum and is being paid less than CUC1 per day. Waiters expect to be tipped 10 percent, even where a service charge has been added to your bill (waiters and staff see only a small fraction of this, if any). Taxi drivers do not need to be tipped; they're all freelancers and have built their profit into your fare.

Museum guides often follow you around in the hope of soliciting a tip. If you don't welcome the service, say so upfront. Musicians in bars and restaurants will usually hover by your table until tipped, after which they usually move on to the next table.

The arrival en masse of U.S. tourists has changed the tipping scenario, as they tend to *overtip* and to tip where it isn't needed. As a result, taxi fares have skyrocketed.

Getting Married in Cuba

It's easy to get married in Cuba if you have the correct documents in place. Civil marriages are handled by the **Bufete de Servicios Especializados** (Calle 23 #501, esq. J, Vedado, Havana, tel. 07/832-6813, www.onbc.cu/bes), the "International Lawyer's Office," which has an office in most major cities. The marriage certificate costs CUC525, plus there are other expenses. Foreigners need to produce their birth certificate, proof of marital status if single, and a divorce certificate (if relevant). These need to be translated into Spanish and authenticated by the Cuban consulate in the country in which they were issued. Marriages in Cuba are recognized in the United States.

Communications and Media

Cuba has one of the most restrictive media policies in the world. A recent study by Washington-based advocacy group Freedom House found that more than 90 percent of Cubans had access *solely* to government media.

POSTAL SERVICE

Correos de Cuba (Av. Rancho Boyeros, Havana, tel. 07/879-6824, Mon.-Sat. 8am-6pm) operates the Cuban postal service, which is slow; delivery is never guaranteed. Mail is read by Cuba's censors; avoid politically sensitive comments. *Never* send cash. Post offices (*correos*) are usually open weekdays 10am-5pm and Saturday 8am-3pm, but hours can vary. Most tourist hotels accept mail for delivery.

International airmail (*correo aereo*) averages one month (savvy Cubans usually hand their letters to foreigners to mail outside Cuba). When mailing from Cuba, write the country destination in Spanish: Inglaterra (England, Scotland, and Wales), Francia (France), Italia (Italy), Alemania (Germany), España (Spain), Suiza (Switzerland), and Estados Unidos (United States, often referred to as "EE.UU.").

International postcards, including prepaid ones, cost CUC0.90 (to all destinations); letters cost CUC1.05. Within Cuba, letters cost from 15 centavos (20 grams or less) to 2.05 pesos (up to 500 grams); postcards cost 10 centavos. Stamps are called *sellos* (SAY-yos).

Parcels from Cuba must be *unwrapped* for inspection. It is far better to send packages through an express courier service, although the same regulation applies.

You can receive mail in Havana by having letters and parcels addressed to you using your name as it appears on your passport or other ID for general delivery to: "c/o Espera [your name], Ministerio de Comunicaciones, Avenida Independencia and 19 de Mayo, Habana 6, Cuba." To collect mail, go to the **Correos de Cuba** (Av. Rancho Boyeros, Havana, tel. 07/879-6824,

"Espera [your name] c/o [your embassy]."

Express Mail
DHL Worldwide Express (www.dhl.com) has offices in major cities. The main office is in Havana (1ra Av., esq. 26, Miramar, tel. 07/204-1876). In 2016, President Obama granted **FedEx** (www.fedex.com) permission to open an office, but no office had yet opened at press time.

Cubapost (Calle P #108, Vedado, tel. 07/836-9790) and **Cubapacks** (Calle 22 #4115, e/ 41 y 47, Miramar, tel. 07/204-2742) offer international express mail and parcel service.

Restrictions
Letters and literature can be mailed from the United States without restriction. Gift parcels can be "sent or carried by an authorized traveler" to an individual or religious or educational organization if the domestic retail value does not exceed US$800. Only one parcel per month is allowed, and contents are limited to food, vitamins, seeds, medicines, medical supplies, clothing, personal hygiene items, computers, software, electronics, and a few other categories. All other parcels are subject to seizure. See http://pe.usps.com/text/imm/ce_017.htm.

TELEPHONE SERVICE
Cuba's modern digital telephone system is the responsibility of the **Empresa de Telecomunicaciones de Cuba** (Etecsa, tel. 07/266-6666 or 118, www.etecsa.cu), headquartered in the Miramar Trade Center in Havana. It has a central office (*telepunto*) with international phone and Internet service in every town (all are open daily 8:30am-7pm). There are still quirks, with some days better than others.

Call 113 for directory inquiries. The national telephone directory is available online at www.pamarillas.cu, and on CD-ROM (Grupo Directorio Telefónico, tel. 07/266-6305). Telephone numbers change often. Trying to determine a correct number can be problematic because many entities have several numbers and rarely publish the same number twice. Most commercial entities have a switchboard (*pizarra*).

Public Phone Booths
Public phone kiosks are ubiquitous. Etecsa operates glass-enclosed telephone kiosks called *micropuntos* (*telecorreos* where they combine postal services). They use phone cards, sold on-site and at tourist hotels and miscellaneous other outlets. They are inserted into the phone and the cost of the call is automatically deducted from the card's value. If the card expires during your call, you can continue without interruption by pushing button C and inserting a new card.

Propia cards use a number specific to each card that is keyed into the telephone when prompted. Propia cards are for local and national calls (blue, 5 pesos and 10 pesos). **Chip** cards (CUC5, CUC10, and CUC20) are used for international calls.

Some phones still accept 5- and 20-centavo coins, which can only be used for local and national calls. When you hear a short "blip," *immediately* put in another coin to avoid being cut off. Public phones do not accept collect or incoming calls.

International Calls

When calling Cuba from abroad, dial 011 (the international dialing code), then 53 (the Cuba country code), followed by the city code and the number. For direct international calls from Cuba, dial 119, then the country code (for example, 44 for the U.K.), followed by the area code and number. For the international operator, dial 012 (Havana) or 180 (rest of Cuba).

Cost per minute varies depending on time of day and location of the call. At last visit, per-minute rates were: CUC1.40 6pm-6am and CUC1.95 6am-6pm to the United States, Canada, Mexico, Central America, Caribbean, and South America; CUC1.50 to Europe and the rest of the world. Rates are much higher for operator-assisted calls and from tourist hotels, most of which have direct-dial telephones in guest rooms.

Domestic Calls

For local calls in the same area code, simply dial the number you wish to reach. To dial a number outside your area code, dial 0, then wait for a tone before dialing the local city code and the number you wish to reach. For the local operator, dial 0. Local calls in Havana cost approximately 5 centavos (about a quarter of a cent). Rates for calls beyond Havana range from 30 centavos to 3 pesos and 15 centavos for the first three minutes, depending on zone—tourist hotels and Etecsa booths charge in CUC equivalent.

Cellular Phones

Cell phone use has rocketed, although the cost of use is high at $0.35 cents a minute locally (7am-11pm; the price drops to $0.10 cents 11pm-7am), CUC2.45 per minute to the United States and the Americas, and CUC5.85 to Europe. Most Cubans use their cell phones for SMS texting (CUC0.9 cents local, or $0.60 cents international). Few Cubans answer incoming calls. They note the number of the caller, then call them back on a landline or phone card, which is much cheaper.

Cell phone numbers in Cuba have eight digits, beginning with 5, and omit the provincial area codes.

Cubacel (Calle 28 #510, e/ 5 y 7, Miramar, tel. 05/264-2266 or 07/880-2222, www.cubacel.com, daily 8:30am-7:30pm, Sat. 8am-noon) operates Cuba's cell phone system and has offices in most major cities. It operates two different cell phone networks (TDMA and GSM) and has roaming agreements with several countries, including the United States. In 2009

President Obama permitted U.S. telecommunications companies to do deals with Cuba. If yours is among them, you can bring your cell phone and expect it to function in Cuba. Cubacel can activate most phones.

Since 2011 foreigners can no longer obtain a permanent local line. A local number can now only be obtained in the name of a Cuban resident (cost CUC40). Hence, you need to find a Cuban who doesn't own a cell phone and is willing to open a line on your behalf, but in their own name. Once set up with a line, you then pay in advance for calling credit and are charged the corresponding rates for all local and long-distance calls. You'll have to use your cell phone to keep your line (the grace period is 30-180 days, depending on how much money is in your account).

Foreign visitors *can* obtain SIM cards and/or rent cell phones (CUC100 deposit, plus CUC10 daily rental—CUC7 for the phone and CUC3 for the line) for the duration of their visit only. In Havana, the only two places where foreigners can get a SIM card or get a cell phone activated are the Cubacel offices at the airport (Terminals 2 and 3) and at the main office in Miramar (Calle 28 #510, e/ 5 y 7, tel. 05/880-2222 or 05/264-2266). You then purchase prepaid cards (CUC10, CUC20, or CUC40, sold at stores and phone centers nationwide) to charge to your account.

The National Geographic Talk Abroad cell phone (www.cellular-abroad.com/travelphone.php) can be rented (from $18 weekly) or purchased (from $99) and will function in Cuba with U.S. and U.K. phone numbers and without any setup being required in Cuba. Several other companies offer similar phone service.

ONLINE SERVICE IN CUBA

Etecsa has a monopoly on Internet service, which it offers using prepaid Nauta cards (since December 2016, CUC1.50 per hour for international access; CUC0.25 domestic access) and can be used at any Etecsa office or wherever Internet service is offered. You may need to present your passport, which may be recorded, along with the number of your prepaid card. Assume that all emails are read directly off the server by security personnel.

The U.S. embargo traditionally banned Cuba from accessing international satellite and telecommunications systems. However, service has improved since 2013, when Cuba activated a new fiber-optic cable connected to Jamaica and Venezuela (replacing slow service via a Russian satellite and vastly increasing bandwidth) and opened 118 Etecsa *telepuntos* nationwide. Most towns of any size have since had Wi-Fi installed in public plazas, and Havana now has scores of Wi-Fi zones. All tourist hotels have Wi-Fi service using Etecsa's system. A few hotels have data ports and Wi-Fi in guest rooms; many also have fixed-line Internet stations. A select few hotels charge their own rates (as high as CUC10 per hour in Havana's Hotel Nacional) and do not accept Nauta cards.

Area Codes and Emergency Numbers

	Area Code	Ambulance	Fire	Police
Havana	07	104	105	106
Havana Province	047			
Artemisa	047	36-2597	105	106
San Antonio de los Baños	047	38-2781	105	106
Mayabeque Province	047			
Batabanó	047	58-5335	105	106
Camagüey	032	104	105	106
Ciego de Ávila	033	104	105	106
Cayo Coco	033	104	30-9102	30-8107
Cienfuegos	043	104	105	106
Granma	023	104	105	106
Pilón	023	104	105	59-4493
Guantánamo	021	104	105	106
Holguín	024	104	105	106
Banes	024	80-3798	105	106
Isla de la Juventud	046			
Cayo Largo	046	24-8238	24-8247	39-9406
Nueva Gerona	046	32-2366	105	106

	Area Code	Ambulance	Fire	Police
Las Tunas	031	104	105	106
Matanzas	045			
Cárdenas	045	52-7640	105	106
Jagüey Grande	045	91-3046	105	106
Matanzas	045	28-5023	105	106
Playa Girón	045	98-7364	105	106
Varadero	045	66-2306	105	106
Pinar del Río	048			
Pinar del Río City	048	76-2317	105	106
Viñales			105	106
Sancti Spíritus	041			
Sancti Spíritus	041	32-4462	105	110
Trinidad	041	99-2362	105	106
Santiago de Cuba	022	185, 62-3300	105	106
Villa Clara	042	104		
Caibarién	042	36-3888	105	106
Remedios	042	39-5149	105	106
Santa Clara	042	20-3965	105	106

Wi-Fi service is erratic and almost always slow. You'll need lots of patience. Skype is prohibited, but IMO is a popular free video call app preferred by Cubans.

In February 2016, Cuba announced it was initiating residential broadband Internet in parts of Havana, and that cafés and restaurants would also get broadband.

NEWSPAPERS AND MAGAZINES
Before You Go
Take all the reading matter you can with you, as there are no newsagents or newsstands in Cuba. *CubaPlus* (www.cubaplusmagazine.com) is an English-language travel magazine, published in Canada but available in Cuba. Likewise, you can subscribe to *OnCuba* (www.oncubamagazine.com), a glossy monthly magazine distributed on charter aircraft flying between Miami and Cuba. By far the most impressive all-around online magazine is LaHabana (www.lahabana.com), covering arts and culture. *Cuba Standard* (www.cubastandard.com) serves investors.

In Cuba
Pre-Castro Cuba had a vibrant media sector, with 58 daily newspapers of differing political hues. The Castro government closed them all down. It's been years since I've seen *any* foreign publications for sale in Cuba. Today domestic media is still almost entirely state controlled. There is no independent press, although things are gradually loosening up under Raúl.

The most important daily—and virtually the sole mouthpiece of international news—is *Granma* (www.granma.cu), the cheaply produced official outlet of the Communist Party (ironically, printed on newssheet imported legally from Alabama). This eight-page rag focuses on denigrating the United States (though that has eased of late) and profiling socialist victories. Until recently, no negatives were reported about domestic affairs, but a forward-thinking editor appointed in 2012 is following a new dictate to permit more realistic and critical coverage, although the paper's international coverage remains heavily distorted. *Granma* is sold on the street but rapidly sells out as many Cubans buy it to resell. A weekly edition published in Spanish, English, and French is sold in hotels. *Habaneros* get their news via *radio bemba,* the fast-moving street gossip or grapevine.

Juventud Rebelde, the evening paper of the Communist Youth League, echoes *Granma.* Similar mouthpieces include the less easily found *Trabajadores* (*Workers,* weekly), *Mujeres* (a monthly magazine for women), and such arts and culture magazines as *Habanera* (monthly), *Bohemia* (weekly), and, best of all, *Temas* (www.temas.cult.cu).

The daily *Granma* and weekly *Cartelera* newspapers print weather forecasts. Cuban TV newscasts have daily forecasts (in Spanish). The Instituto weather information in Spanish online.

RADIO AND TELEVISION

All broadcast media in Cuba are state controlled.

Television

Most tourist hotel rooms have satellite TVs showing international channels such as HBO, ESPN, CNN, and so on (the Cuban government pirates the signals). No Cuban (except the Communist elite) is permitted access to satellite TV. Ordinary Cubans must make do with the national TV networks (Canal 6: CubaVisión and Canal 2: Tele Rebelde, plus Canal Educativo and Canal Educativo-Dos, two educational channels) plus state-run Telesur, from Venezuela.

Programming is dominated by dreary reports on socialist progress (Castro speeches take precedence over all other programming) and the daily *mesa redonda* (roundtable), a political "discussion" that is merely a staged denunciation of wicked Uncle Sam. However, Tele Rebelde features selections from CNN España international news coverage. Cuban television also has some very intelligent programming, emphasizing science and culture (often culled from National Geographic, Discovery Channel, etc.), U.S. series such as *First 48 Hours* and *Friends,* foreign comedy (*Mr. Bean* is a favorite), and sports and foreign movies. There are no advertisements, but five-minute slots might inveigh against abortions or exhort Cubans to work hard, while cartoons aim to teach Cuban youth sound morals. Cubans are so addicted to Latin American *telenovelas* (soap operas) that you can walk through Havana when the *novela* is showing and follow the show as you walk.

Radio

Cuba ranked eighth in the world in number of radio stations in 1958. Today it has only nine national radio stations, including Radio Rebelde (640 and 710 AM, and 96.7 FM) and Radio Reloj (950 AM and 101.5 FM), both reporting news, and Radio Progreso (640 AM and 90.3 FM), featuring traditional music. Radio Taíno (1290 AM and 93.3 FM) caters to tourists with programs in English, French, and Spanish.

There are also provincial and local stations. However, in much of the countryside you can put your car radio onto "scan" and it will just go round and round without ever coming up with a station.

WEIGHTS AND MEASURES

Cuba operates on the metric system. Liquids are sold in liters, fruits and vegetables by the kilo. Distances are given in meters and kilometers. See the chart at the back of the book for metric conversions.

Electricity

Cuba operates on 110-volt AC (60-cycle) nationwide, although a few hotels operate on 220 volts (many have both). Most outlets use U.S. plugs: flat, parallel two-pins, and three rectangular pins. A two-prong adapter is a good idea (take one with you; they're impossible to find in Cuba). Many outlets are faulty and dangerous. Electricity blackouts (*apagones*) are now infrequent. Take a flashlight, spare batteries, and candles plus matches or lighter.

Time

Cuban time is equivalent to U.S. Eastern Standard Time: five hours behind Greenwich mean time, the same as New York and Miami, and three hours ahead of the U.S. West Coast. There is little seasonal variation in dawn. Cuba observes daylight saving time May-October.

CONDUCT AND CUSTOMS

Cubans are respectful and courteous, with a deep sense of integrity. You can ease your way considerably by being courteous and patient. Always greet your host with *"¡Buenos días!"* ("Good morning!") or *"¡Buenas tardes!"* ("Good afternoon!"). And never neglect to say *"gracias"* ("thank you"). Topless sunbathing is tolerated at some tourist resorts, and nude bathing is allowed only on Cayo Largo.

Cubans are extremely hygienic and have a natural prejudice against anyone who ignores personal hygiene.

Smoking is ostensibly prohibited in theaters, stores, buses, taxis, restaurants, and enclosed public areas, but the prohibition is rarely enforced.

Respect the natural environment: Take only photographs, leave only footprints.

Photography

You can take photographs freely (except of military and industrial installations, airports, and officials in uniform). Most museums charge for photography.

Visitors are allowed to bring two cameras plus a video camera. Official permission is needed to bring "professional" camera equipment. Foto Video and Photo Service stores sell instamatic and small digital cameras. However, there are *no* camera stores similar to those found in North America or Europe, and 35mm SLRs, lenses, flash units, filters, and other equipment are unavailable. Bring spare batteries, tapes, and film, which is hard to find. *Snatch-and-grab theft of cameras is a major problem.*

The only camera store in Cuba is in the **Gran Hotel Manzana Kempinski** (Calle San Rafael, e/ Zulueta y Monserrate, Havana, tel), in Havana.

Cubans love to be photographed. However, never assume an automatic right to do so. Ask permission to photograph individuals, and honor any wishing not to be photographed. Cubans often request money for being photographed, as do those Cubans who dress flamboyantly as photo ops: If you don't want to pay, don't take the shot. In markets, it is a courtesy to buy a small trinket from vendors you wish to photograph. *Do* send photographs to anyone you promise to send to.

Several foreigners have been arrested for filming "pornography," which in Cuba includes topless or nude photography.

Business Hours

Bank branches nationwide are open Monday-Saturday 8am-3pm (but 8am-noon only on the last working day of each month). Pharmacies generally open daily 8am-8pm (*turnos permanentes* stay open 24 hours). Post offices are usually open Monday-Saturday 8am-10pm, Sunday 8am-6pm, but hours vary widely. Shops are usually open Monday-Saturday 8:30am-5:30pm, although many remain open later, including all day Sunday. Museum hours vary widely, although most are closed on Monday.

Most banks, businesses, and government offices close during national holidays.

Public Restrooms

Public toilets are few. Many are disgustingly foul. Most hotels and restaurants will let you use their facilities, though most lack toilet paper, which gets stolen. An attendant usually sits outside the door, dispensing pieces of toilet paper. Since 2010, most attendants now pay the state CUC10 for the privilege of cleaning the toilets and collecting tips. CUC0.25 is usually sufficient. Always carry a small packet of toilet tissue with you.

ACCESS FOR TRAVELERS WITH DISABILITIES

Cubans go out of their way to assist travelers with disabilities, although few allowances have been made in infrastructure.

In the United States, the **Society for Accessible Travel & Hospitality** (347 5th Ave. #610, New York, NY 10016, tel. 212/447-7284, www.sath. org) and the **American Foundation for the Blind** (2 Penn Plaza #1102, New York, NY 10001, tel. 212/502-7600 or 800/232-5463, www.afb.org) are good resources, as is Cuba's **Asociación Cubana de Limitados Físicos y Motores** (Cuban Association for Physically & Motor Disabled People, ACLIFIM, Calle 6 #106, e/ 1ra y 3ra, Havana, tel. 07/209-3099, www.acli-fim.sld.cu).

TRAVELING WITH CHILDREN

Cubans adore children and will dote on yours. Children under the age of 2 travel free on airlines; children between 2 and 12 are offered discounts. Children under 16 usually stay free with parents at hotels, although an extra-bed rate may be charged. Children under 12 normally get free (or half-price) entry to museums.

Children's items such as diapers (nappies) and baby foods are scarce in Cuba. Bring cotton swabs, diapers, Band-Aids, baby foods, and a small first-aid kit with any necessary medicines for your child. Children's car seats are not offered in rental cars.

The equivalent of the Boy and Girl Scouts and Girl Guides is the **Pioneros José Martí** (Calle F #352, Vedado, Havana, tel. 07/832-5292), which has chapters throughout the country. Having your children interact would be a fascinating education.

MALE TRAVELERS

The average male visitor soon discovers that Cuban women have an open attitude towards sexuality. They are also much more aggressive than foreign men may be used to, displaying little equivocation.

Romantic liaisons require prudence. Petty robbery (your paramour steals your sunglasses or rifles your wallet while you take a shower) is common. Muggings by accomplices are a rare possibility, and high-class prostitutes have been known to rob tourists by drugging their drinks. Several tourists have even been murdered during sexual encounters.

Men in "sensitive" occupations (e.g., journalists) should be aware that the femme fatale who sweeps you off your feet may be in the employ of Cuba's state security.

WOMEN TRAVELERS

Sexual assault of women is almost unheard of. If you welcome the amorous overtures of men, Cuba is heaven. The art of gentle seduction is to Cuban men a kind of national pastime—a sport and a trial of manhood. They will hiss like serpents in appreciation, and call out *piropos*—affectionate and lyrical epithets. Take effusions of love with a grain of salt; while swearing eternal devotion, your Don Juan may conveniently forget to mention he's married. While the affection may be genuine, you are assuredly the moneybags in the relationship. Plenty of Cuban men earn their living giving pleasure to foreign women looking for love beneath the palms or, like their female counterparts, taking advantage of such an opportunity when it arises.

If you're not interested, pretend not to notice advances and avoid eye contact.

Cuba's **Federación de Mujeres Cubanas** (Cuban Women's Federation, Galiano #264, e/ Neptuno y Concordia, Havana, tel. 07/862-4905) is a useful resource. It publishes *Mujeres,* a women's magazine.

STUDENT AND YOUTH TRAVELERS

Foreign students with the **International Student Identity Card** (ISIC) or similar student ID receive discounts to many museums. You can obtain an ISIC at any student union, or in the United States from the **Council on International Educational Exchange** (tel. 207/553-4000, www.ciee.org) and in Canada from **Travel Cuts** (tel. 800/667-2887, www.travelcuts.com).

The **Federación Estudiantil Universitario** (Calle 23, esq. H, Vedado, Havana, tel. 07/832-4646, www.almamater.cu) is Cuba's national student federation.

SENIOR TRAVELERS

Cuba honors senior citizens, who receive discounted entry to museums and other sights. This may apply to foreign seniors in a few instances. A useful resource is the **American Association of Retired Persons** (tel. 888/687-2277, www.aarp.org).

GAY AND LESBIAN TRAVELERS

Cuba—a macho society—is schizophrenic when it comes to homosexuality. Cuba has made strides, much due to the efforts of Raúl Castro's daughter Mariela Castro Espín, director of the **Centro Nacional de Educación Sexual** (Calle 10 #460, Vedado, Havana, tel. 07/832-2528, www.cenesex. org), which has an ongoing campaign to break down macho attitudes and promote acceptance and equal treatment of the LGBT community.

Useful resources include the **International Gay & Lesbian Travel Association** (tel. 954/630-1637, www.iglta.org). **GayCuba** (tel. 5294-2968, www.gaycuba.me) caters to gay travelers to Cuba.

Tourist Information

TOURIST AND INFORMATION BUREAUS

Cuba's **Ministerio de Turismo** (Av. 3ra y F, Vedado, Havana, tel. 07/836-3245 or 07/832-7535, www.cubatravel.cu) is in charge of tourism. It has offices in nine countries, including Canada (1200 Bay St., Suite 305, Toronto, ON M5R 2A5, tel. 416/362-0700, www.gocuba.ca; 2075 rue University, Bureau 460, Montreal, QC H3A 2L1, tel. 514/875-8004) and the United Kingdom (167 High Holborn, London WC1V 6PA, tel. 020/7240-6655, www.travel2cuba.co.uk). There is no office in the United States; however, the Canadian offices will mail literature to U.S. citizens.

Cuba is a member of the **Caribbean Tourism Organization** (CTO, 80 Broad St., 32nd Floor, New York, NY 10004, tel. 212/635-9530, www.onecaribbean.org), which is a handy information source, and the **Caribbean Hotel Association** (CHA, 2655 LeJeune Rd., Suite 910, Coral Gables, FL 33134, tel. 305/443-3040, www.caribbeanhotelassociation.com). The CTO has an office in the U.K. (22 The Quadrant, Richmond, Surrey TW9 1BP, tel. 0208/948-0057, www.caribbean.co.uk).

Infotur (5ta Av. y 112, Miramar, tel. 07/204-3977, www.infotur.cu), the government tourist information bureau, operates *palacios de turismo* (tourist information booths) in Havana and most major cities and tourist venues nationwide. Every tourist hotel has a *buró de turismo*.

Agencia Cubana de Noticias (Calle 23 #358, esq. J, Vedado, Havana, tel. 07/832-5542, www.acn.cu) dispenses information about virtually every aspect of Cuba but serves primarily as a "news" bureau. The **Oficina Nacional de Estadísticas** (Paseo #60, e/ 3ra y 5ra, Vedado, Havana, tel. 07/830-0053, www.one.cu) provides statistics on Cuba.

MAPS

The best map is National Geographic's waterproof 1:750,000 *Cuba Adventure Map* (http://shop.nationalgeographic.com). A 1:250,000 topographical road map produced by Kartografiai Vallalat, of Hungary, and a similar map by Freytag and Berndt are recommended. Likewise, Cuba's own Ediciones Geo produces a splendid 1:250,000 *La Habana Tourist Map*, plus a 1:20,000 *Ciudad de la Habana* map, sold in Cuba. The superb *Guía de Carreteras* road atlas can be purchased at souvenir outlets.

Resources

Glossary

ache: luck, positive vibe

aduana: customs

agua mala: jellyfish

alfarje: Moorish-inspired ceiling layered with geometric and star patterns

aljibe: well

altos: upstairs unit (in street address)

americano/a: citizen of the Americas (from Alaska to Tierra del Fuego)

animación: entertainment activity involving guests (at hotels)

apagón: electricity blackout

Astro: national bus company

autopista: freeway

azotea: rooftop terrace

babalawo: Santería priest

bagazo: waste from sugarcane processing

bajos: downstairs unit (in street address)

baño: toilet, bathroom

bárbaro: awesome, cool

batido: milkshake

biblioteca: library

bici-taxi: bicycle taxi

bodega: grocery store distributing rations; also Spanish-style inn

bohío: thatched rural homestead

bombo: lottery for U.S. visas

bosque: woodland

botella: hitchhike, graft

buceo: scuba dive

caballería: antiquated land measurement

caballero: sir, respectful address for a male

cabaret espectáculo: Las Vegas-style show

cabildo: colonial-era town council

cacique: Taíno chief

Cadeca: foreign-exchange agency

cajita: boxed meal

calle: street

camarera: maid or waitress

camello: humped mega-bus

camión: truck or crude truck-bus

campesino/a: peasant, country person

campismo: campsite (normally with cabins)

candela: hot (as in a party scene; literally means "flame")

cañonazo: cannon-firing

carne de res: beef

carnet de identidad: ID card that all Cubans must carry at all times

carpeta: reception

carretera: road

carro: automobile

cartelera: cultural calendar

casa de la cultura: "culture house" hosting music and other cultural events

casa de la trova: same as a *casa de la cultura*

casa particular: licensed room rental in a private home

casco histórico: historic center of a city

cayo: coral cay

CDR: Comité para la Defensa de la Revolución; neighborhood watch committees

cenote: flooded cave

central: sugar mill

ciego: blind

cigarillo: cigarette

cimarrón: runaway slave

circunvalación: ring road around a city

claves: rhythm sticks

coche: horse-drawn taxi

coco-taxi: three-wheeled open-air taxi

cola: line, queue

colectivo: collective taxi that runs along a fixed route like a bus

comemierda: literally "shit-eater"; often used to refer to Communist or MININT officials

compañero/a: companion, used as a revolutionary address for another person

congrí: rice with red beans

coño: slang for female genitalia, equivalent to "damn" (the most utilized cuss word in Cuba)

correo: post or post office

criollo/criolla: Creole, used for Cuban food, or a person born in Cuba during the colonial era

cristianos y moros: rice with black beans

Cuba libre: "free Cuba," or rum and Coke

cuentapropista: self-employed person

custodio: guard (as in parking lots)

daiquiri: rum cocktail served with crushed ice

diente de perro: jagged limestone rock

divisa: U.S. dollars or CUC

edificio: building

efectivo: cash

el último: last person in a queue

embajada: embassy

embalse: reservoir

embori: snitch

encomienda: colonial form of slavery giving landowners usufruct rights to Indian labor

entronque: crossroads

escabeche: ceviche, marinated raw fish

escuela: school

esquina caliente: literally "hot corner"; a place where baseball fans debate the sport

estación: station

fábrica: factory

FAR: Fuerza Revolucionaria Militar, or armed forces

farmacia: pharmacy

faro: lighthouse

ferrocarril: railway

Fidelismo: Cuba's unique style of Communism

Fidelista: a Fidel loyalist

fiesta de quince: girl's 15th birthday party

filin: "feeling" music, usually romantic ballads

finca: farm

flota: Spanish treasure fleet

FMC: Federación de Mujeres Cubanas (Federation of Cuban Women)

fruta bomba: papaya (see *papaya*)

fula: U.S. dollars; also a messy situation

G2: state security agency

gasolinera: gas station

gobernador: colonial-era Spanish governor

golpe: military coup

Granma: yacht that carried Fidel Castro and his guerrilla army from Mexico to Cuba in 1956

gringo/a: person from the United States, but can also apply to any Caucasian

guagua: bus

guaguancó: traditional dance with erotic body movements

guajiro/a: peasant or country bumpkin; also used for a type of traditional country song

guaracha: satirical song

guarapería: place selling *guarapo*

guarapo: fresh-squeezed sugarcane juice

guayabera: pleated, buttoned men's shirt

guayabita: fruit native to Pinar del Río

habanero/a: person from Havana

habano: export-quality cigar

heladería: ice-cream store

iglesia: church

ingenio: colonial-era sugar mill

inmigración: immigration

jaba: plastic bag, as at a supermarket

jefe de sector: Communist *vigilante* in charge of several street blocks

jejénes: minuscule sand fleas

jinetera: female seeking a foreign male for pecuniary or other gain

jinetero: male hustler who hassles tourists

joder: slang for intercourse, but also to mess up

libreta: ration book

luchar: to fight; common term used to describe the difficulty of daily life

M-26-7: "26th of July Movement"; Fidel Castro's underground revolutionary movement named for the date of the attack on the Moncada barracks

machetero: sugarcane cutter/harvester

Mambí: rebels fighting for independence from Spain; sometimes referred to as Mambises

maqueta: scale model

máquina: old Yankee automobile

mausoleo: mausoleum

mediopunto: half-moon stained-glass window

mercado: market

mercado agropecuario: produce market

microbrigadista: brigades of unskilled volunteer labor

MININT: Ministry of the Interior

mirador: lookout point or tower

mogote: limestone monoliths

mojito: rum cocktail served with mint

moneda: coins

moneda nacional: Cuban pesos

Mudejar: Moorish (as in architecture)

muelle: pier, wharf

mulatto/a: a person with both black and white heritage

negro/a: black person

norteamericano/a: U.S. or Canadian citizen

Oriente: eastern provinces of Cuba

orisha: Santería deity

paladar: private restaurant

palenque: thatched structure

palestino: derogatory term for a migrant to Havana from Oriente

papaya: tropical fruit; slang term for vagina

parada: bus stop

parque de diversiones: amusement park

PCC: Partido Comunista de Cuba

pedraplén: causeway connecting offshore islands to the Cuban mainland *peninsular:* Spanish-born colonialist in Cuba in pre-independence days

peña: social get-together for cultural enjoyment, such as a literary reading

pesos convertibles: convertible pesos (tourist currency)

piropo: witty or flirtatious comment

pizarra: switchboard

ponchero/a: puncture repair person

presa: dam

prórroga: visa extension

puro: export-quality cigar

quinceañera: girl coming of age

quinta: country house of nobility

quintal: Spanish colonial measure

refresco: "refreshment"; a sugary drink

resolver: to resolve or fix a problem

ropa vieja: shredded beef dish

rumba: a traditional Afro-Cuban dance; also a party involving such

sala: room or gallery

salsa: popular modern dance music

salsero/a: performer of salsa

Santería: a syncretization of the African Yoruba and Catholic religions

santero/a: adherent of Santería

santiagüero/a: person from Santiago de Cuba

sello: postage or similar stamp

sendero: walking trail

servicentro: gasoline station

SIDA: AIDS

son: traditional music as popularized by Buena Vista Social Club

Taíno: the predominant indigenous inhabitants of Cuba at the time of Spanish conquest

taquilla: ticket window

taller: workshop

tarjeta: card, such as a credit card

telenovela: soap opera

telepunto: main telephone exchange

temporada alta/baja: high/low season

terminal de ómnibus: bus station

tienda: shop

tráfico: traffic cop

trago: a shot of rum

tránsito: traffic cop

trova: traditional poetry-based music

UJC: Unión de Jóvenes Comunistas; politically oriented youth Communist group

UNEAC: Unión Nacional de Escritores y Artistas de Cuba; National Union of Cuban Writers and Artists

vaquero: cowboy

vega: patch of land where tobacco is grown
verde: slang for U.S. dollar
Víazul: company offering scheduled tourist bus service
vigilante: community-watch person, on behalf of the Revolution
vitral: stained-glass window
Yoruba: a group of peoples and a pantheistic religion from Nigeria
yuma: slang for the United States
zafra: sugarcane harvest

Cuban Spanish

Learning the basics of Spanish will aid your travels considerably. In key tourist destinations, however, you should be able to get along fine without it. Most larger hotels have bilingual desk staff, and English is widely spoken by the staff of car rental agencies and tour companies. Away from the tourist path, far fewer people speak English. Use that as an excuse to learn some Spanish. Cubans warm quickly to those who make an effort to speak their language.

In its literary form, Cuban Spanish is pure, classical Castilian (the Spanish of Spain). Alas, in its spoken form Cuban Spanish is the most difficult to understand in all of Latin America. Cubans speak more briskly than other Latin Americans, blurring their rapid-fire words together. The diction of Cuba is lazy and unclear. Thought Richard Henry Dana Jr. in 1859: "It strikes me that the tendency here is to enfeeble the language, and take from it the openness of the vowels and the strength of the consonants." The letter "S" is usually swallowed, especially in plurals. Thus, the typical greeting *"¿Como estás?"* is usually pronounced "como-TAH." (The swallowed S's are apparently accumulated for use in restaurants, where they are released to get the server's attention—"*S-s-s-s-s-st!*" Because of this, a restaurant with bad service can sound like a pit full of snakes.) The final consonants of words are also often deleted, as are the entire last syllables of words: "If they dropped any more syllables, they would be speechless," suggests author Tom Miller.

Cubanisms to Know

Cubans are long-winded and full of flowery, passionate, rhetorical flourishes. Fidel Castro didn't inherit his penchant for long speeches from dour, taciturn Galicia—it's a purely Cuban characteristic. Cubans also spice up the language with little affectations and teasing endearments—*piropos*—given and taken among themselves without offense.

Many English (or "American") words have found their way into Cuban diction. Cubans go to *béisbol* and eat *hamburgesas*. Like the English, Cubans are clever in their use of words, imbuing their language with double entendres and their own lexicon of similes. Cubans are also great cussers. The two most common cuss words are *cojones* (slang for male genitalia) and *coño* (slang for female genitalia), while one of the more common colloquialisms is *ojalá,* which loosely translated means "I wish" or "If only!" but which most commonly is used to mean "Some hope!"

Formal courtesies are rarely used when greeting someone. Since the Revolution, everyone is a *compañero* or *compañera* (*señor* and *señora* are considered too bourgeois), although the phrase is disdained by many Cubans as indicating approval of the Communist system. Confusingly, *¡ciao!* (used as a long-term goodbye, and spelled "chao" in Cuba) is also used as a greeting in casual passing—the equivalent of "Hi!" You will also be asked *¿Como anda?* ("How goes it?"), while younger Cubans prefer *¿Que bola?* (the Cuban equivalent of "Wassup?") rather than the traditional *¿Que pasa?* ("What's happening?").

Cubans speak to each other directly, no holds barred. Even conversations with strangers are laced with *"¡Ay, muchacha!"* ("Hey, girl!"), *"¡Mira, chica!"* ("Look, girl!"), and *"¡Hombre!"* ("Listen, man!") when one disagrees with the other. Cubans refer to one another in straightforward terms, often playing on their physical or racial characteristics: *flaco* (skinny), *gordo* (fatty), *negro* (black man), *china* (chinese woman), etc. Cubans do not refer to themselves with a single definition of "white" or "black." There are a zillion gradations of skin color and features, from *negro azul y trompudo* (blue-black and thick-lipped) and *muy negro* (very black), for example, to *leche con una gota de café* (milk with a drop of coffee). Whites, too, come in shades. *Un blanco* is a blond or light-haired person with blue, green, or gray eyes. *Un blanquito* is a "white" with dark hair and dark eyes.

Bárbaro is often used to attribute a positive quality to someone, as in *él es un bárbaro* ("he's a great person"). *Está en candela* ("a flame") is its equivalent, but it's more commonly used to describe an alarming or complicated situation (such as "I'm broke!") or someone who's "hot."

Marinovia defines a live-in girlfriend (from *marido,* for spouse, and *novia,* for girlfriend). An *asere* is one's close friend, though this street term is considered a low-class word, especially common with blacks. A *flojo* (literally, "loose guy") is a lounger who pretends to work. Cubans also have no shortage of terms referring to spies, informers, and untrustworthy souls. For example, *embori* refers to an informer in cahoots with the government. *Fronterizo* is a half-mad person. *Chispa* ("spark") is someone with vitality. To become "Cubanized" is to be *aplatanado.*

When Cubans ask home visitors if they want coffee, it is often diplomatic rather than an invitation. Replying *"gracias"* (thanks) usually signifies "thanks for the thought." *"Si, gracias"* means "yes." Cubans expect you to be explicit.

Spanish commonly uses 30 letters—the familiar English 26, plus four straightforward additions: ch, ll, ñ, and rr, which are explained in "Consonants," below.

Christopher Howard's Official Guide to Cuban Spanish is a handy resource.

PRONUNCIATION

Once you learn them, Spanish pronunciation rules—in contrast to English—don't change. Spanish vowels generally sound softer than in English. (*Note:* The capitalized syllables below receive stronger accents.)

Vowels

a like ah, as in "hah": *agua* AH-gooah (water), *pan* PAHN (bread), and *casa* CAH-sah (house)

e like ay, as in "may:" *mesa* MAY-sah (table), *tela* TAY-lah (cloth), and *de* DAY (of, from)

i like ee, as in "need": *diez* dee-AYZ (ten), *comida* ko-MEE-dah (meal), and *fin* FEEN (end)

o like oh, as in "go": *peso* PAY-soh (weight), *ocho* OH-choh (eight), and *poco* POH-koh (a bit)

u like oo, as in "cool": *uno* OO-noh (one), *cuarto* KOOAHR-toh (room), and *usted* oos-TAYD (you); when it follows a "q" the **u** is silent; when it follows an "h" or has an umlaut, it's pronounced like "w"

Consonants

b, d, f, k, l, m, n, p, q, s, t, v, w, x, y, z, and ch   pronounced almost as in English; **h** occurs, but is silent—not pronounced at all

c like k as in "keep": *cuarto* KOOAR-toh (room), Tepic tay-PEEK (capital of Nayarit state); when it precedes "e" or "i," pronounce **c** like s, as in "sit": *cerveza* sayr-VAY-sah (beer), *encima* ayn-SEE-mah (atop)

g like g as in "gift" when it precedes "a," "o," "u," or a consonant: *gato* GAH-toh (cat), *hago* AH-goh (I do, make); otherwise, pronounce **g** like h as in "hat": *giro* HEE-roh (money order), *gente* HAYN-tay (people)

j like h, as in "has": *Jueves* HOOAY-vays (Thursday), *mejor* may-HOR (better)

ll like y, as in "yes": *toalla* toh-AH-yah (towel), *ellos* AY-yohs (they, them)

ñ like ny, as in "canyon": *año* AH-nyo (year), *señor* SAY-nyor (Mr., sir)

r is lightly trilled, with tongue at the roof of your mouth like a very light English d, as in "ready": *pero* PAY-doh (but), *tres* TDAYS (three), *cuatro* KOOAH-tdoh (four)

rr like a Spanish r, but with much more emphasis and trill. Let your tongue flap. Practice with *burro* (donkey), *carretera* (highway), and *Carrillo* (proper name), then really let go with *ferrocarril* (railroad)

Note: The single small but common exception to all of the above is the pronunciation of Spanish **y** when it's being used as the Spanish word for "and,"

as in "Ron y Kathy." In such case, pronounce it like the English ee, as in "keep":
Ron "ee" Kathy (Ron and Kathy).

Accent

The rule for accent, the relative stress given to syllables within a given word, is straightforward. If a word ends in a vowel, an n, or an s, accent the next-to-last syllable; if not, accent the last syllable.

Pronounce *gracias* GRAH-seeahs (thank you), *orden* OHR-dayn (order), and *carretera* kah-ray-TAY-rah (highway) with stress on the next-to-last syllable.

Otherwise, accent the last syllable: *venir* vay-NEER (to come), *ferrocarril* fay-roh-cah-REEL (railroad), and *edad* ay-DAHD (age).

Exceptions to the accent rule are always marked with an accent sign: (á, é, í, ó, or ú), such as *teléfono* tay-LAY-foh-noh (telephone), *jabón* hah-BON (soap), and *rápido* RAH-pee-doh (rapid).

BASIC AND COURTEOUS EXPRESSIONS

Most Spanish-speaking people consider formalities important. Whenever approaching anyone for information or some other reason, do not forget the appropriate salutation—good morning, good evening, etc. Standing alone, the greeting *hola* (hello) can sound brusque.

Hello. *Hola.*

Good morning. *Buenos días.*

Good afternoon. *Buenas tardes.*

Good evening. *Buenas noches.*

How are you? *¿Cómo está usted?*

Very well, thank you. *Muy bien, gracias.*

Okay; good. *Bien.*

Not okay; bad. *Mal or feo.*

So-so. *Más o menos.*

And you? *¿Y usted?*

Thank you. *Gracias.*

Thank you very much. *Muchas gracias.*

You're very kind. *Muy amable.*

You're welcome. *De nada.*

Goodbye. *Adios.*

See you later. *Hasta luego.*

please *por favor*

yes *sí*

no *no*

I don't know. *No sé.*

Just a moment, please. *Momentito, por favor.*

Excuse me, please (when you're trying to get attention). *Disculpe* or *Con permiso.*

Excuse me (when you've made a boo-boo). *Lo siento.*

Pleased to meet you. *Mucho gusto.*

How do you say . . . in Spanish? *¿Cómo se dice . . . en español?*

What is your name? *¿Cómo se llama usted?*
Do you speak English? *¿Habla usted inglés?*
Is English spoken here? (Does anyone here speak English?) *¿Se habla inglés?*
I don't speak Spanish well. *No hablo bien el español.*
I don't understand. *No entiendo.*
How do you say . . . in Spanish? *¿Cómo se dice . . . en español?*
My name is . . . *Me llamo . . .*
Would you like . . . *¿Quisiera usted . . .*
Let's go to . . . *Vamos a . . .*

TERMS OF ADDRESS

When in doubt, use the formal *usted* (you) as a form of address.

I *yo*
you (formal) *usted*
you (familiar) *tu*
he/him *él*
she/her *ella*
we/us *nosotros*
you (plural) *ustedes*
they/them *ellos* (all males or mixed gender); *ellas* (all females)
Mr., sir *señor*
Mrs., madam *señora*
miss, young lady *señorita*
wife *esposa*
husband *esposo*
friend *amigo* (male); *amiga* (female)
sweetheart *novio* (male); *novia* (female)
son; daughter *hijo; hija*
brother; sister *hermano; hermana*
father; mother *padre; madre*
grandfather; grandmother *abuelo; abuela*

TRANSPORTATION

Where is . . . ? *¿Dónde está . . . ?*
How far is it to . . . ? *¿A cuánto está . . . ?*
from . . . to . . . *de . . . a . . .*
How many blocks? *¿Cuántas cuadras?*
Where (Which) is the way to . . . ? *¿Dónde está el camino a . . . ?*
the bus station *la terminal de autobuses*
the bus stop *la parada de autobuses*
Where is this bus going? *¿Adónde va este autobús?*
the taxi stand *la parada de taxis*
the train station *la estación de ferrocarril*
the boat *el barco*
the launch *lancha; tiburonera*

the dock *el muelle*
the airport *el aeropuerto*
I'd like a ticket to . . . *Quisiera un boleto a . . .*
first (second) class *primera (segunda) clase*
roundtrip *ida y vuelta*
reservation *reservación*
baggage *equipaje*
Stop here, please. *Pare aquí, por favor.*
the entrance *la entrada*
the exit *la salida*
the ticket office *la oficina de boletos*
(very) near; far *(muy) cerca; lejos*
to; toward *a*
by; through *por*
from *de*
the right *la derecha*
the left *la izquierda*
straight ahead *derecho; directo*
in front *en frente*
beside *al lado*
behind *atrás*
the corner *la esquina*
the stoplight *la semáforo*
a turn *una vuelta*
right here *aquí*
somewhere around here *por acá*
right there *allí*
somewhere around there *por allá*
road *el camino*
street; boulevard *calle; bulevar*
block *la cuadra*
highway *carretera*
kilometer *kilómetro*
bridge; toll *puente; cuota*
address *dirección*
north; south *norte; sur*
east; west *oriente (este); poniente (oeste)*

ACCOMMODATIONS

hotel *hotel*
Is there a room? *¿Hay cuarto?*
May I (may we) see it? *¿Puedo (podemos) verlo?*
What is the rate? *¿Cuál es el precio?*
Is that your best rate? *¿Es su mejor precio?*
Is there something cheaper? *¿Hay algo más económico?*
a single room *un cuarto sencillo*

a double room *un cuarto doble*
double bed *cama matrimonial*
twin beds *camas gemelas*
with private bath *con baño*
hot water *agua caliente*
shower *ducha*
towels *toallas*
soap *jabón*
toilet paper *papel higiénico*
blanket *frazada; manta*
sheets *sábanas*
air-conditioned *aire acondicionado*
fan *abanico; ventilador*
key *llave*
manager *gerente*

FOOD

I'm hungry *Tengo hambre.*
I'm thirsty. *Tengo sed.*
menu *carta; menú*
order *orden*
glass *vaso*
fork *tenedor*
knife *cuchillo*
spoon *cuchara*
napkin *servilleta*
soft drink *refresco*
coffee *café*
tea *té*
drinking water *agua pura; agua potable*
bottled carbonated water *agua mineral*
bottled uncarbonated water *agua sin gas*
beer *cerveza*
wine *vino*
milk *leche*
juice *jugo*
cream *crema*
sugar *azúcar*
cheese *queso*
snack *antojo; botana*
breakfast *desayuno*
lunch *almuerzo*
daily lunch special *comida corrida* (or *el menú del día* depending on region)
dinner *comida* (often eaten in late afternoon); *cena* (a late-night snack)
the check *la cuenta*

eggs *huevos*
bread *pan*
salad *ensalada*
fruit *fruta*
mango *mango*
watermelon *sandía*
papaya *papaya*
banana *plátano*
apple *manzana*
orange *naranja*
lime *limón*
fish *pescado*
shellfish *mariscos*
shrimp *camarones*
meat (without) *(sin) carne*
chicken *pollo*
pork *puerco*
beef; steak *res; bistec*
bacon; ham *tocino; jamón*
fried *frito*
roasted *asada*
barbecue; barbecued *barbacoa; al carbón*

SHOPPING

money *dinero*
money-exchange bureau *casa de cambio*
I would like to exchange traveler's checks. *Quisiera cambiar cheques de viajero.*
What is the exchange rate? *¿Cuál es el tipo de cambio?*
How much is the commission? *¿Cuánto cuesta la comisión?*
Do you accept credit cards? *¿Aceptan tarjetas de crédito?*
money order *giro*
How much does it cost? *¿Cuánto cuesta?*
What is your final price? *¿Cuál es su último precio?*
expensive *caro*
cheap *barato; económico*
more *más*
less *menos*
a little *un poco*
too much *demasiado*

HEALTH

Help me please. *Ayúdeme por favor.*
I am ill. *Estoy enfermo.*
Call a doctor. *Llame un doctor.*
Take me to . . . *Lléveme a . . .*

hospital *hospital; sanatorio*
drugstore *farmacia*
pain *dolor*
fever *fiebre*
headache *dolor de cabeza*
stomach ache *dolor de estómago*
burn *quemadura*
cramp *calambre*
nausea *náusea*
vomiting *vomitar*
medicine *medicina*
antibiotic *antibiótico*
pill; tablet *pastilla*
aspirin *aspirina*
ointment; cream *pomada; crema*
bandage *venda*
cotton *algodón*
sanitary napkins use brand name, e.g., Kotex
birth control pills *pastillas anticonceptivas*
contraceptive foam *espuma anticonceptiva*
condoms *preservativos; condones*
toothbrush *cepilla dental*
dental floss *hilo dental*
toothpaste *crema dental*
dentist *dentista*
toothache *dolor de muelas*

POST OFFICE AND COMMUNICATIONS

long-distance telephone *teléfono larga distancia*
I would like to call . . . *Quisiera llamar a . . .*
collect *por cobrar*
station to station *a quien contesta*
person to person *persona a persona*
credit card *tarjeta de crédito*
post office *correo*
general delivery *lista de correo*
letter *carta*
stamp *estampilla, timbre*
postcard *tarjeta*
aerogram *aerograma*
air mail *correo aereo*
registered *registrado*
money order *giro*
package; box *paquete; caja*
string; tape *cuerda; cinta*

border *frontera*
customs *aduana*
immigration *migración*
tourist card *tarjeta de turista*
inspection *inspección; revisión*
passport *pasaporte*
profession *profesión*
marital status *estado civil*
single *soltero*
married; divorced *casado; divorciado*
widowed *viudado*
insurance *seguros*
title *título*
driver's license *licencia de manejar*

AT THE GAS STATION

gas station *gasolinera*
gasoline *gasolina*
unleaded *sin plomo*
full, please *lleno, por favor*
tire *llanta*
tire repair shop *vulcanizadora*
air *aire*
water *agua*
oil (change) *aceite (cambio)*
grease *grasa*
My ... doesn't work. *Mi ... no sirve.*
battery *batería*
radiator *radiador*
alternator *alternador*
generator *generador*
tow truck *grúa*
repair shop *taller mecánico*
tune-up *afinación*
auto parts store *refaccionería*

VERBS

Verbs are the key to getting along in Spanish. They employ mostly predictable forms and come in three classes, which end in *ar, er,* and *ir,* respectively:

to buy *comprar*
I buy, you (he, she, it) buys *compro, compra*
we buy, you (they) buy *compramos, compran*

to eat *comer*

I eat, you (he, she, it) eats *como, come*
we eat, you (they) eat *comemos, comen*

to climb *subir*
I climb, you (he, she, it) climbs *subo, sube*
we climb, you (they) climb *subimos, suben*

Here are more (with irregularities indicated):

to do or make *hacer* (regular except for *hago,* I do or make)
to go *ir* (very irregular: *voy, va, vamos, van*)
to go (walk) *andar*
to love *amar*
to work *trabajar*
to want *desear, querer*
to need *necesitar*
to read *leer*
to write *escribir*
to repair *reparar*
to stop *parar*
to get off (the bus) *bajar*
to arrive *llegar*
to stay (remain) *quedar*
to stay (lodge) *hospedar*
to leave *salir* (regular except for *salgo,* I leave)
to look at *mirar*
to look for *buscar*
to give *dar* (regular except for *doy,* I give)
to carry *llevar*
to have *tener* (irregular but important: *tengo, tiene, tenemos, tienen*)
to come *venir* (similarly irregular: *vengo, viene, venimos, vienen*)

Spanish has two forms of "to be":

to be *estar* (regular except for *estoy,* I am)
to be *ser* (very irregular: *soy, es, somos, son*)

Use *estar* when speaking of location or a temporary state of being: "I am at home." *"Estoy en casa."* "I'm sick." *"Estoy enfermo."* Use *ser* for a permanent state of being: "I am a doctor." *"Soy doctora."*

NUMBERS

zero *cero*
one *uno*
two *dos*
three *tres*

four *cuatro*
five *cinco*
six *seis*
seven *siete*
eight *ocho*
nine *nueve*
10 *diez*
11 *once*
12 *doce*
13 *trece*
14 *catorce*
15 *quince*
16 *dieciseis*
17 *diecisiete*
18 *dieciocho*
19 *diecinueve*
20 *veinte*
21 *veinte y uno* or *veintiuno*
30 *treinta*
40 *cuarenta*
50 *cincuenta*
60 *sesenta*
70 *setenta*
80 *ochenta*
90 *noventa*
100 *ciento*
101 *ciento y uno* or *cientiuno*
200 *doscientos*
500 *quinientos*
1,000 *mil*
10,000 *diez mil*
100,000 *cien mil*
1,000,000 *millón*
one half *medio*
one third *un tercio*
one fourth *un cuarto*

TIME

What time is it? *¿Qué hora es?*
It's one o'clock. *Es la una.*
It's three in the afternoon. *Son las tres de la tarde.*
It's 4 a.m. *Son las cuatro de la mañana.*
six-thirty *seis y media*
a quarter till eleven *un cuarto para las once*
a quarter past five *las cinco y cuarto*
an hour *una hora*

DAYS AND MONTHS

Monday *lunes*
Tuesday *martes*
Wednesday *miércoles*
Thursday *jueves*
Friday *viernes*
Saturday *sábado*
Sunday *domingo*
today *hoy*
tomorrow *mañana*
yesterday *ayer*
January *enero*
February *febrero*
March *marzo*
April *abril*
May *mayo*
June *junio*
July *julio*
August *agosto*
September *septiembre*
October *octubre*
November *noviembre*
December *diciembre*
a week *una semana*
a month *un mes*
after *después*
before *antes*

(Courtesy of Bruce Whipperman, author of *Moon Pacific Mexico*.)

Suggested Reading

ART AND CULTURE

Pérez, Louis A. *On Becoming Cuban: Nationality, Identity and Culture.* New York: Harper Perennial, 2001. Seminal and highly readable account of the development of Cuban culture from colonialism through communism.

BIOGRAPHY

Anderson, Jon Lee. *Che Guevara: A Revolutionary Life.* New York: Grove Press, 1997. This definitive biography reveals heretofore unknown details of Che's life and shows the dark side of this revolutionary icon.

Eire, Carlos. *Waiting for Snow in Havana.* New York: Free Press, 2004. An exquisitely told, heart-rending story of an exile's joyous childhood years in Havana on the eve of the Revolution, and the trauma of being put on the Peter Pan airlift, never to see his father again.

Fuentes, Norberto. *Hemingway in Cuba.* Secaucus, NY: Lyle Stuart, 1984. The seminal, lavishly illustrated study of the Nobel Prize-winner's years in Cuba.

Gimbel, Wendy. *Havana Dreams: A Story of Cuba.* London: Virago, 1998. The moving story of Naty Revuelta's tormented love affair with Fidel Castro and the terrible consequences of a relationship as heady as the doomed romanticism of the Revolution.

Hendrickson, Paul. *Hemingway's Boat: Everything He Loved in Life, and Lost.* New York: Vintage Books, 2012. A brilliant meditation on Hemingway in which his beloved *Pilar* serves as anchor.

Neyra, Edward J. *Cuba Lost and Found.* Cincinnati: Clerisy Press, 2009. A Cuban-American's moving tale of leaving Cuba on the Peter Pan airlift and his eventual return to his roots on the island.

Ramonte, Ignacio, ed. *Fidel Castro: My Life.* London: Penguin Books, 2008. In conversation with a fawning interviewer, Fidel tells his fascinating life story and expounds on his philosophy and passions. This often amusing and eyebrow-raising autobiography reveals Castro's astounding erudition, acute grasp of history, unwavering commitment to humanistic ideals, and his delusions and pathological hatred of the United States.

Sánchez, Juan Reinaldo. *The Double Life of Fidel Castro: My 17 Years as a Personal Bodyguard to El Líder Máximo.* New York: St. Martin's Press, 2015. An explosive, jaw-dropping kiss-and-tell.

Stout, Nancy. *One Day in December: Celia Sánchez and the Cuban Revolution.* New York: Monthly Review Press, 2013. A sympathetic and superbly crafted portrait of this fearless revolutionary—a brilliant organizer, recruiter, and Fidel Castro's most precious aide.

Szulc, Tad. *Fidel: A Critical Portrait.* New York: Morrow, 1986. A riveting profile of the astonishing life of this larger-than-life figure.

CIGARS

Habanos, S.A. *The World of the Habano.* Havana: Instituto de Investigaciones del Tabaco, 2012. Beautifully illustrated coffee-table book that tells you all you want to know about tobacco and its metamorphosis into fine cigars. It comes with a CD and ring gauge.

Perelman, Richard B. *Perelman's Pocket Cyclopedia of Havana Cigars.* Los Angeles: Perelman, Pioneer & Co, 1998. More than 160 pages with over 25 color photos, providing a complete list of cigar brands and shapes. Handy four- by six-inch size.

COFFEE-TABLE BOOKS

Baker, Christopher P. *Cuba Classics: A Celebration of Vintage American Automobiles.* Northampton, MA: Interlink Books, 2004. This lavishly illustrated coffee-table book pays homage to Cuba's astonishing wealth of classic American automobiles spanning eight decades. The text traces the long love affair between Cubans and the U.S. automobile and offers a paean to the owners who keep their weary *cacharros* running.

Barclay, Juliet (photographs by Martin Charles). *Havana: Portrait of a City.* London: Cassell, 1993. A well-researched and abundantly illustrated coffee-table volume especially emphasizing the city's history.

Carley, Rachel. *Cuba: 400 Years of Architectural Legacy.* New York: Whitney Library of Design, 1997. Beautifully illustrated coffee-table book tracing the evolution of architectural styles from colonial days to the Communist aesthetic hiatus and post-Soviet renaissance.

Evans, Walker. *Walker Evans: Cuba.* New York: Getty Publications, 2001. Recorded in 1933, these 60 beautiful black-and-white images capture in stark clarity the misery and hardships of life in the era.

Kenny, Jack. *Cuba.* Ann Arbor, MI: Corazon Press, 2005. Beautiful black-and-white images capture the essence of Cuba and provide an intimate portrait into its soul.

Llanes, Lillian. *Havana Then and Now.* San Diego: Thunder Bay Press, 2004. A delightful collection of images wedding centenary black-and-whites to color photos showing the same locales as they are now.

Moruzzi, Peter. *Havana Before Castro: When Cuba was a Tropical Playground.* Salt Lake City: Gibbs Smith, 2008. This superb book is stuffed with fascinating images and tidbits that recall the heyday of sin and modernism.

GENERAL

Cabrera Infante, Guillermo. *¡Mea Cuba!* New York: Farrar, Straus & Giroux, 1994. An acerbic, indignant, raw, wistful, and brilliant set of essays in which the author pours out his bile at the Castro regime.

Henken, Ted A. *Cuba: A Global Studies Handbook*. Santa Barbara, CA: ABC-CLIO, 2008. A thoroughly insightful compendium spanning everything from history and culture to "Castro as a Charismatic Hero."

Martínez-Fernández, Luis, et al. *Encyclopedia of Cuba: People, History, Culture*. Westport, CT: Greenwood Press, 2004. Comprehensive twin-volume set with chapters arranged by themes, such as history, plastic arts, and sports.

Sánchez, Yoani. *Havana Real: One Woman Fights to Tell the Truth About Cuba*. New York: Melville House, 2009. Sardonic blog posts from "Generation Y" by a leading Cuban dissident paint an unflinching portrait of daily life in Cuba.

Shnookal, Deborah, and Mirta Muñiz, eds. *José Martí Reader*. New York: Ocean Press, 1999. An anthology of writings by one of the most brilliant and impassioned Latin American intellectuals of the 19th century.

HISTORY, ECONOMICS, AND POLITICS

Bardach, Ann Louise. *Cuba Confidential*. New York: Random House, 2002. A brilliant study of the failed politics of poisoned Cuban-U.S. relations, and the grand hypocrisies of the warring factions in Washington, Miami, and Havana.

Bardach, Ann Louise. *Without Fidel*. New York: Scribner, 2009. Bardach reports on Fidel's mystery illness and twilight days, and profiles the new president, Raúl Castro, in raw detail.

Deutschmann, David, and Deborah Shnookal. *Fidel Castro Reader*. Melbourne: Ocean Press, 2007. Twenty of Castro's most important speeches are presented verbatim.

English, T. J. *Havana Nocturne: How the Mob Owned Cuba and then Lost It to the Revolution*. New York: William Morrow, 2008. A fascinating and revealing account of the heyday of Cuba's mobster connections and the sordid Batista era.

Erikson, Daniel. *The Cuba Wars: Fidel Castro, the United States, and the Next Revolution*. New York: Bloomsbury Press, 2008. This seminal and objective work summarizes the U.S.-Cuban relations and "the incestuous relationship between Cuban-Americans and politicians in Washington" in a brilliantly nuanced way.

Frank, Mark. *Cuban Revelations: Behind the Scenes in Havana*. Miami: University Press of Florida, 2013. A U.S. journalist reports on his 25-plus years reporting from Cuba, offering a gripping and nuanced perspective on recent changes and the trajectory ahead.

Gjelten, Tom. *Bacardi and the Long Fight for Cuba.* New York: Viking, 2008. A superb and sweeping distillation of the fortunes of the Bacardi family and corporation and its relations to the epochal transition to Cuban independence, the toppling of the Batista regime, and Castro's Communism.

Gott, Richard. *Cuba: A New History.* New Haven, CT: Yale University Press, 2005. Erudite, entertaining, and concise yet detailed tour de force.

Latell, Brian. *After Fidel: The Inside Story of Castro's Regime and Cuba's Next Leader.* New York: Palgrave Macmillan, 2005. A former senior CIA analyst profiles the personalities of Fidel and Raúl Castro, providing insights into their quixotic, mutually dependent relationship and the motivations that have shaped their antagonistic relationship with the United States.

LeoGrande, William and Peter Kornbluth. *Back Channel to Cuba.* North Carolina: University of North Carolina Press, 2015. A fascinating assessment of secret efforts over decades to normalize relations between Cuba and the USA.

Morais, Fernando. *The Last Soldiers of the Cold War: The Story of the Cuban Five.* New York: Verso, 2015. A fascinating and objective account of how Cuba's intelligence agents infiltrated Cuban-American organizations to thwart terrorism.

Oppenheimer, Andres. *Castro's Final Hour.* New York: Simon and Schuster, 1992. A sobering, in-depth exposé of the uglier side of both Fidel Castro and the state system.

Smith, Wayne. *The Closest of Enemies.* New York: W. W. Norton, 1987. Essential reading, this personal account of the author's years serving as President Carter's man in Havana during the 1970s provides insights into the complexities that haunt U.S. relations with Cuba.

Sweig, Julia E. *Cuba: What Everyone Needs to Know.* Oxford: Oxford University Press, 2009. A reference to Cuba's history and politics, addressed in a clever question and answer format.

Thomas, Hugh. *Cuba: The Pursuit of Freedom, 1726-1969.* New York: Harper and Row, 1971. A seminal work—called a "magisterial conspectus of Cuban history"—tracing the evolution of conditions that eventually engendered the Revolution.

Thomas, Hugh. *The Cuban Revolution*. London: Weidenfeld and Nicolson, 1986. The definitive work on the Revolution, offering a brilliant analysis of all aspects of the country's diverse and tragic history.

Wyden, Peter. *Bay of Pigs: The Untold Story*. New York: Simon and Schuster, 1979. An in-depth and riveting exposé of the CIA's ill-conceived mission to topple Castro.

LITERATURE

Cabrera Infante, Guillermo. *Three Trapped Tigers*. New York: Avon, 1985. A poignant and comic novel that captures the essence of life in Havana before the ascendance of Castro.

García, Cristina. *Dreaming in Cuban*. New York: Ballantine Books, 1992. A poignant and sensual tale of a family divided politically and geographically by the Cuban revolution and the generational fissures that open.

Greene, Graham. *Our Man in Havana*. New York: Penguin, 1971. The story of Wormold, a British vacuum-cleaner salesman in prerevolutionary Havana. Recruited by British intelligence, Wormold finds little information to pass on, and so invents it. Full of the sensuality and tensions of Batista's last days.

Gutiérrez, Pedro Juan. *Dirty Havana Trilogy*. New York: Farrar, Straus & Giroux, 2001. A bawdy semi-biographical take on the gritty life of Havana's underclass—begging, whoring, escaping hardship through sex and Santería—during the Special Period.

Hemingway, Ernest. *Islands in the Stream*. New York: Harper Collins, 1970. An exciting triptych set in Cuba during the war, it draws on the author's own experience hunting Nazi U-boats.

Hemingway, Ernest. *The Old Man and the Sea*. New York: Scribner's, 1952. The simple yet profound story of an unlucky Cuban angler won the Nobel Prize for Literature.

TRAVEL GUIDES

Lightfoot, Claudia. *Havana: A Cultural and Literary Companion*. Northampton, MA: Interlink Publishing, 2001. The author leads you through Havana past and present using literary quotations and allusions to add dimension to the sites and experiences.

Rodríguez, Eduardo Luis. *The Havana Guide: Modern Architecture 1925-65*. New York: Princeton Architectural Press, 2000. A marvelous guide to individual structures—homes, churches, theaters, government buildings—representing the best of modern architecture (1925-1965) throughout Havana.

TRAVEL LITERATURE

Aschkenas, Lea. *Es Cuba: Life and Love on an Illegal Island*. Emeryville, CA: Seal Press, 2006. Told with gentle compassion for a culture and country, *Es Cuba* reveals how the possibilities and hopes of the heart can surmount obdurate political barriers.

Baker, Christopher P. *Mi Moto Fidel: Motorcycling through Castro's Cuba*. Washington, D.C.: National Geographic's Adventure Press, 2001. Winner of the Lowell Thomas Award Travel Book of the Year, this erotically charged tale of the author's 7,000-mile adventure by motorcycle through Cuba offers a bittersweet look at the last Marxist "utopia."

Cooke, Julia. *The Other Side of Paradise: Life in the New Cuba*. Berkeley, CA: Seal Press, 2014. This exquisite memoir paints a vivid and sympathetic narrative of Cubans whose most common dream is of escaping a sclerotic Communist system.

Corbett, Ben. *This Is Cuba: An Outlaw Culture Survives*. Cambridge, MA: Westview Press, 2002. This first-person account of life in Castro's Cuba is a stinging indictment of the havoc, despair, and restraints wrought by *fidelismo*.

Miller, Tom. *Trading with the Enemy: A Yankee Travels through Castro's Cuba*. New York: Basic Books, 1996. Told by a famous author who lived in Cuba for almost a year, this travelogue is thoughtful, engaging, insightful, compassionate, and told in rich narrative.

Miller, Tom, ed. *Travelers' Tales: Cuba*. San Francisco: Travelers' Tales, 2001. Extracts from the contemporary works of 38 authors provide an at times hilarious, cautionary, and inspiring account of Cuba.

Tattlin, Isadora. *Cuba Diaries: An American Housewife in Havana*. Chapel Hill, NC: Algonquin Books, 2002. A marvelous account of four years in Havana spent raising two children, entertaining her husband's clients (including Fidel), and contending with chronic shortages.

Before Night Falls (2000). A poignant adaptation of Reinaldo Arenas's autobiography, in which the persecuted Cuban novelist recounts his life in Cuba and in exile in the United States. Says film critic Lucas Hilderbrand, "It's an intoxicating, intensely erotic account of sexual discovery and liberation, and a devastating record of the artist's persecution under the Castro regime."

Buena Vista Social Club (1999). An adorable documentary look at the reemergence from obscurity of veteran performers Ruben González, Omara Portuondo, Ibrahim Ferrer, Eliades Ochoa, and Compay Segundo, culminating in their sellout concert at Carnegie Hall.

Death of a Bureaucrat (1966). Tomás Gutiérrez Alea's questioning portrait of the absurdities of the Cuban bureaucratic system and people's propensity to conform to absurd directives that cause misery to others.

El Cuerno de Abundancia (2008). The "Horn of Plenty" is Juan Carlos Tabio's tale of how a million-dollar inheritance upsets an entire town in Cuba's interior.

Fresa y Chocolate (1994). Nominated for an Oscar, Tomás Gutiérrez Alea's classic skit ("Strawberry and Chocolate") about the evolving friendship between a cultured gay man and the ardent revolutionary he attempts to seduce is an indictment of the treatment of homosexuals and liberals in the gray 1970s.

Guantanamera (1997). A road movie with a twist, this rueful romantic comedy by Tomás Gutiérrez Alea and Juan Carlos Tabio begins to unfold after an elderly dame dies from an excess of sexual stimulation. The farce of returning her body to Havana for proper burial provides the vehicle for a comic parody of an overly bureaucratic Cuba.

Los Diosas Rotas (2008). An enthralling, beautifully filmed tale of pimps and prostitutes in contemporary Havana. Nominated for a 2008 Oscar as Best Foreign Film.

Memories of Underdevelopment (1968). Director Tomás Gutiérrez Alea's sensual, wide-ranging masterpiece revolves around an erotically charged, intellectual "playboy" existence in early 1960s Cuba, pinned by the tragedy of the central character's alienation from the "underdeveloped" people around him and his own inability to attain a more fulfilled state.

Miel para Oshún (2003). Humberto Solas's "Honey for Oshún" tells the tale of a Cuban-American who, aided by a taxi driver, embarks on a wild road trip through Cuba to search for the mother he thought had abandoned him as a child.

Paradise Under the Stars (1999). Set around a star-struck woman's dream of singing at the Tropicana nightclub, this buoyantly witty comedy combines exuberant musical numbers, bedroom farce, and some satiric jabs at Cuban machismo.

¡Soy Cuba! (1964). Filmed by Russian director Mikhail Kalatozov, "I Am Cuba" is a brilliant, melodramatic, agitprop black-and-white, anti-American epic to Communist kitsch that exposes the poverty, oppression, and decadence of Batista's Havana.

Suite Habana (2003). The hit of the 25th Havana Film Festival, this emotionally haunting silent documentary records a single day in the life of 10 ordinary Cubans in Havana.

Tomorrow (2006). Alejandro Moya's video-clip style insight into contemporary Cuban reality as revealed by the nation's youthful intelligentsia.

Internet Resources

GENERAL INFORMATION

Cuba Sí
www.cubasi.cu
Generic Cuban government site with sections on travel, culture, news, etc.

Cuba Standard
www.cubastandard.com
Excellent news site focused on economics, business, and politics.

Etecsa
www.etecsa.cu
The website of Cuba's telephone corporation.

Gobierno de la República de Cuba
www.cubagob.cu
Official website of the Cuban government.

Havana Journal
www.havanajournal.com
A news bulletin and forum on everything Cuban related.

www.paginasamarillas.cu
Online Yellow Pages for commercial entities.

BLOGS

The Cuban Triangle
http://cubantriangle.blogspot.com
Politically focused posts by Phil Peters, of the Lexington Institute.

Generation Y
http://lageneraciony.com
Blog of Yoani Sánchez, Cuba's internationally known dissident, with biting insights into daily life.

CULTURE

Cubarte
www.cubarte.cult.cu
Cuban cultural site.

LaHabana
www.lahabana.com
A superb online magazine covering travel, culture, and the arts.

On Cuba
www.oncubamagazine.com
Excellent magazine spanning culture and travel.

TRAVEL INFORMATION

Christopher P. Baker
www.cubatravelexpert.com
Website of the world's foremost authority on travel and tourism to Cuba.

Infotur
www.infotur.cu
Information on tourist information centers in Havana.

Ministerio de Turismo
www.cubatravel.cu
Portal of Cuba's Ministry of Tourism.

Oficina del Historiador de la Ciudad Habana
www.habananuestra.cu
Spanish-only site (Office of the City Historian) relating to restoration projects, museums, hotels, and sites of interest in Habana Vieja.

U.S. Treasury Department (OFAC)
www.treas.gov/ofac
What you need to know about U.S. law and Cuba, direct from the horse's
mouth.

Víazul
www.viazul.com
Website of Cuba's tourist bus company with online reservations.

NOP

List of Maps

Also Available

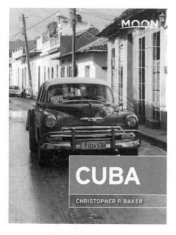

MOON

CUBA

CHRISTOPHER P. BAKER

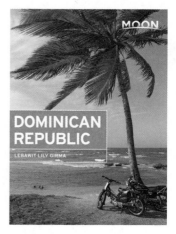

MOON

DOMINICAN REPUBLIC

LEBAWIT LILY GIRMA

MOON

JAMAICA

OLIVER HILL

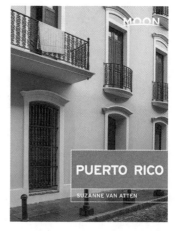

MOON

PUERTO RICO

SUZANNE VAN ATTEN

MAP SYMBOLS

▦ Expressway	★ Highlight	✗ Airfield	⌕ Golf Course
═ Primary Road	○ City/Town	✈ Airport	☐ Parking Area
▦ Secondary Road	◉ State Capital	▲ Mountain	⬟ Archaeological Site
┄ Unpaved Road	◉ National Capital	✛ Unique Natural Feature	⛪ Church
┅ Trail	★ Point of Interest	☂ Waterfall	⛽ Gas Station
┉ Ferry	● Accommodation	⚑ Park	〰 Glacier
┉ Railroad	▼ Restaurant/Bar	☐ Trailhead	🍃 Mangrove
▦ Pedestrian Walkway	■ Other Location	⛷ Skiing Area	Reef
⟁ Stairs	▲ Campground		Swamp

CONVERSION TABLES

°C = (°F - 32) / 1.8
°F = (°C x 1.8) + 32
1 inch = 2.54 centimeters (cm)
1 foot = 0.304 meters (m)
1 yard = 0.914 meters
1 mile = 1.6093 kilometers (km)
1 km = 0.6214 miles
1 fathom = 1.8288 m
1 chain = 20.1168 m
1 furlong = 201.168 m
1 acre = 0.4047 hectares
1 sq km = 100 hectares
1 sq mile = 2.59 square km
1 ounce = 28.35 grams
1 pound = 0.4536 kilograms
1 short ton = 0.90718 metric ton
1 short ton = 2,000 pounds
1 long ton = 1.016 metric tons
1 long ton = 2,240 pounds
1 metric ton = 1,000 kilograms
1 quart = 0.94635 liters
1 US gallon = 3.7854 liters
1 Imperial gallon = 4.5459 liters
1 nautical mile = 1.852 km

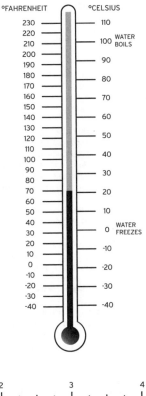

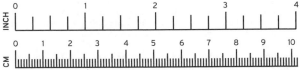

MOON HAVANA
Avalon Travel
Hachette Book Group
1700 Fourth Street
Berkeley, CA 94710, USA
www.moon.com

Editor: Sabrina Young
Series Manager: Kathryn Ettinger
Copy Editor: Brett Keener
Production and Graphics Coordinator: Darren Alessi
Cover Design: Faceout Studios, Charles Brock
Interior Design: Domini Dragoone
Moon Logo: Tim McGrath
Map Editor: Mike Morgenfeld
Cartographers: Austin Ehrhardt, Larissa Gatt
Proofreader: Alissa Cyphers
Indexer: Greg Jewett

ISBN-13: 978-1-63121-717-3
Printing History
1st Edition — 2015
2nd Edition — February 2018
5 4 3 2 1